Preventing Terrorism and Violent Extremism

Preventing Terrorism and Violent Extremism

Andrew Staniforth

Consultant Editors:
Lord Carlile of Berriew CBE QC
and
John Parkinson OBE

UNIVERSITY PRESS

Great Clarendon Street, Oxford, OX2 6DP,
United Kingdom

Oxford University Press is a department of the University of Oxford.
It furthers the University's objective of excellence in research, scholarship,
and education by publishing worldwide. Oxford is a registered trade mark of
Oxford University Press in the UK and in certain other countries

First Edition published in 2014

Impression: 1

Published in the United States of America by Oxford University Press
198 Madison Avenue, New York, NY 10016, United States of America

British Library Cataloguing in Publication Data

Data available

Library of Congress Control Number: 2013955380

ISBN 978–0–19–870579–6

Printed and bound by
Lightning Source UK Ltd

Foreword

I was delighted to be asked to provide a foreword for *Preventing Terrorism and Violent Extremism*, a valuable contribution to the still sparse literature to which the serious student—and the practitioner—of counter-terrorism can refer. After 9/11 I was appointed to the new post of UK Security and Intelligence Coordinator in the Cabinet Office in London and set in motion work on developing a comprehensive national counter-terrorism strategy. It was clear to all of the team that worked on the strategy that the characteristics of jihadist terrorism, with its vaulting ambitions, strident ideology—and total contempt for all who did not share it with a corresponding disregard for civilian casualties—and the willingness of some of their adherents to give their lives in their attacks, represented very new challenges for Parliament and public, government, and law enforcement alike.

The UK counter-terrorism strategy that emerged from our work, which I labelled with the acronym CONTEST, had a clear strategic aim: to make it possible for society to maintain conditions of normality so that people could go about their normal business, freely and with confidence, even in the face of suicidal terrorist attacks. The conditions, freely and with confidence, are an important reminder that we should seek security in ways that uphold values such as liberty and freedom under the law and that, in the end, feeling secure is a psychological state of mind on the part of the public.

The compelling logic of risk management was at the heart of the CONTEST strategy, acknowledging that governments could not, and should not, promise a risk-free world but recognising that it is possible by harnessing all our national capabilities significantly to reduce the risks faced by the public when confronted with a phenomenon like international terrorism: through simultaneously acting to reduce the likelihood of attack (Pursue the terrorists to uncover their networks, disrupt their activities, and bring them to justice, and Prevent the radicalisation of a new generation of violent extremists); reducing our vulnerabilities to attack (Protect our critical infrastructure, aviation, and other transport systems and other crowded places); and reducing the impact and duration of an attack should it occur (Prepare the emergency services and build national resilience to enable the nation to recover quickly from the disruption caused by an attack). This strategy is easily understood as a logical narrative, translated into specific programmes of action across government, the private sector, and the voluntary sector, and as has been shown over succeeding years under three Prime Ministers (and a much larger number of Home Secretaries), is capable of being updated and extended in response to developments in the terrorist threat and in our technologies for countering it.

Police officers will always find themselves at the sharp end of managing terrorism, whether gathering the evidence for prosecutions, providing protection for the public and the critical infrastructure from attack, or taking the initial brunt of dealing with the horrific aftermath of an attack. The police service will thus always have to plan on having an integral role in delivering CONTEST and must play their full part across the operating landscape of Prevent, Pursue, Protect, and Prepare. It is important for the continued development of counter-terrorism policing that police officers of all roles, ranks, and responsibilities have access to authoritative resources to guide them through the complexities of higher policing. This new book fills a lacuna in police counter-terrorism literature, combining both practical and theoretical elements to support the operational implementation and interpretation of national strategies. No area of policing is more critical to the maintenance of national security. The author has compiled a valuable reference for front-line, public-facing officers working within communities, as well as for those officers assigned to specialist counter-terrorism roles.

To get to the roots of terrorism and violent extremism it is essential that all members of the police family understand more about the structure, delivery mechanisms, and key characteristics of Neighbourhood Policing that are in operation today. The police service has come to learn that it is not specialist counter-terrorism police officers working from New Scotland Yard who are likely to be the first to find themselves confronting a terrorist on the street, but a Neighbourhood Police Officer or Police Community Support Officer. If these officers are to support and contribute towards the prevention of terrorism and violent extremism they must raise their awareness of terrorist threats in their locality and understand more about the process of radicalisation, as well as what to do when such issues are discovered. At its simplest level, police interaction with the public through Neighbourhood Policing reassures communities about the risk from terrorism and reminds the public to remain vigilant. But the individual and collective efforts of a professional and positive Neighbourhood Policing Team, who are both informed of the terrorist threats in their locality and conduct their duties through the lens of counter-terrorism, can directly prevent terrorism and protect the communities they serve.

A team of dedicated police officers, visible, accessible, and most importantly, familiar within the community, remains the fundamental building-block for all policing, including counter-terrorism policing. Engagement with all communities at a local level is the key to building capacity to challenge and resist violent extremism which can lead to terrorism, and is also the optimal way of gaining valuable community intelligence which serves to inform the policing response to terrorism and violent extremism at all levels.

Through positive, open, and informative dialogue with the public, Neighbourhood Policing Teams can encourage and support people to come forward with information to help keep their own neighbourhood safe. They can also relay messages to reassure their communities following police operations, terrorist events, and concerns in the community. That being said, none of that guarantees a risk-free life. Bad things will still happen. The ideology of terrorist groups operating in the United Kingdom still, as this volume explains, is a virulent one, with domestic extremism remaining a problem in many countries across the world, creating a serious level of terrorist threat that must be tackled by a dedicated and determined police service.

Professor Sir David Omand GCB
Visiting Professor, War Studies Department, King's College London

Editor's Notes

The UK continues to face threats from extremists who believe they can advance their aims through acts of terrorism. This threat is both serious and enduring, is international in scope, and involves a variety of groups, networks, and individuals who are driven by violent and extremist beliefs.

In response to this threat and to support the work of the security and intelligence agencies, the police service has constructed a counter-terrorism network that is now fully constituted and operational across the UK. Developing this specialist network marked a period of unprecedented change and growth in the history of policing terrorism and is now a model considered across the world. As an operational practitioner, being involved in designing the components and infrastructure of the network meant that the most effective arrangements were developed.

The police and intelligence agencies now combine their expertise in what is a new era of collaboration in counter-terrorism. This joint organisational working is essential to protect the public from the threats of terrorism and violent extremism but it cannot prevent terrorism in isolation. The continuing commitment of the wider police service, other responsible authorities, and the public are vital in order to infuse neighbourhood-level activity with an international perspective.

Over recent years, senior counter-terrorism leadership across all organisations has recognised that national security is increasingly reliant upon neighbourhood safety. It is important to note though that the police service represents just one of many bodies who can improve the safety and quality of lives for individuals and communities. It is local and direct contact that is necessary not just to tackle crime and anti-social behaviour, but also to identify those who encourage extremist views and engage in terrorist-related activity.

We must, however, keep the threat from terrorism and violent extremism in perspective. When compared with other types of criminal activity, terrorism remains a relatively rare occurrence, but the impact of a terrorist attack leaves an enduring legacy. This demands a focused and determined response from the whole police service and partner agencies. As a senior officer involved in the aftermath of the 7 July bombings investigating those responsible, the impact on the wider communities remains tangible.

This new publication is a welcome introduction to the Blackstone's Practical Policing series by Oxford University Press. It will be a trusted companion for police officers, the extended police network, and partners who share in the task of keeping communities safe through preventative counter-terrorism measures and activities. It will not only help navigate a clear course through the complexities of concepts of terrorism and violent extremism, but will also provide guidance on the structures, tactics, and motivations of terrorist organisations that threaten public safety.

This important contribution to preventing terrorism and violent extremism is written by a counter-terrorism practitioner and police academic whose research has been supported by colleagues at CENTRIC (Centre of Excellence in Terrorism, Resilience, Intelligence and Organised Crime Research). CENTRIC is a multidisciplinary and end-user-focused research network linking both academic and professional expertise across a range of disciplines and professional practice in the security domain. This new book fulfils the operating ethos of CENTRIC, serving to bridge the gap between research and operational realities to inform operational policy, practice, and procedure while making a positive contribution to citizen safety.

The author has compiled an excellent operational reference guide for preventing terrorism, which is the very first of its kind. I commend it to police officers and those involved in community safety, as it will serve to develop collective knowledge and understanding of preventing terrorism and violent extremism. This important contribution to policing will make practitioners better prepared today to meet the challenges of tomorrow.

John D Parkinson OBE, M.St (Cantab)
Chair of CENTRIC Advisory Board
Centre of Excellence in Terrorism, Resilience, Intelligence & Organised Crime Research (CENTRIC)

Preface

Preventing terrorism is no longer the hidden dimension of statecraft. It has, over recent years, moved out of the shadows and into the public spotlight, driven by the nature of new-era global terrorism. While the UK government has made strides towards an increasingly open and public-facing domestic national security apparatus, the very nature of counter-terrorism remains enshrined in a preventative ethos. To prevent terrorism and to render visible what violent extremists do not want us to know, counter-terrorism must be intelligence-led and so necessitates a covert approach. However, not all counter-measures need to be cloaked in secrecy in order to be effective, and the contemporary phase of counter-terrorism has evolved important new trends alongside moves towards expansion and localism. This sudden development in the long history of policing terrorism, extremism, and political violence in the UK has served to place the police service at the centre of national counter-terrorism policy.

Preventing terrorism today is a collaborative approach. No single government agency or department can protect the nation from the wide range of threats we face at home and overseas. To ensure a holistic response, everyone in authority must now bring their expertise to bear in concert with one another in the nation's interest. Collaboration in counter-terrorism is essential, as the discovery of the home-grown terrorist threat, embedded citizens living in our communities, has challenged the traditional pursuit of terrorists. The police now seek to ensure that mechanisms are in place to be able to draw upon the valuable information, cooperation, and goodwill of communities from which extremists may be recruited and radicalised. A major shift towards harnessing the capacity of the public to support the broader counter-terrorism effort has been an important development, and community-based intelligence to prevent terrorism at its source has come to the fore. Thus, preventing terrorism and violent extremism is the responsibility for all the police, for all its partners, and all the public.

Of critical concern for the security of our nation is the way in which members of our own communities are being influenced by the extreme single narrative of the political and religious ideologies promoted by terrorist and extremist groups. Such harmful narratives, when combined with complex social and economic factors, serve to nudge individuals towards extremist perspectives, cultivating violent lone actors who present a clear and present danger to a free and democratic way of life. Understanding why and how individuals within communities move towards extremist perspectives, and creating an alternative to allow them to resist adopting such views, remains the key challenge for preventing the contemporary terrorist threat.

To prevent terrorism effectively, police officers are required to develop their knowledge and understanding of terrorism as a concept, and as a crime, if they are to be able to interpret and apply an increasingly complex and growing body of anti-terror powers properly. There are unique challenges that confront police officers when attempting to learn more about terrorism and violent extremism. The perceived complexity of the subject, the sensitivity of operational information, and the nature of specialist roles are contributory factors. Recognising these challenges, *Preventing Terrorism and Violent Extremism*, for the very first time, provides an authoritative and accessible guide for counter-terrorism policing, designed for the front-line patrol officer, police sergeant, and inspector, as well as senior managers, members of Neighbourhood Policing Teams, and those officers designated to deliver preventative counter-terrorism policing in support of specialist detectives from intelligence and investigative disciplines of Special Branch, Counter Terrorism Intelligence Units, Counter Terrorism Units, and the Metropolitan Police Service Counter Terrorism Command.

Police training professionals will find this new contribution to preventative counter-terrorism policing a valuable classroom reference and resource, which will serve to inform programmes of study for all officers, including new student officers, Police Community Support Officers, Special Constables, and the growing body of police volunteers. This book will also be of significant interest and value to all police partners, stakeholders, organisations, groups, and individuals in government and wider society who share in the task of delivering community safety. This book has been informed and supported by a multidisciplinary network of experienced operational police practitioners, policy-makers, legislators, trainers, and globally recognised academics in the fields of security, law, sociology, politics, informatics, policing, and psychology from the UK, Europe, and the United States.

An important message for everyone in authority woven through the very fabric of this work is that complacency based upon the absence of a major terrorist event remains misplaced and unwise. Terrorism continues to demand a determined, yet proportionate and justified response from a police service that is well trained, well equipped, and properly resourced. The history of terrorism in the UK reveals with alarming regularity that terrorist plotters achieve their intended objectives, and can defeat the state's security measures. Unfortunately, this pattern is not about to change. The police and intelligence machinery of the state will prevent further terrorist atrocities but there is a very strong likelihood that they will not stop them all. In this light, the police must dedicate themselves to developing new and innovative ways of embedding the prevention of terrorism into mainstream policing activity with the support of partners and the consent and cooperation of the public. This new contribution to preventing terrorism and violent extremism literature seeks to plug that gap, so all police officers can carry out their duties through the lens of counter-terrorism to protect the communities they serve.

Dr Andrew Staniforth
Detective Inspector and Senior Research Fellow
Centre of Excellence in Terrorism, Resilience, Intelligence and Organised Crime Research (CENTRIC)

Acknowledgements

The author wishes to acknowledge the support of Lord Carlile of Berriew, CBE QC (Independent Reviewer of National Security Policy in Northern Ireland and former Independent Reviewer of Terrorism legislation 2001–2011) as consultant editor alongside John Parkinson, OBE, Chair of Advisory Board, Centre of Excellence in Terrorism, Resilience, Intelligence and Organised Crime Research (CENTRIC) and former Chief Constable of West Yorkshire Police and Head of the North East Counter Terrorism Unit (NE CTU). Thanks are also extended to Professor Sir David Omand, GCB of King's College London for supporting this new volume and for providing the Foreword.

No work of counter-terrorism scholarship can be completed without a multidisciplinary approach, and the author wishes to acknowledge the contributions and support provided by an extended network of experts including Clive Walker, Professor of Criminal Justice Studies, School of Law, University of Leeds; Nigel Hughes, Head of the Police National Legal Database (PNLD); Rozila Kana, Prevent Delivery Officer, National Prevent Delivery Unit (NPDU), Association of Chief Police Officers (Terrorism and Allied Matters); Dr Rupali Jeswal, terrorism analyst, operational psychologist and Chief Executive Officer of Xiphos-ISS (Intelligence and Security Solutions); Babak Akhgar, Professor of Informatics and Director of CENTRIC; Dr Petra Saskia Bayerl, Post-Doctoral Researcher, Erasmus University, Netherlands; and Gregory Saathoff MD, Executive Director, Critical Incident Analysis Group (CIAG), University of Virginia, USA.

The author is also indebted to the Community Engagement Field Officers (CEFOs), Prevent Delivery Officers, Neighbourhood Policing Team officers, and Counter-Terrorism police officers who assisted in the development of this volume.

And finally, thanks are also extended to the team at Oxford University Press, especially Peter Daniell, Lucy Alexander, and Sally Pelling-Deeves for sharing their expertise, together with the support provided by the team at CENTRIC, who have provided the author with a platform to undertake research.

Contents

Tables		xix
Figures		xxi
Special Features		xxiii
Abbreviations		xxv
1	**Terrorist Threat to the United Kingdom**	**1**
1.1	Introduction	2
1.2	Global Context of Terrorism	2
1.3	National Security Today	4
1.4	National Risks	5
1.5	Assessing National Threats	7
1.6	National Threats	8
1.7	Summary	30
2	**Concept of Terrorism and Extremism**	**32**
2.1	Introduction	33
2.2	Defining Terrorism	33
2.3	Understanding Terrorism	35
2.4	Typology of Terrorism	43
2.5	Characteristics of Terrorism	46
2.6	Terrorist Motivations	50
2.7	Summary	52
3	**Terrorist and Extremist Methodology**	**54**
3.1	Introduction	55
3.2	Terrorist Organisations	55
3.3	Terrorist Tactics	64
3.4	Domestic Extremist Tactics	79
3.5	Summary	81
4	**Counter-terrorism Strategy**	**83**
4.1	Introduction	84
4.2	Responses to Counter-terrorism	84

4.3 The UK Counter-terrorism Strategy 87
4.4 Summary 103

5 Pursuing Terrorists and Extremists 105

5.1 Introduction 106
5.2 Intelligence Machinery 106
5.3 Counter-terrorism Policing 111
5.4 Prosecuting Terrorists 114
5.5 Code for Crown Prosecutors 115
5.6 Summary 116

6 Anti-terror Legislation 118

6.1 Introduction 119
6.2 Operational Reality 120
6.3 Anti-terror Legal Framework 121
6.4 Independent Oversight 124
6.5 Key Definitions 126
6.6 Stop and Search 129
6.7 Power of Arrest 140
6.8 Cordons 145
6.9 Parking 148
6.10 Terrorism Prevention and Investigation Measures 150
6.11 Officers' Powers and Duties 153
6.12 Summary 155

7 Terrorism Offences 157

7.1 Introduction 158
7.2 Encouraging Terrorism 158
7.3 Terrorist Training 161
7.4 Summary 165

8 Preventing Terrorism and Violent Extremism 166

8.1 Introduction 167
8.2 'Prevent' Priorities 168
8.3 'Prevent' Cycle 168
8.4 'Prevent' in Communities 168
8.5 Delivering 'Prevent' 173
8.6 Summary 179

9 Radicalisation **181**

9.1 Introduction 182
9.2 Defining Radicalisation 183
9.3 Drivers of Radicalisation 184
9.4 Models of Radicalisation Processes 191
9.5 Online Radicalisation 196
9.6 Social Media Radicalisation 202
9.7 Summary 203

10 Neighbourhood Policing **206**

10.1 Introduction 207
10.2 Evolution of Neighbourhood Policing 208
10.3 Implementing Neighbourhood Policing 209
10.4 Defining 'Neighbourhood' and 'Community' 212
10.5 Neighbourhood Policing Principles 212
10.6 Neighbourhood Policing Works 226
10.7 Neighbourhood Policing Plus 228
10.8 Summary 234

Appendix 1 List of Proscribed Terrorist Organisations 237

Appendix 2 Terrorism Act 2000 (Issued under S47AB as amended by the Protection of Freedoms Act 2012)
Code of Practice (England, Wales and Scotland) for the Exercise of Stop and Search Powers under Sections 43 and 43A of the Terrorism Act 2000, and the Authorisation and Exercise of Stop and Search Powers Relating to Section 47A of and Schedule 6B to the Terrorism Act 2000 243

Bibliography 267

Index 273

Tables

1.1	Rapport's 'four waves of terrorism'	3
1.2	National threat level system	7
2.1	Typology of single issue extremism	45
2.2	Human Rights Articles	49
3.1	Primary and secondary sites	80
3.2	Tactics used by extremist groups in the UK	80
4.1	Twelve Rules for Preventing and Combating Terrorism	86
4.2	CONTEST roles and responsibilities	100
6.1	Lord Lloyd Guiding Principles for the introduction of terrorism legislation	121
6.2	Designation of areas to be cordoned	146
6.3	Section 48 authorising officers	149
6.4	Schedule 1—Terrorism Prevention and Investigation Measures	151
6.5	Summary of officers' powers and duties	154
9.1	Radicalisation process models	191
10.1	Ten Neighbourhood Policing Principles	212
10.2	Positive outcomes of collaborative working	220
10.3	Evidence to support the positive outcomes of Neighbourhood Policing	227

Figures

1.1	The National Security Cycle	5
1.2	Threat and Risk Formula	8
1.3	Terrorist threats to the UK	9
1.4	The threat to the UK from Al Qa'ida	10
1.5	Comparison of terrorist threats of Northern Irish-related terrorism and Al Qa'ida-related terrorism	26
2.1	Core motivations of terrorism	36
2.2	Terrorism, audience, and victim relationship	37
3.1	Duo-cell structure	57
3.2	Tri-cell structure	58
3.3	Corporate cell structure	58
3.4	Link cell structure	60
3.5	Star cell structure	61
3.6	Fused cell network structure	61
3.7	Primary role of hostile reconnaissance	71
4.1	Mechanics of the CONTEST strategy	89
4.2	'Prevent' key objectives	91
4.3	'Pursue' key objectives	93
4.4	'Protect' key objectives	96
4.5	'Prepare' cycle	98
4.6	'Prepare' key objectives	99
5.1	Intelligence machinery	106
6.1	UK Anti-terror legal framework	123
6.2	Terrorist definition: commission, preparation, instigation	128
6.3	Stop and search 'PLAN'	138
8.1	The 'Prevent' cycle	168
8.2	Reducing risk of radicalisation in universities—4R 'Prevent' model	172
9.1	Radicalisation factors	185
9.2	The six steps of Moghaddam's staircase to terrorism model	194
9.3	European Commission radicalisation pyramid	195
9.4	The Radicalisation-Factor Model (RFM)	199
10.1	Delivery mechanisms of Neighbourhood Policing	210
10.2	Neighbourhood Policing timeline	211
10.3	Neighbourhood Policing public priority cycle	218
10.4	The SARA process cycle	223
10.5	The components of community engagement for preventing terrorism and violent extremism	225
10.6	Effective counter-terrorism contact management	232

Special Features

This book contains a number of special features intended to assist the reader. These are explained here.

Case studies

To provide illustrative examples of certain key points and issues from real life incidents, events, and investigations.

Checklists

To provide a list of key issues and considerations those practitioners might consider useful when planning, managing, and interpreting the application of legal powers.

Definitions

Where appropriate, definitions of key terms and concepts are provided.

Figures

To provide illustrative examples in diagrammatic form of key issues and concepts.

Further reading

These features direct readers towards sources cited or used in the text, and to additional material that will amplify and elaborate the content of the book.

Key points

Information requiring particular emphasis is summarised in key points.

Tables

Some information or concepts have been tabulated for ease of illustration and presentation.

Abbreviations

ACPO	Association of Chief Police Officers
ACT NOW	All Communities Together Now
ALARP	As Low As Reasonably Practicable
AMISOM	African peacekeeping force
AQ	Al Qa'ida
AQ-AP	Al Qa'ida in the Arabian Peninsula
AQ-I	Al Qa'ida in Iraq
AQ-KB	Al Qa'ida Kurdish battalions
AQ-M	Al Qa'ida in the Maghreb
ASB	Anti-Social Behaviour
ATCSA	Anti-Terrorism Crime and Security Act 2001
BIS	Department for Business, Innovation and Skills
BPC	Border Policing Command
CBRNE	Chemical, Biological, Radiological, Nuclear or Explosive
CCTV	Closed Circuit Television
CEC	Conflict-Engaged Citizens
CEFOs	Community Engagement Field Officers
CEOP	Child Exploitation and Online Protection Centre
CIA	Community Impact Assessment
CIRA	Continuity Irish Republican Army
CO	Cabinet Office
COBR	Cabinet Office Briefing Room
CONTEST	COuNter-TErrorism STratgey
CPI	commission, preparation, or instigation
CPNI	Centre for the Protection of the National Infrastructure
CPS	Crown Prosecution Service
C-TACT	Counter-Terrorism Act 2008
CTB	Police Counter Terrorism Board
CTD	Counter Terrorism Division
CTIRU	Counter Terrorism Internet Referral Unit
CTIU	Counter Terrorism Intelligence Units
CTLEOs	Counter Terrorism and Extremism Liaison Officers
CTLP	Counter Terrorism Local Profile
CT SIO	Counter Terrorism Senior Investigating Officer
CTU	Counter Terrorism Units
CyT	Cyber Terrorism
DCLG	Department for Communities and Local Government
DE	Domestic Extremism

DECC	Department of Energy & Climate Change
DEFRA	Department for Environment, Food and Rural Affairs
DfE	Department for Education
DFID	Department for International Development
DfT	Department for Transport
DH	Department of Health
DIS	Defence Intelligence Staff
DSO	Distinguished Service Order
DT	Domestic Terrorism
ECC	Economic Crime Command
ECtHR	European Court of Human Rights
EKP	Economic Key Points
ETA	Euskadi Ta Askatasuna
EVA	Environments Visual Aids
FATA	Federally Administered Tribal Areas (Pakistan)
FBI	Federal Bureau of Investigation
FCO	Foreign and Commonwealth Office
FEMA	Federal Emergency Management Agency
GCHQ	Government Communications Headquarters
GDP	Gross Domestic Product
GLO	Government Liaison Officer
GO-S	Government Office for Science
HEIs	Higher Education Institutions
HME	Home-Made Explosives
HMIC	Her Majesty's Inspectorate of Constabulary
HO	Home Office
IED	Improvised Explosive Device
INLA	Irish National Liberation Army
INPTs	Integrated Neighbourhood Policing Teams
IRTL	Independent Reviewer of Terrorism Legislation
ISAF	International Security Assistance Force
ISG	Internet Strategy Group
ISOC	student union Islamic society
JTAC	Joint Terrorism Analysis Centre
KDF	Kenya Defence Forces
KIN	Key Individual Network
KINEL	Key Individual Networks Extended List
LeT	Lashkar-e-Tayyiba
LGD	Lead Government Department
LSE	London Stock Exchange
MC	Military Cross
MI5	Security Service (Military Intelligence section 5)
MI6	Secret Intelligence Service (Military Intelligence section 6)
MoD	Ministry of Defence

MoJ	Ministry of Justice
MPS	Metropolitan Police Service
NaCTSO	National Counter-Terrorism Security Office
NCA	National Crime Agency
NCTT	National Community Tension Team
NDET	National Domestic Extremism Team
NDEU	National Domestic Extremism Unit
NDPB	Non-Departmental Public Body
NECTU	North East Counter Terrorism Unit
NETCU	National Extremism Tactical Coordination Unit
NGO	Non Governmental Organizations
NIM	National Intelligence Model
NIO	Northern Ireland Office
NIRT	Northern Ireland-Related Terrorism
NPDU	National Prevent Delivery Unit
NPOIU	National Public Order Intelligence Unit
NPP	Neighbourhood Policing Programme
NPT	Neighbourhood Policing Teams
NRPP	National Reassurance Policing Programme
NSC	National Security Council
NSRA	National Security Risk Assessment
OBE	Officer of the Order of the British Empire
OCC	Organised Crime Command
OCG	Overseas CONTEST Group
OSCT	Office of Security and Counter-Terrorism
PACE	Police and Criminal Evidence Act 1984
PACT	Partners and Communities Together
PCC	Police and Crime Commissioners
PCSO	Police Community Support Officer
PIRA	Provisional Irish Republican Army
PNCTN	Police National Counter Terrorism Network
PNLD	Police National Legal Database
POP	Problem-Orientated Policing
PoT	Prevention of Terrorism Act 2005
PSNI	Police Service of Northern Ireland
RFM	Radicalisation-Factor Model
RIPA	Regulation of Investigatory Powers Act 2000
RIRA	Real Irish Republican Army
SARA	Scanning, Analysis, Response, and Assessment model
SB	Special Branch
SCCTD	Special Crime and Counter Terrorism Division
SIS	Secret Intelligence Service
SOCA	Serious Organised Crime Agency
SPR	Strategic Policing Requirement

TACT	Terrorism Act 2000
TACT 2006	Terrorism Act 2006
TAM	Terrorism and Allied Matters
TCMJ	Terrorism Case Management Judge
TPIMS	Terrorism Prevention and Investigation Measures
TTP	Taliban (Tehrik–e Taliban Pakistan)
UKBA	UK Border Agency
VBIED	Vehicle-Borne Improvised Explosive Devices
VSS	Vulnerable Sites and Sectors
WTC	World Trade Center
XLW	Extreme Left-Wing
XRW	Extreme Right-Wing

1

Terrorist Threat to the United Kingdom

1.1	Introduction	2
1.2	Global Context of Terrorism	2
1.3	National Security Today	4
1.4	National Risks	5
1.5	Assessing National Threats	7
1.6	National Threats	8
1.7	Summary	30

1.1 Introduction

All police officers, the extended police family, including Police Community Support Officers (PCSOs) and Special Constables alongside police partners, must understand the threat to the United Kingdom from all forms of contemporary terrorism and violent extremism in order to protect the communities they serve. Police officers remain the most important tool of the state for tackling terrorism. They are best placed to uncover terrorist plotters living within communities and they can encourage and support people to share relevant information to help keep their own neighbourhood safe. They can also relay messages to reassure the public following counter-terrorism operations and terrorist events, and allay concerns that exist in the community. Police officers gather intelligence, preserve evidence, and conduct covert and overt operations against terrorist individuals and groups. They arrest, detain, and investigate terrorist matters, building complex criminal cases to remove violent extremists from civil society, and they are prepared to put themselves in harm's way while responding to terrorist attacks in order to save life and protect property. No other arm of the state has such a broad and important role in tackling contemporary terrorism and violent extremism.

For a long time, terrorist groups pursuing their political, religious, and ideological beliefs have planned and executed attacks on the free and democratic communities of the Western world. The UK in particular has a long history of tackling terrorists and extremists who have had cause to challenge and violently oppose the values of tolerance, human rights, and the rule of law. At every juncture of modern history where the domestic safety and security of the UK has been threatened by violent extremists, it has been police officers who have been at the forefront of protecting the public and preserving the peace. Central to combating the long and violent struggle with terrorism in the UK is a police officer who is visible, accessible, publicly accountable, and most importantly, a familiar face within the community.

1.2 Global Context of Terrorism

In the long history of preserving the UK's security, previous governments have grappled with anarchists, nationalists, Nazism, and, more recently, the brutal certainties of the Cold War, with its existential threat clear and omnipresent, the Soviet army arrayed across half of Europe, and the constant shadow of nuclear confrontation between the superpowers hovering overhead. These historical phases of terrorism are now widely accepted by scholars and defined in David Rapport's wave theory, arguably one of the greatest contributions to the study of terrorism. Rapport's waves, shown in Table 1.1, span more than a century and include four broad political movements, each of which produced a plethora of related terrorist groups.

Table 1.1 Rapport's 'four waves of terrorism'

Focus	Primary strategy	Target identity	Precipitant	Special characteristics
First wave: *Anarchists 1870–1920s*	Elite assassinations, bank robberies	Primary European states	Failure and slow pace of political reform	Developed basic terrorism strategies and rationales
Second wave: *Nationalists 1920s–1960s*	Guerrilla attacks on police and military	European empires	Post-1919 de-legitimisation of empire	Increased international support
Third wave: *New left/Marxist 1960s–1980s*	Hijackings, kidnappings, assassination	Governments in general; increasing focus on USA	Viet Cong successes	Increased international training, cooperation, and sponsorship
Fourth wave: *Religious 1970s–2020s*	Suicide bombings	USA, Israel, UK, and secular regimes with Muslim populations	Iranian Revolution, Soviet invasion of Afghanistan	Casualty escalation. Decline in the number of terrorist groups

Rapport's wave theory has proven useful not only as it divided terrorist initiatives into four distinct periods, but also via its observation that the motivation for violence in each wave affected the nature and quality of the violence employed by groups in successive movements. Rapport does not imply that the four waves represent discrete categories where one era consisted of one, and only one, form of terrorism; on the contrary, there is quite a degree of overlap from one wave to the next. However, a dominant movement, spurring in turn a proliferation of like-minded groups, defines each wave. Rapport observed that very few organisations were able to outlive their epoch, each of which lasted roughly one generation, which is important for understanding the contemporary context of the kinds of terrorist threats we face today.

1.3 National Security Today

Contemporary Britain faces a complex range of threats from a myriad of sources. Terrorism, cyber attack, unconventional attacks using chemical, nuclear, or biological weapons, as well as large-scale accidents or natural hazards; any one of these could inflict grave damage on citizens and the UK's interests at home and abroad. New threats can emanate from states, but also from non-state actors: terrorists, home-grown or foreign, insurgents, or criminals, as well as the threat to the security of our energy supplies which increasingly comes from fossil fuels located in some of the most unstable parts of the world. Increasing nuclear proliferation continues to pose a threat to us, as well as our vulnerability to the effects of climate change and its impact on food and water supplies. In summary, the landscape of threats which have the potential to undermine or destroy our way of life is very different now than as it appeared ten, twenty, let alone fifty, or one hundred years ago.

1.3.1 Impact of globalisation

In order to protect our interests at home, we must extend our influence abroad. As the global balance of power shifts, it will become harder for the UK to do just this. But we should be under no illusion that our national interest requires our continued full and active engagement in world affairs. Our economy must compete with the strongest economies throughout the world, requiring the government and private enterprise to expend a massive and continuing effort to promote trade, the lifeblood of our economy, with the rest of the world.

1.3.2 Delivering security to the nation

To help coordinate the UK's security response, the British government has published a *National Security Strategy* which provides a cohesive, pan-government response to the variety of threats the nation faces. The *National Security Strategy* sets out three key steps for a secure and prosperous Britain: to use all our national capabilities to build the UK's prosperity, to extend the UK's influence in the world, and to strengthen national security (see Figure 1.1).

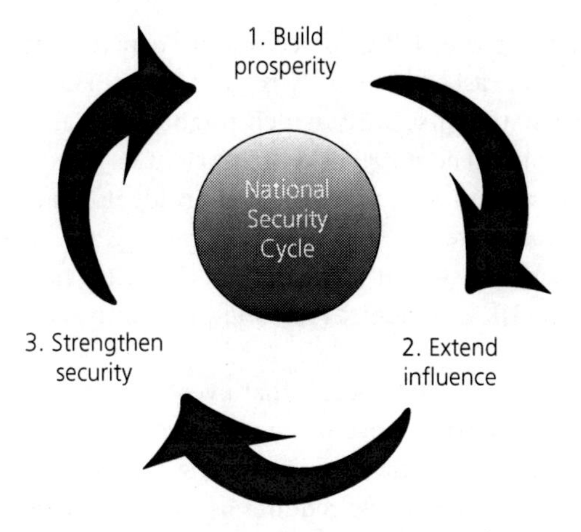

Figure 1.1. The National Security Cycle.

KEY POINTS—NATIONAL SECURITY COUNCIL

By creating the National Security Council (NSC) in 2010, the UK government has placed national security at the very highest level. The creation of the NSC marks a key change in the security machinery of government, bringing together all senior governmental ministers concerned under the chairmanship of the Prime Minister. The NSC ensures a strategic and tightly coordinated approach across the entire government to the risks and opportunities the country faces.

1.4 National Risks

The *National Security Strategy* requires all agencies of government engaged in law enforcement, security, intelligence collection, and civil protection to identify the most pressing risks to our security, and to put in place appropriate ways to address them. As well as by malicious attacks, the UK's national interest can also be threatened by natural disasters and man-made accidents. These risks create widely different impacts if and when they may occur, and some are more likely to occur than others.

1.4.1 National Security Risk Assessment

A truly strategic approach to national security requires governments to go further than just simply assessing domestic civil emergencies. The *National Security Strategy*, as well as looking at short-term domestic risks, also considers aspects of national security. It is an 'all-hazards' strategy which is underpinned by the first ever National Security Risk Assessment (NSRA) which assesses and prioritises all major areas of national security risk, from both domestic and overseas sources.

In order to develop the NSRA, subject-matter experts, analysts, and intelligence specialists were asked to identify the full range of existing and potential risks to the UK's national security which might materialise over a five- and twenty-year horizon. All potential risks of sufficient scale or impact as to require action from government and/or which had an ideological, international, or political dimension were assessed based on relative likelihood and relative impact. The impact assessment was based on the direct harm a potential risk could cause to the UK's residents, territories, economy, key institutions, and infrastructure.

The results of the first NSRA suggest that over the next twenty years, the UK could face risks from a wide range of sources, and that the means available to our adversaries to enact these threats are increasing in number, variety, and impact. Our increasingly networked world requires us to protect virtual assets and networks on which our economy and way of life now depend so heavily. This has rapidly become just as important as protecting physical assets, marking a seismic shift in the focus of national security planning.

The NSRA serves to inform strategic judgements. It is not a forecast, but rather the result of informed choices of which risks to include as serious enough to warrant government attention. This helps the UK government to identify the actions and resources needed to deliver suitable responses to those risks.

The NSRA was presented to the NSC and on that basis, the NSC identified fifteen generic priority risk types and divided them into three tiers. Terrorism and cyber terrorism were highlighted as being tier one threats, as shown in the following box.

National Security Strategy: Tier One Priority Risks

Tier One: The National Security Council considered the following groups of risks to be those of highest priority for future UK national security, taking account of both likelihood and impact.

- ***International terrorism*** affecting the UK or its interests, including a chemical, biological, radiological, or nuclear attack by terrorists; and/or a significant increase in the levels of terrorism relating to Northern Ireland.
- ***Hostile attacks upon UK cyber space*** by other states and large-scale cyber crime.

1.5 **Assessing National Threats**

Prior to 1 August 2006, the public was not privy to information about national terrorism threat levels nor how they operated, but from this date, the government made information available to the public on the terrorism threat level system in the UK.

This decision recognised the important role the public plays in countering terrorism when confronted with such a sustained and heightened threat. The government continues to maintain a state of readiness in response to this kind of threat. It remains the government's policy to issue public warnings or advice if it becomes necessary to protect the public in the event of a specific and credible terrorist threat. However, there is a delicate balance to maintain between keeping the public informed of current threats, whilst ensuring the secrecy and security of covert operations. Information which is made available to the public is also available to terrorists, and the challenge is to keep the public informed whilst not providing an unnecessary advantage to terrorist cells.

POINT TO NOTE—INFORMING THE PUBLIC

It is important that the public is informed about terrorist activity, but in doing so it should not increase the public's fear of terrorism which may become disproportionate to the actual threat, thereby potentially provoking an overreaction which may be neither necessary nor justified. The police service has an important role to play in relaying these messages to reassure communities following any police counter-terrorism operation or terrorist event.

1.5.1 **National threat level system**

The Joint Terrorism Analysis Centre (JTAC) provides analysis and assessment of information relating to the threats from international terrorism. A new system has been created to keep the public informed and it is designed to give a broad indication of the likelihood of a terrorist attack. The threat levels are shown in Table 1.2.

Table 1.2 National threat level system

Threat level	Descriptor
CRITICAL	An attack is expected imminently
SEVERE	An attack is highly likely
SUBSTANTIAL	An attack is a strong possibility
MODERATE	An attack is possible but unlikely
LOW	An attack is unlikely

KEY POINT—THREAT LEVEL

The UK threat level may change. The current threat to the UK from international terrorism is kept up to date and reported on the Home Office website: <http://www.homeoffice.gov.uk/security/current-threat-level>.

1.5.2 **Threat analysis**

Judgements about the threat are based on a wide range of information which is often fragmented. Data must be collated, including analysis of previous attacks and similar events in other countries. Intelligence is not an exact science and it will never reveal absolutely everything about a given threat, which is why information supplied by police officers, other authorities, and members of the public is important. No matter how insignificant it may appear to be at the time, it just might provide vital corroboration of a particular piece of information and might help strengthen analytical judgements.

Assessing the threat includes the gathering and analysis of information around four core areas: the terrorist's intention, capabilities, timescales, and the vulnerability of the chosen target. Intelligence gathered concerning the desired result of terrorist activities and an assessment of whether the terrorists' aims are achievable or realistic given their capabilities are key to this process. Timescales are also a crucial element of assessing threat levels, as knowing when a terrorist group is to strike may provide a greater degree of urgency in the proposed response to unfolding events. Once these data are captured, an analysis of the potential vulnerability to such an attack can be made. Compiling relevant data in order to make an accurate assessment of the actual threat is a real challenge and one that requires a thorough understanding of terrorism-related activity. The 'threat' and 'risk' formula illustrated in Figure 1.2 is used to assess specific terrorist-related threats.

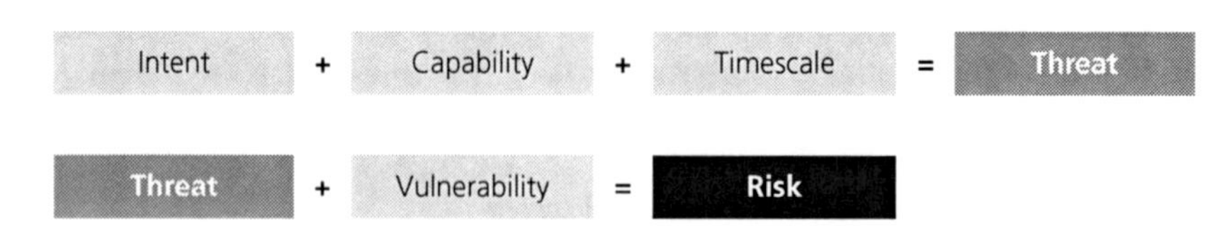

Figure 1.2. Threat and Risk Formula.

1.6 **National Threats**

The contemporary terrorist threat to the UK derives from four primary sources: Al Qa'ida (AQ), Northern Ireland-Related Terrorism (NIRT), domestic Extreme Right-Wing (XRW) terrorism, and cyber terrorism (CyT) (see Figure 1.3). Each of these specific threats shall be examined in more detail.

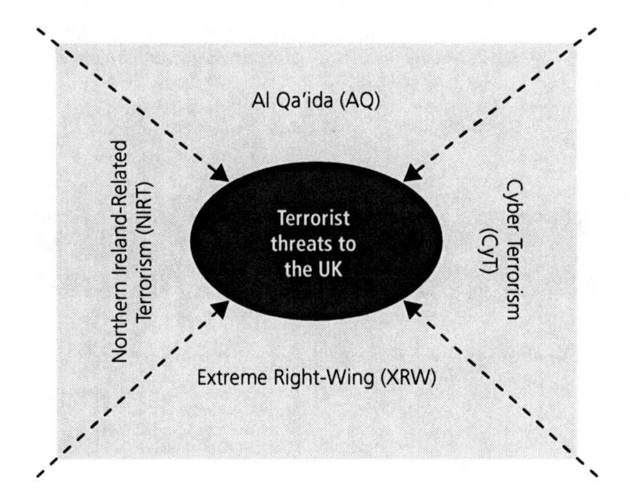

Figure 1.3. Terrorist threats to the UK.

1.6.1 Al Qa'ida

In 2009 there were approximately 11,000 terrorist attacks around the world causing nearly 15,000 casualties. Attacks took place primarily in Pakistan, Afghanistan, and Iraq. The victims of the attacks were mainly Muslim and the perpetrators primarily Al Qa'ida-linked terrorist groups. In 2010 over 11,500 terrorist attacks caused more than 13,000 fatalities; the vast majority of the attacks were still carried out by Al Qa'ida and associated terrorist groups. Most attacks continue to take place in Afghanistan, Pakistan, and Iraq, as well as Somalia, and the majority of victims remain Muslim. The UK assesses that Al Qa'ida is the principal source of terrorist threats to the country which stem from the leadership of Al Qa'ida, terrorist groups affiliated to Al Qa'ida, and self-starting networks, lone actors, and terrorist groups following the Al Qa'ida ideology (see Figure 1.4).

Al Qa'ida leadership

In recent years the leadership and core of Al Qa'ida (based primarily in the Federally Administered Tribal Areas—FATA—of Pakistan) has been severely weakened by the operations of the Pakistani military and security agencies, the United States, and the International Security Assistance Force (ISAF) in Afghanistan. The operational capability of Al Qa'ida's leadership is now less than at any time since 11 September 2001. Many have been killed or captured, or have dispersed. Communications, training, and planning have all been significantly disrupted. Al Qa'ida's senior leadership has been forced to increase its reliance on other terrorist groups for operational support and has begun to make more frequent calls for extremists to conduct independent attacks without further guidance or instruction.

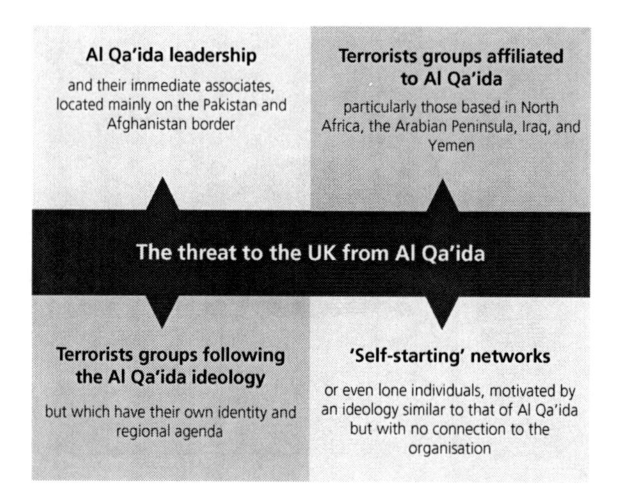

Figure 1.4. The threat to the UK from Al Qa'ida.

The death of Osama Bin Laden on 2 May 2011 dealt a significant blow against Al Qa'ida. This event disrupted Al Qa'ida operations and decision making, and seems to have left a leadership gap which has not been filled effectively. Al Qa'ida has long sought to overturn what it has regarded as un-Islamic governments throughout those countries in which the majority of the population follows the Muslim faith. It claims that the only way to do this is via indiscriminate violence against these 'un-Islamic' regimes and those who support them. Although it has yet to play out in full, the current phenomenon of an Arab Spring may well demonstrate that Al Qa'ida is wrong. Change has followed popular and largely non-violent protest. The tactics of terrorism have not been universally adopted, and Al Qa'ida has been relegated to a minor role in many countries experiencing transformation, despite evidence that it has made a number of attempts to broaden its popular appeal.

Since Bin Laden's death, Al Qa'ida's senior leadership has continued to plan and attempt terrorist attacks in the West and in other countries. Hundreds of people originally from European countries (including the UK) have joined Al Qa'ida in Pakistan, and the organisation has continued to try to send operatives back into Western countries where plots have been discovered and disrupted. Above all, Al Qa'ida has continued to try to attack the US and its interests abroad.

Al Qa'ida affiliates

An unintended consequence of the disruption of the Al Qa'ida leadership in Pakistan that stemmed from the death of Bin Laden was the increase in threat from Al Qa'ida affiliates. This small number of groups use the Al Qa'ida name but often operate without reference to the Al Qa'ida leadership. These groups include:

- Al Qa'ida in the Arabian Peninsula (AQ-AP);
- Al Qa'ida in the Maghreb (AQ-M);
- Al Qa'ida in Iraq (AQ-I);
- Al Qa'ida Kurdish battalions (AQ-KB).

The most significant of these groups has proved to be Al Qa'ida in the Arabian Peninsula (AQ-AP), formed in January 2009 when members of Al Qa'ida fled Saudi Arabia and joined an Al Qa'ida network based in Yemen. Nine tourists were kidnapped in Yemen by AQ-AP in June 2009. Seven of these, including a British citizen, were killed. AQ-AP also attempted to assassinate the Deputy Interior Minister in Saudi Arabia in August 2009 and since then has conducted further attacks in Yemen. However, the group's most ambitious attack was over Detroit during 2009.

Case Study—Al Qa'ida in the Arabian Peninsula

On 25 December 2009, 23-year-old Nigerian-born Umar Farouk Abdulmutallab boarded Northwest Airlines Flight 253 at Amsterdam's Schipol airport. Identified as suspicious for being in possession of hand luggage only for a transatlantic flight and carrying no coat, Abdulmutallab nevertheless evaded all the sophisticated security screening that is in place at one of Europe's premier international aviation hubs, and is alleged to have successfully concealed an improvised explosive device (IED) in his clothing. Abdulmutallab took his reserved seat, 19A, which was directly located over the wings and fuel tanks of the aircraft which departed without incident. As the aircraft made its descent over Detroit, Abdulmutallab is believed to have attempted to detonate the IED consisting of a primary and secondary explosive sealed in a plastic package in the crotch of his underwear. As the device ignited it failed to detonate, but the ignition alerted passengers and crew extinguished flames coming from Abdulmutallab who was hidden beneath a travel blanket in an attempt to conceal his actions. Abdulmutallab was restrained on board the flight and was later arrested by US authorities upon arrival in Detroit. On 2 January, US President Barack Obama addressed the world's media stating that Abdulmutallab 'joined an affiliate of Al Qa'ida, and that this group, Al Qa'ida in the Arabian Peninsula, trained him, equipped him with those explosives and directed him to attack the plane headed for America'.

This failed attack demonstrates that Al Qa'ida still intends to use commercial passenger jets to deliver death and destruction on an innocent civilian population, a stark reminder of the threat we continue to face. Al Qa'ida in the Arabian Peninsula (AQ-AP) was formed in January 2009 by a merger between two regional offshoots of the international Islamist militant network in neighbouring Yemen and Saudi Arabia. AQ-AP vowed to attack oil facilities, foreigners, and security forces as it seeks to topple the Saudi monarchy and Yemeni government in order to establish an Islamic caliphate. It has claimed responsibility for a number of attacks in Saudi Arabia and Yemen including the murder, kidnapping, and beheading of a number of foreign nationals. After news of the failed attempt to destroy the Northwest Airlines plane emerged, AQ-AP released a statement saying it had sought to avenge recent raids by Yemeni security forces that they suspected of being supported by US intelligence. 'We tell the American people that since you support the leaders who kill our women and children we have come to slaughter you and will strike you with no warning, our vengeance is near'. They continued: 'We call on all Muslims to throw out all unbelievers from the Arabian Peninsula by killing crusaders who work in embassies or elsewhere in a total war on all crusaders in the Peninsula of Muhammad'.

The failed attack over Detroit did not curb the ambitions of AQ-AP. On 31 October 2010 it tried to conduct two further attacks on commercial cargo aircraft en route to the US. These failed narrowly. The explosive devices were discovered before they detonated, one found during a search at East Midlands Airport. AQ-AP continues to conduct operations against both internal and Western diplomatic targets in Yemen. Terrorist attacks against all targets increased by more than 250 per cent during 2009 and 2010; 11 UK diplomats were attacked in April and October 2010 alone. The breakdown of law and order in parts of Yemen and the departure to Saudi Arabia of President Saleh on 4 June 2011 enabled AQ-AP to seize territory and weapons from the Yemeni armed forces. The death of Osama Bin Laden has made no difference to AQ-AP's operational capability: its internal and external operations have not been closely coordinated with the Al Qa'ida leadership.

Operational activity by Al Qa'ida in the Maghreb (AQ-M) has been confined to the Maghreb and sub-Saharan Africa and has not extended to Europe or the US. But AQ-M has repeatedly taken Western hostages, including many from Europe, and in June 2009 seized and then murdered a UK national. In some cases these operations have been coordinated with the Al Qa'ida leadership, unlike those by AQ-AP. Funds raised from ransom payments have significantly enhanced AQ-M's operational capability and have enabled it to operate more widely through Mali and Niger. Recent instability in Libya has also enabled AQ-M to seize weapons from military sources. Further south, AQ-M has established contact with the Nigerian terrorist group, Boko Haram, and extended its reach into the volatile region of northern Nigeria. This area has long been of interest to the leadership of Al Qa'ida.

Case Study—Boko Haram

On 8 July 2013 the UK Home Office announced that the Nigerian-based jihadist terrorist group, Boko Haram, was to be banned from operating in the UK from the 12 July onwards. Home Secretary Theresa May had asked for the radical Islamist organisation to be banned under terrorism laws. Flagging Boko Haram as a potential threat to UK interests in a speech on terrorism during July 2011 she said: 'Increasingly, the threat to Britain comes not just from Al Qa'ida's core leadership itself, but from the so-called Al Qa'ida affiliates in places like Yemen and North Africa, from associated groups like Boko Haram'.

Boko Haram are the latest organisation to join a growing list of terrorist groups now outlawed in the UK under provisions provided by Schedule 2 of the Terrorism Act 2000. Police officers and the extended police family should be aware of the terrorist groups that are banned in the UK, as well as the mechanisms in place to proscribe them under the law.

Boko Haram (the name means 'Western education is forbidden') was founded in 2001, and took as its official name '*Jamā'at Ahl as-Sunnah lid-da'wa wal-Jihād*', which translated from Arabic means 'Congregation of the People of Tradition for Proselytism and Jihad'. This group is strongly opposed to Western influence, culture, and education, and has waged an insurgency in Nigeria for more than a decade, seeking to establish Sharia law.

Boko Haram has cemented its place as one of the deadliest terrorist groups in operation today. While many of their victims are fellow Muslim citizens who oppose their violent interpretation of Islam, the group is renowned for attacking Christians, bombing churches, and attacking schools.

Nigerian authorities believe that Boko Haram has been responsible for some grotesque crimes against humanity, including fatal clashes related to sectarian violence in Nigeria and mass shootings of innocent people praying at mosques in the north-east of the country. It is claimed that Boko Haram were responsible for at least 450 killings in Nigeria during 2011, and over 620 deaths over the first six months of 2012. Since its founding in 2001, these jihadist terrorists are believed to have been responsible for 10,000 deaths, the vast majority being innocent civilians.

Why the British government should proscribe a terrorist group which primarily operates in the poorest areas of northern and central Nigeria may not at first be clear to front-line police officers. However, specialist counter-terrorism practitioners believe that distant events have the potential to compromise national security and neighbourhood safety closer to home.

In 2013 Boko Haram was responsible for the kidnapping of a French family in Cameroon. A Nigerian government report revealed the group was paid more than £2 million before releasing its hostages. This has raised concerns about the group's increasing international reach, and appears to mark a departure from its focus on conducting terrorist activity on Nigerian nationals only. Fears that the success of this recent change of tactic may have enhanced the group's appetite for kidnapping Western citizens is well founded.

While there is little evidence to suggest that Boko Haram is operating in the UK, the group's potential to recruit and radicalise British citizens remains a real concern of security authorities.

KEY POINT—PROSCRIBED TERRORIST ORGANISATIONS

The proscription of terrorist organisations certainly contributes towards making the UK a hostile environment for terrorists, sending a strong message that the UK will not tolerate such organisations and their claims to legitimacy.

There are forty-nine international terror organisations proscribed under the UK Terrorism Act 2000, and in Northern Ireland fourteen organisations remain proscribed under previous legislation. A list of proscribed organisations currently outlawed in the UK is shown in Appendix 1. (For updates of this list, see the Home Office website, following the links at: <http://www.homeoffice.gov.uk>.)

The proscription of terrorist groups has the effect of outlawing previously lawful activity, and police officers must be aware that once an organisation is proscribed it is a criminal offence to belong to, support, or display support for a proscribed organisation.

In deciding to proscribe any organisation, the Home Secretary takes into account a number of factors including the nature and scale of its activities; the specific threat it poses to the UK; the specific threat it poses to British nationals overseas; the extent of its presence in the UK; and the need to support other members of the international community in the global fight against terrorism.

Increasing police officers' awareness of how terrorist groups are proscribed will help the legislation work as it was intended, to prevent terrorism and protect the communities the police serve. Both knowledge about and understanding of terrorist organisations, including how they operate in UK communities, are essential elements in being able to deliver the policing of terrorism and violent extremism at a local level.

Al Qa'ida followers

There is a small number of terrorist groups who follow the ideology of Al Qa'ida but who have their own identity and regional agenda. These groups include the Pakistan Taliban (Tehrik-e Taliban Pakistan (TTP), meaning 'student movement of Pakistan'), which has grown significantly in recent years, at one point seizing control not only of significant areas of the FATA but also areas closer to Islamabad, and it occasionally collaborates with Al Qa'ida and other local militant groups. In May 2010 TTP claimed responsibility for the attempted detonation of an explosive device in Times Square, New York. In September 2010, the group made explicit threats against both the US and EU member states, and, following the death of Osama Bin Laden, led a wave of retaliatory attacks in Pakistan.

Many other terrorist groups remain active in the FATA and more widely in Pakistan. Some have a purely sectarian agenda; others regard the West, India, and Indian-administered Kashmir as priority targets. Of all these groups, Lashkar-e-Tayyiba (LeT, meaning 'Army of the Pure or Righteous') is the most capable terrorist group. In Pakistan, Jama'at-ud-Da'wa engages in relief work, social welfare, and education programmes, but is in fact a front for LeT which in theory has been banned since 2002. It conducts attacks in Afghanistan. In the West, it recruits, raises funds, and has also planned operations, including the armed assault in Mumbai in 2008.

Case Study—Massacre in Mumbai

The terrorist attack in Mumbai during 2008 was an armed assault operation incorporating a series of coordinated shootings and bombings conducted in India's largest city and its financial capital. The attacks, which began on 26 November and lasted until 29 November, killed 175 people and wounded at least 308. The killings drew widespread condemnation across the world. Eight separate attacks occurred in south Mumbai at Chhatrapati Shivaji airport Terminus, the Oberoi Trident and the Taj Mahal Palace hotels, Leopold Cafe, Cama Hospital, Nariman House, the Metro Cinema, and a lane behind the Times of India building and St Xavier's College. There was also an explosion at the Mazagaon docks in Mumbai's port area, and one in a taxi at Vile Parle. By early morning 28 November, all sites except for the Taj Mahal Palace hotel had been secured by Mumbai police and security forces. An operation conducted by India's national security guards on 29 November resulted in the death of the remaining suspected terrorists at the Taj Mahal Palace, ending the assault. One suspected terrorist, Mohammed Ajmal Amir Kasab, was captured alive.

Investigations by Indian authorities revealed that ten terrorists had arrived in Mumbai from Pakistan via a stolen boat before dispersing into the city in five separate pairs. The terrorists, armed with grenades and semi-automatic weapons, used modern communication satellite technology which allowed terrorists in Pakistan to command and control their activities. A dossier of evidence compiled by the Indian investigators revealed that the terrorists in Pakistan commanding the operation monitored news coverage, and relayed information to the attackers on the ground in Mumbai. As they monitored the media coverage, one terrorist told an attacker inside the Taj Mahal Hotel, 'There are three ministers and one secretary of the cabinet in your hotel. Find those three or four persons and get whatever you want from India'. He then said, 'Throw one or two grenades on the navy and police teams which are outside'. It remains unclear from the investigators' dossier if any specific media report contributed in any way to the death of civilians or security forces personnel, but the constant encouragement and guidance provided by the commanders assisted in sustaining the operation. In addition to relaying information from media reports, the terrorists in Mumbai took direction from their commanders in Pakistan. A terrorist in the Oberoi Hotel said, 'We have five hostages', a commander replied, 'Kill all hostages, except the two Muslims. Keep the phone switched on so that we can hear the gunfire'. Throughout the armed assault the terrorists appeared to make few operational decisions themselves, taking direct orders from those in Pakistan.

Following the attack, the Indian government announced a 'major overhaul' of the country's internal security which included measures to establish a federal investigation agency, strengthening of coastal security, training of additional commandos, increasing anti-terror laws, and recruiting to fill the vacancies within depleted intelligence agencies.

Other groups following Al Qa'ida's ideology include the clan-based militia, al-Shabaab (meaning 'the Youth') in Somalia, which continues to control significant parts of the south and centre of the country, conducting regular attacks against the African peacekeeping force (AMISOM). Parts of al-Shabaab have adopted the global jihadist ideology associated with Al Qa'ida, and these have attracted hundreds of foreign fighters, including UK nationals. They have links to Al Qa'ida and to AQ-AP and operate more widely in east Africa. In June 2010 al-Shabaab carried out its first terrorist attack outside Somalia, killing seventy-four people in suicide bombings in Kampala, Uganda. In September 2013, it carried out its most ambitious attack at a shopping mall in Nairobi in Kenya.

Case Study—Al-Shabaab Armed Assault

At midday on Saturday 21 September 2013, al-Shabaab militants stormed Nairobi's premier shopping centre in Kenya, throwing grenades and firing indiscriminately at shoppers. The Westgate Shopping Centre was packed with shoppers and people having lunch. The multi-storey mall contained restaurants, cafes, banks, a large supermarket, a cinema, and a casino.

The armed assault began when a number of gunmen entered the mall from three separate entrances. According to witnesses sitting outside ArtCaffe on the ground floor, one group armed with assault weapons drove up to the main entrance firing indiscriminately and throwing grenades, causing panic.

Simultaneously, witnesses observed a second group of armed terrorists making their way onto the second floor of the building via a rooftop car park. A children's cooking competition was taking place in the car park at the time of the initial assault, during which a number of children and adults were killed.

The third group of attackers is believed to have entered the building down a ramp into a basement area. In the period leading up to the assault, the terrorists had hired a shop in the mall which gave them unrestricted access to service lifts, enabling them to stockpile weapons and ammunition.

The attackers set up a base using a ventilation shaft on the first floor, supported by an unidentified vehicle in the basement which was used as a command and control centre. When police and security forces arrived on the scene, their efforts initially focused on rescuing those people trapped inside the building, as gunfire and explosions continued to echo around the mall. A number of citizens were believed to have been taken hostage and held in a cinema and a casino on the second floor, while others were held hostage in the basement.

Witness reports claim that the first police officers did not arrive at the mall until 12.30 p.m. At around 3 o'clock, the Kenya Defence Forces (KDF) troops were deployed. Gun battles raged throughout Saturday afternoon. Having positioned weapons in the preceding days, the attackers were able to re-arm quickly and repel Kenyan security forces.

The operation to free the hostages and capture the militants continued into the night and throughout the next day, with sporadic gunfire and explosions. At 6.45 p.m. on Sunday 22 September, two helicopters landed on the roof in an attempt to retake the mall. Shortly afterwards a large explosion was heard from inside, but the militants proved resilient and the battle continued throughout Monday 23 September, despite the launch of a series of assaults by Kenyan security forces.

By the evening of Tuesday 24 September, Kenyan President Uhuru Kenyatta declared the siege to be over. The Somali militant group, al-Shabaab, claimed responsibility for the attack in retaliation for Kenya's army carrying out operations on Somali territory. The armed assault and subsequent siege lasted eighty hours, resulting in at least sixty-seven deaths. The number of gunmen involved in the attack is still in dispute. Initially, security forces had estimated there to be between ten and fifteen terrorists but later reports suggested the attack may have been conducted with just four to six militants. Kenyan Interior Minister, Joseph Ole Lenku, revealed that the possibility that when security forces were evacuating people in the first stages of the operation that some of the attackers may have escaped could not be ruled out.

Governments around the world were quick to condemn the violent attack, Prime Minister David Cameron describing it as 'an absolutely sickening and despicable attack of appalling brutality'.

Lone Al Qa'ida terrorists

Al Qa'ida and some of its affiliates have increasingly encouraged acts of terrorism by individuals or small groups independent of the Al Qa'ida chain of command and without reference to, or guidance and instruction from, the leadership. The Internet has helped to enable this type of terrorism by providing material which encourages and informs radicalisation and provides easy access to instructions on how to plan and conduct operations. In practice, some attacks have been conducted or attempted by groups or sole individuals apparently using their own initiative; in other cases they have had some contact with terrorist networks. In cases where lone actors have activated the final stages of their attack planning operations, it was found that the assailants had read propaganda on the Internet from an Al Qa'ida affiliate and they had corresponded with an Al Qa'ida member, but the attacks seem to have been planned and conducted without formal guidance or instruction. Such attacks by lone actors are of real concern to security forces in the UK and throughout the West.

Case Study—Online Radicalisation of Lone-Actor Al Qa'ida Terrorists

Denis Mamadou Cuspert, born in Berlin during 1975 in the borough of Kreuzberg, had a German mother. His Ghanaian father left the family shortly after his birth. Cuspert had a troubled childhood and an argumentative relationship with his stepfather, a former member of the US armed forces. At the age of only 8, Cuspert began stealing toy cars. As a teenager, he and his gang were involved in dealing drugs and committing armed robberies. After shooting a friend in the face with a gas pistol, Cuspert was sentenced to three years' imprisonment, during which time he decided to start a new career as a rap musician.

Upon release from prison, Cuspert changed his name during 2002 to Deso Dogg and became a successful 'gangster rapper'. His new-found career lasted until 2009, and although he never reached the top ranking of musical artists, he was well known and respected amongst his peers and had many fans. During his musical career he forged contacts with radical Islamist groups including the Kaplan group, the Hizb ut-Tahrir, and the Tablighi Jamaat. During 2010, Cuspert announced his retirement from music in order to continue new work as an Islamic preacher. He changed his name again, this time calling himself Abu Maleeq. Leading Salafist preachers in Germany, including Pierre Vogel, believed that given the recognition he had achieved as a musician, Cuspert offered a unique opportunity to promote their cause and engage in their missionary work. Salafist preachers expected Cuspert's music fans would continue to follow him and convert to their version of Islam. Guided by extremist preachers, Cuspert became increasingly radical and forged a close association with Abu Nagie, an extremist preacher from the organisation, *Wahre Religion* (true religion). He began to produce *nasheeds* (religious chants) to glorify jihad which were broadcast on the Internet. Cuspert produced Salafist online propaganda for the jihadist movement, extending his efforts by working for an organisation called Millatu Ibrahim. It was during this time that his activities came to the attention of the police. Following an incident in May 2012 in Bonn where a police officer was seriously injured by a knife wielded by an Islamist extremist during a clash with members of the right-wing political movement, 'pro Köln', police conducted eighty raids on premises suspected of being occupied by members of the Salafist movement. In one of the flats raided, officers discovered a vest filled with explosives which had been prepared by Cuspert. While forensic examinations revealed that the improvised device would not have detonated, it provided a clear signal to authorities that Cuspert was prepared to pursue his extremist beliefs through acts of violence.

The public disorder in Germany between Salafists and right-wing groups resulted in Millatu Ibrahim being banned. Cuspert disappeared with associates shortly after the raids, suspected of making his way to Egypt. During September 2012, he produced an online video asking all Muslims in Germany to fight against the German government and bring jihad to Germany. The German authorities were concerned at the speed at which Cuspert had adopted such extreme views, most likely as a result of the high-level support he received from leading Islamist preachers. His online *nasheeds* and propaganda videos would have damaging consequences, serving to radicalise others. During February 2011, Arid Uka, a native Albanian who grew up in Germany and was aged 22, killed two US soldiers at Frankfurt Airport. At his trial, Uka revealed that he had been radicalised by jihadist propaganda videos he had watched online. As part of their investigations, German authorities investigated his Facebook profile and found that just days before the shooting, Uka had written alongside one of Cuspert's videos, 'I love you for Allah Abu Maleeq'. As an online terrorist recruiter and radicaliser, Cuspert could not be ignored by authorities.

1.6.2 **Conflicts overseas**

Terrorists exploit instability in countries overseas. This instability can easily spread from one country to another, and lawless regions provide a haven for terrorist groups and organised criminal networks alike.

The UK armed forces are fighting in Afghanistan because of this threat, supporting the Afghani government in the attempt at preventing Afghan territory from again being used by Al Qa'ida as a secure base from which to plan attacks on the UK or its allies. The UK is supporting an Afghan-led process to develop its own security forces and build a more effective state that can control its own security and, ultimately, achieve a lasting political settlement with the diverse groups that seek to control that complicated country. Afghan security forces are now 260,000 strong. The transition of national security responsibility from ISAF to the Afghans is underway, and joint Afghan and international operations continue to suppress insurgent forces. The Afghan economy is growing rapidly and the Afghan government's ability to deliver key services such as health and education has significantly improved. The UK government continues to work with the Afghans to ensure further progress is made to tackle corruption, stimulate regional engagement and political and economic reform, but it must not be complacent. The insurgency remains strong.

UK engagement in conflicts overseas, both in Afghanistan and Iraq, and more recently in Syria, has provoked a series of unintended consequences that threaten the safety of communities in the UK and overseas, among these the migration of foreign fighters, radicalised British citizens from British communities travelling to conflict zones overseas, the exportation of terrorism overseas by British citizens, and the challenges confronting Conflict-Engaged Citizens (CEC) on their return home following exposure to the brutality of conflict.

Foreign fighters

Throughout the long and violent history of terrorism in the UK, its citizens have left home shores to join various causes and fight for their beliefs in foreign lands. During 2006 the International Institute for Strategic Studies published a report entitled *The Military Balance*. It estimated that 'one in ten of the 20,000 insurgents fighting the conflict in Iraq were foreign-born'. It also revealed that up to 150 radicals from Britain had travelled to Iraq to join up with a 'British Brigade' that had been established by Al Qa'ida leaders to fight coalition forces. It appeared that the flow of young men from Western Europe to Iraq was increasing. The supply chain of volunteers to join the ranks of the insurgency was not just restricted to the UK. In France, Pierre de Bousquet de Florian, the head of the French domestic security service, revealed that fifteen young French men remained in and around Iraq and of these, at least nine had been killed. This raised two key issues for the security authorities: first, how were these men travelling to Iraq and receiving their training? The second was the realisation that while many of these kinds of volunteers may run the risk of dying in conflicts overseas, some may return to the UK. These Conflict-Engaged Citizens could put their skills to unlawful use when they return to their local communities in the UK by continuing violent jihadist aims. Overseas conflicts in Iraq, Afghanistan, and Syria draw UK citizens to support insurgent groups in these countries. This is of real concern for UK security forces as the number of foreign fighters is increasing with each uprising and conflict overseas.

Case Study—Call to Arms in Syria

Since the beginning of the Syrian uprising in March 2011, the International Centre for Study of Radicalisation (ICSR) has compiled a database of foreign fighters travelling to the country. Based on an update of their earlier estimates published in April, ICSR now believes that between 200 and 350 UK citizens have travelled to Syria with the intention of becoming fighters. This figure includes deceased individuals and those who later left the conflict and have returned to their communities in the UK.

The ICSR continue to monitor the flow of foreign fighters from Western countries as part of an ongoing project exploring this aspect of the Syrian conflict. Although it may be too early to draw general conclusions, the ICSR project provides an insight to better understand the threats and risks posed by foreign fighters. ICSR data suggests that many of those UK citizens travelling to Syria as foreign fighters are male, in their twenties, of Muslim faith and of South Asian ethnic origin, with recent connections to higher education and with links to individuals or groups who have international connections.

The reasons why some British Muslims would seek to engage in violent jihadist activity abroad remain varied. However, the ICSR suggests that some general observations about the key drivers which either serve to push or pull individuals towards fighting in Syria can be made. These include what has become known as the 'ummah consciousness', a viewpoint which advises Muslims that they belong to a global fraternity where issues such as loyalty and allegiance are defined through confessional identity. Some Muslims may, therefore, feel obliged to defend their 'brothers and sisters' in Syria.

The proximity of the Syrian conflict to Europe also makes it particularly attractive to potential fighters. Moreover, the main transit country, Turkey, does not require UK citizens to have a visa and it is also relatively inexpensive to reach. While UK involvement in previous conflicts over the last decade may have proved contentious, there was nonetheless an alternative narrative which counselled young Muslims against travelling abroad for jihad. With the present conflict in Syria, would-be jihadists find themselves adopting a not dissimilar view to Western governments—that Assad is guilty of committing atrocities against civilians, and that he should be removed.

Exporting terrorism

The UK government is committed to ensuring national security and its primary responsibility remains the safety of citizens at home. However, in our increasingly globalised and interdependent world, the government also has a responsibility to ensure that Britain does not become a staging post in which extremists can plan their next attacks. The government also has a responsibility to protect other nations from any terrorist activity which might emerge from our native soil. Everyone should be aware of this particular danger.

Case Study—Exporting Home-Grown Terrorists

The first significant attack by a UK home-grown suicide bomber occurred thousands of miles from British territory, in Israel, two years before the multiple suicide terrorist attacks in London on 7 July 2005. At 1 o'clock in the morning on 30 April 2003, a suicide bomber attacked Mike's Place, a bar on the Tel Aviv seafront. Three people were killed and a further sixty were injured. Waiting outside the bar was another suicide bomber whose device failed to detonate. As the emergency services arrived, the second bomber fled. In a nearby rubbish-bin police later found two UK passports. One of the suicide bombers, Asif Mohammed Hanif, aged 21, died at the scene whilst his accomplice, Omar Khan Sharif, aged 27, escaped. Two weeks later Sharif's body was found floating off the coast of Tel Aviv. Both men had travelled to Israel from their native Derby. The Palestinian militant group, Hamas, claimed responsibility for the attack, having recruited Hanif and Sharif.

Conflict-Engaged Citizens

Whether armed forces personnel, charitable organisation volunteers, or citizens working for non-governmental organisations (NGOs), the return to the UK from conflict zones of Conflict-Engaged Citizens (CECs) raises concerns about public safety.

Case Study—Terror Threats at Central Mosque

At 4 o'clock on 23 September 2012, Fraser Rae, a 28-year-old male from Johnstone in Renfrewshire, Scotland, walked towards the central mosque in Glasgow shouting, 'I will blow this place up'. Wearing a backpack, Rae walked through the mosque car park to the main entrance, terrifying a 15-year-old by telling him, 'Run, run, run, I've got a bomb'. Rae made his way into the mosque where the caretaker heard him shouting and swearing as he walked through corridors towards the main prayer room. As Rae entered the prayer room, in which thirty adults and children were present, he yelled, 'Christians can do it too'. As he was approached by adults in the prayer room Rae, who held a bottle in his left hand, his right hand tucked into the waistband of his trousers, under his jacket and behind his back, said, 'Stay back, I've got a gun', quickly followed by, 'I'll shoot you'. He then launched into a tirade of racist abuse aimed at those present in the prayer room, and implied he had a bomb in his backpack. Despite threats to their personal safety, members of the mosque restrained Rae and physically escorted him off the premises. Police officers attending the incident arrested Rae and searched his backpack seizing a number of items including a mask, gloves, and scissors. Rae was taken to

Cathcart police station to be interviewed. The police investigation did not discover any firearms, and a search by a dog trained to identify traces of explosives discovered no bomb-making materials.

On 20 December 2012, Fraser Rae appeared at Glasgow Sheriff Court. The court heard that Fraser James Watson Rae, born 8 August 1984, was a former soldier and Iraq veteran, serving with the Argyll and Sutherland Highlanders. Defence lawyer Mark Chambers said his client was remorseful and that his actions were out of character, although it was revealed that Rae had suffered psychologically after leaving the Army and that he had become abusive towards the presence of Pakistani people in the UK, suggesting that these people were responsible for the bombings in Iraq. The court also heard that Rae had said to the police, 'I was in Iraq and all they did was bomb. My brothers in the army got blown up'. Procurator fiscal deputy, Adam Roberts, informed the court that a friendly competition involving around 300 adults and children had finished shortly before Rae had entered the mosque.

Rae pleaded guilty to threatening to blow up the mosque and for inferring that he had a bomb. He also admitted to carrying scissors, shouting and swearing and making racist remarks to police. Rae was sentenced to twenty-eight months' imprisonment for contravening section 38 (1) of the Criminal Justice and Licensing (Scotland) Act 2010 (threatening and/or abusive behaviour), and section 49 (1) Criminal Law (Consolidation) (Scotland) Act 1995 (carrying a knife). Following sentencing, John Dunn, Procurator fiscal for West Scotland, said:

> Everyone has the right to live free from violence, threats, intimidation or the fear of harassment or abuse stemming from the prejudice of another person. Hopefully the conviction of and sentencing of Fraser Rae will encourage the public to report all hate crimes to the police. They can have the confidence that all such hate crimes will be investigated carefully and prosecuted robustly.

Reinforcing this, Strathclyde Police Detective Inspector Joe Mckerns said, 'We will not tolerate any acts targeted against minority ethnic communities and will take robust and prompt action'.

The actions of Rae were abhorrent, causing unnecessary alarm and distress to innocent members of the public. Surprisingly, little media coverage or comment was offered by authorities about exactly what had pushed Rae to such an extreme act. Whatever the specific circumstances in this case, it is evident that engagement in conflict overseas had led to psychological damage from which acts providing danger to the public had arisen. Whether through failure of authorities to assess the potential threat to the public he posed, or through a lack of support and appropriate intervention by relevant professionals, Rae may consider himself a victim too. He is not the first UK citizen to return home following engagement in conflicts overseas to have suffered psychologically from his experiences, nor will he be the last. Exposure to significant conflict can be deeply affecting. CECs require full support, which includes preparing for their return and for their long-term resettlement and reintegration to civil society.

1.6.3 **Northern Ireland-Related Terrorism**

The UK has a long experience of Northern Ireland-Related Terrorism (NIRT). Between 1969 and 1999 (the thirty-year period referred to as the 'Troubles') there were 3,667 deaths related to political violence in Northern Ireland; 303 of these were police officers, 709 were soldiers, 536 were terrorists (although this figure is disputed). The remainder and vast majority were civilians. Following the Good Friday Agreement made in 1998, many Northern Ireland terrorist groups agreed a ceasefire and a subsequent decommissioning of their weapons. Despite progress in stabilising the political situation in Northern Ireland, some terrorist groups continue to carry out terrorist attacks. Support for NIRT remains low, but the frequency of these attacks has increased from twenty-two in 2009, to forty in 2010.

Case Study—Murder at Massereene Barracks

At 9.20 p.m. on Saturday 7 March 2009, soldiers from 38 Engineer Regiment at the Massereene Barracks in County Antrim ordered pizzas from a local take-away restaurant. The soldiers were due to depart the following morning for Afghanistan. When the pizza delivery arrived at the main barracks gates, four soldiers came out to collect them. As they did, two gunmen opened fire from a nearby car. From the sixty shots fired, two soldiers, Sapper Mark Quinsey, aged 23 and from Birmingham, and Sapper Patrick Azimkar, aged 21 from north London, were killed. Four other people were also injured in the shooting, including the pizza-delivery man.

In a statement claiming responsibility for the attack, the South Antrim Brigade of the Real Irish Republican Army (RIRA), made no apology for shooting the delivery man, accusing him of 'collaborating' with the British army by delivering food to the base. Politicians and communities across the political spectrum were united in their condemnation of the attack. In an historic moment for Northern Ireland, Sinn Féin's Gerry Adams and Martin McGuinness backed the police manhunt to catch the killers and denounced the terrorists. McGuinness, the Deputy First Minister, said: 'I was a member of the IRA, but that war is over now. The people responsible for last night's incident are clearly signalling that they want to resume or restart that war. Well, I deny their right to do that'. Adams said: 'Sinn Féin has a responsibility to be consistent. The logic of this is that we support the police in the apprehension of those involved in last night's attack'.

Lieutenant Colonel Roger Lewis, the regiment's commanding officer, said of Azimkar that he was 'shocked and stunned by the death of this very promising young soldier', and described Quinsey as a 'mature, reliable and hugely capable young soldier with a bright future ahead of him'.

POINT TO NOTE—RE-EMERGENCE

Following the terrorist attack at the Massereene Barracks, then Northern Ireland's First Minister and Democratic Unionist Party leader Peter Robinson, spoke to the Irish Assembly: 'The events of Saturday evening were a throwback to a previous era. We must never return to such terrible days. The police need the support and cooperation of the entire community. Let the answer be loud and clear: We are not turning back'.

These words failed to prevent a further terrorist incident that occurred two days later.

Case Study—Murder of Police Constable Stephen Caroll

At 9.45 p.m. on Monday 9 March 2009, police officers responded to a request for assistance from a member of the public at Lismore Manor in Craigavon, Northern Ireland. Two police vehicles arrived in the area and as officers alighted, gunshots were fired, resulting in the death of Police Constable Stephen Caroll. On Tuesday 10 March in a coded message, the dissident terrorist group, the Continuity Irish Republican Army (CIRA), claimed responsibility for the shooting which was conducted by its North Armagh battalion. CIRA stated that 'As long as there is British involvement in Ireland, these attacks will continue'.

Then Chief Constable of the Police Service of Northern Ireland, Sir Hugh Orde, appealed for the community to help police bring those responsible to justice:

> Shortly before 10 o'clock officers in Craigavon were going about their duty, serving the public of Northern Ireland, answering a call for help. Sadly one of those officers paid the ultimate price when cowards and criminals gunned him down. I pay tribute to him and send my deepest sympathy to his family. My officers joined the police service to serve the community here. Every day and night they respond to reports of burglary, domestic abuse, missing persons, vehicle theft, rape . . . the list goes on. Last night in Craigavon it was a call to a broken window. Such is the desire within my organisation to win the support of all within the community my officers responded knowing the threat to their lives was a very real possibility. But last night their commitment was met with the very worst in human nature. This morning the Police Service of Northern Ireland has lost an officer. But I say to you—the people living on this island—you have lost a member of your community. This was not only an attack on the peace process, it was an attack on the community here. Children today do not remember the horrors of the past. Let us not repeat that pointless loss of life with them.

KEY POINT—RESURGENCE

On the first anniversary of the murder of Police Constable Stephen Caroll on 10 March 2010, colleagues from the Police Service of Northern Ireland (PSNI) stated that, 'Stephen Caroll was a highly respected and very experienced police officer. He, like his colleagues, never shied away from his responsibility to serve the people of Northern Ireland'. The resurgence of politically motivated violence on the streets of Northern Ireland during March 2009 must serve as a reminder to all in authority of the devastating impact of terrorism.

There were also sixteen attacks alone from January to June 2011 including the murder of Police Constable Ronan Kerr in April 2011. Many more attacks have been successfully stopped. Between January 2009 and December 2010, there were 316 arrests in connection with terrorism-related activity in Northern Ireland. Over the same period there were ninety-seven charges for terrorist offences and nine people were convicted of terrorist activity, but not all paramilitary operations have been disrupted.

In May 2011 a number of coded warnings were received which suggested a bomb had been left somewhere in central London. These were the first coded warnings in the UK from Northern Ireland terrorist groups for ten years.

1.6.4 **Responding to domestic and international terrorism**

Since the attacks in the US which took place on 11 September 2001, the UK police service has undergone a complete change in its understanding of the terrorist threat. For many years police officers had been facing a deadly campaign of terrorism conducted by ruthless individuals intent on causing havoc in Northern Ireland, but the emergence of Al Qa'ida-inspired terrorism presented a new type of threat. The terrorism conducted by the IRA had clear political objectives and the organisation itself had a military structure. It adopted recognisable military tactics and methods of operating. The IRA avoided the loss of its own operatives. This threat is different to the one posed by Al Qa'ida and its affiliates. Al Qa'ida today has little formal organisational structure, and is best described as a network of networks operating globally. These networks have a wide range of targets and have no defined method of operating. They have no particular signature that can be attributed to their activities. Most importantly, they seek mass casualties in order to maximise the impact of their attacks. They also enthusiastically embrace the use of suicide operations. The key differences between the threats posed by the IRA and Al Qa'ida are shown in Figure 1.5.

Figure 1.5. Comparison of terrorist threats of Northern Irish-related terrorism and Al Qa'ida-related terrorism.

1.6.5 **Extreme right-wing terrorism**

Right-wing, political, violent extremism leading to terrorism can take various forms. Some individuals and groups seek strong centralised government and the preservation of their national domestic culture. Others, such as certain militia in the US, believe in the preservation of individual rights, including militant protection of personal property and privacy, and the right to bear arms, the responsibility for preserving these rights resting less with central government than with individuals themselves. Extreme right-wing views are often associated with fascism and racism. There are individuals and groups who advocate severe, stringent, and immoderate measures using violence and intimidation to promote their beliefs and their beliefs' priority over other cultures and communities presents a clear and present danger to UK national security.

Case Study—Right-Wing Terrorism

During November 2007 police officers were conducting searches for child pornography but as they raided Martin Gilleard's East Yorkshire flat, they uncovered ammunition, weapons, home-made bombs, and a large amount of extremist literature promoting racist views. They seized a diary belonging to Gilleard, which read, 'I'm so sick and tired of hearing Nationalists talk of killing Muslims, of blowing up Mosques, of fighting back, only to see these acts of resistance fail to appear. The time has come to stop the talk and start to act'.

Gilleard seemed to be preparing for a kind of ethnic war, his aim to protect the purity of Caucasians. He had started to collect dozens of weapons. He had made four nail bombs and hidden them underneath the bed where his son slept whenever he came to visit. At the time his premises were searched, Gilleard was not at home prompting a large manhunt. Police officers successfully located him three days later in Dundee, Scotland, where he was arrested for terrorism offences.

This case showed that counter-terrorist units and their local force Special Branch counterparts are increasingly having to investigate far right groups. Gilleard was one of the first right-wing extremists to be prosecuted under counter-terrorism legislation. Then Head of the North East Counter-Terrorism Unit, Assistant Chief Constable John Parkinson said:

> Martin Gilleard is a very dangerous individual and not only did he express his intentions to carry out acts of terrorism, he had the capacity to do so. Terrorism in its rawest form is someone who possesses those extreme views who then moves on to violence or threats of violence for an ideological or political cause and that is equally applicable to right-wing extremism or to an Islamist cause.

The judge at Leeds Crown Court stated that he believed that Martin Gilleard intended to cause havoc with the devices found by police under his bed. Gilleard was found guilty of terrorist offences and possessing child pornography and was sentenced to sixteen years' imprisonment.

KEY POINT—DOMESTIC EXTREMISM LEADING TO TERRORISM

The police service, which has traditionally retained responsibility for investigating domestic extremism issues, is discovering that UK extremists have moved from protest, direct action, and committing low level crimes to committing terrorism-related offences, as a result of the stimulus successful acts of international terrorism have brought about. In his review of terrorism legislation published in August 2010, Lord Carlile reported that there had been a significantly greater increase in the activities of right-wing extremism, warning that those tempted by it should be aware that they face the prospect of very long prison sentences.

The boundaries between domestic terrorism (DT) and domestic extremism (DE) are becoming increasingly blurred, and elements of violent DE are now finding their way into the realm of DT and the sphere of national security.

1.6.6 **Cyber-terrorism**

The burgeoning role cyberspace plays in everyday life has revealed new threats as well as new opportunities. A growing number of adversaries are looking to use cyberspace to steal, compromise, or destroy critical data. Governments have no choice but to find ways to confront and overcome these threats if they are to flourish in an increasingly competitive and globalised world. As citizens place more dependence on online products and services, this matters increasingly. The scale of our dependence now means that our economic well-being, our key infrastructure, our places of work and our homes can all be directly affected.

The use of the Internet by terrorist recruiters and radicalisers concerns national security professionals, but violent extremists have also harnessed the power of the web to conduct remote hostile reconnaissance and other planning activities designed for use in a terrorist attack.

Case Study—Cyber Terrorist 007

When Metropolitan Police officers raided a flat in west London during October 2005, they arrested a young man, Younes Tsouli. The significance of this arrest was not immediately clear but investigations soon revealed that the Moroccan-born Tsouli was the world's most wanted 'cyber-terrorist'. Tsouli adopted the user name 'Irhabi 007' (*Irhabi* means 'terrorist' in Arabic), and his activities grew from posting advice on the Internet on how to hack into mainframe computer systems, to assisting those in planning terrorist attacks. Tsouli trawled the Internet searching for home movies made by US soldiers in Iraq and Afghanistan that revealed the layout of US military bases. Over time, these small pieces of data were collated and passed to those planning attacks against these bases. This virtual reconnaissance provided data illustrating how it was no longer necessary for terrorists to conduct physical reconnaissance if relevant information could be captured and collated direct from publicly available sources on the Internet.

Police investigations subsequently revealed that Tsouli had €2.5 million of fraudulent transactions passing through his accounts which he used to support and finance terrorist activity. Pleading guilty to charges of incitement to commit acts of terrorism, Tsouli received a sixteen-year custodial sentence to be served at Belmarsh High Security Prison in London where, unsurprisingly, he has been denied access to the Internet. The then National Coordinator of Terrorist Investigations, Deputy Assistant Commissioner Peter Clarke, said that Tsouli 'provided a link to core Al Qa'ida, to the heart of Al Qa'ida and the wider network that he was linking into through the internet', going on to say, 'what it did show us was the extent to which they could conduct operational planning on the internet. It was the first virtual conspiracy to murder that we had seen'.

The case against Tsouli was the first in the UK which showed that cyber-terrorism threatened national security. Law-enforcement practitioners understood that the

Internet was clearly a positive force for good, but it could also be hijacked and exploited by terrorists not only to plan attacks but also to be used in the radicalisation and recruitment of new operatives to their cause. The core and affiliated networks of Al Qa'ida were quick to realise and to exploit this.

KEY POINT—CYBER THREATS

Some crimes exist only in the digital world, in particular those targeting the integrity of computer networks and online services. But cyberspace is also being used as a platform for committing 'terrestrial' crimes such as fraud, and often on an industrial scale. Identity theft and fraud online now dwarf their offline equivalents. The Internet has provided new opportunities for those who seek to exploit children and the vulnerable. Cyberspace allows criminals to target countries from other jurisdictions across the world, making it harder to enforce the law. As businesses and government services move more of their operations online, potential targets increase in number. Some of the most sophisticated threats to cyberspace come from foreign states which seek to conduct espionage with the aim of spying on or compromising government, military, industrial, and economic assets, as well as monitoring opponents of their own regimes. 'Patriotic' hackers can act upon states' behalf, to spread disinformation, disrupt critical services, or seek advantage during times of increased tension. In times of conflict, vulnerabilities in cyberspace could be exploited by an enemy to reduce a nation's military's technological advantage, or to attack domestic critical infrastructures.

Cyberspace is now a domain where strategic advantage—industrial or military—can be won or lost. The Internet underpins the complex systems used by commerce and the military, from the National Grid on which our electricity supply depends, to the mechanisms safeguarding sophisticated military targets, including those housing our nuclear weapons. The growing dependence on cyberspace means that its disruption can affect nations' ability to function effectively in a crisis. Nearly two-thirds of critical infrastructure companies report regularly finding software designed to sabotage their systems. Some states regard cyberspace as providing a way to commit hostile acts 'deniably'. Alongside existing defence and security capabilities, nations must be capable of protecting their national interests in cyberspace. Iain Lobban, the Director of the Government Communications Headquarters (GCHQ) has stated that 'There are over 20,000 malicious emails on UK government networks each month, 1,000 of which are deliberately targeting them'. These kinds of attack are increasing. The number of emails with malicious content detected by government networks in 2010 was double the number seen in 2009, and law-enforcement agencies are themselves being targeted.

1.7 Summary

The threat the UK faces continues to change, and the police service has an important role to play in tackling contemporary terrorist threats. Although Al Qa'ida is still capable of terrorist attacks in the UK, it is weaker now than it ever has been since 9/11. It has thus far failed to achieve its objectives, and has been marginalised by events in the Middle East and North Africa. But persistent longer-term factors—fragile and failed states, technology, radicalisation—will continue to sustain terrorist groups. The UK must not underestimate the resilience of Al Qa'ida. Complacency based upon the absence of large-scale terrorist attacks is both misplaced and unwise. Other groups, some affiliated to Al Qa'ida, now pose a very high threat to UK national security. The threat from lone-actor terrorism is significant. Individual terrorists who operate in isolation very often come to the attention of intelligence agencies and law enforcement only once their attacks have been mounted, or through a failing of their own security, not because they have been discovered by law enforcement agencies.

Terrorist attacks in Northern Ireland have increased in recent years. The uncomfortable truth is that terrorists and violent extremists are already present and operating in the UK, embedded within our local communities. The priority of UK counter-terrorism practice remains as high as ever. All ranks in the police service must discharge their responsibilities to ensure that the people they serve can go about their lives freely, and with confidence that they are indeed safe.

The police service continues to be the most important tool of the state for tackling the threat from terrorism and violent extremism. The police are the most appropriate and suitable people to uncover terrorist plotters living within communities, and they can build local partnerships to encourage and support people to come forward with information to help keep their own neighbourhood safe. They can also relay messages to reassure the public following police counter-terrorism operations, terrorist events, and allay concerns in the community. Police officers gather intelligence, preserve evidence, conduct covert and overt operations with armed support against terrorist individuals and groups. They can arrest, detain, and investigate terrorist matters, building complex criminal cases to remove violent extremists from civil society, and they are prepared to put themselves in harm's way to respond to terrorist attacks to save life and protect property. No other arm of the state has such a broad and important role in tackling contemporary terrorism and violent extremism. It is a role that not only serves to make communities safer, but it preserves freedom, democracy, tolerance, and the respect for human rights and civil liberties, values that characterise the UK and make it a very desirable place in which to live.

Further reading

- Baylis, J, and Smith, S, *The Globalization of World Politics: An Introduction to International Relations* 2nd edition (Oxford: Oxford University Press, 2007).
- Chandler, M, and Gunaratna, R, *Countering Terrorism: Can We Meet the Threat of Global Violence?* (London: Reakton Books Ltd, 2007).
- Coogan, P, *The IRA* (London: Harper Collins, 1995).
- HM Government, *Threat Levels—The System to Assess the Threat from International Terrorism* (2006).
- HM Government, *A Strong Britain in an Age of Uncertainty: The National Security Strategy* (2010).
- HM Government *Countering International Terrorism—The United Kingdom's Strategy* CONTEST (2011).
- HM Government, *The UK Cyber Security Strategy—Protecting and Promoting the UK in a Digital Age* (2011).
- Schmid, AP, *The Routledge Handbook of Terrorism Research* (Oxford: Routledge, 2011).
- Staniforth, A, *The Routledge Companion to UK Counter-Terrorism* (Oxford: Routledge, 2012).
- Staniforth, A, and PNLD, *Blackstone's Counter-Terrorism Handbook* 3rd edition (Oxford: Oxford University Press, 2013).

2

Concept of Terrorism and Extremism

2.1 Introduction 33
2.2 Defining Terrorism 33
2.3 Understanding Terrorism 35
2.4 Typology of Terrorism 43
2.5 Characteristics of Terrorism 46
2.6 Terrorist Motivations 50
2.7 Summary 52

2.1 Introduction

The way in which the UK counters terrorism is developing in response to current threats. Protecting the public from acts of terrorism is no longer only the responsibility of specialist agencies, organisations, or departments. It now requires a multi-agency approach with each organisation bringing its expertise to bear on the problem, in concert with others. To counter the threat effectively, all those in authority are now required to broaden their knowledge and understanding of terrorism in order to prevent it from taking root in our communities, to investigate terrorist-related matters, set policy, devise strategy, and make informed decisions. Developing an understanding of terrorism will ensure that all police practitioners are better prepared than ever before to protect the public from a diverse range of terrorist-related activities.

2.2 Defining Terrorism

Terrorism is not new. Its origins can be traced back many centuries but it remains a much contested concept to this day. Lord Carlile of Berriew CBE QC, the UK's former independent reviewer of terrorism legislation said, '[t]here is no single definition of terrorism that commands full international approval'. There are hundreds of definitions in use today which emphasise a variety of attributes of terrorism. These include terrorism's symbolic character, its often indiscriminate nature, its typical focus on civilian and non-combatant targets of violence, its sometimes provocative, sometimes retributive aims, and the disruption of public order, and endangering public security. In addition, definitions of terrorism in use today include its creation of a climate of fear to influence audiences beyond its target victims, its disregard for the rules of war and justice, and its asymmetric character, where terrorists oppose state authorities whose military power far exceeds the capacity and capability of terrorists groups. Many definitions also refer to the fact that terrorism is usually an instrument for the attempted realisation of a political or religious project that perpetrators lacking mass support are seeking, that it generally involves a series of punctuated acts of demonstrative public violence, followed by threats of more such acts in order to impress, intimidate, and/or coerce target audiences. Yet a listing of the elements of terrorism is not a suitable definition.

In most situations, the adoption of a standard meaning of any given concept is simply a matter of convenience. This is not the case with such a value-laden term as terrorism, which not only refers to a special form of violence, or special type of criminal offence, but is also used as a pejorative term, expressing moral condemnation in official and public discourse. Despite numerous attempts to define terrorism, many of the definitions in use today lack the legal credibility required to be applicable in domestic or international law. In March 2007, Lord Carlile presented a report to the UK parliament which focused on the legal definition of terrorism. The report highlighted the fact that a definition of terrorism is of real practical and operational significance because it triggers many legal powers as well as contributing to the description of offences and the understanding of the security threat to be tackled.

POINT TO NOTE—OPERATIONAL REQUIREMENTS FOR DEFINING TERRORISM

Defining terrorism is important. Stating that the threat from terrorism is severe, or that terrorist-related incidents are increasing annually, has little meaning unless we know precisely what terrorism actually is. Defining terrorism provides a focus for those with the responsibility of making key strategic decisions. It ensures that police officers, police partners, and government agencies understand from the outset what it is they are protecting the public from. A clear definition is also important for international cooperation, as 'terrorism' may have a different meaning in other countries. A clear definition is also vital so that the police can adequately distinguish between legitimate and illegitimate activities, especially those related to political policies. The special laws devised to deal with terrorism, often draconian compared to other laws, should not affect legitimate political activity, even if this activity is aggressive or unpopular. Most importantly, it is not enough to declare war on what one deems to be terrorism without giving a precise definition of what one is fighting. An objective definition of terrorism must not only prove possible, it is also indispensable to any serious attempt to prevent terrorism.

As a starting point for his report, Lord Carlile highlighted the definition of terrorism which was included in the Prevention of Terrorism (Temporary Provisions) Act 1989. It described terrorism as: 'the use of violence for political ends, and includes any use of violence for the purpose of putting the public or any section of the public in fear'.

This definition had major drawbacks as new forms of terrorist activity began to emerge during the 1990s. Most importantly, the definition did not include mention of a serious level of violence, serious damage to property, risk to health and safety, or electronic disruption. In a review of terrorism legislation during 1996, Lord Lloyd of Berwick recommended that an alternative definition should be adopted. He suggested the operational definition used at the time by the US Federal Bureau of Investigation (FBI) would be better suited for UK legislation which defined terrorism as, 'The use of serious violence against persons or property, or threat to use such violence, to intimidate or coerce a government, the public or a section of the public, in order to promote political, social or ideological objectives'.

The definition used by the FBI extends the description of terrorism to promote political, social, and ideological causes. Following much debate legislators concluded that it did not cover issues associated with vital electronic systems such as damage to air traffic control or other critical infrastructure systems. The pursuit of a more accurate description continued as independent reviewers of terrorism legislation agreed that there were great difficulties in finding a single satisfactory definition. Following substantial research, analysis, and debate, the legal definition of terrorism can be found in Section 1 of the Terrorism Act 2000, which has over recent years been amended by the Terrorism Act 2006 and the Counter-Terrorism Act 2008.

Legal Definition of Terrorism

Section 1 of the Terrorism Act 2000 states, '"terrorism" means the use or threat of action where;

a) it involves serious violence against a person, involves serious damage to property, endangers a person's life (other than that of the person committing the action), creates a serious risk to the health or safety of the public, or a section of the public, or is designed seriously to interfere with or seriously to disrupt an electronic system;
b) it is designed to influence the government, or an international government organisation, or to intimidate the public or a section of the public;
   and;
c) is made for the purpose of advancing a political, religious, racial or ideological cause'.

The legal definition provided by Section 1 is necessarily broad in order to capture the diverse range of activities associated with terrorism. The influence of previous definitions from UK and US legislation can be clearly seen by the inclusion of phrases such as 'serious violence' and 'section of the public in fear'. These key phrases can also be found in many other legal definitions of terrorism operating throughout the world which have often used the UK Act as a precedent. Section 1 provides a detailed description of what acts comprise terrorism, what these acts are designed to do and to what purpose, but does the definition really help clarify what terrorism actually is?

2.3 Understanding Terrorism

First and foremost, terrorism is a crime. It is a crime which has serious consequences and one which needs to be distinguished from other types of crime. Individuals who commit terrorist-related offences contrary to UK law are subject to the processes of the criminal justice system, and those who are otherwise believed to be involved in terrorism are subject to restrictive executive actions. However, the key features of terrorism that distinguish it from other forms of criminality are its core motivations. Terrorism may be driven, as the legal definition provided in Section 1 of the Terrorism Act 2000 states, by:

- politics;
- religion;
- race;
- ideology.

These objectives are unlike other criminal motivations such as personal gain or revenge. Terrorists may be driven by any of the four core motivations, alone or in combination, but the primary motivator is political (see Figure 2.1).

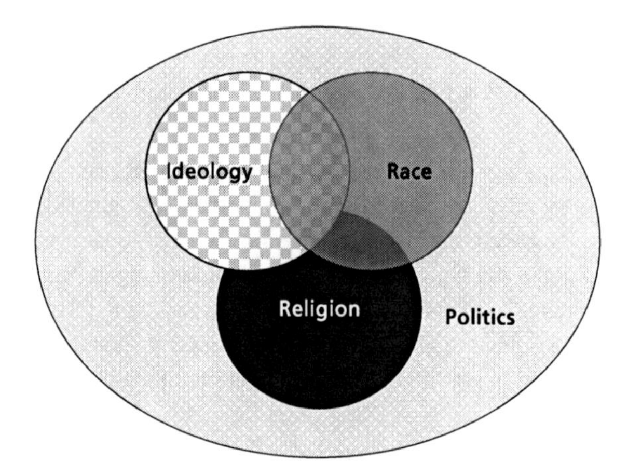

Figure 2.1. Core motivations of terrorism.

Individuals who are driven by religious, racist, or ideological beliefs must gain some political credibility and do so by explaining and justifying their position in order to compel others to conform to their point of view. Despite violence being used to pursue their religious, racist, or ideological beliefs, terrorists frame their arguments and grievances within a political context to support and underpin their views providing relevance and currency to their position. Terrorists operating within or intending to influence a democratic society are driven by political motivations to compel others to conform to their point of view.

Whether motivated by politics, religion, race or ideology, acts of terrorism convey a message. This message attempts to persuade its audience or force them to accept the terrorist's views and beliefs. The specific victims of terrorism are often distinct from this audience. Victims may be passers-by on a train or those travelling on a plane, but the wider audience is a government or the public. Terrorism therefore has a three-way relationship between the terrorist, the victim, and the audience as Figure 2.2 illustrates.

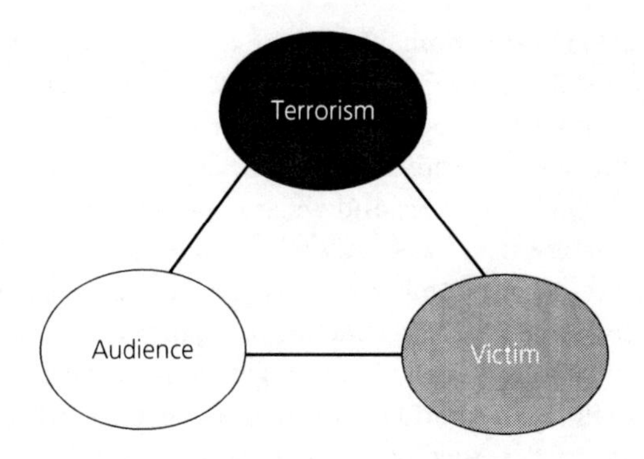

Figure 2.2. Terrorism, audience, and victim relationship.

This three-way relationship is not usually found in other types of crime. Most of these comprise a simple two-way relationship: perpetrator and victim. The wider audience does not come into play. The relationship between the terrorist, the victim, and the audience calls for a greater degree of control and oversight to counter terrorist acts, in order to protect innocent and non-combatant victims.

KEY POINT—STATE LEGITIMACY

Terrorism is a very powerful way in which to promote beliefs. The consequences of acts of terror are potentially serious for the whole of society. If allowed to flourish, it can undermine national security, can cause instability to a country, and in the most extreme of circumstances, can lead to war. Terrorism seeks to undermine state legitimacy, freedom, and democracy. A very different set of motivations and outcomes are involved in terrorist activities when compared to other types of crime. This is the reason why tackling terrorism is a very different matter to countering other types of criminality, and why it requires a very different, dedicated approach to preventing it.

2.3.1 **Impact of terrorism**

Following the death and destruction of the coordinated strikes by Al Qa'ida suicide terrorists on 11 September 2001 in the US, 3,051 children lost a parent on that day. The social impact on local New York communities after the fall of the World Trade Center Twin Towers is evidence of the ripple effect terrorist acts have. Alcohol consumption in Manhattan in the week that followed 9/11 increased by 25 per cent when compared to the same week a year earlier. Tobacco consumption rose by 10 per cent, marijuana consumption by 3.2 per cent, and church and synagogue attendance rose by 20 per cent. The devastating attacks of 9/11 affected people's lives in many different ways; a total of seventeen babies were subsequently born whose fathers died in the attacks, and nine months thence, the number of births in New York was 20 per cent greater than those in September 2000.

The victims of 9/11 came from all over the world. The vast majority were US citizens. Among the 2,973 that perished that day, sixty-seven were UK nationals, the largest number of UK civilians ever killed in a terrorist attack.

Police officers are all too aware of the immediate devastation and longer-term consequences for family, friends, and wider communities following the most violent crimes, but terrorism transcends normal boundaries. The human cost of terror is just one result. Economic repercussions have been grave. Business suffers, insurance costs rise, vital infrastructure like transport links and telecommunications links are affected. Many Western governments began to conduct risk analysis of these effects, in addition to the traditional focus on the general causes of attacks, trends, tactics, theoretical predictions, and political recommendations, in the immediate aftermath of 9/11.

The economic effects of terrorism centre on evaluating the costs of the attacks in their entirety, both direct and indirect. Examining the full economic impact of 9/11, the terrorist attacks in Madrid on 11 March 2004 (3/11), and in London on 7 July 2005 (7/7), reveal the importance of distinguishing terrorism from other types of crime.

Case Study—Economic Impact of Major Terrorist Attacks

11 September 2001 (9/11)

The direct economic impact of the coordinated strikes of 9/11 has been estimated at $47,000 million, equivalent to 0.46 per cent of US gross domestic product (GDP). In addition, an estimated $1.5 billion was needed to clean up and restore Ground Zero, an effort that was finally completed in June 2002 and was paid for by the Federal Emergency Management Agency (FEMA). The World Trade Center (WTC) Twin Towers also contained an art collection whose estimated value was $100 million. The entire collection was of course lost when the towers collapsed.

The issue of insurance was also a major issue in the immediate aftermath of the WTC collapse. During April of 2001, property developer Larry Silverstein bought the ninety-nine-year lease on the WTC for $3.2 billion. His investment was privately insured but the physical space—14 million square feet of office and commercial space— was lost in 102 minutes that September morning.

Many of the companies in the WTC sustained huge losses, both personal and financial. Cantor Fitzgerald, who occupied floors 101 to 105 in the North Tower, lost 658 employees in the attack. Among other companies who lost employees were Morgan Stanley, the Atlantic Bank of New York, Bank of America, Fuji Bank, Lehman Brothers, and Ashai Bank. The economic repercussions of Al Qa'ida's attack were significant.

The economic impact of the attacks also damaged the federal purse. Taxpayers would be required to find $850 million to repair the subway, $550 million to replace the Port Authority Trans-Hudson rail station, and a total of $2.3 million was required to repair the supply of gas, electricity, and water.

The impact on the stock market was equally great. Altogether, the US stock market posted losses in terms of $1.7 billion. There were longer-term financial losses as well. The New York Stock Exchange shed 18,000 jobs, banks lost a total of 9,000, and restaurants and hotels lost in excess of 15,000. While some of these jobs were relocated to other areas of New York in the weeks, months, and years that followed 9/11, some simply disappeared completely.

Chinatown in New York suffered loss of expected sales of between 60 and 100 per cent in the two-week period following the collapse of the Twin Towers. In the three months which followed, a slow recovery began, but business witnessed an accumulated loss of sales in the three months which followed 9/11 of between 30 to 70 per cent directly due to the absence of tourists, the loss of office staff at the WTC complex, and difficulties in making telephone bookings and reservations. Although the financial cost of the attacks proved challenging for many, the US economy made an eventual full recovery.

11 March 2004 (3/11)

The immediate multi-agency emergency response to the coordinated train bombings carried out by Al Qa'ida in Madrid on 11 March 2004 cost the Spanish authorities an estimated €2.1 million. There were 1,584 casualties. The longer-term cost of care for the 1,298 injured citizens who required hospital treatment from the Spanish healthcare system a further €5.1 million. The longer-term psychological support of victims, their friends and families, and others caught up in the horror cost Spanish authorities an additional €4.9 million.

Beyond the loss and injury to human life, the economic impact of responding to and recovering from the immediate attacks on 3/11 caused serious damage and disruption to the suburban railway infrastructure of Madrid. A number of houses were destroyed and damaged in the blasts, and the total damage to Madrid's infrastructure and housing was estimated to be €5.2 million.

An often hidden, yet direct cost associated with assessing the true economic impact of contemporary terrorist attacks is the amount of compensation awarded to victims. The loss of human life and the damages for pain, suffering, and loss of amenity to those injured in terrorist attacks comprise an increasingly important cost for the relevant communities in an increasingly litigious culture. In Spain, the compensation for the terrorist victims of 3/11 was paid by the state based on the applicable legislation, which established a scale of minimum compensation that could, under certain circumstances, be increased by judicial discretion. The total award of compensation to the terrorist victims of 3/11 was €134 million, but the true financial impact of the attacks was far greater.

On 12 March 2004, the day after the bombings, more than 2 million citizens of Madrid took part in a demonstration on the streets of the Spanish capital. Access roads to Madrid were completely blocked by the vast number of people who came from the surrounding towns and villages, united in their determination to show their abhorrence of terrorist violence. Many companies suspended all their activities for the entire day in order to facilitate the attendance of employees at the demonstration. When calculated by the number of working hours lost, this temporary cessation of economic activity cost the Spanish economy an estimated €57.3 million. Combining all the financial impacts of the 3/11 attacks, including the initial rescue and recovery, damage to infrastructure, compensation of victims, the loss of working hours due to the solidarity demonstration, and other associated direct costs, Al Qa'ida's impact upon local and state finances amounted to €211 million.

7 July 2005 (7/7)

Within moments of the terrorist attack in London on 7 July 2005, news had reached the London Stock Exchange (LSE). The main index, the FTSE 100, lost 3.5 per cent of its total value within just 90 minutes of the opening of trading, equivalent to a total decapitalisation of around £44,000,000,000. This immediate economic impact was staggering in and of itself. The 'return' on the 'investment' by Al Qa'ida of £1,000 to deliver the attacks is staggering.

In the immediate aftermath of 7/7, investors concentrated their sales orders on shares related to the tourist sector, fearful of travellers opting to cancel their stay in London. However, and even though major airlines and tour operators gave their customers the option of cancelling or postponing their trips to London, there was no significant number of cancellations. The LSE recovered its losses very quickly and by close of trading on 7 July they had been clawed back.

There were, however, three important factors that were considered instrumental in restoring trading confidence. The first was that the British government suggested to the LSE that it suspend electronic trading in order to avoid a 'deluge of orders'. This measure undoubtedly contributed to reducing losses, although the stock exchange operators had to face the difficult task of dealing with all orders only by telephone. Secondly, the impact of the attacks on the LSE was slight when compared to 9/11, and disruption was kept to one single session of trading. Finally, in the wake of 9/11, most financial institutions headquartered in London had developed 'emergency evacuation plans' which enabled them to transfer their business quickly from central London locations to premises outside the urban area. These crisis contingencies, derived from responses to the 9/11 and 3/11 attacks, restored confidence to investors and traders.

KEY POINT—ECONOMIC REPERCUSSIONS OF TERRORISM

The economic impact of terrorist attacks reveals the short-, medium-, and long-term consequences of terrorism. The sheer size, scale, and scope of the economic repercussions of terrorism provide evidence to support the notion that terrorism in itself needs to be distinguished from other types of criminality, as it reaches far beyond the human, social, and economic impact of other crimes.

2.3.2 **Politics**

Understanding the political motivations of terrorist groups is key to countering their activities. Politics is central in society; it is the way in which governance and authority within society is managed.

Definition of Politics

The *Oxford English Dictionary* defines politics as follows:

1. (a) the art and science of government;
   (b) public life and affairs as involving authority and government.
2. (a) particular set of ideas, principles or commitments in politics;
   (b) activities concerned with the acquisition or exercise of authority or government.

POINT TO NOTE—DISTINGUISH BETWEEN EXTREMISM AND TERRORISM

Everyone in positions of authority, and especially police officers who have direct contact with the communities they serve, must continue to distinguish between extremism and terrorism. One does not necessarily lead to another, and simply to hold extremist views is not an offence and does not constitute terrorism. To qualify as a terrorist act, there must be elements of violence or intimidation or the planning of it.

Unlike terrorism, there is no equivalent legal definition for domestic extremism (DE). This is because the crimes committed by those considered to be domestic extremists already exist in common law or statute. The term is generally used to describe the activity of individuals or groups carrying out criminal acts of direct action to further their protest campaigns. Clearly, the majority of people exercising their lawful and democratic right to campaign and peacefully protest are never considered to be extremists. The term only applies to individuals or groups whose activities go outside the normal democratic process and who engage in crime and disorder in order to further causes. Extremists may operate independently, but will sometimes try to mask their activities by associating closely with legitimate campaigners. The police work hard to ensure that the majority of protesters can campaign peacefully while stopping the few individuals who break the law.

Extreme right-wing

Extreme right-wing terrorist acts are covered in section 1.6.5 of this book.

Extreme left-wing

Left-wing political extremism also takes various forms. A common theme amongst these is to bring about what extremists perceive as a more equal distribution of power and wealth, whether in a particular locality, in the country as a whole, or on an international scale. Existing instruments for the distribution of power and wealth, such as governmental structures and international organisations, therefore become targets.

2.3.3 **Religion**

Recent history shows that religion can be a key motivator of terrorist acts. An awareness of world faiths and cultures is very useful for those who seek to counter terrorism and extremism effectively. The powerful beliefs of followers of different faiths need to be recognised and acknowledged by all those in a position of authority, especially as extremists can twist the truth of religious teachings and scriptures to legitimise the pursuit of their aims.

Definition of religion

A clear definition of religion can be found in the *Oxford English Dictionary*:

1. the belief in a superhuman power, in a personal God of gods entitled to obedience and worship;
2. the expression of this in worship;
3. a particular system of faith and worship;
4. life under monastic vows;
5. a thing to which one is devoted.

Most terrorist action based on religious grounds could be attributed to political aims, and so the definition of terrorism has been expanded to include religious motivations. Religion can be a major motivation for terrorist organisations. However, the full extent to which the appeal of religion assists in recruiting and radicalising individuals has yet to be fully determined. Religious motivation continues to be the subject of much analysis and research by authorities and academics around the world, who hope that by understanding it, one may be able to 'de-radicalise' these individuals and thus help to prevent extremist views whose eventual outlet may well be acts of extreme violence.

KEY POINT—RELIGION IN VIOLENT RADICALISATION DEVELOPMENT

The problem with assessing the role played by religion in terrorism is that while religious extremism may serve as a powerful driving force, and/or be effectively used to guide, support, underpin, or justify terrorist activity, it does not necessarily or automatically lead to terrorism, or indeed, to violence. Police officers must recognise this important difference. It must be stressed that individuals and groups using terrorist means in the name of religion do not necessarily represent 'deviant sects', but are often guided by a radical interpretation of religion's basic tenets.

2.3.4 **Ideology**

An ideology is an organised collection of ideas. Understanding the context of a particular ideology will help tackle the justifications offered by terrorists who seek to legitimise their actions.

Definition of Ideology

1. the system of ideas at the basis of an economic or political theory;
2. the manner of thinking characteristic of a class or individual;
3. visionary speculation;
4. the science of ideas.

The key purpose of an ideology is to offer a fundamental change in society that believers feel is for the betterment of that society. Individuals or organisations that promote their ideology do so believing the ideology offers the chance for a better life, or a better society. Most terrorists do not simply yearn for a change in society; they believe they are absolutely justified in acting to cause a trigger that will advance the kind of change which they want.

2.4 **Typology of Terrorism**

Terrorism and extremism can be classified into six broad categories which include:

- political;
- religious;
- ideological;
- nationalist;
- state-sponsored;
- single issue.

POINT TO NOTE—IDENTIFYING TYPES OF TERRORISM AND/OR EXTREMISM

Identifying the type of terrorism or extremism an individual or group belongs to is an important step in understanding what it is the individual or group wishes to achieve. This understanding informs determining appropriate countermeasures. It provides an insight into the key characteristics of the individual or group and what tactics they may use to convey their message and promote their beliefs.

2.4.1 **Political and religious terrorism**

Those who perpetrate political and religious terrorism perceive themselves to be acting upon orders of a higher or divine authority. They are often the most violent terrorists who believe that their actions are sanctioned by this higher authority, are morally justified, and that they will be vindicated of any wrongdoing when carrying out orders in pursuit of their objectives.

2.4.2 **Ideological terrorism**

Ideological terrorism and extremism seeks to change the social, economic, and political systems of a given nation. Ideological terrorists are violent individuals and groups who can come from either the extreme left-wing or extreme right-wing of the political spectrum. Objectives are extreme, and in order to achieve them, a full-scale social revolution is envisaged. The term 'social-revolutionary' is often used to describe this grouping.

2.4.3 **Nationalist terrorism**

Nationalist terrorist groups claim to be the authentic voice of a national culture. Through acts of violence they seek a restoration of their nations or lands to some original state, a unified country, or they may seek an entirely new, separate state. Well-known nationalist terrorist organisations include the Irish Republican Army (IRA) and Euskadi Ta Askatasuna (ETA) of Spain.

2.4.4 **State-sponsored terrorism**

State-sponsored terrorism requires a state to support terrorism activities in pursuit of achieving its political objectives. These terrorist activities are sometimes carried out in the state's own territory, or they may be conducted in a second or neighbouring country. This tactic is often used to fulfil the home state's own political agendas because any allegations of state involvement in terrorism can be easily denied by the relevant state or disassociated from political parties, especially when terrorist acts are conducted in other countries.

2.4.5 **Single-issue terrorism and extremism**

Single-issue terrorism and extremism focuses on a specific policy, practice, or procedure. The key objective is to change, block, or at the very least disrupt or deter one issue from continuing in its present form. Unlike purely ideological terrorism and extremism, single-issue groups do not seek a full-scale political revolution but they do want real action and changes to be made.

There is a broad range of single-issue causes. There are those who oppose globalisation, animal experimentation, medical research, genetically modified crops, the pharmaceutical and food industries, hunting, sports involving animals, and the financial industry, for example. Single-issue causes can be divided into the following subcategories shown in Table 2.1.

Table 2.1 Typology of single issue extremism

Anarchism
Anarchism is the belief that society should have no government, laws, police, or other authority, but should instead be a free association of all its members. It rests on the doctrine that no man has a right to control by force the action of any other man.
Animal rights
Animal rights, sometimes referred to as animal liberation, is an ideology based on the perceived basic interests of animals. There are a wide variety of individual belief structures within this movement, but in general, people who support this cause believe that animals should be afforded the same consideration as humans. They should not suffer harm. They should not be considered as property, used as food, clothing, or be the subject of experimental research. Nor should they be used primarily as entertainment. A widely accepted view amongst animal rights activists is that all animals should be regarded as legal persons and members of the moral community.
Capitalism
Capitalism is a term used to describe the economic system which promotes private ownership for profit, operating within a free market. Those who oppose this system of economics are described as anti-capitalists who seek a centralised power and economic system based on the principles of safeguarding individual employees' rights.
Globalisation
Globalisation is the term used to describe the process or transformation of local or regional issues into world-wide phenomena. Anti-globalisation is the term used to describe those individuals who oppose what is often an economic issue concerning the power, influence, and impact of large multinational corporations, and who may oppose immigration, transnational investment, and technologies that extend beyond national borders.
Anti-war
Anti-war protestors should be distinguished from 'peace' activists. Anti-war activists are engaged in protest activities which aim to put an end to a nation's decision to start or become involved in an armed conflict involving another nation. There are a variety of belief strands within this category of domestic extremism. Some anti-war protestors may believe that both sides of the conflict should stop their activities while others may support the withdrawal of only one side in the conflict, often the more powerful body which is widely seen as the aggressor or invader.
Environmentalism
The protection of our planet has become a social movement centred upon the conservation and improvement of the natural environment. An extreme environmentalist is a person who would advocate unlawful activity to sustain the management of resources and stewardship of the natural environment through changes in policy, or individual or group direct action.

(*continued*)

Table 2.1 Continued

Fascism
Fascism is a political ideology that seeks to regenerate the social, economic, and cultural life of a country by basing it on a heightened sense of national belonging or ethnic identity. Fascists reject liberal ideas, such as freedom and individual human rights and democracy. Fascism is often associated with right-wing fanaticism, racism, and violence. Nazism, the shortened name for national socialism, is considered to be a form of fascism, focusing upon the belief in the superiority of an Aryan race. 'Neo-Nazism' refers to post-Second World War activities, and neo-Nazis are those who seek to resurrect social movements and ideologies in place during that time.

KEY POINT—EXCERCISING DEMOCRATIC RIGHTS AND FREEDOMS

It is important to stress again that the vast majority of individuals who exercise their lawful and democratic right to campaign and peacefully protest in the name of their chosen cause ought never to be considered 'extremist'. The term only applies to individuals or groups whose activities go beyond the normal democratic process and engage in crime and disorder, and in the most extreme cases commit offences contrary to terrorist-related legislation. Single-issue violent extremists may operate independently or as part of a small faction, but will sometimes attempt to mask their activities by closely associating with legitimate campaigners, using them as cover. Police officers must be careful to distinguish between terrorists, extremists, and those citizens who are demonstrating peacefully.

2.5 Characteristics of Terrorism

Terrorist acts may be the sole tactic used by an individual or group to further their particular cause but it may also be used as part of a much wider strategy which includes non-violent or legitimate components. Terrorists have been associated with legitimate political movements, such as the Irish Republican Army (IRA) and Sinn Fein. There are three common characteristics of terrorism wherever it is used throughout the world, that it is:

- pre-meditated;
- indiscriminate; and it
- breaches human rights.

2.5.1 Pre-meditated

It is clear from every example of a terrorist act that it is, first and foremost, pre-meditated. Consider, for example, the activities of the terrorist cell responsible for the Madrid train bombings in 2004.

Case Study—Madrid, Spain, 2004

On the morning of Thursday 11 March 2004, Al Qa'ida terrorist cell members placed thirteen improvised explosive devices (IEDs) containing 10 kg of explosives packed with nails in rucksacks on four separate commuter trains in Madrid. Within three minutes all the devices were detonated on busy carriages during the rush hour at El Pozo Station, Calle Téllez, Atocha Station, and Santa Eugenia Station. The coordinated explosions claimed 191 lives, leaving more than 1,584 people injured. The victims were nationals of seventeen countries. In total, 5,000 people participated in the authorities' efforts to rescue and recover the victims of the attack.

The coordinated bombings became known as 3/11, and were believed to have been planned to coincide with the Spanish general election, occurring just three days before national voting began. The Spanish government was swift to accuse the terrorist group ETA of carrying out the strikes, but police investigations soon revealed that this was not the case. On the morning of the attacks, police discovered a van parked near the rail network which contained detonators, traces of explosives, and audio cassettes with recordings of recitations from the Koran. The timing of the attack also had great significance beyond coincidence with the general elections, being committed exactly 911 days after the 9/11terrorist attacks in the United States. 3/11 allowed Al Qa'ida to mark the anniversary of 9/11 in this pre-meditated attack (Staniforth, 2012). Police investigations accelerated following the discovery of three of the devices that had failed to detonate, two of which were placed in the rail carriages, one left on a railway platform. Bomb-disposal experts were able to defuse the IEDs successfully, providing crucial evidence with which to identify the bombers. Spanish authorities later revealed that the rucksack devices had been detonated by means of mobile phones. The phones were identified as being the same brand and model of those used in a similar way in the November 2002 Al Qa'ida bombings in Bali in which 202 people had been killed.

On 3 April 2004, just three weeks after the attacks, police mounted a raid on a flat in Leganes in south Madrid where the terrorist suspects were believed to be hiding. During the raid, one officer was killed, a further eleven were injured as seven suspects committed suicide in an explosion which ripped through the premises. The suspects who died included the alleged plot mastermind, Serhane ben Abdelmajid Fakhet who was a Tunisian national. In total, the Spanish authorities accused twenty-nine people of being involved in the train bombings. The defendants were brought to trial in Madrid on 15 February 2007 to face charges of murder and belonging to a terrorist group.

Ahead of both the trial and the third anniversary of the attacks on 11 March, Spanish officials raised the country's security alert level from low to medium. Extra police and soldiers were stationed in key public areas and at water supply and power plants. A bullet-proof chamber was constructed in the courtroom to house the eighteen suspects. Seven of the men were from Morocco, eight from Spain, and one each from Algeria, Syria, and Lebanon. The first defendant, Rabei Osman, also known as 'Mohamed the Egyptian', denied any links to the bombings and Islamic extremists: 'Obviously I condemn these attacks unconditionally and completely'. On 31 October

2007 twenty-one suspects were convicted of offences ranging from murder to forgery of documents. Judge Juan del Olmo said, 'Local cells of Islamic extremists inspired through the internet' were responsible for the attack. Al Qa'ida terrorist cell ringleaders Jamal Zougam, Otman el Ghanoui, and José Emilio Suárez Trashorras were given multiple life sentences for committing what remains Europe's worst terrorist atrocity this century.

2.5.2 **Indiscriminate**

The second characteristic common to acts of terrorism throughout the world is their indiscriminate nature. Even if a terrorist organisation selects what it perceives to be a 'legitimate target', such as a military installation or government building, innocent civilians are often killed or injured. The means used to deliver these attacks are similarly indiscriminate—for example, car bombs or suicide bombers.

Case Study—Warrington Bombings, 1993

At 4 a.m. on Friday 26 February 1993, residents in Warrington in Cheshire were evacuated from their homes following explosions at the local gas works on Winwick Road. Several hours before the explosions, Police Constable Mark Toker was shot and injured following a routine vehicle check of a van. The van sped away from the scene, and the occupants later hijacked a Ford Escort, forcing the car's driver into the boot. Following the incident, members of the Provisional Irish Republican Army (PIRA), Pairic MacFhloinn, John Kinsella, and Denis Kinsella were arrested and later jailed for their part in the attack. Possibly in retaliation for the arrests, members of PIRA returned to Warrington on Saturday 20 March 1993, just twenty days after the original attack. Explosive devices were placed in two waste bins on Bridge Street, both outside busy shops. A warning was given, but alas too late for action to be taken by the emergency services. The bombs exploded at 12.12 p.m. Two children died, the only fatalities. The first victim, 3-year-old Jonathan Ball, died at the scene. The second victim, Timothy Parry died in Liverpool's Walton Hospital five days later as a result of his injuries. A further fifty-six people were injured, many of them seriously. Despite a massive police investigation, the perpetrators of the attack have never been prosecuted.

POINT TO NOTE INDISCRIMINATE BOMBINGS

The case study of the two Warrington bombings shows how terrorist organisations are indiscriminate in their choice of targets and methods of operating. On both occasions, no concern was shown for the potential loss of innocent life. It is not only military personnel, government officials, and police officers who have been murdered by acts of terrorism on the UK mainland most recently, but also, and in far greater numbers, members of the public.

2.5.3 **Human rights**

The third common characteristic to be found in acts of terrorism throughout the world is their disregard for fundamental human rights. Many of those rights, now enshrined in the Human Rights Act 1998, are breached by terrorist attacks. The rights contained in separate Articles of the Act are shown in Table 2.2.

Table 2.2 Human Rights Articles

Article 2	Right to life
Article 3	Prohibition of torture
Article 4	Prohibition of slavery and forced labour
Article 5	Right to liberty and security
Article 6	Right to a fair trial
Article 7	No punishment without law
Article 8	Right to respect for private/family life
Article 9	Freedom of thought, conscience, and religion
Article 10	Freedom of expression
Article 11	Freedom of assembly and association
Article 12	Right to marry
Article 14	Prohibition of discrimination

Operating beyond the boundaries of domestic and international law, terrorist organisations pursue their extremist causes and influence governments to change policy. They may breach human rights but in combating them, security authorities, including the police, must not follow their example, no matter how provoked. Prohibition of torture under Article 3, and a right to a fair trial under Article 6, have both emerged as key issues for international policy-makers arising as a direct consequence of the efforts to counter global terrorism. Torture, illegal detention, and threats against political activists are counterproductive to the aim of upholding the values of a liberal, pluralist democracy, and adopting such tactics damages confidence in the police and security forces, especially amongst the communities from which the terrorists are drawn and which might otherwise help the authorities. Article 3's prohibition on the use of torture has been severely tested in most recent times. Some countries obtain information claimed to be essential in combating terrorism through torture or through other methods condemned elsewhere as unacceptable. How should such information be treated when received by a government in a liberal democracy? This situation creates a real dilemma for those responsible for protecting a nation from an imminent terrorist attack. The correct moral and ethical response would be to reject the information on the basis that to accept it would be to condone the methods used in its acquisition. However, it is often uncertain how information is obtained, and authorities have claimed that the subject matter may be so compelling that it demands action irrespective of the methods to obtain it. The public deserves to be protected, but at what moral cost? The potential tangle of tacit, reciprocal exchanges of information between agencies and nations can lead to a very dubious relationship indeed. In any case, courts can find evidence obtained under duress inadmissible. It is vital for the integrity of democracy that no matter what the prevailing circumstances there must be no derogation from Article 3, as the European Convention on Human Rights clearly states. On 10 May 2010, Foreign Secretary William Hague, clarified the position of the UK government: 'We condemn torture without reservation. We do not torture, and we do not ask others to do so on our behalf. We are clear that officials must not be complicit in mistreatment of detainees'.

KEY POINT—POLICE ABUSE OF POWER AND AUTHORITY

It is also important to acknowledge the potential for the treatment of individuals at the hands of government agencies can also give rise to extremist behaviour. Where police officers' actions fall below the professional standards and expectations set by the communities they serve, their abuse of authority and poor interpretation and application of anti-terror powers may also be used to convince vulnerable others that the police are the aggressors. This is obviously, and extremely, counterproductive to the broader efforts to prevent terrorism and violent extremism.

2.6 Terrorist Motivations

Taking steps to understand why terrorists act the way they do is an important aspect of countering terrorism. Understanding elements of terrorist beliefs may facilitate tackling those drawn to commit acts of terrorism. Identifying what drives people towards committing acts of terrorism and identifying the climate which allows extreme beliefs to grow and flourish may present an opportunity to tackle terrorism at its source.

2.6.1 Justification

Belief systems provide justifications for any given action. And so with terrorism. Individuals who teach, preach, and promote extremist beliefs often provide a single narrative of events. They are able to convince individuals that their version of events is the only true reflection of reality, and all alternative opinions are false. The greatest contemporary terrorist threat emanates from Al Qa'ida. What does this group want, and why are they so adamantly against Western culture?

Case Study—The Belief System Of Al Qa'Ida

In February 1998 from headquarters in Afghanistan, Osama Bin Laden, and his second-in-command, Ayman al Zawahiri, arranged for an Arabic newspaper in London to publish a fatwa, issued in the name of a 'World Islamic Front'. The fatwa, normally an interpretation of Islamic law provided by a respected Islamic authority, claimed that America had declared war against God, and called for the murder of any American, anywhere in the world as the 'individual duty for every Muslim'. Although novel for its open endorsement of indiscriminate killing, this fatwa was only the latest in a long series of Bin Laden's public and private calls that singled out the US and its allies for attack.

Seizing upon symbols of Islam's past greatness, Bin Laden promised to restore pride to people who considered themselves the victims of successive foreign masters. He employed a dense web of cultural and religious allusions to paint a picture of Islam's decline, and to justify unprovoked mass murder as a righteous defence of an embattled faith, repeatedly calling for his followers to embrace martyrdom.

POINT TO NOTE—JUSTIFICATION OF BELIEFS

Whatever their motivation, terrorists believe they can justify their acts. Indeed, they believe that their acts are 'just'. Many terrorist organisations view themselves as victims, their enemy as the stronger body, the more dominant power. Usually, this assessment is true; their ability to access and use force, and the apparatus of force is far less than the means possessed by the states and nations they are attempting to overthrow. But in viewing and presenting themselves as the weaker of the combatants, terrorists enlist a kind of sympathy that can be extremely persuasive.

2.6.2 **Profile**

A personality profile of a terrorist, or a person vulnerable to the process of radicalisation, would be extremely useful to the police, partner agencies, and communities in trying to identify potential individuals. Alas, there is no single profile that exists. Indeed, in its official account of the bombings in London on 7 July 2005, the UK government states that: 'there is not a consistent profile to help identify who may be vulnerable to radicalisation'.

POINTS TO NOTE—DANGERS OF A SINGLE PROFILE OF A TERRORIST PERSONALITY

Every individual who engages in terrorist activity does so for a variety of reasons, but all are singular to each person. The real danger in establishing a generic profile of a terrorist is that whilst seeking positive indicators on a profile, one may overlook an individual or group, failing to identify them as a potential threat.

No definition of the 'terrorist personality' as a specific psychological type has been made. In fact, most terrorists have been found to be clinically quite normal, despite their impetus to decidedly extra-normal violence. No empirical evidence has been collected to support the existence of universal terrorist personality traits across nationalities, boundaries, cultures, political contexts, and roles. But no serious attempt has been made thus far to find out whether such commonalities exist. All that scholars claim now is that it is unlikely that there exist common universal personality traits for terrorists, although the likelihood that some common personality traits are shared by terrorists within the same culture, nationality, and political context may be greater than the likelihood that common traits can be found universally.

2.7 Summary

A clear understanding of what terrorism is and what it is not is essential for all police officers, the extended police family, and police partners. Everyone in authority is required to be able to distinguish between legitimate and illegitimate activities related to political, religious, and ideological beliefs. The special laws devised to deal with terrorism and violent extremism must not affect legitimate political activity, even if this legitimate activity is highly aggressive or unpopular. In a liberal, pluralist, and democratic society, a wide range of political views are acceptable and desirable, even those views which may offend others. A sophisticated democracy allows room for these views to be held and expressed, but often extreme views do not allow for the existence or legitimacy of other perspectives. It is important to distinguish between extremism and terrorism; one does not necessarily lead to another, and simply to hold extremist views is not an offence and does not constitute terrorism.

A key message arising from this chapter should be reiterated here. Where police officers' actions fall below the professional standards and expectations set by the communities they serve, abuse of authority and poor interpretation and application of anti-terror policy may be used to convince others vulnerable to being recruited to those very causes the police are keen to combat.

A greater understanding of the concept of terrorism and violent extremism, including the possible motivation and justification for terrorism by individuals and groups, will significantly reduce—if not entirely eradicate—the discriminatory stereotyping of potential suspects from minority ethnic groups. It should come as no surprise to senior police officers and counter-terrorism practitioners that a poor understanding of terrorism and extremism as concepts, when combined with poorly briefed and poorly trained officers working within communities, only leads to the limited effectiveness of counter-terrorism measures. This contributes to mistrust of the police, damaging a community's confidence in the very people they ought to trust to protect them from harm.

Further reading

- Awan, I, and Blakemore, B, *Extremism, Counter-Terrorism and Policing* (Surrey: Ashgate Publishing Ltd, 2013).
- Baumert, T, and Buesa, M, *The Economic Repercussions of Terrorism* (New York: Oxford University Press, 2010).
- Berman, P, *Terror and Liberalism* (London: WW Norton & Company, 2003).
- Davies, B, *Terrorism: Inside a World Phenomenon* (London: Virgin Books Ltd, 2003).
- Eatwell, R, and Goodwin, M, *The New Extremism in 21st Century Britain* (Oxford: Routledge, 2010).
- HM Government *The Definition of Terrorism—A Report by Lord Carlile of Berriew Q.C. Independent Reviewer of Terrorism Legislation* (2007).
- Masferrer, A, and Walker, C, *Counter-Terrorism, Human Rights and the Rule Of Law Crossing Legal Boundaries in Defence of the State* (London: Edward Elgar Publishing, 2013).
- Nasiri, O, *Inside Global Jihad* (London: Hurst & Company, 2006).
- Schmid, A, *The Routledge Handbook of Terrorism Research* (Oxford: Routledge, 2011).
- Staniforth, A, *The Routledge Companion to UK Counter-Terrorism* (Oxford: Routledge, 2012).
- Staniforth, A, and PNLD, *Blackstone's Counter-Terrorism Handbook* 3rd edition (Oxford: Oxford University Press, 2013).
- *The 9/11 Commission Report: Final Report of the National Commission on Terrorist Attacks Upon the United States* (Authorised edition) (Washington DC: WW Norton & Company, 2004).

3

Terrorist and Extremist Methodology

3.1	Introduction	55
3.2	Terrorist Organisations	55
3.3	Terrorist Tactics	64
3.4	Domestic Extremist Tactics	79
3.5	Summary	81

3.1 Introduction

The purpose of this chapter is to provide police officers, the extended police family, and police partners with an introduction to terrorist and extremist methodology. Understanding how terrorists operate, alone or in groups, their structures, lines of communication, and command and control systems, provides an opportunity to assess the level of threat they pose, and potentially identify vulnerabilities which may help target countermeasures to detect, deter, and disrupt their activities.

An important part of this chapter is its exploration of the 'lone actor', who continues to pose the most potent threat of any terrorist organisational structure in operation today. A dedicated and determined individual, who plans and prepares attacks in isolation, with limited contact, direction, or control from terrorist groups, can emerge without warning, hidden from intelligence and law enforcement agencies. Identifying potential early indicators of lone actor terrorist activity presents the greatest challenge to the police, their partners, and the public.

Countering terrorism is not a level playing field. Terrorists and their organisations do not respect the norms of law, human rights, and civil liberties. The choice of target is influenced by a wide range of factors, including the nature of the intended target, the capabilities the terrorists have at their command, and the environment in which they operate. No single technique can be attributed to a specific group. There is no evidence to suggest that certain tactics are delimited from being used in any environment. Violent and indiscriminate attacks that were once considered the preserve of terrorists operating in some of the poorest and least industrialised countries in the world have been used in the UK to threaten the safety of the civilian population.

3.2 Terrorist Organisations

Schedule 2 of the Terrorism Act 2000 provides a list of terrorist organisations that are banned in the UK (see Appendix 1). These range from global networks such as Al Qa'ida, to nationalist groups such as the Provisional Irish Republican Army (PIRA/IRA).

The command and control systems within terrorist organisations vary. Many nationalist terrorist groups are well structured and conduct their activities under tight operational security. Organisations often demand that their operatives are well trained, that they have military discipline, that they are able to follow complex plans, and can successfully overcome tactical and technical challenges during operations. However, all this is not always the case. Al Qa'ida, for example, operates with a much looser network basis. The core group provides ideology and assistance, but individuals or cells may be self-forming and are autonomous, using the name of the core group as if it were a franchise.

POINT TO NOTE—TERRORIST ORGANISATIONS

Understanding how terrorist organisations operate, focusing on their structure, lines of communication, and command and control systems, will provide an opportunity to assess the level of threat they pose. Increased understanding will also help to identify effective ways to counter terrorist operations.

Terrorist organisations can be broadly categorised as being either centralised or decentralised.

3.2.1 Centralised organisations

Centralised organisations tend to have a hierarchical, often military command and control, structure. This structure permits a high degree of control from the leadership, but its very regimentation also makes it vulnerable to attack. Their command and control functions can be predictable, offering law enforcement and intelligence agencies an opportunity to counter future threats.

Case Study—Irish Republican Army

The Irish Republican Army (IRA) has a centralised structure with defined procedures and specific roles for its operatives. It is led by a General Army Council which passes instructions through the command chain to the Army Executive, the Army Council, and the General Headquarters staff, who deliver the agreed strategies. Senior IRA members sanction operations. The IRA is generally regarded as being disciplined and its attack planning thoroughly researched, providing it with a high level of certainty that its activities will achieve the desired ends.

Terrorist attacks by the IRA are designed to increase political pressure on the government and to gain additional support for its cause. An effective example of this includes the vehicle bomb that was detonated on Whitehall in London during 1991. The location of the device showed that the IRA was able to strike at the very heart of government when it pleased. This attack gained considerable republican support at the time and was clearly a very tightly controlled operation but other attacks have not attracted such support.

Case Study—Omagh Bombing 1998

On 15 August 1998 members of the Real IRA (RIRA) parked a stolen Vauxhall Cavalier containing 500 pounds of explosives outside a shop on Omagh's Market Street. The device detonated at 3 o'clock on a crowded shopping day. A series of warnings were provided but the location of the bomb was not made clear. To add to the confusion, it appeared that the car had been parked some distance away from its intended target. The police led members of the public away from what was thought to be the location of the device, but in fact they were leading people directly towards the bomb.

It is still not clear as to whether the primary intention of RIRA was to maximize casualties from the outset, or whether a series of mistakes about the exact location of the vehicle had been made. Twenty-nine people were killed in the attack, including Protestants and Catholics, men and women, and nine children. There was huge public condemnation of RIRA for this attack. The then Prime Minister, Tony Blair, described the attack as an 'appalling act of savagery and evil'. The very peace RIRA sought to destabilise subsequently gained significant public support.

There are a number of centralised structures which terrorist organisations have adopted, athough it should be recognised that structures often cohere around personalities and friendships, so what follows is something of a generalisation. Some of these structures will have formed naturally, but others will have been purposefully created. There are three key centralised structures:

- Duo-cell;
- Tri-cell;
- Corporate cell.

Duo-cell

A Duo-cell (Figure 3.1) is difficult to detect and penetrate as the activities of only two members can be easily concealed. The primary advantage for the leader of a Duo-cell is that if their activities have been well planned, Terrorist A can withdraw and disengage from Terrorist B at any time without detection.

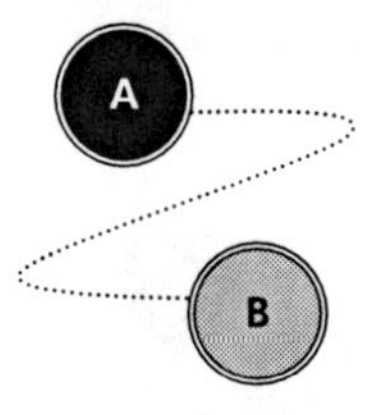

Figure 3.1. Duo-cell structure.

Tri-cell

A Tri-cell (Figure 3.2) is another simple centralised structure, but it allows the cell to engage in more than a single activity. Terrorist A can provide orders to Terrorists B and C independently so that each is not aware of the other's activities. In certain circumstances, Terrorists B and C may never meet and may never know each other's identity. Operational security is thus tight, and informants can be swiftly identified. If the cell's activities have been well planned, Terrorist A can withdraw from Terrorist B or Terrorist C at any time without detection. If two independent or simultaneous attacks are being planned, the exposure of only one attack will not prevent the second attack from occurring.

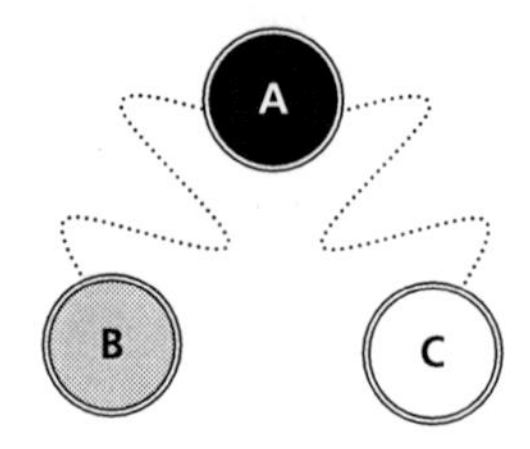

Figure 3.2. Tri-cell structure.

Corporate cell

The corporate cell (Figure 3.3) is the most sophisticated centralised terrorist structure in operation today. It encompasses the advantages of both the Duo-cell and the Tri-cell. A corporate cell provides its leader or leaders with great operational scope. The corporate cell of major centralised terrorist organisations can be as complex as any organisational structure of commercial companies. A corporate cell relies upon clear lines of communication, and each member has a specific role and defined responsibilities. Activities undertaken by one member can be completely isolated from those undertaken by another. Having multiple members provides numerous opportunities for agents to infiltrate the group, each terrorist acting as a link in a chain, but sheer scale of these structures can help to ensure the group's immunity from detection. The key disadvantage of such a large centralised terrorist organisation is the effective management of its members in order to ensure that no activity is conducted without the appropriate approval. To keep its members in line, large terrorist groups generally have robust internal methods of security and policing.

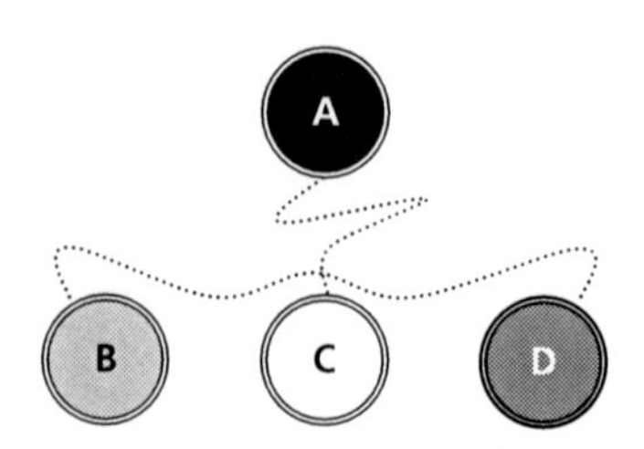

Figure 3.3. Corporate cell structure.

3.2.2 **Decentralised organisations**

Decentralised organisations are described as networks with no vertical chain of command. They require a minimum degree of control by their leaders and are extremely difficult to locate and to penetrate. A network structure offers flexibility to terrorist groups with opportunities to plan and conduct multiple attacks, stretching law enforcement resources. Al Qa'ida is the most prominent group which currently operates a decentralised structure, and can be described as an amorphous 'network of networks'.

Case Study—Al Qa'ida Organisational Structure

Al Qa'ida has been forced to change the way in which it is structured in order to survive. Throughout the 1980s, following the Soviet invasion and occupation of Afghanistan, Al Qa'ida operated using a centralised structure but the US-led military operation in Afghanistan during 2001, launched in direct response to the 9/11 terrorist attacks, resulted in Al Qa'ida losing its footing in Afghanistan, being forced to physically disperse, leading to a review of its operating structures. A centralised structure for the fractured post-9/11 Al Qa'ida was no longer effective as communication channels to its operatives now dispersed across the world would not be easily achieved. The loss of central command and control of its operatives and their activities was inevitable but a decentralised structure not only offered an alternative solution for Al Qa'ida to continue its operations but has presented new challenges for security authorities across the world to detect, deter, and disrupt their decentralised networks.

Multiple attacks in numerous countries became possible once Al Qa'ida reshaped itself into a loose coalition of networked groups. Prior to this, its vertical structure had made these kinds of attacks difficult to mount without being detected. The military section focused upon recruitment, training, procurement of weapons, and operations. The finance section raised revenue and religious and legal sections drafted the requisite justification for their extreme ideology.

It became clear during the 1990s that Al Qa'ida had spread into Europe and the UK. Khalid-al-Fawwaz was arrested in London for the US embassy bombings in Kenya and Tanzania in 1998 which claimed 300 lives. Prior to his arrest Khalid-al-Fawwaz was managing the group's European press and public relations office, operating from London.

Al Qa'ida now operates as a series of networks which makes it very difficult to track. It is reported to be operating in over sixty countries across the world. Cells dotted all over the world can now operate independently, each claiming to have conducted attacks in its name.

POINT TO NOTE—DECENTRALISED STRUCTURES

The development of terrorist cells poses one of the most potent threats to public safety and national security today. They can emerge anywhere, form quickly, and do not require any formal or prior approval from the core leadership of Al Qa'ida to exist. They can conduct their operations from within their own local communities; indeed, home-grown terrorism is one of the most worrying threats.

Decentralisation limits the opportunities for intelligence agencies to intercept and disrupt attack planning activity, as multiple terrorist operations can be conducted simultaneously with no direct links between terrorist plotters. Moreover, decentralised structures serve to protect the core terrorist leadership from being directly identified with given attacks whilst allowing them to take place in Al Qa'ida's name.

There are a number of different kinds of decentralised structures which terrorist organisations have adopted. Some of these structures have formed organically as groups grow and gain support, but others will have been purposefully crafted. There are four key decentralised structures:

- Link cell;
- Star cell;
- Fused cell; and
- Lone actor.

Link cell

A Link cell (Figure 3.4) is a simple linear network with no hierarchy. It relies on its members to trust the authority of the cell's leaders, asking no questions about where instructions have originated. The anonymity of Terrorist A is almost completely assured, as lines of communication flow in one direction only, as instructions, guidance, and information passes through the links to Terrorist D. If they follow strict security protocols, a Link cell need never know each other's identities. The Link cell is common amongst organised criminal gangs, especially in the movement of drugs and firearms.

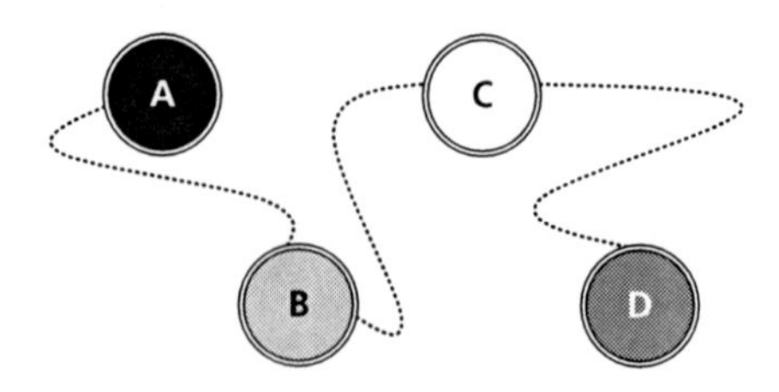

Figure 3.4. Link cell structure.

Star cell

The Star cell (Figure 3.5) is a decentralised structure which has a prominent leader at its centre. Information from Terrorist A is communicated to other members, flowing around the structure of the star, and feeding back to the centre. The leader is the key driver of this structure, often providing propaganda, guidance, and encouragement for the network to develop and deliver terrorist attacks. There are no formal lines of communication between each member, making the identification of the network by authorities difficult. The primary advantage of a Star cell lies in its ability to regenerate following the disruption or compromise of any of its members. As one member is removed, attacks can continue to be mounted by other members. If the cell's leader is removed, any one of the other members can assume this position. To disrupt or eliminate a Star cell, all of its component parts have to be tackled simultaneously.

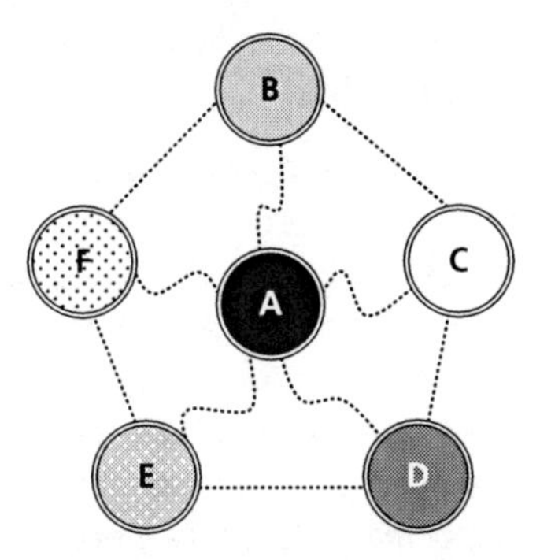

Figure 3.5. Star cell structure.

Fused cell

A Fused cell (Figure 3.6) is the most complex of decentralised structures. There is no identifiable leader. It is best described as a fully linked network of networks where each member is linked to another by numerous lines of communication. Members of fused terrorist cells do not take direction from any specific individual, but instead make their own decisions about the activities they wish to undertake. The key advantage of a Fused cell is that membership can increase organically as the group's ideology takes hold of different individuals, different publics. They pose a major challenge for law enforcement agencies.

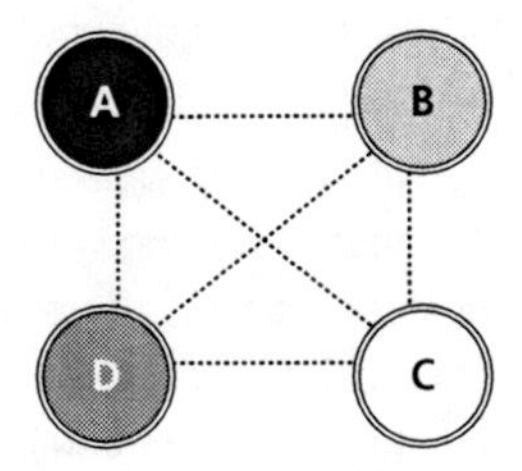

Figure 3.6. Fused cell network structure.

Lone actor

The most alarming of all structures is that of a lone individual who has no direct line of communication with any terrorist group. A single individual can plan, prepare, and mount an attack in complete isolation if tight operational security measures are followed. Individual terrorists who operate alone often first come to the attention of intelligence agencies and law enforcement only once their attacks have been conducted or through a failure of their own operational security. However, without a network of support the capabilities of the lone actor are constrained. It is worth bearing in mind that lone actors can, and have mounted successful attacks in the UK.

Case Study—London Nail Bomber

On Saturday 17 April 1999, David John Copeland, a 22-year-old engineer from Farnborough in Hampshire, began a three-week reign of terror targeting minority groups in London with home-made bombs. During that afternoon, he made his way to Brixton Market carrying a sports bag which contained a home-made bomb packed with 1,500 four-inch nails. At the corner of Electric Avenue, Copeland planted and primed the device leaving it outside a supermarket. Nearby market traders and other members of the public became suspicious of the sports bag and reported it to the police. At 5.25 p.m., just as the police arrived, the bomb exploded. Fifty people were injured in the blast, many of them seriously. Anti-terrorism Branch detectives at Scotland Yard began searching through CCTV footage in order to identify the bomber. Their efforts did not prevent Copeland from carrying out his second attack.

On Saturday 24 April 1999, one week after the Brixton bombing, Copeland made his way to Brick Lane, the centre of the Bengali community in the east end of London. Once again, he carried a home-made nail bomb strapped to the inside of a sports bag. He left the device on Hanbury Street where it exploded injuring thirteen people. Metropolitan Police Officers found CCTV images of a suspect they believed to be the bomber, which they circulated to the media on 29 April 1999. Copeland, having seen the CCTV image, decided to bring forward his third and final attack.

During the evening of Friday 30 April 1999, Copeland planted and detonated another home-made nail bomb after leaving it inside the crowded Admiral Duncan pub in Old Compton Street in Soho. The explosion ripped the pub apart, killing three people and injuring a further 129, four of whom required amputations.

Shortly before the third attack, Paul Mifsud, one of Copeland's work colleagues, recognised him from the CCTV images circulating in the media. He alerted the police and later that evening they arrested Copeland in his rented room in Farnborough. When entering his bedroom police officers discovered a Nazi flag draped on his wall together with a macabre selection of clippings of bombings. During police interviews Copeland maintained he had worked alone and had not discussed his plans with anyone. He openly declared that he held neo-Nazi views, telling police that: '[m]y main intent was to spread fear, resentment and hatred throughout this country, it was to cause a racial war'. He also stated, '[t]here'd be a backlash from the ethnic minorities, I'd just be the spark that would set fire to this country'. As a former member of the British National Party before joining the smaller, violent, and openly neo-Nazi National Socialist Movement, Copeland became its regional leader for Hampshire just weeks before the start of his bombing campaign. Although Copeland was diagnosed by five psychiatrists as having paranoid schizophrenia, and one consultant concluded he had a personality disorder, his plea of diminished responsibility was not accepted by the prosecution. At the Old Bailey in London on 30 June 2000, Copeland was convicted of murder and given six concurrent life sentences. Mr Justice Burton, who described the bombings as a 'really exceptional case of deliberate, multiple murder', spoke of his doubt that it would ever be safe to release Copeland. Seven years after his conviction, on 2 March 2007 the High Court decided that Copeland should remain in prison for at least fifty years, effectively ruling out his release until at least 2049 at the age of 73.

The terrorist acting alone is potentially vulnerable to those who seek to recruit and radicalise new operatives to their cause. These new operatives can be drawn from our very own communities.

POINTS TO NOTE—TERRORIST ORGANISATIONAL STRUCTURES

A consideration of organisational structures provides a simple analysis of terrorist organisations. The list presented is by no means complete, and new structures may emerge. It is also important to note that any single terrorist organisation may be made up of one or any combination of the structures. Al Qa'ida, for example, may operate as a Star cell in some countries, but it may also have connecting nodes to a series of Fused cells in other locations. Its ideology has also attracted many lone actors.

Terrorist organisations can also change and adapt their structures and methods of operating, particularly if they sense their operational security is under threat. This was observed during 1977 when the IRA, believing that its organisation had been infiltrated by agents working for the government, changed its structure from organised companies and brigades to small cells that, although taking instructions from the centre, had increased autonomy. This new structure was implemented quickly—another key advantage of a centralised structure as decisions are followed and translated throughout the organisation swiftly.

3.3 **Terrorist Tactics**

There are many factors which influence which tactics to take, including the nature of the intended target, the capabilities of the organisation's operatives, and the environment in which they operate. Over time, by trial and error, often by accident rather than design, terrorist organisations tend to develop a preferred method of operating. This is often referred to as their 'signature' or 'hallmark', a trusted tactic that they have refined through operational experience. Today's international terrorist groups, however, use a variety of tactics and no single technique can be solely attributed to a specific group. Nor can any given group be definitively identified from tactics used. Armed assaults, bombings, hijacking, infiltration, sabotage, kidnap, and suicide missions are all part of the panoply of the techniques of terrorism, and organisations may use these activities alone or as part of a much broader strategy. Other tactics include producing published propaganda, threats, or hoaxes, deployed to increase fear and raise tensions within communities. Criminal activities are also often used to support terrorist organisations, in particular financial crimes for raising terrorist funds.

3.3.1 **Armed assaults**

Armed assaults are a particularly lethal tactic in the armoury of the terrorist. They take advantage of the element of surprise and have been used by terrorist organisations for many years, primarily as a precursor to wider kidnap, assassination, or siege operations. More recently, however, armed assaults have combined with suicide martyrdom missions.

Case Study—Armed Assaults of Lashkar-e-Tayyiba

At 8.45 a.m. on Tuesday 3 March 2009, the Sri Lankan cricket team travelled to the Gaddafi Stadium in Lahore in preparation for the third day of their second test match against Pakistan. Having left the Pearl Continental Hotel moments earlier, the team coach, together with a smaller twelve-seater minibus carrying cricket umpires, was escorted in a convoy of three police vehicles. As the convoy entered Bank Alfalah Square, two white cars intercepted and terrorists fired a grenade that narrowly missed the coach. At the same time, more terrorists arrived in three rickshaws travelling from different directions. They opened fire on the police escorts with assault rifles. A total of twelve terrorists, working in pairs, shot at the coach, first targeting the wheels and then its main body. Wearing backpacks over civilian clothing, the terrorists were clearly identifiable on images captured by CCTV, communicating with hand-held walkie-talkies. As the cricket players threw themselves to the ground, a terrorist launched a grenade that rolled underneath the coach but which failed to detonate. Despite being under heavy gunfire, the driver of the coach managed to steer his way around the terrorists' vehicles and accelerated to the nearby stadium, crashing through its entrance barriers to safety.

The twelve terrorists retreated down four main roads leading off Bank Alfalah Square as the cricket team were airlifted from the stadium pitch to an army base by Pakistani Air Force helicopters. Seven members of the Sri Lankan cricket team, including six players and a British assistant coach, were injured in the attack. Eight Pakistanis were killed including the driver of the minibus, a member of the public caught up in the attack, and six police officers assigned to protect the sportsmen. As Pakistani police defused two car bombs and recovered grenades, explosives, a pistol, and detonator cable from the scene of the attack, Habib-ur Rahman, Chief of Police in Lahore, said that, 'The plan was apparently to kill the Sri Lankan team, but the police came in their way and forced the attackers to run away'. He went on to say that 'They appeared to be well-trained terrorists'. Pakistani authorities said that the attack bore the hallmarks of the outlawed terrorist group Lashkar-e-Tayyiba (LeT), the same militant organisation blamed for the armed assault in Mumbai during 2008, in which 173 people were killed.

3.3.2 Assassinations

Some terrorist organisations have gained considerable operational expertise in delivering successful assassination operations. The use of suicide bombers has been used to murder political figures, a tactic predominantly deployed by terrorist organisations operating in the Middle East. In Northern Ireland, a common tactic has been to use vehicle-borne improvised explosive devices (VBIEDs).

Case Study—Assassination of Airey Neave

At 2.58 p.m. on 30 March 1979, the Shadow Secretary for Northern Ireland, Airey Neave, was killed by a car bomb as he left the House of Commons. The 63-year-old Conservative MP, known for taking a tough line on security, was cut free from the wreckage and taken to Westminster Hospital. Despite efforts of the emergency services to save his life, the extent of his injuries proved fatal, and he died soon after arriving in hospital. Police officers immediately closed Parliament Square and a series of searches was conducted.

In the preceding months, despite increasing threats to MPs from Irish dissident groups, not all cars were checked as they entered the Westminster car park. The Metropolitan Police Commissioner, Gilbert Kellard, said that Neave was aware of the dangers and was 'happy and content' with his security. The inquest into the assassination was told that the bomb was attached to the car by magnets and the timer had been started by a wrist-watch. A sophisticated tilt-switch was used to activate the bomb when the car started. Then Prime Minister, James Callaghan, said, 'No effort will be spared to bring the murderers to justice and to rid the United Kingdom of the scourge of terrorism'.

Airey Neave, a soldier, barrister, politician, and recipient of the Distinguished Service Order (DSO), Officer of the Order of the British Empire (OBE), and the Military Cross

(MC), was no stranger to violent conflict. He was one of the few servicemen to escape from Colditz Castle in 1942. During January of that year, having been wounded and captured by the Germans in Calais two years earlier, he escaped from the enemy a second time by disguising himself as a German soldier. He made his way out of the prison, and fled to Switzerland via Leipzig, Ulm, and Singen. Neave returned to Britain through France, Spain, and Gibraltar.

Five months after the assassination of Neave, the Irish National Liberation Army (INLA) issued a statement saying that, 'In March, retired terrorist and supporter of capital punishment, Airey Neave, got a taste of his own medicine when an INLA unit pulled off the operation of the decade and blew him to bits inside the "impregnable" Palace of Westminster'.

POINTS TO NOTE—SECURITY OF PUBLIC OFFICIALS

The assassination of Neave serves as a reminder of the dangers that politicians, civil servants, and other public officials encountered from Irish dissidents wishing to advance their political agenda during 'The Troubles'. The resurgence of violence and terrorist events in Ireland over recent years, which has included the murder of British soldiers and a police constable, reinforces the need to place the safety and security of our public officials as paramount. A successful assassination of a leading public and political figure offers terrorists an obvious victory, and the fear this instils in the public's mind may force governments to react and respond. There is no room for complacency in the fight against terrorism, and all officers must follow the operational security measures and guidance put in place to protect them.

3.3.3 **Bombings**

A wide variety of bombing techniques continues to be used: letter bombs designed to target an individual, concealed pipe bombs to attack small groups in specific locations, and vehicle-borne devices, and suicide bombers. Knowledge, expertise, and access to the relevant materials are required before a bombing attack of any nature can be conducted. This preparatory phase provides an opportunity for authorities to identify and intercept terrorist attack planning. Industrial and military-grade explosives are tightly controlled and regulated in the UK, but terrorists may also use chemicals found in non-commercial and non-military products to make home-made explosives (HMEs).

The most devastating terrorist attack in the UK was achieved through the use of a bomb located on Pan Am Flight 103 during December 1988.

Case Study—Pan Am Flight 103

At 6.25 p.m. on 21 December 1988, Pan American Flight 103, a Boeing 747 took off from Heathrow destined for JFK airport in New York. Moments after 7 o'clock, as the flight was over Scotland, the airliner's transponders stopped replying. At that time, the 747 was calculated to be flying at 31,000 feet and at a speed of 580 kilometres per hour. The subsequent investigation revealed that an explosion tore through the front fuselage section of the aircraft causing it to break into several pieces. Investigators believe that within three seconds of the explosion, the cockpit, fuselage, and the third engine fell separately to the ground. The fuselage continued a gradual descent until it reached 19,000 feet, at which point it dived. As the aircraft fell it broke into smaller pieces, debris was scattered over an area of two square kilometres over the town of Lockerbie. The explosion resulted in the death of 270 people, all passengers and crew. Eleven people in Lockerbie were killed as large sections of the fuselage fell in and around the town. Lockerbie resident, Bunty Galloway lived on Rosebank the street most affected by the fallen debris. Parts of the aircraft landed in her garden. She was watching television when she heard an awful noise that seemed to come closer and closer. She ran to the front of her house:

> There were spoons, underwear, headscarves, and everything on the ground. A boy was lying at the bottom of the steps on to the road. A young laddie with brown socks and blue trousers on. Later that evening my son-in-law asked for a blanket to cover him. I didn't know he was dead. I gave him a lamb's-wool travelling rug thinking I'd keep him warm. Two more girls were lying dead across the road, one of them bent over garden railings. It was just as though they were sleeping. The boy lay at the bottom of my stairs for days. Every time I came back to my house for clothes he was still there. 'My boy is still there', I used to tell the waiting policeman. Eventually on Saturday I couldn't take it no more. 'You got to get my boy lifted', I told the policeman. That night he was moved.

The subsequent police investigation was the largest ever mounted in Scotland. Police officers were quickly drafted in to manage the disaster. Police Constable Raymond Platt, then a young officer in Strathclyde Police stationed in Glasgow, recalls his tour of duty in Lockerbie that fateful evening:

> On the night of the bombing I, along with my colleagues, were called back to our police station and informed of the plane crash. At first we all thought it was an exercise but we were told that a jumbo jet had crashed on the town and that the town was on fire. We were advised to phone home as we couldn't be told at that time when we would be returning home. On the journey down there were dozens of police, fire and ambulances racing down to the town. On our arrival we at first went to a local hall and then went out to locate the bodies. I along with a number of others were sent to Sherwood Crescent. My first impression was of the overwhelming smell of aviation

> fuel and the utter devastation of the houses. As the electricity had been knocked out we were working by torchlight and the scene that we found will remain with me. As I only found body parts the scale of the disaster began to hit home and I will never forget the sights which I encountered that are too horrific to mention.

Victims on the aircraft came from twenty-one countries, including 180 from the US, and forty-one from the UK. The attack remains the deadliest terrorist incident in the UK, and until the events of 9/11, was the largest loss of American life due to an act of terrorism. The explosion was believed to have been caused by a bomb concealed in a suitcase that was placed on the flight by the interline baggage system. The suitcase was unaccompanied at the time of detonation. On 3 May 2000 two Libyans were tried for murder, Abdelbaset Ali Mohmed Al Megrahi and Lamin Khalifah Fhimah. Fhimah was found not guilty but Megrahi was convicted of murder on 31 January 2001 and sentenced to life imprisonment. Although his first appeal was rejected on 14 March 2002, Al Megrahi was freed on compassionate grounds and was returned to Libya by the Scottish government on 20 August 2009. Al Megrahi died at home in Tripoli on 20 May 2012 at the age of 60, two years and nine months after his release.

During a Memorial Service held at Dryfesdale Parish Church on 4 January 1989, Right Reverend James Whyte addressed the congregation.

> It is not only pain and grief that we feel at this catastrophe, it is also indignation. For this was not an unforeseeable natural disaster, such as an earthquake. Nor was it the result of human error or carelessness. This, we know now, was an act of human wickedness. That such carnage of the young and of the innocent should have been willed by men in cold and calculated evil is horror upon horror. What is our response to that? The desire, the determination, that those who did this should be detected and, if possible, brought to justice, is natural and right. The uncovering of the truth will not be easy, and evidence that would stand up in a court of law may be hard to obtain. Justice is one thing. But already one hears in the media the word 'retaliation'. As far as I know, no responsible politician has used that word, and I hope none ever will, except to disown it. For that way lies the endless cycle of violence upon violence, horror upon horror. And we may be tempted, indeed urged by some, to flex our muscles in response, to show that we are men. To show that we are what? To show that we are prepared to let more young and more innocent die, to let more rescue workers labour in more wreckage to find grisly proof, not of our virility, but of our inhumanity. That is what retaliation means. I, for one, will have none of it, and I hope you will not either. . . .

3.3.4 **Chemical, biological, radiological, nuclear, and explosive**

Terrorist organisations are pursuing the use of chemical, biological, radiological, nuclear, and explosive (CBRNE) agents as weapons to deliver terror. While other forms of tactics successfully deliver mass casualties, they do not compare with the potentially devastating consequences of CBRNE agents if they were to be effectively developed. A terrorist operation involving the use of these materials not only has the potential to deliver destruction on an unimaginable scale, but it also threatens to have a long-term impact on public health. The secure storage of CBRNE materials remains an important element in protecting the public from harm.

Case Study— Al Qa'ida Ricin Plot

On 5 January 2003 anti-terror police officers raided a flat on High Road, Wood Green in North London. They found twenty-two castor-oil beans, the raw material for the poison ricin, alongside equipment and recipes for ricin, cyanide, and several other poisons. Seven people were arrested at the scene but other suspected cell members fled to Bournemouth where they were later arrested on 11 and 12 January 2003. One terrorist cell member with alleged links to Al Qa'ida, Kamel Bourgass, travelled to Manchester. On 14 January 2003, Greater Manchester Police conducted a raid on a flat in the Crumpsall district of Manchester to investigate suspected immigration offences. Bourgass was staying in the flat and during the police operation, in a desperate attempt to evade capture, he grabbed a six-inch kitchen knife from a nearby kitchen. He stabbed four officers, including Detective Constable Stephen Oake who died as a result of the injuries he sustained.

As the police operation to disrupt and detect the ricin plot continued, officers arrested seven people at the Finsbury Park mosque in north London on 20 January 2003. Police found weapons, and forged passports and identity cards. Police believed that Bourgass, a failed asylum-seeker, was an Al Qa'ida operative who had discussed various ways of spreading poison, including smearing it on car door handles in the Holloway Road area of north London. On 30 June 2004, Bourgass was convicted of the murder of Detective Constable Stephen Oake at the Old Bailey in London. He was sentenced to life imprisonment. On 8 April 2005 Bourgass was also convicted of conspiracy to cause a public nuisance, and other cell members were convicted of possessing false passports. Peter Clarke, the then Deputy Assistant Commissioner of the Metropolitan Police and Head of the Anti-Terrorist Branch at New Scotland Yard, said, 'We must remember that this case was about a conspiracy between a small group of terrorists', revealing that a 'real and deadly threat' had been averted. He added, '[i]t would be hard to underestimate the fear and disruption this plot could have caused across the country'. Paying tribute to Detective Constable Stephen Oake, Clarke said that 'He died protecting the public from a vicious terrorist'. Assistant Chief Constable Whatton of Greater Manchester Police said, '[t]he death of Stephen Oake was the first example of the type of a new danger facing British officers'.

3.3.5 **Fundraising**

To finance their activities, terrorist organisations engage in a variety of criminal activities, not unlike other organised criminal groups. This may also involve fundraising from legitimate sources, such as personal donations and profits from businesses, as well as by criminal means, such as fraud, extortion, theft, and the smuggling of weapons and other goods.

The techniques of money launderers are commonly used by terrorists to conceal sources of money to be used for terrorist purposes. Such money laundering activities may include the running of cash-intensive businesses, the evasion of tax, currency exchanges, and the physical smuggling of cash to another jurisdiction. However, financial transactions associated with terrorist financing tend to be in smaller amounts than is the case with other criminal money laundering methods. When funds are raised from legitimate sources, it is well nigh impossible to detect and track them. To move funds, terrorists use the formal banking system, informal value-transfer systems, and the physical transportation of cash and valuable goods through smuggling routes. The routing of funds through traditional banking centres to countries with major financial hubs is common practice, in an effort to conceal their final destination.

Over recent years terrorists operating in the UK have raised finances from a variety of sources. The use of cheque and credit-card fraud was identified by authorities as a preferred method of operating. Fundraising is a secondary activity in support of the primary function of attack planning. It is a real challenge for those in authority to identify terrorists, who generally do not openly display the profits of their activities, unlike those involved in organised crime.

The complexity of terrorist financing across national and international jurisdictions has forced governments to recognise the need to mount a sustained effort to disrupt and dismantle all terrorist-funding sources. In October 2002, then Chancellor of the Exchequer, Gordon Brown said:

> The United Kingdom is a leading world participant in efforts to counter the financing of terrorism. Our response to the funding of terrorist acts must be every bit as clear, as unequivocal and as united as our response to the terrorist acts themselves. The Government is determined to maintain that advantage over all those who seek to threaten the UK, its economy and all its people.

POINTS TO NOTE—TERRORIST FINANCE

Finance is the lifeblood of terrorists. Without money, they cannot operate. It may seem an obvious point to make, but any suspicion of financial crimes ought to be reported immediately to the relevant authorities.

3.3.6 **Hostile reconnaissance**

Hostile reconnaissance involves the gathering of information for use in a terrorist attack. It forms an integral part of the attack planning process as terrorists seek to obtain a profile of a target. Hostile reconnaissance involves gathering information to determine whether a given attack is feasible, the best method of attack, and the preferred time of attack. The three objectives of hostile reconnaissance are illustrated in Figure 3.7.

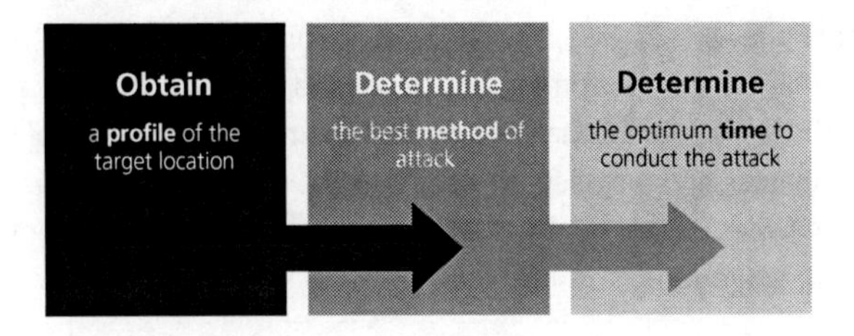

Figure 3.7. Primary role of hostile reconnaissance.

Identifying hostile reconnaissance is important as it very often provides the first indication that an attack is planned. A number of terrorist plots in the UK and across Europe that have been disrupted by security forces have been discovered via evidence of hostile reconnaissance.

Case Study—Al Qa'ida Hostile Reconnaissance

On 23 December 2000, members of an Al Qa'ida terrorist cell travelled by car from Frankfurt in Germany, to Strasbourg in France on a reconnaissance mission. As they approached the French border one of the terrorists began to film the journey through the front windscreen using a hand-held video recorder. German anti-terror police were already monitoring the Frankfurt-based terrorist cell and two days later they raided two apartments in Frankfurt where the suspected terrorists were staying. Police officers discovered several pressure cookers and 30 kilograms of chemicals that could be used to make explosives. They also seized a notebook detailing how to construct home-made bombs. They also found the reconnaissance video still inside the recorder which revealed that the intended target was the Strasbourg Christmas market, and not the European Parliament complex, as the police had originally suspected it might be. The video not only showed families walking through the market but it also captured the quickest escape route out of the city.

In March 2003, the core leaders of the Frankfurt Al Qa'ida cell were found guilty of planning a terrorist attack in Strasbourg. The Frankfurt court heard that the group had planned to blow up pressure cookers packed with explosives, a technique they allegedly learned in terrorist training camps in Afghanistan. Cell members Mohamed Bensakhria and Rabah Kadri, both aged 37, and Slimane Khalfaoui, aged 29, were sentenced to ten years' imprisonment. The fourth member, Mohamed Yacine Aknouche, aged 30, was sentenced to eight years' imprisonment. In December 2004, ten other suspected violent extremists were jailed in Paris for their part in the failed plot. These suspects, both Algerian and French-Algerian, were sentenced to terms of up to ten years' imprisonment. This wider terrorist cell was clearly providing logistical support for the attack, and its members were convicted of criminal association with a terrorist enterprise, which according to the French state prosecutor Christophe Tessier, had links to Al Qa'ida-inspired networks in Britain, Italy, and Spain. This particular case provides evidence that Al Qa'ida were conducting relatively sophisticated operations across Europe before the events of 9/11, and Al Qa'ida-inspired terrorism had put down roots in Europe long before the devastating attacks in Madrid in March 2004, and in London in July 2005. The Frankfurt Al Qa'ida terrorist cell also provides evidence of hostile reconnaissance techniques and provided an insight to the important role of reconnaissance and the reconnaissance team which would become increasingly important to Al Qa'ida attack-planning operations.

POINTS TO NOTE—REPORTING SUSPICIOUS ACTIVITY

By reporting suspicious activity to the police terrorist attacks can be prevented. Members of the public should be encouraged by police to report any information which they believe to be unusual and out of place.

Members of the public should be encouraged to contact the confidential anti-terrorism hotline number, which in the UK is: 0800 789321. For any incident that requires an immediate response, the Emergency Services should be contacted on 999.

3.3.7 **Infiltration**

Terrorist organisations seek information about their enemies, and are only too aware that infiltrating the ranks of their intended target is an extremely effective way to gather this kind of detail. As part of hostile reconnaissance, they will attempt to elicit information about an identified target or test security measures to analyse reaction and responses.

Case Study—Castlereagh, Belfast, 2002

On St Patrick's Day, just after 10 o'clock on Sunday 17 March 2002, intruders entered Castlereagh Police Station in Belfast. They made their way to 'Room 2-20', allegedly an area designated for the storage of sensitive Special Branch files. A police officer was overpowered and documents were stolen. Initial investigations revealed no sign of a forced entry.

As media speculation grew it emerged that 'Room 2-20' had recently been moved to that location from another part of the building. All indications suggested that the intruders had received details about this move from an insider. The stolen documents were believed to contain highly sensitive information concerning covert human intelligence source activities of the police.

Following the attack, Sammy Wilson, a member of the Policing Board of Northern Ireland stated that he had serious concerns about security at Castlereagh, which up until 1999 was believed to have been used to conduct interviews with terrorist suspects. He said,

'People who have given information to Special Branch and understood it was given in the strictest confidence would have grave concerns', concluding that, 'if a police station can be robbed in this way, what chance do the ordinary punters have who are manning petrol stations late at night and people manning post office counters'.

Suspicions were directed to the potential involvement of the Provisional Irish Republican Army (PIRA) and the then Secretary for Northern Ireland, Dr John Reid, was swift to appoint a former civil servant, Sir John Chilcot to head a government inquiry which was to run in parallel with the criminal investigation. Dr Reid stated that: 'it is essential that we establish the facts surrounding this incident as quickly as possible and ensure, in the national interest, that all necessary steps have been taken'.

The attack put pressure on the already fragile peace process, particularly as the IRA was at that time planning a second round of weapons decommissioning, and any IRA involvement in the theft would be a clear breach of the complete cessation of military operations which was outlined as an integral part of the peace process. Ulster Unionist MP David Burnside declared that: 'if the Provisional IRA are inside this process and are in the government of Northern Ireland, then unionists and my party colleagues are going to have to re-examine their whole approach'. The BBC reported that Sinn Féin had said that republicans played 'no part in the raid on Castlereagh'.

3.3.8 **Kidnap**

Throughout the history of terrorism, terrorist organisations have used kidnapping to draw attention to their cause. Kidnapping operations require detailed planning. If terrorists have planned their operations well, are appropriately equipped, and are trained to execute this type of operation, it can be carried out swiftly with little resistance offered by the target.

During the conflicts in Iraq and Afghanistan, many types of kidnap operations have been mounted, especially by insurgent groups who have targeted not only the military and police but also government officials, contractors, security guards, and journalists. Some of these kidnap operations have resulted in the brutal murder and beheading of those kidnapped, some of which have been recorded and shown on the Internet. It is worth noting that this tactic is readily available to terrorists operating in the UK.

Case Study—Operation Gamble

Not long back from his six-month tour in Iraq, a young Muslim soldier was puzzled when police called at his family home in Birmingham. Officers described how a gang from his home town was allegedly plotting to abduct the soldier and then force him on film to 'apologise' for what he had done in Iraq. After instigating this propaganda coup, the gang planned to video the execution of their hostage, a warning to other British Muslims regarded by the kidnappers as 'traitors' of the faith.

On 31 January 2007 in the combined Operation GAMBLE, the police and MI5 arrested Pervaiz Khan, the leader of the kidnapping plot. Khan, aged 36, was born in Derby and had turned from a young man whose main passions were Sunday league football and cricket into a radical jihadist after making several trips to Pakistan. Now married with three young children, Khan's involvement with Al Qa'ida changed him into a homicidal obsessive who spoke of the 7 July bombers as 'brothers'. In February 2008, Pervaiz Khan, together with four other individuals, was found guilty of committing terrorism offences. Khan admitted his guilt to charges of conspiracy to murder and kidnap and was sentenced to life imprisonment.

3.3.9 **Siege**

A siege is best described as an operation carried out to capture a specific site by surrounding and blockading it in order to either retain or remove its occupants. Sieges require meticulous planning and preparation, and is a tactic fraught with challenges for the terrorist not least as they have multiple captives to keep under control whilst they are working towards their objectives. Although a well-planned siege may attract substantial media coverage, they very often conclude in unpredictable ways either as a direct result of terrorist actions, but also the reactions of security forces who seek to resolve such events.

Case Study—Beslan Siege

On 1 September 2004, the Beslan school siege began when the Riyadus-Salikhin Reconnaissance and Sabotage Battalion of Chechen Martyrs took 1,200 people, including over 700 children, hostage. Led by Shamil Basayev, the group of Chechen armed separatists was believed by Russian authorities to be demanding an end to the second Chechen war. The timing of the attack was planned to coincide with the 'Day of Knowledge', the first day of the new school year, regarded as a local festival. At School Number One in the town of Beslan in the north Caucasus region of the Russian Federation, the terrorists led hostages into a small gym, not much bigger than a basketball court, in the centre of the school complex. Mines and bombs connected by cables were placed around them on the floor. Improvised explosive devices were taped to the walls and suspended from the ceiling. Two larger devices were placed in the basketball hoops. Periodically, the attackers fired guns in order to terrify the hostages. They placed children along the windows to act as human shields. As the late summer temperatures soared, many hostages began to faint. They stripped their clothes in an effort to stay cool, and many drank urine to try to stave off dehydration.

During the siege, which lasted three days, the thirty-two terrorists released twenty-six hostages, but they refused to allow food or water supplies into the school which was surrounded by Russian Special Forces. The terrorists agreed to let emergency workers in to retrieve bodies of those who had been killed when the school was seized. On the third day of the standoff, security forces stormed the building using tanks, rockets, and other heavy weapons. A series of explosions shook the school, followed by a fire which engulfed the building. A chaotic gun battle ensued between the terrorists and Russian security forces. As troops moved in, half-naked and bloodied children began running out of the school. Others were carried out by adults. Those who were not seriously hurt were desperate for water. They were first treated at a field hospital set up nearby. Military and civilian ambulances, as well as civilian cars commandeered by soldiers, were used to take the injured to different hospitals. Later, hundreds of bodies, many of them children, were found in the debris of the school gym. Amid the chaos after the storming of the school, there was confusion about the fate of the hostage-takers. Some of the attackers reportedly fled south and took refuge in a nearby house, where they were surrounded by Special Forces, and killed.

By 5 September, the full horror of what had taken place at the school became clear. Emergency workers, sifting through the debris of the burnt-out gymnasium, uncovered the remains of some of those who had been killed. The siege left 331 people dead, including 186 children. More than 700 people were injured. Many of the bodies were charred beyond recognition and some parents had to wait for DNA tests to confirm the fate of their children. The tragedy led to security and political repercussions in Russia, most notably a series of government reforms consolidating power in the Kremlin and the strengthening of the powers of the President. Many aspects of the crisis remained disputed, including the number of militants involved, details regarding the planning of the attack, and whether any of the attackers had escaped. Questions about the government's management of the crisis have also persisted.

Many of the surviving children from School Number One in Beslan were too young or too traumatised to recount their experiences at the time, but survivors are now beginning to reveal their accounts. Bella Gubyeva was twelve years old when she was taken hostage with her brother Vladimir, then ten, who also survived.

> The events on that day changed so much in my life. Now I know what life is worth. I know what it means to be free. When people talk about freedom, it's when you can do what you want to do. It's about being able to breathe fresh air, to have good friends.

3.3.10 **Suicide bombings**

Suicide bombers command attention. Research indicates that suicide attacks kill four times more individuals than conventional tactics. It is effective, inexpensive, and symbolic, drawing considerable attention to the perpetrators' cause. No strategy or planning for withdrawal from a given attack scene is required, saving considerable time and effort. Scant evidence is left. Once the preserve of terrorist organisations operating in the least industrialised countries in the Middle East, the potential for these kinds of attacks now threaten every country in the world.

Case Study—7 July 2005

At 3.58 a.m. on 7 July 2005, a light-blue Nissan Micra car was caught on closed circuit television (CCTV) cameras in Hyde Park Road in Leeds, West Yorkshire. The Nissan picked up the M1 motorway, driving south. It had been hired by Shehzad Tanweer, aged 22, who had lived most of his life in the area of Beeston in Leeds. Neighbours would later describe the sports' science graduate as a 'nice lad' who 'got on with anyone'. Friends would say that Tanweer was very religious, but that he did not express an interest in politics. That July morning, Tanweer was in the car with two of his closest associates from Leeds, Mohammed Sidique Khan and Hasib Hussain. Mohammed Sidique Khan, aged 30, was married and had one child. He was a teaching assistant in the local community. Khan was raised in Beeston and was the youngest of six children born to Pakistani immigrants who had taken British citizenship. Friends from his teenage years would recall him as a highly Westernised young man who insisted on being called 'Sid'. Hasib Hussain, aged 18, was a quiet student with few friends, whose life attracted little outside attention during his early years. Hussain was a second-generation UK citizen whose parents were of Pakistani origin. He grew up in the Holbeck area of Leeds and was still living at home with his parents. All three men knew each other. They had been planning that morning's journey for some time.

At 4.54 a.m. the car stopped at Woodhall Services to fill up with petrol. Tanweer walked to the petrol station shop to pay. At this time he was wearing a white T-shirt, dark jacket, white tracksuit bottoms, and a baseball cap. He bought some snacks and quibbled with the cashier over his change, looking directly at the CCTV camera before he left. Tanweer, Khan, and Hussein then headed south towards Luton where they would meet up with another man.

At approximately 5.07 a.m., a red Fiat Brava arrived at the train station car park in Luton. The Fiat was driven by Germaine Lindsay, aged 19, a Jamaican-born UK resident who had spent his childhood in Huddersfield in West Yorkshire. Lindsay converted to Islam during 2000 and took the name 'Jamal'. At school he was disciplined for handing out leaflets in support of Al Qa'ida. His wife was pregnant with their second child. Waiting for his friends to arrive, he got out of the car and walked around, entered the station, looked at the departure board, left the station, and moved the car a couple of times. There were only a handful of other cars in the car park; London commuters had not yet started their early morning journey.

At 6.49 a.m. the blue Nissan arrived at Luton station and parked next to the Fiat. Khan, Tanweer, Hussain, and Lindsay got out of their cars, looked in the boots of both vehicles, and appeared to move items between them. They put on rucksacks, which CCTV footage showed were large and full. Witnesses said they thought the men were off on a camping holiday. They were, in fact, Al Qa'ida-inspired suicide bombers making their final preparations to deliver a deadly attack which the UK authorities had no idea was about to be mounted.

When police officers later seized the cars they would discover a variety of explosive devices of a different and smaller kind from those contained in the rucksacks. It remains unclear what these were intended for, but speculation by authorities suggests that they were intended for use in self-defence or diversion in case of interception during their journey to the rendezvous at Luton station. This speculation was based on a number of factors, including the size of the devices discovered, and the fact that they were seized from inside the car rather than the boot, and the fact that they were left behind.

Also left in the Nissan Micra were other items consistent with the use of explosives. A 9-millimetre handgun was also seized by police from the Fiat. The Nissan had a day-long parking ticket displayed in its window, perhaps to avoid swift detection. The Fiat had no ticket at all.

The four bombers entered the station and went through the ticket barriers together. It is not known where they bought their tickets or what sort of tickets they possessed. At 7.21 a.m. Khan, Tanweer, Hussain, and Lindsay were all captured on CCTV cameras heading together to the platform for the King's Cross Thameslink train. They were casually dressed, apparently relaxed. Tanweer's posture and the way he pulled the rucksack onto his shoulder as he walked, suggested that the contents were heavy. It is estimated that each rucksack contained two to five kilos of high explosive. By this time, Tanweer was wearing dark tracksuit bottoms, not the white tracksuit bottoms he was wearing earlier. No explanation for this change of clothing has been provided. At 7.40 a.m. the train left Luton station. There are conflicting accounts of the men's behaviour on the train. Some witnesses report noisy conversations, another believes he saw two of them standing silently by a set of train doors. The four men did not stand out from other commuters enough to cause suspicion or attract particular attention, but it was, after all, the beginning of the summer tourist period and the train station served Luton Airport at which many tourists arrive.

The train arrived at King's Cross at 8.23 a.m. At 8.36 a.m. Khan, Tanweer, Lindsay, and Hussain were captured on CCTV cameras on the concourse close to the Thameslink platform, heading in the direction of the London Underground system. A few moments earlier, at around 8.30 a.m. four men matching the description of the bombers were seen hugging. They appeared happy, even euphoric. They then separated. Khan appears to have walked to board a westbound Circle Line train, Tanweer an eastbound Circle Line train, and Lindsay a southbound Piccadilly Line train. Hussain appears to have walked towards the Piccadilly Line entrance. From their movements at this time, it appears that a coordinated north, south, east, and west strike was planned, a calculated attack designed to maximise chaos amid the 3.4 million passenger journeys made on the Underground every day.

At 8.50 a.m. CCTV cameras show the platform at Liverpool Street with the eastbound Circle Line train alongside seconds before the explosion. Tanweer was not visible, but he must have been in the second carriage from the front. The images show commuters rushing to get onto the train from a busy platform. Some get onto the train, some just miss it. The train pulls out of the station. Seconds later, smoke billows from the tunnel. People on the platform are clearly shocked and confused, some run for the exits. Forensic evidence later suggested that Tanweer was sitting towards the back of the second carriage with the rucksack next to him on the floor. When he detonated his device, the blast killed eight people, including Tanweer himself, and injured a further 171 innocent members of the public.

At Edgware Road Khan was in the second carriage from the front, mostly likely near the standing area by the first set of double doors. He was probably also seated with the bomb next to him on the floor. Shortly before the explosion, Khan was seen fiddling with the top of the rucksack. The explosion killed seven people, including Khan, and injured a further 163.

On the Piccadilly Line, Lindsay was in the first carriage as it travelled between King's Cross and Russell Square. The crowded train had 127 people in the first carriage alone. Forensic evidence later suggested that the explosion from the device occurred on or close to the floor of the standing area between the second and third set of seats. This, the most devastating of the blasts on the morning of 7 July, killed twenty-seven people including Lindsay, leaving a further 340 people injured.

At 8.55 a.m. Hussain walked out of King's Cross Underground onto Euston Road. Telephone records show that he tried unsuccessfully to contact his co-conspirators on his mobile telephone over the next few minutes, but they were already dead. His demeanour over this period appeared relaxed and unhurried. Five minutes later, he returns to King's Cross station through a chemist, walking into a newsagency on the station concourse. It appears that he bought a 9-volt battery. Speculation continues as to why he purchased a battery, and why he left the station, but at 9.06 a.m. he walked into the McDonald's restaurant on Euston Road, directly across from King's Cross station, leaving approximately ten minutes later. At 9.19 a.m. Hussain is seen on Gray's Inn Road. Around this time, a man fitting his description is seen on a Number 91 bus travelling from King's Cross to Euston Station, looking nervous and pushing past people. It was almost certainly at Euston that Hussain boarded a Number 30 bus travelling east from Marble Arch. This bus was crowded following closures on the Underground caused by the other attacks. Hussain sat on the upper deck towards the back. Forensic evidence later suggested that the bomb was placed next to him in the aisle or between his feet on the floor. A man fitting his description was seen on the lower deck earlier, fiddling repeatedly with his rucksack.

At this time, Annette Rosenberg called her partner, John Falding, to say that there were problems on the Underground. John advised her to catch a bus. He recalls that, 'she got on a Number 30 bus and she had even got a seat, and then she called to say that it was being diverted down Tavistock Square but she was confident that it would then eventually make its way north to where she worked in Highbury. And as she talked, suddenly I heard ghastly screams in the background, nothing from Annette and no explosion, just these awful screams and the phone went dead'.

Hussain had detonated his rucksack device at 9.47 a.m., killing fourteen people, including Annette, and injuring a further 110 passengers. John tried desperately to call Annette back, remembering that 'it was just going to voicemail all of the time and the fact that I hadn't heard from her and that she didn't come back to me, I just knew I think then that the worst had happened'. Within a mere fifty-seven minutes, fifty-two lives were lost and 784 people were injured. Four otherwise unremarkable British citizens, inspired by Al Qa'ida, had managed to deliver an attack of military proportion in the middle of the nation's capital, totally undetected by the state's security apparatus.

3.4 Domestic Extremist Tactics

Non-terrorist demonstrations and protests may not reach the threshold of terrorist activity or seriously threaten issues of national security, but they can cause harm to communities and the economic well-being of the UK. It is important to keep the threat from 'domestic extremists' in perspective. The majority of protests in the UK are perfectly peaceful, lawful, and undertaken in pursuance of the right of assembly and freedom of speech that we all enjoy as part of living in a democratic society. There is, however, a more complex side to extremists who wish to further their cause by committing criminal acts, become involved in incidents of public disorder, and use violence and intimidation. It is these individuals who are of concern to the police service. Some extremists will, under certain circumstances, adopt a 'soft' style of protest, behaving in a perfectly law-abiding manner as part of a legitimate and peaceful protest. Their attendance at such events may, however, stem from very different motives than the majority of those engaged in lawful democratic activities.

Extremist groups use a wide variety of tactics. They adopt very creative approaches to disrupting the activities of businesses and targeting employees. Police officers need to be aware of these tactics when deciding on and developing responses. Protest activity comprises the following, which are directed towards 'primary' or 'secondary' sites:

- **Day-to-day activities**—protests by local group members at the primary and sometimes secondary sites; and
- **Regional and national days of action**—where substantially larger numbers of protesters gather together or in organised groups. They will target both primary and secondary sites. Often the majority of the protesters are not local people and there is more likelihood of more extremist involvement.

'Primary' and 'secondary' sites are defined as per Table 3.1:

Table 3.1 Primary and secondary sites

Primary	Primary sites consist of the main target premises or organisation where the activity of that business is the primary issue against which the protest is directed. It has to be recognised that protesters will sometimes deliberately target another site, which is less well prepared for such an eventuality. If a place is identifiable as being connected or associated to a particular organisation, protesters may regard it as a target.
Secondary	Secondary sites consist of all other sites, which are linked in any way whatsoever to the primary target site. For example, home addresses of directors, shareholders, employees of primary and secondary targets, suppliers or customers of primary and secondary targets, local authorities, solicitors, banks, shops, and public places. The list of potential secondary targets is extensive. It is generally any target that will have a direct impact or assist in the continuing and increasing pressure to bring about the closure of the primary target organisation.

Domestic extremist groups have used a wide variety of tactics to advance their cause. Table 3.2 provides examples of some of the tactics that have been used by extremist groups in the UK.

Table 3.2 Tactics used by extremist groups in the UK

Mass Demonstrations	Organised and pre-planned mass demonstrations covering a large area, for example, city-centre May Day protests.
Spontaneous Demonstrations	Spontaneous or pre-planned demonstrations at specific locations, for example, outside company addresses.
Home Address Demonstrations	Pre-planned or spontaneous demonstrations at an individual's home address, or immediate neighbourhood.
Bomb Telephone Threats	Bomb or other malicious telephone threats to a third party, company premises, or an individual's home address.
Improvised Explosive Devices	Improvised explosive devices (IEDs), for example in shops or upon vehicles at distribution centres.
Hoax Devices	Real or hoax devices left at company premises or an individual's home address.
Intrusions	Intrusions into company premises for 'sit ins', obtaining information, for example, details of staff, or supplying companies, or releasing or stealing animals.
Malicious Mail	Real, hoax, or malicious mail sent to company premises or an individual's home address.
Harassment	Harassment of staff at or away from company premises.
Intimidation	Intimidation of staff at or away from company premises.
Unsolicited Goods	The sending of unsolicited goods to company and individual employee addresses.

Assault	Physical assault on individuals.
Switchboard Jamming	Telephone switchboard-jamming campaigns.
Fax Machine Blockades	Fax machine blockade—a continuous piece of black paper is faxed to the machine.
E-mail Saturation	E-mail saturation campaigns.
Infiltration	Social engineering and infiltration, for example, organisations unwittingly employing extremists or sympathisers.

3.5 **Summary**

The case studies throughout this chapter serve to highlight the wide range of methods terrorists have used to advance their political, ideological, or religious causes. Everyone in positions of authority should not be surprised by the creativity and ingenuity that terrorists bring to their search for inflicting mass murder on a community, nor should they believe that tactics used overseas will not be used in towns and cities across the UK.

Given the severity of the terrorist threat in the UK, it is no longer acceptable to simply prepare to respond to the types of terrorist attack already encountered. This reactive approach will not protect the public. A creative approach must be employed to identify potential attacks that have not yet occurred. Practitioners and policy-makers must make every effort to understand how terrorists think, what their tactical options are, and how they are able to deliver successful attacks. Preparedness built around assessing risk and making solid contingency plans in the event of future terrorist events form an essential part of tackling terrorism in the UK now.

The police service and individual officers should work to understand terrorist methodologies. Through an increased awareness of terrorist hostile reconnaissance operations, officers can understand the importance of reporting suspicious activity, and encourage members of the public to do so. They will also be in a better position to reassure the public, advising them to remain vigilant, which is an important step in preserving the security of neighbourhoods from terrorist activity.

In the long struggle with terrorists in the UK, far too many police officers have been killed and seriously injured on duty at the hands of terrorists. At all times, police officers must remember that they also are prime targets for terrorists. There is no room for complacency in counter-terrorism and officers must follow the operational security measures and guidance put in place to protect them. If the protectors cannot protect themselves against terrorists, the public will lose confidence in the ability of the police to keep them safe. The highest professional levels of police operational security must continue to be embedded into the very culture of policing contemporary terrorism and violent extremism.

Further reading

- Bergen, P, *The Longest War: America and Al-Qaeda since 9/11* (London: The Free Press, 2011).
- Bongar, B, Brown, L, and Beutler, L, *Psychology of Terrorism* (Oxford: Oxford University Press, 2006).
- Burke, J, *Al-Qaeda: The True Story of Radical Islam* (London: Penguin, 2007).
- Burke, J, *On the Road to Kandahar: Travels through Conflict in the Islamic World* (London: Penguin, 2007).
- Burke, J, *The 9/11 Wars* (London: Penguin, 2012).
- Crenshaw, M, *Explaining Terrorism: Causes, Processes and Consequences* (Oxford: Routledge, 2010).
- English, R, *Armed Struggle: The History of the IRA* (London: Pan, 2012).
- Harnden, T, *Bandit Country: The IRA and South Armagh* (London: Hodder, 2000).
- Jackson, R, *Terrorism: A Critical Introduction* (London: Palgrave Macmillan, 2011).
- Kegley, C, *The New Global Terrorism: Characteristics, Causes, Controls* (London: Pearson, 2002).
- Lambert, R, *Countering Al-Qaeda in London: Police and Muslims in Partnership* (London: C Hurst & Co Publishers Ltd, 2011).
- Moloney, E, *A Secret History of the IRA* (London: Penguin, 2007).
- Neumann, P, *Old and New Terrorism* (London: Polity Press, 2009).
- Taylor, P, *The Provos: The IRA and Sinn Fein* (London: Bloomsbury, 1998).

4

Counter-terrorism Strategy

4.1	Introduction	84
4.2	Responses to Counter-terrorism	84
4.3	The UK Counter-terrorism Strategy	87
4.4	Summary	103

4.1 Introduction

The prevention of terrorist attacks remains the primary objective of counter-terrorism strategies operating throughout the world today, but they must also prepare emergency services to respond to the consequences of terrorism. In addition, counter-terrorism strategies need to be able to protect the public, and a robust criminal justice system must be in place to arrest and prosecute terrorists. The balance between affording the same human rights and civil liberties to would-be terrorists as to law-abiding citizens is extremely challenging.

An effective counter-terrorism strategy must also be capable of implementation by multiple organisations, departments, and agencies of government. The purpose of this chapter is to provide all police practitioners with an introduction to the numerous models used to develop contemporary counter-terrorism strategies. It explains the development, structure, strategic aim, and objectives of the UK's counter-terrorism strategy which offers a framework for all police counter-terrorism activity.

Contemporary counter-terrorism machinery now cuts across government departments, law enforcement and intelligence agencies. A better understanding of the role of the police in counter-terrorism will serve to contextualise their contribution to national strategies and to reinforce the collaborative approach required to tackle terrorism today.

4.2 Responses to Counter-terrorism

Governments around the world approach the design of their counter-terrorism strategies by considering three broad responses to tackle the problem: the military, criminal justice, and the community responses.

4.2.1 Military response

A military counter-terrorism response is used by governments to tackle terrorists who pose a significant threat to national security. Terrorist groups who possess and use conventional weapons, and aspire to possess chemical, biological, radiological, or nuclear capabilities, require a robust response which the military can offer. A military system for countering terrorism may also be required when domestic law enforcement agencies can no longer contain a specific terrorist threat. Governments allow the armed forces to plan and implement counter-terrorism strategies in such circumstances.

POINTS TO NOTE—MILITARY RESPONSE

Deciding to use the military to combat a terrorist threat is a significant step for any government to take. This may, however, be absolutely necessary to protect innocent civilians and preserve national security. The current 'war on terror' has made governments review their military response, as military interventions can raise expectations of an early success. In general, military force on its own does not successfully counter the threat.

4.2.2 **Criminal justice response**

The criminal justice system provides the means for trial and conviction of suspected terrorists. The foundation of a democratic criminal justice system is the premise that an individual is innocent until proven guilty, and the process is conducted in a recognised court of law, following a fair trial with legal representation. Founding the battle against terrorism on the tenets of the criminal justice system protects the democratic values of the prosecuting states while ensuring that the rights of all concerned are maintained.

POINTS TO NOTE—CRIMINAL JUSTICE RESPONSE

A criminal justice approach has a number of key advantages, none more so than the element of trust in a system that ensures an individual's human rights are respected.

A criminal justice system depends upon effective domestic law enforcement agencies and their ability to conduct complex terrorist investigations. Countering a global terrorist threat via a criminal justice system also depends upon efficient bi-lateral and multinational cooperation between law enforcement agencies and via the use of agencies such as Interpol.

It is important to ensure that robust legislation is in place that has the scope to keep pace with new and emerging terrorist threats, but is mindful of what is an appropriate and proportionate response.

4.2.3 **Community response**

Current events have shown that communities are good at exposing terrorism and violent extremism. The political and socio-economic issues that give rise to anti-social behaviour and low-level criminality are also those which give rise to serious and organised crime and to terrorism, and these begin at the most fundamental local level. Terrorists live within local communities and operate there. The community response harnesses the collective attributes of communities seeking to create long-term trusted relationships between charities, groups, residents, schools, clubs, and associations, all of which can have a role in challenging unacceptable behaviours and extremist views. It can feed information to authorities where a potential threat is identified.

The community response highlights the fact that communities as well as governments have a direct responsibility for increasing cohesion in their own community.

POINTS TO NOTE—COMMUNITY MODEL

An effective counter-terrorism strategy should be underpinned by a community approach, because national security depends now upon neighbourhood security. Empowering communities, listening to their grievances and concerns, and supporting their activities and aspirations will serve to build confident communities that are robust, resilient, and ready to reject not just anti-social behaviour or low-level criminality but also terrorism and violent extremism. The community response is based upon the trust and confidence existing between all of its partners, who work together united in the rejection of extremist rhetoric. Encouraging an effective community response requires time, dedication, and commitment from everyone in authority, but especially the police and local authorities who are very often the public face of this counter-terrorism approach.

POINTS TO NOTE—MODEL STRATEGIES

An effective counter-terrorism strategy to tackle all forms of contemporary terrorism will effectively fuse the community, criminal justice, and military approaches. Authorities then have a range of options that can be appropriately deployed in justified, proportionate, and legitimate responses to terrorist threats.

4.2.4 Twelve rules of counter-terrorism strategy

As part of a major study which synthesised more than two decades of scholarly research in the field, Professor Alex P Schmidt, Director of the Terrorism Research Initiative (TRI), identified twelve rules for preventing and combating terrorism. The twelve rules, illustrated in Table 4.1, were drawn from the responses of one hundred experts in twenty countries who shared their experiences of counter-terrorism and the lessons they had learnt from the counter-measures they had deployed. These rules provide policy-makers with a framework to construct effective counter-terrorism strategies, and support the interpretation and implementation of strategies by police officers and their partners.

Table 4.1 Twelve Rules for Preventing and Combating Terrorism

	Twelve Rules for Preventing and Combating Terrorism
1	Try to address the underlying conflict issues exploited by the terrorists and work towards a peaceful solution while not making substantive concessions to the terrorists themselves.
2	Prevent alienated individuals and radical groups from becoming terrorist extremists by confronting them with a mix of 'carrot' and 'stick' tactics, and searching for effective counter-motivation models.

3 Stimulate and encourage defection and conversion of free and imprisoned terrorists and find ways to reduce the tacit or open support of aggrieved constituencies for terrorist organisations.

4 Deny terrorists access to arms, explosives, false identification documents, safe communication, and safe travel and sanctuaries; disrupt and incapacitate their preparations and operations through infiltration, communications intercepts, and espionage, and by limiting their criminal and other fund-raising capabilities.

5 Reduce low-risk/high-gain opportunities for terrorists to strike by enhancing communications security, energy security, and transportation security, by hardening critical infrastructures and potential sites where mass casualties can occur, and by applying principles of situational crime prevention to the countering of terrorism.

6 Keep in mind that terrorists seek publicity and exploit the media and the Internet to gain recognition, propagate their cause, glorify their attacks, win recruits, solicit donations, gather intelligence, disseminate terrorist know-how, and communicate with their target audiences.

7 Prepare for crisis and consequence management for both 'regular' and 'catastrophic' acts of terrorism in coordinated simulation exercises, and educate first responders and the public on how best to cope.

8 Establish an all-sources early detection and early warning intelligence system against terrorism and other violent crimes on the interface between organised crime and political conflict.

9 Strengthen coordination of efforts against terrorism both within and between states; enhance international police and intelligence cooperation, and offer technical assistance to those countries that lack the know-how and means to upgrade their counter-terrorism instruments.

10 Show solidarity with, and offer support to, victims of terrorism at home and overseas.

11 Maintain the moral high ground in the struggle with terrorists by defending and strengthening the rule of law, good governance, democracy and social justice, and by matching deeds with words.

12 Counter the ideologies, indoctrination, and propaganda of secular and non-secular terrorists, and try to get the upper hand in the war of ideas—the battle for the hearts and minds of those the terrorists claim to speak and fight for.

4.3 The UK Counter-terrorism Strategy

Up until 11 September 2001, the UK, like the US and many other countries in the developed world, had no sophisticated or coherent cross-departmental strategy to counter international terrorism. Of course, the UK security apparatus had long experience of terrorism in Northern Ireland which offered some foundation to potential emergency terrorism legislation. Collaboration between government departments had been key to the success of many counter-terrorism operations, and the intelligence community had learned the value of close cooperation with the police service. Nevertheless, violent jihadist terrorism represented new challenges for parliament and public, government and law enforcement alike.

In the immediate aftermath of 9/11, Sir David Omand was appointed in the new position of UK Security and Intelligence Coordinator at the Cabinet Office. He began developing a comprehensive national counter-terrorism strategy. The threat from Islamist terrorism had been assessed as severe and numerous plots affecting British interests both overseas and at home were taken very seriously indeed. Sir David called his strategy CONTEST (COuNter-TErrorism STratgey), which was launched in November 2002 and adopted in 2003. Details remained confidential and were not published by the government until 2006. An updated version, CONTEST 2, was published in 2009, and CONTEST 3 was published in 2011.

4.3.1 **Constructing CONTEST**

Building the CONTEST strategy started with assessing the strategic risks to the UK. The first steps were to establish the ends, ways, and means of Al Qa'ida's intentions. Al Qa'ida seeks to liberate and unite the global community of Islamic believers in a Caliphate covering all 'Muslim' lands. The ways it seeks to achieve this are to weaken the enemy by building strength through global alliances with existing terrorist organisations. It seeks to complete its aims by means of extreme acts of terrorism to expose the weakness of the West, to create confidence that resistance to US influence is possible, and to inspire an 'awakening' of revolutionary consciousnesses.

An important and implicit assumption contained in CONTEST from the outset was that there was no complete defence against determined terrorists, especially as they continued to develop new ways in which to deliver death and destruction, often on an unimaginable scale.

Omand's aim was for the country to take sensible steps to reduce the risk to the public at home and to UK interests overseas, based on the principle known as ALARP (As Low As Reasonably Practicable). CONTEST provided measures to counter each of the identified ends, means, and ways of Al Qa'ida's terrorist strategy. To mitigate the ends of Al Qa'ida's intentions, CONTEST must protect the UK and its interests from security risks, including terrorism in all of its forms. The way in which to do this was to reduce terrorism risk through concerted action by government. From these were mapped what became known as the '4Ps' campaigns which included:

Pursue, to stop terrorist attacks;
Prevent, to stop people becoming terrorists, or supporting violent extremists;
Protect, to strengthen protection against terrorist attack; and
Prepare, where an attack cannot be stopped, to mitigate its impact.

The means to achieve this was to be seen to uphold human rights, the rule of law, legitimate and accountable government, and the core values of justice, and freedom. The strategic aim was to make it possible for society to maintain conditions of normality so that people could go about their normal business, freely and with confidence, even in the face of suicidal terrorist attacks.

KEY POINT—STRATEGIC AIM OF CONTEST

The strategic aim of CONTEST is to reduce the risk to the UK and its interests overseas from terrorism, so that people can go about their lives freely and with confidence.

4.3.2 CONTEST strategy structure

The CONTEST strategy continues to be divided into four key pillars which provide the scope to counter terrorism effectively. The four pillars are commonly known as the four Ps, cited earlier.

Sir David believed that the strategy for countering terrorism was best understood as a logical narrative that could be translated into specific programmes of action across government, the private sector, and the voluntary sector, capable of being updated and extended in response to developments in the threat and in the kinds of technologies for countering it. It was important that complexities were simplified, and a joined-up approach across the many agencies involved was reinforced. The creation of CONTEST has given clarity and direction to all agencies and provided the framework via which separate organisations can allocate resources and assets for a combined and successful effort.

Of the four Ps, 'Prevent' and 'Pursue' both focus upon the actual human threat from terrorists designed to reduce the risk by stopping them. 'Protect' and 'Prepare' focus upon the capability of the UK to reduce vulnerability of attacks when they occur. By simultaneously tackling areas to reduce the risk and to minimise vulnerability, collectively serves to reduce the threat (see Figure 4.1).

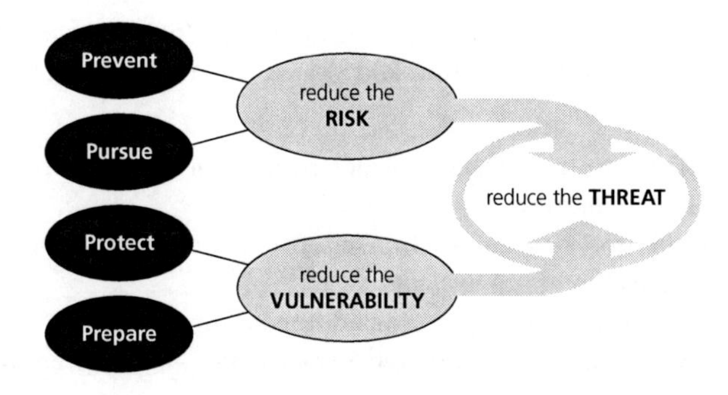

Figure 4.1. Mechanics of the CONTEST strategy.

4.3.3 'Prevent'

The 'Prevent' strand of CONTEST is concerned with tackling the radicalisation of individuals. It aims to do this by addressing structural problems in the UK and overseas that may contribute to the process of radicalisation development, such as inequalities and discrimination. A long-term approach is clearly required. The strategy seeks to deter those who facilitate terrorism as well as those who encourage others to become terrorists. This strand also aims to engage in the battle of ideas, to win hearts and minds by challenging the ideologies that extremists believe justify the use of violence.

Preventing violent extremism, often referred to as the 'PVE' agenda, is a key area of CONTEST. Preventing terrorism and extremism is the proactive element of the strategy. The government believes that the UK, like many other countries, faces a challenge from terrorism and violent extremism from a minority who seek to harm innocent people in the name of an ideology which causes division, hatred, and violence. The role of the government is to take tough security measures needed to keep people safe, but a security response alone is not enough; a response led and driven by local communities is vital. The very essence of the 'Prevent' strategy seeks to engage partners to work together to challenge and expose the ideology that sanctions and encourages indiscriminate violence. The strategy identifies the need to expose and isolate the apologists for violence and safeguard from them the places where they may operate. It states that local authorities, the police, and their partners in schools, other educational institutions, and elsewhere all have a critical role in preventing violent extremism as these groups understand the local context and are in a unique position to talk to local communities, hear their concerns, and galvanise action against the threat.

A fresh focus

During June 2011 the UK government published a review of 'Prevent'-related work, followed by a new strategy. This review concluded that the UK government does not believe that it is possible to resolve the threats simply by arresting and prosecuting more people. A new version of the strategy places greater emphasis on the delivery of successful integration, which seeks to establish a stronger sense of common ground and shared values. The key objectives of 'Prevent' are to:

- Respond to the ideological challenge of terrorism and the threat presented by those who promote it;
- Prevent people from being drawn into terrorism and ensure that they are given appropriate advice and support; and
- Work with a wide range of sectors (including education, criminal justice, faith, charities, technology, and health) where radicalisation is a current risk.

The government believes that success in delivering 'Prevent' will mean that:

- There is a reduction in support for terrorism of all kinds in the UK and in states overseas whose security is linked with the UK's;
- There is more effective challenge to those extremists whose views are shared by terrorist organisations and used by terrorists to legitimise violence; and
- There is more of a direct challenge to, and isolation of, extremists and terrorists operating on the Internet.

The strategic aim of 'Prevent', its key objectives, and critical success factors are shown in Figure 4.2.

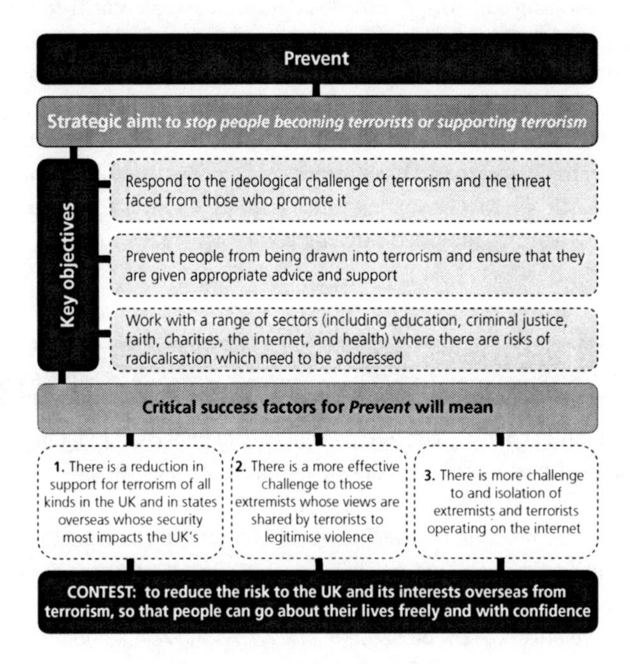
Prevent
Strategic aim: to stop people becoming terrorists or supporting terrorism
Key objectives
Respond to the ideological challenge of terrorism and the threat faced from those who promote it
Prevent people from being drawn into terrorism and ensure that they are given appropriate advice and support
Work with a range of sectors (including education, criminal justice, faith, charities, the internet, and health) where there are risks of radicalisation which need to be addressed
Critical success factors for Prevent will mean
1. There is a reduction in support for terrorism of all kinds in the UK and in states overseas whose security most impacts the UK's
2. There is a more effective challenge to those extremists whose views are shared by terrorists to legitimise violence
3. There is more challenge to and isolation of extremists and terrorists operating on the internet
CONTEST: to reduce the risk to the UK and its interests overseas from terrorism, so that people can go about their lives freely and with confidence

Figure 4.2. 'Prevent' key objectives.

4.3.4 **'Pursue'**

The purpose of 'Pursue' is to stop terrorist attacks in the UK and against UK interests overseas. This means detecting and investigating threats at the earliest possible stage, disrupting terrorist activity before it can endanger the public, and, wherever possible, prosecuting those responsible. The key objectives of 'Pursue' are to:

- Continue to assess the UK's counter-terrorism powers and ensure they are both effective and proportionate;
- Improve the ability to prosecute and deport people for terrorist-related offences;
- Increase the capabilities required to detect, investigate, and disrupt terrorist threats;

- Ensure that judicial proceedings in the UK are equipped to handle sensitive and secret material to serve the interests of both justice and national security; and
- Work with other countries and multilateral organisations to improve efforts to tackle threats at their source.

To achieve its objectives, 'Pursue' focuses on gathering intelligence and improving the ability to identify and understand the terrorist threat. It also aims to take action to frustrate terrorist attacks and to bring terrorists to justice through developing a fit-for-purpose legal framework. New anti-terrorism legislation has greatly assisted the pursuit of terrorists, but bringing them to justice involves international cooperation. 'Pursue' recognises the dependence the UK intelligence agency and law enforcement departments have on international partners, many less experienced than the UK in countering terrorism. To support 'Pursue', the government has provided significant assistance and capability building in over twenty countries in a range of counter-terrorism skills and techniques, which has included offering advice on legal structures and human rights.

POINTS TO NOTE—ACQUAINTANCE WITH ANTI-TERROR POWERS

It is important for counter-terrorism practitioners to understand that given the current level of threat from international terrorism, stopping terrorist activity prior to gathering sufficient evidence to secure a conviction at court is sometimes going to be essential. The Home Office is currently seeking to increase detection and investigation capacity and capability, increase the effectiveness of the prosecution process from evidential collection to post-prison supervision, and develop more effective non-prosecution actions. All those in authority, and in particular operational police officers of all ranks, roles, and responsibilities should know what these provisions are. They are powers to be utilised by all police officers and not just those assigned to specialist counter-terrorism units. Taking time to study these laws will serve the efficiency of investigations where officers may be asked to carry out duties in support of achieving objectives of a counter-terrorism operation.

While anti-terror provisions have helped counter-terrorism officers to disrupt terrorist activity at an early stage where required, it is not always possible to prosecute people simply because intelligence indicates that they are engaged in terrorist-related activity. For this very reason, anti-terror law includes a range of alternative non-prosecution actions to protect the public. They include T-PIMS orders, the exclusion of foreign nationals from entering the UK, revocation of citizenship, and deportation.

The government believes that success in delivering 'Pursue' will mean that:

- UK authorities are able to disrupt terrorist related activity at home, and prosecute or deport those responsible;
- Overseas, the UK can reduce the threat from Al Qa'ida, its affiliates, and other terrorist organisations and has disrupted attacks planned against it; and
- UK counter-terrorism work is effective, proportionate, and consistent with its commitment to human rights.

The strategic aim of 'Pursue', its key objectives, and critical success factors are shown in Figure 4.3.

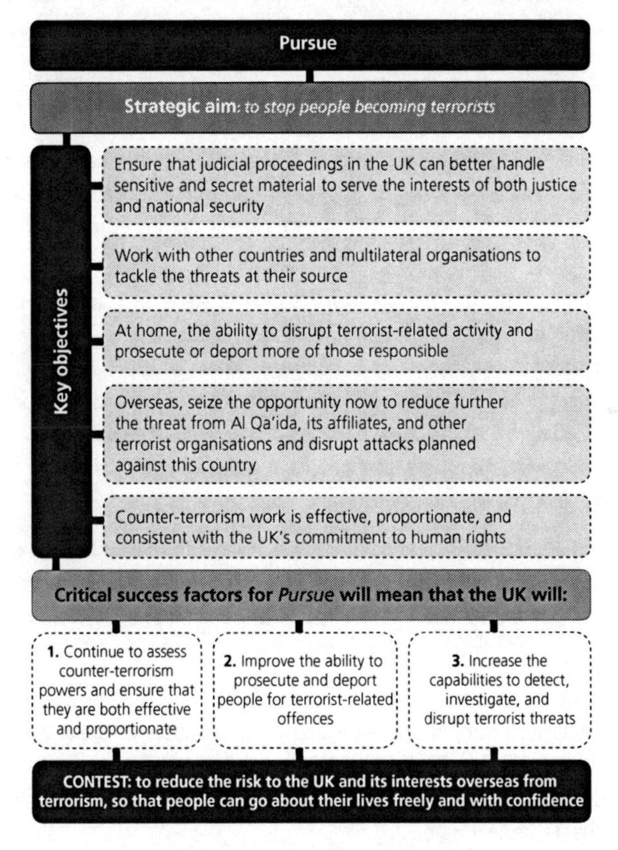

Figure 4.3. 'Pursue' key objectives.

4.3.5 **'Protect'**

Reducing the vulnerability of the UK and its interests overseas to a terrorist attack is the purpose of 'Protect'. It aims to strengthen border security, protect key utilities, transport infrastructures, and crowded places. Our national infrastructure is the underlying framework of facilities, systems, sites, and networks necessary for the functioning of the country and the delivery of essential services. They are often taken for granted and include water, energy, and food supplies which if attacked could lead to severe economic loss, social damage, or, in the most extreme cases, large-scale loss of life. Key sites within the UK include airports.

Case Study—Operation Seagram

At 3.11 p.m. on Saturday 30 June 2007, a dark-green Jeep Cherokee loaded with propane cylinders was driven into the glass doors of the Glasgow International Airport terminal. Initial reports indicated that protective security steel bollards had prevented the vehicle from entering the terminal. The vehicle contained two men, Kafeel Ahmed and Bilal Talal Samad Abdullah, who were both arrested at the scene. Ahmed suffered 90 per cent burns to his body and died at Glasgow Royal Infirmary as a result of his injuries several days later. Although people assisting police officers at the scene of the attack suffered injuries themselves, no other casualties arose from this attempted suicide attack.

The attack came a day after the Metropolitan Police were also engaged in a counter-terrorism investigation following a controlled explosion carried out on a car also packed with gas cylinders in Haymarket in London on 29 June 2007. An ambulance crew reported seeing smoke coming from a green Mercedes which had been parked near a nightclub at 1.30 a.m. that day. Two major incidents within the space of two days raised fears that the UK was the target of a potential series of coordinated terrorist attacks. Alex Salmond, the First Minister of Scotland, said,

> The incident at Glasgow Airport today as well as recent events in London show that we face threats both north and south of the border, and both the Scottish and UK Governments are united in our determination to stand up to that threat and protect our communities.

The attack was the first specifically to target Scotland. Images of the events at Glasgow Airport were televised throughout the world within minutes of the attack. Airports in the UK were quick to respond, taking measures to increase their security. Other countries also implemented their counter-terrorism contingency plans. US Secretary of Homeland Security, Michael Chertoff, said:

> We have been in close contact with our counterparts in the UK regarding today's incident at the Glasgow airport and yesterday's car bomb discoveries in London. Our law enforcement and intelligence officials are closely monitoring the ongoing investigations.

POINT TO NOTE—REVIEW OF 'PROTECT'

As a direct result of the failed terrorist attacks in London and Glasgow in June 2007, Lord West, then Minister for Homeland Security and Counter-Terrorism, conducted a review of security within the UK. The review specifically focused on the protection of strategic infrastructure, stations, ports and airports, and other crowded places. There were three key findings from the review:

- A need for a new 'risk-based' strategic framework to reduce vulnerability of crowded places;
- Focused effort on reducing the vulnerability of the highest risk crowded places by working with private and public sector partners at a local level;
- New efforts to 'design in' counter-terrorism security measures are needed, building on good practice from crime prevention.

These findings have been developed over recent years to strengthen the protection from terrorism provided to the public still further.

The key objectives of 'Protect' are to:

- strengthen UK border security;
- reduce the vulnerability of the transport network;
- increase the resilience of the UK's infrastructure; and
- improve protective security for crowded places.

The government believes that success in delivering 'Protect' will mean that:

- The UK will be able to judge how it is vulnerable to terrorist attack and will be able to reduce those vulnerabilities to an acceptable and a proportionate level;
- governmental priorities can be shared with the private sector and the international community, and, wherever possible, these parties can act in concert to address them.

The strategic aims of 'Protect', its key objectives, and critical success factors are shown in Figure 4.4.

4.3.6 'Prepare'

The purpose of 'Prepare' is to mitigate the impact of a terrorist attack in the event that the attack cannot be stopped. This includes efforts to bring a terrorist attack to an end and to increase resilience so that recovery is possible. An effective and efficient response will save lives, reduce harm, and aid recovery. Preparing for emergency incidents and planning for worst-case scenarios will reduce the impact of a terrorist attack. The primary government department responsible for delivering the national objectives of 'Prepare' is the Home Office, in particular its Office of Security and Counter-Terrorism (OSCT).

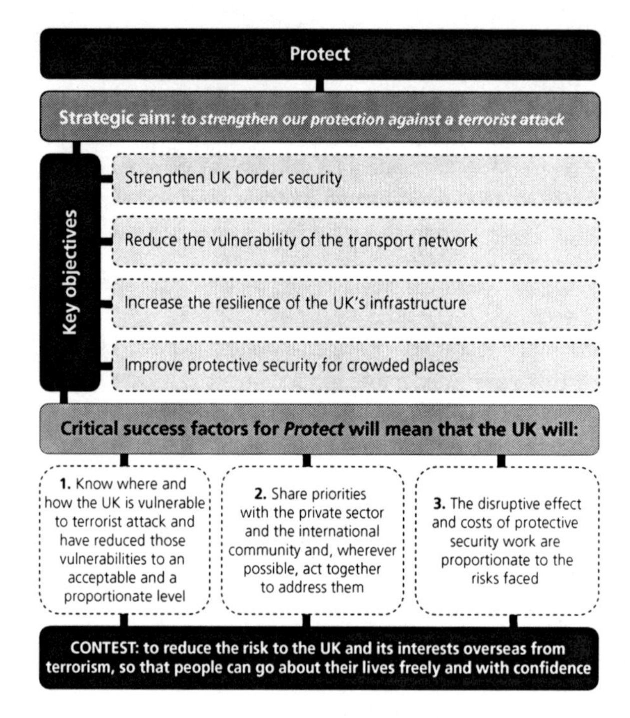

Figure 4.4. 'Protect' key objectives.

Case Study—The Role of the Office of Security and Counter-Terrorism

For over thirty years, the Office of Security and Counter-Terrorism (OSCT) has led the work on counter-terrorism in the UK in collaboration with the police and security services. The OSCT reports directly to the Home Secretary. The OSCT currently has responsibility for:

- developing and coordinating the CONTEST Strategy;
- implementing the UK's response to a terrorist incident;
- developing security measures and protection packages for public figures;
- ensuring that the UK's critical national infrastructure is protected from attack (including cyber attack);
- ensuring the UK is prepared to deal with a chemical, biological, or nuclear release;
- liaising with government and emergency services during terrorist incidents and counter-terrorism operations;
- overseeing the Regulation of Investigatory Powers Act 2000 (RIPA);
- overseeing the Security Service Acts 1989 and 1996;
- overseeing Home Office-related elements of the Intelligence Services Act 1994.

POINT TO NOTE: NATIONAL COUNTER TERRORISM EXERCISE PROGRAMME

One of the primary functions of the OSCT is to implement the UK's response to a terrorist incident. OSCT works with the police, security, and intelligence agencies, other government departments, and the armed forces to devise, maintain, and test capabilities and responses which would be used in the event of a terrorist incident. The OSCT's National Counter Terrorism Exercise Programme reflects the changing nature of the terrorist threat we face, and aims to improve the ability of the police service and other key partners to prepare for, respond to, and manage terrorist investigations and incidents.

The National Counter Terrorism Exercise Programme delivers a mix of exercises, usually including three major national counter-terrorism exercises each year. In recent years, major exercises have been completed in most regions of the UK. Since 2009, major exercises have employed scenarios which feature responses to aviation, CBRN, marauding gunmen, maritime, and hostage-taking threats. Some exercises test the ability to disrupt an imminent attack. Others test the response to an attack in progress or to an attack that has occurred. A key element is the testing of both the command chain (from government down to the lowest level of police command), and the coordination between emergency services during an incident. Ministers regularly participate in national counter-terrorism exercises, ensuring that the highest level of strategic decision-making is tested, via the government's COBR processes.

National counter-terrorism exercises are the culminating event in a structured series of smaller scale preparatory exercises, which may include live or simulated activity aimed at developing greater counter-terrorism preparedness. Progress is assessed through CONTEST structures and at the Police Counter Terrorism Board (which includes senior police officers and Home Office Ministers).

The 'Prepare' cycle

To stop terrorist attacks and to recover effectively when attacks succeed requires a cycle of sustained effort. This includes first identifying the potential risks, then assessing the potential impact of those risks. Appropriate capabilities can then be devised to respond effectively to the risks followed by programmes of evaluation and testing of preparedness to respond to risks should they come to pass. The cycle of 'Prepare' is illustrated in Figure 4.5.

The key objectives of 'Prepare' are to:

- continue to build generic capabilities to respond to and recover from a wide range of terrorist and other civil emergencies;
- improve preparedness for the highest impact risks in the National Risk Assessment;

- improve the ability of the emergency services to work together during a terrorist attack; and
- enhance communications and information-sharing regarding terrorist attacks.

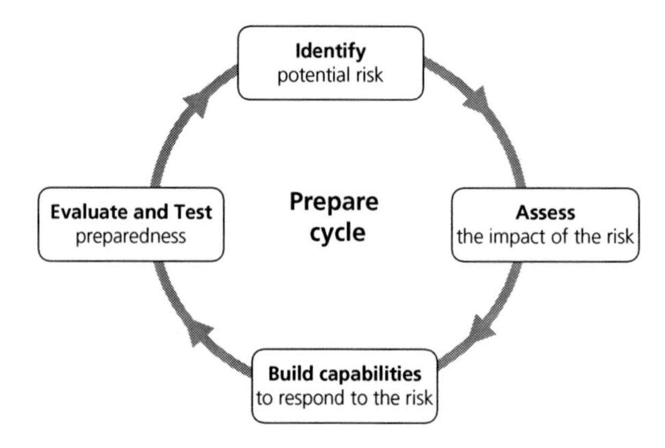

Figure 4.5. 'Prepare' cycle.

The government believes that success in delivering 'Prepare' will mean that:

- planning for the consequences of all civil emergencies provides the capabilities to respond to and recover from the most likely kinds of terrorist attacks in the UK;
- additional capabilities to manage ongoing terrorist attacks wherever required are safely in place; and
- additional capabilities to respond to the highest impact risks are provided.

The strategic aim of 'Prepare', its key objectives, and critical success factors are shown in Figure 4.6, demonstrating its contribution towards the overall aim of CONTEST to reduce the risk to the UK and its interests overseas from terrorism, so that people can go about their lives freely and with confidence.

4.3.7 **CONTEST governance**

The National Security Council (NSC), chaired by the Prime Minister, has oversight of CONTEST, and receives regular reports on its progress. The Home Secretary continues to lead on domestic counter-terrorism, and is a member of and accountable to the NSC. The NSC regularly reviews progress of CONTEST, considering specific risks and agreeing the appropriate response and resources. The Home Secretary also has oversight of the Security Service and is accountable for the activities of the police service in England and Wales.

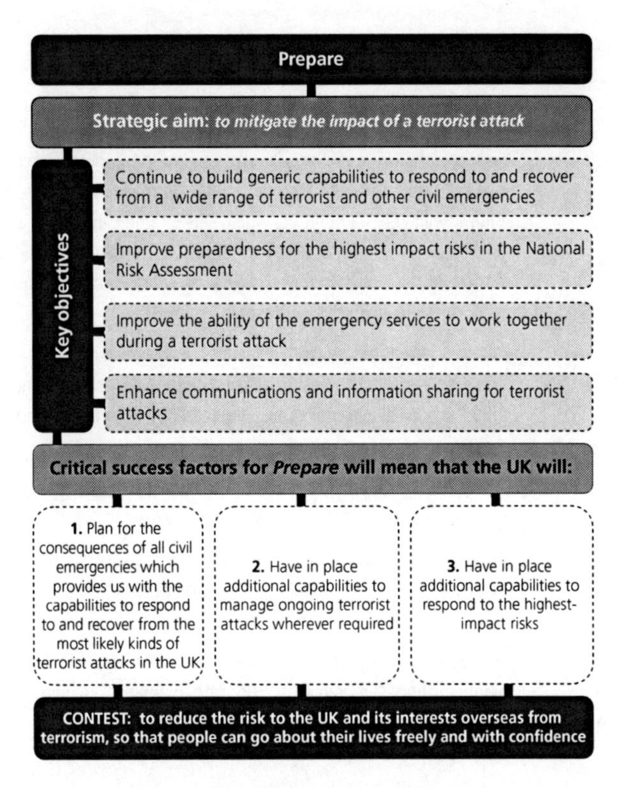

Figure 4.6. 'Prepare' key objectives.

The CONTEST Board is responsible for developing and monitoring implementation of the strategy. The Board includes officials from key government departments, the police, security and intelligence agencies, and the Scottish and Welsh governments to ensure that all those involved in countering terrorism are included in decision making. To ensure effective oversight of the strategy, sub-Boards are responsible for 'Pursue', 'Prevent', 'Protect', and 'Prepare'. There are also separate oversight boards for a range of cross-cutting issues, including the Overseas CONTEST Group (OCG), the Police Counter Terrorism Board (CTB), and the Internet Strategy Group (ISG).

4.3.8 **CONTEST roles and responsibilities**

Developing and delivering CONTEST involves numerous departments from across government including the emergency services, as well as voluntary organisations, representatives from the commercial sector, and diverse partners from around the world. A full list of government departmental roles and responsibilities to support and contribute towards achieving the strategic aim of CONTEST is shown in Table 4.2.

Table 4.2 CONTEST roles and responsibilities

Department	Roles and Responsibilities
Cabinet Office (CO)	Supports the National Security Council and the Cabinet Office Briefing Room (COBR), oversees the Single Intelligence Account, and services the Joint Intelligence Committee, which sets strategic intelligence gathering priorities and delivers strategic intelligence assessments. The Civil Contingencies Secretariat of the Cabinet Office leads cross-government work on many aspects of *Prepare*.
Centre for the Protection of the National Infrastructure (CPNI)	Provides integrated protective security advice (covering physical, personnel, and cyber security) to businesses and organisations across the national infrastructure aimed at reducing vulnerability to terrorism and other threats.
Crown Prosecution Service (CPS)	The government department responsible for prosecuting criminal cases investigated by the police in England and Wales.
Department for Business, Innovation and Skills (BIS)	In connection with CONTEST provides guidance and support to higher and further education sectors on tackling violent extremism.
Department for Communities and Local Government (DCLG)	Sets policy on supporting local government, communities, and neighbourhoods; regeneration; housing; planning, building, and the environment; and fire. As part of its work on the Big Society, DCLG is developing a new approach to integration.
Department for Education (DfE)	Has responsibility for ensuring that young people are protected from exposure to extremism and extremist views in or outside schools.
Department of Energy & Climate Change (DECC)	Contributes to the *Protect* and *Prepare* strands of CONTEST as lead government department for energy. DECC is responsible for ensuring the security of the nation's energy supplies (electricity, gas, and oil) and civil nuclear sites from all risks, including malicious attack. The department's work also includes contributing to the UK's policy on nuclear safeguards and non-proliferation issues, sponsoring the Civil Nuclear Police Authority and Civil Nuclear Constabulary, and managing the nuclear and radiological elements of the UK's Global Threat Reduction Programme.
Department for Environment, Food and Rural Affairs (DEFRA)	Responsible for dealing with the impact of a terrorist incident on the natural environment, plant and animal health, food and drinking water supplies, waste management (excluding radioactive waste), farming, fisheries, and rural communities. DEFRA has lead government departmental responsibility for the recovery phase of a chemical, biological, radiological, and nuclear (CBRN) incident.
Department for International Development (DFID)	Manages Britain's aid to developing countries. DFID uses its resources for the purpose of poverty reduction overseas. Its activities can contribute to CONTEST by addressing underlying social and economic issues, helping governments in key countries to improve governance and security, economic stability and employment opportunities, and access to basic services.

Department for Transport (DfT)	The security regulator of most of the transport sector including aviation, maritime, and rail. It aims to protect the travelling public, transport facilities, and those employed in the transport industry from acts of terrorism.
Department of Health (DH)	Oversees the health sector's commitment and contribution to CONTEST. The sector's key priorities include improving, protecting, and maintaining the health of the population by ensuring the country's ability to respond to and cope with threat-derived mass casualty emergencies, including catastrophic acts of terrorism (CBRN). Its activities contribute to the crowded places and hazardous substances work, and as one of the nine national infrastructure sectors, it also contributes to the UK's Critical National Infrastructure programme.
Devolved Administrations	Responsible in Northern Ireland, Scotland, and Wales for the functions which have been devolved to them according to their different devolution settlements. All three devolved administrations are responsible for health, education, and local government. Policing and justice are devolved in Scotland and Northern Ireland.
Foreign and Commonwealth Office (FCO)	Has overall responsibility for coordinating the delivery of CONTEST overseas, and chairs the cross-Government Overseas CONTEST Group (OCG).
Government Communications Headquarters (GCHQ)	Has two important missions, Signals Intelligence (known as SIGINT) and Information Assurance (IA). SIGINT work provides vital information to support government policy-making and operations in the fields of national security, military operations, law enforcement, and economic well-being. Information Assurance is about protecting government data (communications and information systems) from hackers and other threats.
Government Office for Science (GO-Science)	Headed by the Government Chief Scientific Adviser, this is responsible for ensuring that all levels of government, including the Prime Minister and Cabinet, receive the best scientific advice possible. GO-Science is engaged across CONTEST to ensure it is underpinned by robust science, including peer review.
HM Treasury	Leads on asset freezing and is the joint lead with OSCT on terrorist financing. In 2007, HM Treasury set up a dedicated asset-freezing unit to handle counter-terrorist and other asset-freezing work. HM Treasury's Financial Crime Team, with OSCT, coordinates the delivery of the UK's strategy for tackling terrorist finance.
Home Office: the Office for Security and Counter-Terrorism (OSCT)	Has overall responsibility for coordinating the CONTEST strategy. OSCT's primary responsibilities are to support the Home Secretary and other ministers in developing, directing, and implementing CONTEST across government; to deliver aspects of the counter-terrorism strategy directly, e.g. legislation, policing (in England and Wales), UK border security, protective security policy; to facilitate oversight of the Security Service, its operations and police counter-terrorism operations, and coordinate counter-terrorism crisis management.

(*continued*)

Table 4.2 Continued

Department	Roles and Responsibilities
Joint Terrorism Analysis Centre (JTAC)	The UK's centre for the all-source analysis and assessment of international terrorism. JTAC sets threat levels and issues analytical reporting to Government Departments and agencies.
Ministry of Defence (MOD)	Contributes to CONTEST using its military capability and supports *Pursue* through its capability to disrupt terrorist groups overseas, as well as through intelligence collection counter-terrorism capacity building for partner nations, and support to overseas law enforcement and security agencies. Its support to conflict prevention work also contributes to CONTEST objectives. In the event of a terrorist attack that exceeds the capability or immediate capacity of the UK civilian response, the MOD can provide support to *Prepare* through military aid to the civil authorities.
Ministry of Justice (MoJ)	Responsible for ensuring there is sufficient capacity in the criminal justice system to deal with terrorism cases, and that they are dealt with efficiently, effectively, and securely. The National Offender Management Service (an agency of the MoJ) manages the risks posed by terrorist offenders, in partnership with the police and security and intelligence agencies. The Youth Justice Board is a Non-Departmental Public Body (NDPB) which is sponsored by the MoJ, and is responsible for delivering a range of prevention programmes designed to support individuals who are vulnerable to recruitment by violent extremists.
National Security Council (NSC)	Brings together key ministers, and military and intelligence chiefs, under the chairmanship of the Prime Minister. The NSC ensures a strategic and coordinated approach across the whole of government to national security issues.
National Crime Agency (NCA)	Strengthens the operational response to organised crime and better secures the border through more effective national tasking and enforcement action delivered through four commands, including Organised Crime Command (OCC), Border Policing Command (BPC), Economic Crime Command (ECC), and the Child Exploitation and Online Protection Centre (CEOP).
National Counter-Terrorism Security Office (NaCTSO)	A police unit co-located with CPNI. NaCTSO's work is divided into three areas: protection of crowded places, protection of hazardous sites and dangerous substances, and assisting the CPNI to protect the critical national infrastructure.
Northern Ireland Office (NIO)	The government department that supports the Secretary of State for Northern Ireland.
Police, Police National Counter Terrorism Network (PNCTN), and Special Branch (SB)	The police service responsible for disrupting or responding to terrorist incidents in the UK.
Scotland Office	The government department that supports the Secretary of State for Scotland.

Secret Intelligence Service (SIS)	Collects intelligence overseas to promote and defend the national security and the economic well-being of the UK. It supports Security Service work in the UK.
Security Service (MI5)	Responsible for protecting the UK against threats to national security, notably terrorism (it leads the investigation of terrorism in the UK), espionage, and sabotage, the activities of agents of foreign powers, and actions intended to overthrow or undermine parliamentary democracy by political, industrial, or violent means.
UK Border Agency (UKBA)	UK Border Force—A law enforcement command within the Home Office with responsibility to secure the UK border by carrying out immigration and customs controls for people and goods entering the UK.
Wales Office	The government department that supports the Secretary of State for Wales.

KEY POINT—CONTEST CHALLENGES

CONTEST has matured since the first classified version was published in 2003. Developing the strategy has become a real challenge in itself. Designing CONTEST can be broken down into three areas: scope, scale, and duration, and the strategy underpins the UK government's efforts both at home and abroad. In previous years, domestic efforts have dominated the agenda, but this changed in 2009 and again in 2011 when a more concerted effort was made to widen the scope to international efforts. Developing CONTEST has the potential to overwhelm government planners unless efforts are made to prioritise areas of activity, and this is helped by developing a more robust intelligence- and evidence-based approach, and use of 'Prevent', 'Pursue', 'Protect', and 'Prepare' to set objectives. Developing CONTEST requires support from a range of Whitehall departments, intelligence and law enforcement agencies, local government, and the voluntary sector. Ensuring everyone agrees on the approach, is prepared to invest resources, and sustain the project and programme requires a great deal of time and effort. The tension between investing in short-term initiatives and long-term policy is ever-present, however, CONTEST has nevertheless produced successful results, providing policy-makers with encouraging signs that their efforts across government are achieving the overarching aim of the strategy.

4.4 Summary

The CONTEST strategy provides a framework for coordinating, directing, and shaping the UK government's response to the threat from terrorism. A decade since its first presentation to the Cabinet in 2003, it continues to provide focused direction. Over time, it has grown in size, scale, and scope, and the latest version (published in July 2011 as CONTEST 3), comprises 236 pages, some sixty-two pages longer than its 2009 iteration, and 203 pages longer than that of 2006. This expansion reflects the increasing breadth and depth of the UK's counter-terrorism policy, and its gradual emergence from the veil of governmental secrecy.

Further reading

- English, R, *Terrorism: How to Respond* (Oxford: Oxford University Press, 2010).
- Hewitt, S, *The British War on Terror – Terrorism and Counter-terrorism on the Homefront since 9/11* (London: Continuum, 2008).
- HM Government *A Strong Britain in an Age of Uncertainty: The National Security Strategy* (2010).
- HM Government *Countering International Terrorism—The United Kingdom's Strategy CONTEST* (2011).
- HM Government *Prevent Strategy* (2011).
- Lum, C, and Kennedy, L, *Evidence-Based Counterterrorism Policy* (London: Springer, 2012).
- Omand, D, *Securing the State* (London: Hurst & Co Publishers Ltd, 2012).
- Sageman, M, *Leaderless Jihad: Terror Networks in the Twenty-first Century* (Pennsylvania: University of Pennsylvania Press, 2000).
- Sageman, M, *Understanding Terror Networks* (Pennsylvania: University of Pennsylvania Press, 2004).
- Spalek, B, *Counter-Terrorism: Community-Based Approaches to Preventing Terror Crime* (London: Palgrave Macmillan, 2012).
- *The 9/11 Commission Report: Final Report of the National Commission on Terrorist Attacks Upon the United States* (Authorised edition) (Washington DC: WW Norton & Company, 2004).

5

Pursuing Terrorists and Extremists

5.1	Introduction	106
5.2	Intelligence Machinery	106
5.3	Counter-terrorism Policing	111
5.4	Prosecuting Terrorists	114
5.5	Code for Crown Prosecutors	115
5.6	Summary	116

5.1 **Introduction**

The purpose of this chapter is to explain the role and responsibilities of all operational counter-terrorism stakeholders who support and contribute towards the pursuit of terrorists and extremists. Police officers joining the specialist counter-terrorism units for the first time may find their new operational environment is a crowded space when compared to the pursuit of other criminals, but the collaborative approach to countering contemporary terrorism and jointly gathering intelligence and evidence for prosecution is essential.

While a greater perspective is required of all police investigators when investigating terrorists cases, it must also be remembered that countering terrorism also requires a local community focus. Many police officers, police partners, and members of the public may not fully appreciate their own role in countering terrorism. Information passed by members of the public and the police across the UK assists specialist police departments and partner agencies in countering terrorism. Police officers may underestimate the importance of the information they provide, but the effective pursuit of terrorists now demands an efficient process of intelligence collection from all sources of information which must be readily shared across all departments who are concerned in the pursuit of terrorists and extremists.

5.2 **Intelligence Machinery**

The 'intelligence community' is the collective name for the group of agencies who gather and assess secret intelligence to preserve national security on behalf of the government. It includes the Cabinet Office (CO), Secret Intelligence Service (SIS), Government Communications Headquarters (GCHQ), Security Service (MI5), Defence Intelligence Staff (DIS), and the Joint Terrorism Analysis Centre (JTAC), shown in Figure 5.1.

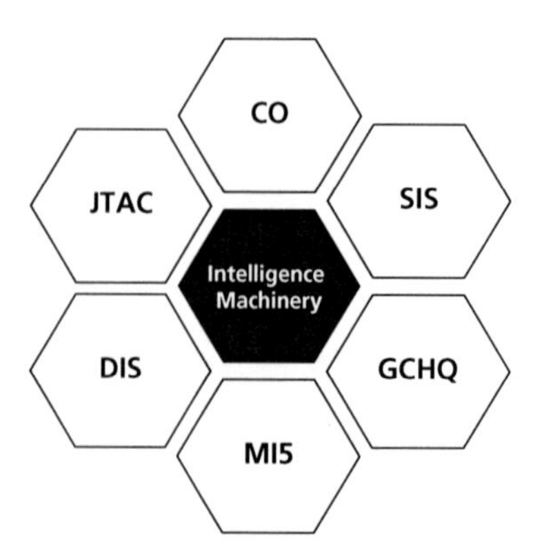

Figure 5.1. Intelligence machinery.

Each agency has a specific function in the support of and contribution towards the strategic aim of the UK government's strategy to counter terrorism (CONTEST). All the intelligence machinery agencies naturally act within the law and their operations are conducted within a framework of legislation that defines their roles and activities.

POINT TO NOTE—COMMUNITY FOCUS

Whilst it is true that countering international terrorism requires a united and coordinated response, a local focus is vital. Police officers and members of the public may not fully appreciate their role in countering terrorism, but it is extremely important. Information passed by members of the public and the police across the UK can directly assist in countering the threat. Often, the value of information received from the public is underestimated, and receipt of information may not be readily acknowledged. This does not mean that information is not acted upon, or that it is not significant. Information is useful in an enormous number of ways: it may be used to provide background details, provide new lines of enquiry, or corroborate existing intelligence. It is important to encourage the public to come forward with any details that may be relevant, no matter how insignificant they seem.

5.2.1 Cabinet Office

The Cabinet Office (CO) exists to support the executive machinery of government, namely the Prime Minister and the Cabinet, including its sub-committees, across the spectrum of government activities, managing the flow of business requiring collective ministerial consideration, brokering agreements between departments, and ensuring a common understanding of issues. As part of its work, the Cabinet Office engages with central, local, and regional partners to prepare for emergencies and to coordinate the central government response to major disruptive challenges.

Organisation of the Cabinet Office Briefing Rooms

The UK central government response to a terrorist event or emergency is underpinned by the Cabinet Office Briefing Rooms (COBR), from which the central response is activated, monitored, and coordinated. COBR provides a focal point for the government's response and responses from there are given top priority by local agencies. Within COBR, a senior decision-making body oversees the government's response, supported as necessary by subgroups and specific sources of specialist advice.

In practice, the actual response to a given emergency will need to take into account the nature of the challenge and circumstances at the time. Where COBR is activated in response to an incident which has occurred without any warning, its default strategic objectives are to:

- protect human life and, as far as possible, property and the environment;
- alleviate suffering;
- support the continuity of everyday activity;
- restoration of disrupted services at the earliest opportunity;
- uphold the rule of law and the democratic process.

These objectives are listed in no particular order of priority. In reality they will evolve and their relative priority may shift as the emergency develops. In addition, not all the set objectives may be achievable at the outset of an emergency. Ministers will advise on the appropriate balance to strike in light of the circumstances at the time. This interpretation of the objectives may also need to be refined and developed as the emergency unfolds.

When COBR is activated, the early priorities are to ensure clear lines of communication and to establish a common view of the issues, along with an understanding of immediate and emerging priorities, and to identify and take any urgent decisions that are required. The pressure on government and local responders in the first few hours will be intense, and immediate action will be required on a variety of fronts, which will need careful consideration and coordination, and in some cases, prior planning of how information needs to flow from agency to agency.

When COBR is activated or in other situations where there is a significant central government role, a Government Liaison Officer (GLO) will normally be despatched immediately to act as the primary liaison channel between departments and local responders in the local Strategic Coordination Centre. The GLO will normally be from the relevant government office in England or the Lead Government Department (LDG).

POINT TO NOTE—A NATIONAL RESPONSE

COBR underpins the central government response. Ministers and senior officials from relevant UK government departments and agencies, as well as representatives from other relevant organisations, are brought together here to ensure a common appreciation of the situation, and to facilitate effective and timely decision-making.

History has taught the police service and the government to expect the unexpected. Events can, and do take place that by their nature cannot be anticipated. While police officers engaged in countering terrorism continue to tackle a severe threat with the aim of pursuing terrorists and preventing their activities, it is right that the government possesses a contingency response should another attack break through the web of countermeasures.

5.2.2 Secret Intelligence Service

The Secret Intelligence Service (SIS) is commonly known as MI6 (Military Intelligence section 6). It is Britain's secret service and provides the government with a global covert capability to promote and defend the national security and economic well-being of the UK. SIS operates throughout the world collecting secret foreign intelligence in accordance with the requirements and priorities established by the Joint Intelligence Committee. It collects intelligence through human and technical sources, and liaises with a wide range of intelligence and security service agencies overseas.

SIS was established in 1909 in response to German espionage activity and the threat of Germany's military and naval expansion. The first tasks of SIS were to counter foreign espionage in the UK and to collect secret intelligence abroad. To meet these demands SIS was divided into two sections, the Home Section, which later became the Security Service (MI5), and the Foreign Section, which later became SIS as we know it today. The role of SIS is now governed by the Intelligence Service Act 1994 which placed SIS on a statutory basis for the first time. The Act formalises the Foreign Secretary's responsibility for the work of SIS as it protects national security, with particular reference to government defence and foreign policy.

5.2.3 **Security Service (MI5)**

The Security Service (MI5) is responsible for protecting the UK against the threats to national security. The focus of this work is domestic. The Security Service has broad responsibilities. It aims to frustrate terrorism, prevent damage to the UK from foreign espionage, and to frustrate the proliferation of materials, technologies, and expertise relating to the development of weapons of mass destruction. In addition to watching out for new and re-emerging types of threat, it offers security advice to a range of organisations, and protects government assets.

The role of the Security Service is defined by the Security Service Act 1989 which put the Service onto a statutory footing for the first time. In collecting and assessing intelligence the Service is guided by the requirements and priorities established by the Joint Intelligence Committee. Since the creation of the Serious Organised Crime Agency (SOCA), the Service has delegated its work on serious crime in order to concentrate more resources to counter terrorism. The work of the Security Service requires considerable secrecy. It is only in recent years, following the growth of international terrorism and subsequent threats to the UK, that the Service has embarked upon a new era of openness.

5.2.4 **Government Communications Headquarters**

The Government Communications Headquarters, commonly known as GCHQ, is an intelligence and security organisation. It has two key missions, Signals Intelligence and Information Assurance. Signals Intelligence relates to the interception of communications, and GCHQ is often described as the UK's listening post. Signals Intelligence protects the vital interests of the UK by providing information to support government decision-making processes in the fields of national security, military operations, and law enforcement. Information Assurance supports the government communications and information systems, and keeps them safe from hackers and other terrorist-related cyber-threats.

As a civil service department, GCHQ reports to the Foreign Secretary, and like SIS, it was also placed on a statutory basis by the Intelligence Services Act 1994. This Act defines the boundaries of GCHQ activities. Within these boundaries the choice of what to intercept and report to the government and military commands is based on the intelligence requirements established by the Joint Intelligence Committee.

5.2.5 **Defence Intelligence Staff**

The Defence Intelligence Staff (DIS) is very different to the other agencies forming part of the 'intelligence community'. The DIS is a constituent part of the Ministry of Defence which brings together expertise from the army, air force, and navy. It conducts intelligence analysis of both overt and covert sources providing intelligence assessments which are used by the military and the government. The DIS collects intelligence in direct support of military operations as well as supporting operations by members of the 'intelligence community'. The DIS is an integral part of the 'intelligence community', providing access to intelligence collected during military operations.

5.2.6 **Joint Terrorism Analysis Centre**

The Joint Terrorism Analysis Centre (JTAC) was established in 2003 to analyse and to assess all intelligence relating to international terrorism, at home and overseas. The creation of JTAC brought together expertise from the police and key government departments and agencies. As a truly joint organization, it ensures that the efficient sharing of information across separate organisations is achieved. Poor information sharing between agencies was highlighted by the 9/11 Commission as a deficiency of the US Government during the build-up to the terrorist attacks in 2001, a deficiency that the UK Government was quick to identify and to rectify at home with the creation of JTAC.

JTAC also sets the threat levels for the UK posed by international terrorism. It issues warnings of threats and other terrorist-related subjects for customers from a wide range of government departments and agencies. JTAC also produces in-depth reports on trends, terrorist networks, and capabilities. It is an integral part of the intelligence machinery, and is where information gathered by the police service is fed into the national picture for analysis.

5.3 Counter-terrorism Policing

Counter-terrorism policing in England and Wales is delivered through the Police Counter Terrorism Network. The network, which consists of four Counter Terrorism Units (CTUs) and four smaller Counter Terrorism Intelligence Units (CTIUs), was established to complement the work of local force Special Branches and the London-based Counter Terrorism Command. It links front-line police officers with regional counter-terrorism hubs, and thereby effects national counter-terrorism policing. The Police Counter Terrorism Network and Special Branches have close and effective working relationships with the Security Service which is the result of joint working and joint intelligence assessments. In Scotland, the ACPOS Coordinator of Counter Terrorism coordinates all police counter-terrorism-related duties to ensure that Scottish Police counter-terrorism capability is effective and remains an integral part of the UK Police CT Network. Coordination is delivered by a police unit, which is broadly similar in capability to CTIUs in England and Wales. Counter-terrorism policing contributes to all four work streams of the UK's counter-terrorism strategy CONTEST by:

- 'Pursue': identifying and disrupting terrorist activity;
- 'Prevent': working with communities and local authorities to identify and to divert those involved in or vulnerable to radicalisation;
- 'Protect': policing the UK border, critical national infrastructure, civil nuclear sites, transport systems, and the public; and
- 'Prepare': leading the immediate response after or during a terrorist attack, including responding to CBRNE incidents.

Counter-terrorism policing requires oversight because of its large budget and significant police powers. The Home Secretary is accountable to Parliament for the provision and funding of counter-terrorism policing in England and Wales, and is responsible for setting strategic priorities.

POINTS TO NOTE—TEAM EFFORT

The new counter-terrorism structure supports the intelligence machinery of the UK. However, neither specialist counter-terrorism policing units nor the intelligence agencies can detect, disrupt, or deter terrorist activity without the commitment of the wider police service.

A key development in the response to tackling terrorism has been the introduction of terrorism and extremism as key issues on local policing plans. Countering terrorism on a local level relies on the practical policing skills of all police officers, who are therefore required to identify and to report any unusual or suspicious activity. This is not easy. A knowledge and understanding of how terrorists and their organisations operate is required, together with a detailed understanding of the communities that local policing serves—a vital role of

Neighbourhood Policing Teams (NPTs). Communities can be enlisted to help defeat terrorism, and NPTs and their partners are at the forefront of this battle. They are the first point at which a new terrorist cell, or an individual starting to become radicalised, can be identified. Everyone in authority must note that countering terrorism must be a team effort.

5.3.1 **Policing domestic extremism**

Over recent years, domestic extremism has become an increasing concern to government, the police, and many private sector organisations because it targets individuals and their homes, as well as business premises. Domestic extremists move beyond the bounds of legitimate protest to intimidate individuals engaged in lawful activity and to impose great economic costs on legal businesses. As such, it presents a threat that is national in scope.

In January 2011 the Chief Constables' Council, the senior decision-making body for the Association of Chief Police Officers (ACPO), ratified the decision for the Metropolitan Police Service (MPS) to become the lead force for the National Domestic Extremism Unit (NDEU). The NDEU remains a national policing unit, under governance arrangements, and sits under the Specialist Operations business group of the MPS. It was created following a merger of the National Public Order Intelligence Unit (NPOIU), the National Domestic Extremism Team (NDET), and the National Extremism Tactical Coordination Unit (NETCU). The NDEU supports all police forces to help reduce the criminal threat from domestic extremism across the UK. It works to promote a single and coordinated police response by providing tactical advice to the police service alongside information and guidance to industry and government.

One of the key responsibilities of the NDEU is to provide intelligence on domestic extremism and strategic public order issues in the UK. Police will always engage to facilitate peaceful protest, prevent disorder, and minimise disruption to local communities. Where individuals' actions cross over the legal line into criminality and violence, the police act swiftly and decisively to uphold the law.

5.3.2 **Strategic policing requirements**

From November 2012 the Strategic Policing Requirement (SPR) set by the Home Secretary, empowers and enables Police and Crime Commissioners (PCC) to deliver their important role of holding their chief constable to account for the totality of their policing—both local and national—which includes tackling the terrorist threat. PCCs and chief constables are now expected to drive collaboration between police forces and to ensure that forces can work effectively together and with their partners to address terrorism. The SPR supports chief constables and PCCs to ensure they fulfil forces' national responsibilities. It:

- helps police and crime commissioners, in consultation with their chief constable, to plan effectively for policing challenges that go beyond single-force boundaries;
- guides chief constables in the exercise of these functions; and
- enables and empowers police and crime commissioners to hold their chief constable to account for the delivery of these functions.

In doing so, chief constables and PCCs must demonstrate that they have taken into account the need for appropriate capacity to contribute to the government's counter-terrorism strategy (CONTEST) by:

- identifying, disrupting, and investigating terrorist activity, and prosecuting terrorist suspects;
- identifying and diverting those involved in or vulnerable to radicalisation;
- protecting the UK border, the critical national infrastructure, civil nuclear sites, transport systems, and the public;
- leading the immediate response after or during a terrorist attack, including responding to incidents involving chemical, biological, radiological, nuclear, firearms, and explosive material; and
- ensuring the appropriate capacity to respond adequately to a major cyber incident through the maintenance of public order.

5.3.3 National Crime Agency

The new National Crime Agency (NCA) established in 2013 serves to strengthen the operational response to organised crime and help secure borders through effective national tasking and enforcement action. The government is clear that counter-terrorism policing already has effective national structures, and is considering how to ensure these strengths are maintained and enhanced alongside its new approach to fighting crime. The creation of the NCA marks a significant shift in the UK's approach to tackling serious, organised, and complex crime, with an emphasis on greater collaboration across the whole law enforcement landscape. The NCA will build effective two-way relationships with police forces, law enforcement agencies, and other partners, and is to comprise four commands:

- The **Organised Crime Command (OCC)** targets organised crime groups operating across local, national, and international borders. The command works with police forces and other agencies to ensure that prioritised and appropriate action is taken against every organised crime group identified.
- The **Border Policing Command (BPC)** ensures that all law enforcement agencies operating on the border work to clear, mutually agreed priorities, ensuring illegal goods are seized, illegal immigrants are dealt with, and networks of organised criminals are targeted and disrupted, both overseas and at ports throughout the UK.

- The **Economic Crime Command** (ECC) provides an innovative and improved capability to deal with fraud and economic crimes, including those carried out by organised criminals.
- The **Child Exploitation and Online Protection Centre** (CEOP) works with industry, government, children's charities, and law enforcement to protect children from sexual abuse and to bring offenders to account.

All four commands will also benefit from:

- an intelligence hub, which develops and maintains a comprehensive picture of the threats to the UK from organised crime;
- a national cyber-crime centre, providing expertise, support, intelligence, and guidance to police forces and the commands of the NCA.

POINT TO NOTE—WIDENING POLICE PORTFOLIO

Substantial specialist police skills and resources are required to tackle terrorism, and the need to do this has widened the broad sweep of responsibilities the police force already shoulder.

5.4 Prosecuting Terrorists

The threat from Al Qa'ida-inspired terrorism has served to shape how governments respond to protect its citizens. The UK has constructed a new police counter-terrorism network and strengthened its intelligence machinery. It has also ushered in some unprecedented changes within the wider criminal justice system, not only by the introduction of a series of anti-terror powers necessary to pursue terrorists effectively, but also changes to the structures within the Crown Prosecution Service (CPS) itself.

5.4.1 Crown Prosecution Service

In 2004 the CPS began reviewing how it could best deliver on serious casework. Out of this review came three new casework divisions, including the Counter Terrorism Division (CTD) which was primarily established to deal with prosecuting terrorism cases which had been rapidly increasing in terms of size and complexity. During April 2011, the CTD merged with the Special Crime Division to create a new Special Crime and Counter Terrorism Division (SCCTD) at the CPS.

Special Crime and Counter Terrorism Division (SCCTD)

The Special Crime and Counter Terrorism Division (SCCTD) is responsible for advising the police in all terrorism cases, and is often consulted whilst evidence is still being gathered. The SCCTD subsequently undertakes the prosecution of those terrorism offences, and it also deals with all allegations of incitement to racial and religious hatred, war crimes and crimes against humanity, official secrets cases, and hijacking.

Specialist prosecutors work closely with colleagues in the CPS to support tackling terrorism through due legal process and to improve the management of terrorism cases both before and after the initial charge is brought. Prosecutors begin from the perspective that terrorists are criminals and use the full gamut of both criminal and terrorism offences to prosecutions. Strong relationships exist between the police, prosecutors, and the intelligence services, and are facilitated by developments in case management through the use of the Terrorism Case Management Protocol, designed to clarify each agency's role and responsibility in the prosecution phases of counter-terrorism investigations, and the role of the Terrorism Case Management Judge (TCMJ).

Prosecutors are of course independent but they work very closely with the police and others to build up strong cases. The need for an early arrest for public safety reasons often means that a full evidential picture does not develop until shortly before or after an arrest takes place. Such cases need to be investigated and built quickly as the evidence unfolds within the pre-charge detention period. Prosecutors give advice on the effects of the proposed investigative action, ensure the developing case is complete, accurate, and consistent by considering the intelligence picture, and help identify evidentially weak cases to bring them to an early conclusion before a great deal of time and effort is wasted. Prosecutors prefer to present charges at the earliest opportunity using the Code for Crown Prosecutors. When more time is required to pursue a case, they are involved in making some applications for warrants of further detention.

Robust management is essential to ensure the case moves efficiently through the criminal justice process. The prosecutor has a key role in this. Shortly after charge, the defence and the court are provided with an outline of the prosecution case and a proposed timetable. Following representations from both parties at an early preliminary hearing, the TCMJ gives directions for service of the evidence, disclosure of unused material, service of defence statements, and an estimate for trial. Thereafter he or she monitors progress of the timetable.

The joint protocols and systems which have been developed to complement the legal framework assist in successfully delivering justice through efficient but fair and transparent case management in what is a very complex area of practice.

5.5 Code for Crown Prosecutors

Although cases against those suspected of terrorism may be specialist in nature, they are actually managed by CPS in the same way as any other criminal case. All decisions are made in accordance with the Code for Crown Prosecutors which states that a prosecutor needs to have sufficient evidence to afford a realistic prospect of a conviction before he or she can go on to consider the wider public interest. Commonly referred to as the 'evidential test', the CPS must be satisfied first of all that there is enough evidence to provide a realistic prospect of conviction against each defendant on each charge. This means that a jury or a bench of magistrates, properly directed in accordance with the law, is more likely than not to convict the defendant of the alleged charge. For there to be a conviction, the CPS has to prove the case so that the court is sure of the defendant's guilt. If the case does not pass the Evidential Test based on the strength of the evidence, it must not go ahead, no matter how important or serious it may be.

If the case does pass the evidential test, CPS must then decide if a prosecution is needed in the public interest. A prosecution will usually take place unless there are public interest factors tending against prosecution which clearly outweigh those tending in favour. When considering the public interest test, one of the factors CPS should always take into account are the consequences for the victim of the decision whether or not to prosecute, and any views expressed by the victim or the victim's family.

POINTS TO NOTE—CRIMINAL JUSTICE

Pursuing terrorists through the criminal justice system preserves and protects the democratic values of the prosecuting state while ensuring that the rights of all concerned are maintained. The role and responsibility of the SCCTD is fundamental to this. Key to the success of the criminal justice system is the degree of collaboration between all agencies and departments who share the common goal of protecting the public from terrorism. Everyone in authority should be aware that the nature of the severe threat from terrorism demands that intelligence and evidence be gathered simultaneously, as potential attacks uncovered today may need to be disrupted tomorrow.

5.6 Summary

Terrorism undermines the basis of state legitimacy—the capability and capacity to protect its citizens. Protecting the public from those who seek to destroy the UK's free and democratic way of life remains the primary responsibility, and therefore the primary challenge, for all servants of the state, and the police service plays a vital role in this, by pursuing terrorists and extremists and bringing them to justice.

For many years the citizens of the UK have enjoyed protection from terrorism under the aegis of various departments and agencies across the landscape of government, but critical to the success of domestic counter-terrorism has been the collaborative approach between the Security Service and the police service. This collaboration in counter-terrorism is unique. There are no other partnership models that are directly comparable, unmatched elsewhere in the world. Together, these very different emanations of state power have served the public well.

The regionalisation of the National Police Counter-Terrorism Network, supported by the regional deployment of the Security Service, working closely with police officers, ensures that a locally focused and coordinated approach is maintained to exploit intelligence gathering opportunities in order to identify and respond to threats.

The interdependence of the police service and Security Service is vital. Each is the other's most important partner but they remain independent of each other. It is a relationship that has existed for over 100 years, but has never been more important than today.

A key message woven through the very fabric of this chapter is that the police service, indeed any arm of the state, cannot effectively tackle contemporary terrorism or violent extremism alone. Collaboration in counter-terrorism is vital. An inter- and multidisciplinary approach is required to pursue terrorists, and the maintenance and continued development of strong strategic partnerships across the full operating landscape of the police service, intelligence machinery, and prosecutors is essential.

Further reading

- Andrew, C, *The Defence of the Realm: The Authorised History of M15* (London: Penguin, 2009).
- Chandler, M, and Gunaratna, R, *Countering Terrorism: Can We Meet the Threat of Global Violence?* (London: Reakton Books Ltd, 2007).
- HM Government *A Strong Britain in an Age of Uncertainty: The National Security Strategy* (2010).
- HM Government *Countering International Terrorism—The United Kingdom's Strategy CONTEST* (2011).
- Masferrer, A, and Walker, C, *Counter-Terrorism, Human Rights and the Rule of Law: Crossing Legal Boundaries in Defence of the State* (London: Edward Elgar Publishing Ltd, 2013).
- Schmid, AP, *The Routledge Handbook of Terrorism Research* (Oxford: Routledge, 2011).
- Staniforth, A, *The Routledge Companion to UK Counter-Terrorism* (Oxford: Routledge, 2012).
- Staniforth, A, and PNLD, *Blackstone's Counter-Terrorism Handbook* 3rd edition (Oxford: Oxford University Press, 2013).

6

Anti-terror Legislation

6.1	Introduction	119
6.2	Operational Reality	120
6.3	Anti-terror Legal Framework	121
6.4	Independent Oversight	124
6.5	Key Definitions	126
6.6	Stop and Search	129
6.7	Power of Arrest	140
6.8	Cordons	145
6.9	Parking	148
6.10	Terrorism Prevention and Investigation Measures	150
6.11	Officers' Powers and Duties	153
6.12	Summary	155

6.1 Introduction

The purpose of this chapter is to introduce all police officers, community support officers, and special constables to the primary powers and provisions of anti-terror legislation. From the growing body of increasingly complex counter-terrorism powers passed by Parliament to tackle the terrorist threat, the legislation outlined in this chapter represents the primary provisions to be encountered by police officers while carrying out their routine duties. Supported by data provided by the Police National Legal Database (PNLD), this chapter also includes the anti-terror laws which police officers across the United Kingdom most frequently use.

Police officers and the wider police network must understand the extent and limitations of counter-terrorism laws. Recent history informs us that when new anti-terror powers are enacted they are very often poorly applied by law enforcement officers. This poor interpretation and operational application of legislation arises not only because the laws are deemed to be unique and special provisions, but also because attempting to apply complex legislation direct from the statute books with little training or explanation is a real challenge for the officer working on the front line, especially given the multitude of other tasks officers must undertake to protect the public. This challenge is amplified as new anti-terror laws are very often drafted in direct response to a specific terrorist event when the nation is still either under serious threat or recovering from a terrorist attack. Of course, new legislation must be interpreted by the practitioner without the safeguards of precedents set by previous cases. This adds a degree of uncertainty to legal applications, and the accumulaton of both case law and officers' experience in applying the law can lead to some fragile interpretations of the law being made.

There are a number of other challenges that confront police officers when they are attempting to increase their knowledge and understanding of terrorism and the application of the law. The perceived complexity of the subject, the sensitivity of operational information, and the nature of specialist counter-terrorism roles are just some contributory factors. The key challenge for the police service and its officers remains the professional delivery of anti-terror powers without isolating them from those individuals, groups, and communities with which they wish to engage and from which the next terrorist cell may very well emerge. If the police service is to sustain and develop public confidence in its use of specialist powers, lessons must be learned from the past. The incidence of stops of innocent members of the public should not be repeated nor exacerbated by a misguided attempt to balance the statistics by interventions against those who plainly are not terrorists. Poorly trained and poorly briefed officers can apply anti-terror powers badly and this has resulted in public complaints. Such complaints are unwelcome, unnecessary, and time-consuming, and they detract from the positive efforts made by the police service and partner agencies to tackle the terrorist threat.

KEY POINT—EFFECTIVE APPLICATION OF ANTI-TERROR LAWS

The most important guiding principle for the effective use of all anti-terror legislation by police officers is that terrorism law ***must*** be used ***only*** for the purpose of tackling terrorism. Everyone in positions of authority is required to remember that these laws reach beyond the norms of criminal justice legislation: for example, obtaining authority to cordon off an area is a potentially serious interference with the private and economic lives of law-abiding citizens. The right to stop and search in the street in a manner different from, and more invasive than, an intervention with a non-terrorist suspect is a power to be exercised with great caution. While police officers must use the powers provided to them to protect the public from acts of terrorism, due consideration must be afforded to the potential long-term damage to community relations when the appropriate and proportionate use of anti-terror powers is over-extended.

6.2 Operational Reality

Police officers will face terrorism issues from time to time during their public service. In the decade that followed the terrorist attacks in the US on 11 September 2001, UK law enforcement authorities made 1,963 terrorism arrests. From 2001 to 2011, an average of 206 individuals per year were arrested for terrorism-related matters. An unprecedented volume of suspected terrorists are being stopped, arrested, and detained for their alleged involvement in terrorism-related activities. This sudden rise has been fuelled by the severity of the terrorist threat to UK national security from Al Qa'ida-inspired terrorism, and this requires police officers to rapidly develop their counter-terrorism knowledge. Many officers may only have served in Special Branch or other specialised Counter Terrorism Units for a short time—especially promoted senior officers—when critical incidents and key stages of major counter-terrorism investigations occur. The nature of prevalent threats suggests that it is not a specialist counter-terrorism officer based at New Scotland Yard who is most likely to confront a terrorist; it is a local neighbourhood police officer or a local community support officer. Custody officers and detention staff may also find themselves receiving arrested terrorist suspects with complex detention issues surrounding their initial reception and continued detention. Advance revision and training of powers and offences will repay itself fully for any officer in the tense atmosphere after terrorism arrests, very often as part of an ongoing multi-agency operation being conducted under the glare of media attention.

A further challenge for the police service arrives in the immediate aftermath of a major terrorist incident, or an event which is taking place that has the potential to attract increased levels of terrorist threat. As part of cross-border mutual support and mobilisation arrangements between police forces—now made manifest for counter-terrorism by the Strategic Policing Requirements (SPRs) introduced by the Home Secretary during 2012—police officers are drafted in from outside forces, with little local knowledge and only a basic acquaintance with counter-terrorism law. Sometimes they will have to be briefed very quickly indeed. A better understanding of the law will also help the efficiency of the legislation, the effectiveness of individual officers, and the collective policing response. All police officers must therefore acquaint themselves with the powers they have been provided as part of their policing toolkit. Advanced reading of the powers described in this chapter will ensure that all police officers can protect the communities they serve to the very best of their ability.

6.3 Anti-terror Legal Framework

To pursue terrorist organisations effectively, successive UK governments have found it necessary to introduce new powers and new provisions. Over many years, the UK government has gained substantial legislative experience of tackling different forms of terrorism. In responding to the threats from terrorism relating to the struggle in Northern Ireland, legislators had over time created five separate pieces of legislation. These included the Prevention of Violence (Temporary Provisions) Act 1913, and the Prevention of Terrorism (Temporary Provisions) Acts of 1974, 1976, 1984, and 1989. While the separate and specific powers presented a swift response to the terrorist threats at the time of their enactment, and had served to arm law enforcement and the military with greater provisions to tackle dissidents and paramilitaries, post-9/11 terrorism was considered to represent a very different threat to national security and public safety.

6.3.1 Guiding principles

During 1995 Lord Lloyd of Berwick was given responsibility by the government to review existing legal provisions for counter-terrorism. In his report, published in 1996, he set out four guiding principles for the introduction of any new anti-terror legislation which continue to be used today (see Table 6.1).

Table 6.1 Lord Lloyd Guiding Principles for the introduction of terrorism legislation

Approximate	New legislation against terrorism should *approximate* as closely as possible to ordinary criminal laws and procedures
Justify	The introduction of additional statutory offences and powers may be *justified* but only if they were deemed *necessary* to meet the anticipated threat; if so, they must strike the right balance between the needs of security and the rights and liberties of the individual

(continued)

Table 6.1 Continued

Safeguard	Additional *safeguards* should be considered alongside any additional powers
Comply	New legislation must *comply* with the UK's wider obligations in international law

6.3.2 **A new legal framework**

In his review, Lord Lloyd concluded that although the threat of terrorism within Northern Ireland could be expected to diminish, the *global* terrorist threat was likely to intensify. Therefore, refreshing outdated provisions and consolidating them in a single piece of legislation with a broader range of new contemporary powers seemed the best way to protect the future national security interests of the UK, at home and overseas. This was achieved through the introduction of the Terrorism Act 2000 (TACT 2000), enacted by Parliament in February 2001. The Terrorism Act 2000 was created following the largest overhaul of terrorism legislation in UK legal history and it remains the primary piece of terrorism legislation in operation today. Not only does the 2000 Act define what 'terrorism' and 'terrorist' are, it also outlaws terrorist organisations, provides new offences and procedures for the detention of terrorist suspects and examinations at port and border controls. In direct response to the events of 9/11 and the subsequent wars against terrorism overseas, new legislation was swiftly introduced. These new pieces of legislation included the Anti-Terrorism, Crime and Security Act 2001 (ATCSA), designed to cut off terrorist funding and protect the aviation and nuclear industry. This was followed by the introduction of Control Orders established by the Prevention of Terrorism Act 2005 (PoT) to monitor and restrict the movements of suspected terrorists. The loss of life on 7 July 2005 in the London bombings, combined with the realisation that home-grown suicide terrorists were being recruited from within UK communities, led to the enactment of the Terrorism Act 2006 (TACT 2006). This Act extended police powers, created nine new offences, and significantly lowered the threshold for individuals to be arrested for terrorism offences. To tighten controls on terrorist finances and fundraising as well as introducing measures for post-charge questioning of terrorist suspects charged with specific terrorism-related offences, the Counter-Terrorism Act 2008 (C-TACT 2008) was added to the expanding legal framework. During December 2010 legislators introduced the Terrorist Asset-Freezing etc. Act 2010, repealing the Terrorist Asset-Freezing (Temporary Provisions) Act 2010 designed to provide provision for the imposing of financial restrictions on, and in relation to, persons suspected of involvement in terrorist activity, and for connected purposes.

In December 2011, the Terrorism Prevention and Investigation Measures Act 2011, introduced the new system of Terrorism Prevention and Investigation Measures (TPIMs). These measures, which replaced the controversial Control Orders, were designed to improve the protection of the public from a small number of people who pose a real terrorist threat to the UK but who cannot be prosecuted due to insufficient evidence to secure a likely conviction at court, or in the case of foreign nationals, deported. The current UK anti-terror legal framework is summarised in Figure 6.1.

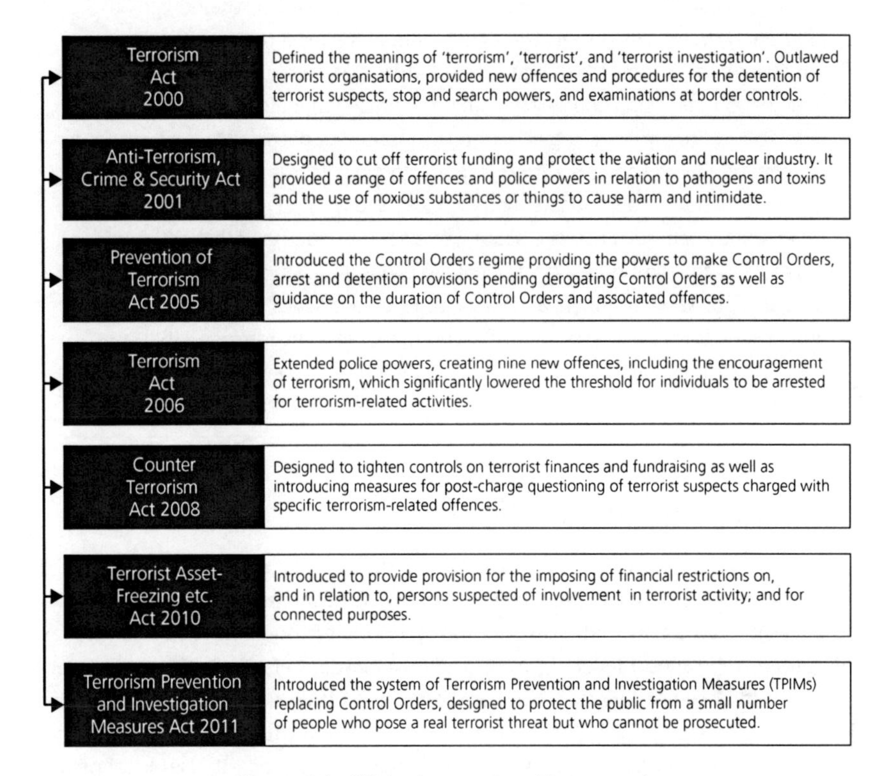

Figure 6.1. UK Anti-terror legal framework.

The introduction of the post-9/11 anti-terror powers served to negate some of Lord Lloyd's anticipated gains from consolidating previous provisions into the Terrorism Act 2000. The pace of legal change was, like that of the threat that spawned it, unprecedented. The five previous anti-terror Acts of temporary provisions had been brought to the statute book over a period of eighty years; the government's legislative response to Al Qa'ida's tactics of mass casualties stemming from indiscriminate attacks forced the introduction of seven pieces of legislation within just ten years.

KEY POINT—LEGISLATORS, PARLIAMENT, AND THE POLICE

In the aftermath of terrorist events, political stakes are high: legislators fear being seen as lenient or indifferent and often grant the executive broader powers without thorough debate. New special provisions intended to be temporary turn out to be permanent, and police officers are then forced to interpret and apply complex and sometimes poorly thought-through legislation. Embedded within the UK's new post-9/11 legal framework are broad powers and provisions. Perhaps predictably, these new powers contained some of the most controversial aspects of the government's response to new-era global terrorism including detention, examinations, and stop and search without the requirement of reasonable suspicion. Police officers charged with the responsibility of using these powers must understand that the powers at their disposal continue to generate profound questions about the appropriate moral, ethical, and political response to terrorism. When armed with such powers, police officers must understand that anti-terrorism laws remain the most draconian of legal provisions and as such, are powers that must be applied with caution, and which require continuous independent oversight and review. Everyone in positions of authority ought to be reminded that counter-terrorism legislation and its enforcement remain controversial topics, but that these tools are provided for very real reasons, and are there to be used.

6.4 Independent Oversight

The UK government has always understood the value of independent review of its anti-terror legislative regime. Regular reviewing began in the 1970s, and reporting was put on an annual basis in 1983. The role of independent reviewer was designed to provide a level of public and independent accountability, to be carried out by a senior lawyer whose key responsibilities are to scrutinise the use made of terrorism legislation and to advise the government, Parliament, and other interested parties of its relative efficacy. The reviewer criticises legal provisions where necessary, suggests changes in the law, and offers comments on any proposed changes in the law. In short, the reviewer's contribution to the counter-terrorism effort is to help mould and monitor a proportionate, justifiable, and acceptable approach to a legitimate outcome.

In order to conduct a rigorous review, the independent reviewer has access to both open and classified material, and travels the country to talk to politicians, spies, officials, police, prosecutors, judges, lawyers, non-governmental organisations (NGOs), suspected terrorists, and community representatives. The resulting report also contains recommendations, which can range from legislative amendments to changes in operational practice. Originally, the reports provided by the independent reviewer informed the yearly debates on renewing the Prevention of Terrorism Acts of 1984 and 1989, as well as the emergency provisions in Northern Ireland, but following the introduction of the Terrorism Act 2000 and the further legislation that followed the 9/11 attacks, the reviewer's role took on additional functions. Lord Carlile of Berriew CBE QC was the first independent reviewer following 9/11. From 2001 to 2011, Lord Carlile viewed his responsibility as reviewing the operation of the Terrorism Act 2000, especially its compatibility with the needs of national security and standards of human rights.

6.4.1 **Statutory functions**

The Independent Reviewer of Terrorism Legislation (IRTL) has a number of statutory obligations which include reporting on the Terrorism Acts, Terrorism Prevention and Investigation Measures (TPIMs), and asset-freezing initiatives.

Terrorism Acts

The IRTL has a statutory obligation to conduct annual reviews of the operation of the Terrorism Act 2000, and Part 1 of the Terrorism Act 2006 as required by section 36 of the Terrorism Act 2006. Reviews cover the calendar year and are normally published in June or July of the following year. These reviews cover the following:

- definition of terrorism;
- proscribed organisations;
- terrorist property;
- terrorist investigations;
- arrest and detention;
- stop and search;
- port and border controls;
- terrorist offences.

Since August 2012, the review has included a specific power to monitor the conditions of detention of persons detained for more than forty-eight hours under section 1 of the Terrorism Act 2000.

Terrorism Prevention and Investigation Measures

The annual review of the operation of the Terrorism Prevention and Investigation Measures Act 2011 (TPIMs) is required by section 20 of that Act. TPIMs replaced the system of Control Orders in the Prevention of Terrorism Act 2005. It allows a series of constraints, reviewable in the courts, to be imposed in the interests of public protection on persons whom the Home Secretary believes to have been involved in terrorism-related activity. Reviews cover the calendar year and are normally published in February or March of the following year.

Asset-freezing

The annual review of the Terrorist Asset-Freezing etc. Act 2010 (Part 1) is required by section 31 of the Act. The Act, which implements the United Nations Security Council Resolution 1373, gives the Treasury power to freeze assets of individuals and groups believed to have been involved in terrorism, and to deprive them of access to financial resources. Reviews cover the year to 17 September and are normally published in December of that same year.

Other statutory functions

Other statutory functions that may in the future have to be performed by the independent reviewer are:

- reporting or commissioning a report on any detention prior to charge in excess of fourteen days (should the law be changed so as to permit such detentions), as per section 36 of the Terrorism Act 2006;
- advising whether the system of TPIMs should continue beyond 2016, as per Terrorism Prevention and Investigation Measures Act 2011, section 21;
- advising whether the system of enhanced TPIMs should continue more than two years after its introduction, as per Draft Enhanced Terrorism Prevention and Investigation Measures Bill, clause 9.

6.4.2 **Non-statutory functions**

The IRTL may at the request of ministers or on his own initiative conduct reviews and produce reports on specific issues. 'Snapshot' reports, presented to ministers and laid before Parliament, have included:

- the Definition of Terrorism (June 2007);
- Operation PATHWAY (October 2009);
- Operation GIRD (May 2011).

POINT TO NOTE—INDEPENDENT REVIEWER OF TERRORISM LEGISLATION

David Anderson QC was appointed in January 2011 as the Independent Reviewer of Terrorism Legislation. A leading barrister in private practice, David Anderson is provided with security clearance by the government, but remains independent of it, in order to fulfil his responsibilities. Regular reviews of the UK anti-terror legal framework can be found at: <https://terrorismlegislationreviewer.independent.gov.uk>.

The latest news and opinions concerning UK terrorism legislation can also be found via the Independent Reviewer of Terrorism Legislation on Twitter, at: <@terrorwatchdog>.

6.5 Key Definitions

The Terrorism Act 2000 is the primary piece of anti-terror legislation in operation today. As part of the review of UK anti-terror legislation, the meaning of key terms such as 'terrorist', 'terrorism', and 'terrorist investigation', were defined for the purposes of the Act, definitions which continue to be used throughout legalisation within the anti-terror legal framework. They are essential terms for police officers to understand, serving to facilitate the effective interpretation and operational application of related powers.

6.5.1 **The meaning of 'terrorism'**

Definition of terrorism

Terrorism is defined by section 1(1) and 1(2) of the Terrorism Act 2000. In summary, the term 'terrorism' in the 2000 Act means the use or threat of action where it:

- involves serious violence against a person or serious damage to property;
- endangers a person's life, other than that of the person committing the action;
- creates a serious risk to the health or safety of the public or a section of the public; or
- is designed seriously to interfere with or seriously to disrupt an electronic system; and
- the use or threat is designed to influence the government or an international governmental organisation, or intimidate the public or a section of the public; and,
- the use or threat is made for the purpose of advancing a political, religious, racial, or ideological cause.

This definition covers terrorism both within the UK and abroad and the planning for any such action.

- 'Action' includes action outside the UK;
- 'Person' and 'property' means any person, or property, wherever situated;
- 'The public' includes the public of a country other than the United Kingdom;
- 'The government' means not only the United Kingdom government but also the government of any country.

This definition of terrorism is not only used in the Terrorism Act 2000, but also in the Anti-Terrorism, Crime and Security Act 2001, Prevention of Terrorism Act 2005, Terrorism Act 2006, and the Counter-Terrorism Act 2008. It has also been included in a number of different Acts, such as the Civil Contingencies Act 2004.

6.5.2 **The meaning of 'terrorist'**

Definition of terrorist

For the purposes of the exercise of counter-terrorism powers, a terrorist is defined under section 41 of the Terrorism Act 2000 as either a person who is or has been concerned in the **commission, preparation,** or **instigation** (CPI) of acts of terrorism, as defined in the Act, or has committed an offence under any of the following sections of the Terrorism Act 2000;

- Section 11—membership of a proscribed organisation
- Section 12—support of a proscribed organisation
- Section 15—invite, receive, provide funds
- Section 16—use, possess money/property
- Section 17—being concerned in the raising of funds
- Section 18—money laundering
- Section 54—weapons training
- Section 56—directing a terrorist organisation
- Section 57—possession for terrorism purposes
- Section 58—collection of information
- Section 59—inciting terrorism overseas (England and Wales)
- Section 60—inciting terrorism overseas (Northern Ireland)
- Section 61—inciting terrorism overseas (Scotland)
- Section 62—terrorist bombing
- Section 63—terrorist finance offences

In practice, an individual's involvement in the commissioning, preparation, or instigation of acts of terrorism may be linked, illustrated in Figure 6.2.

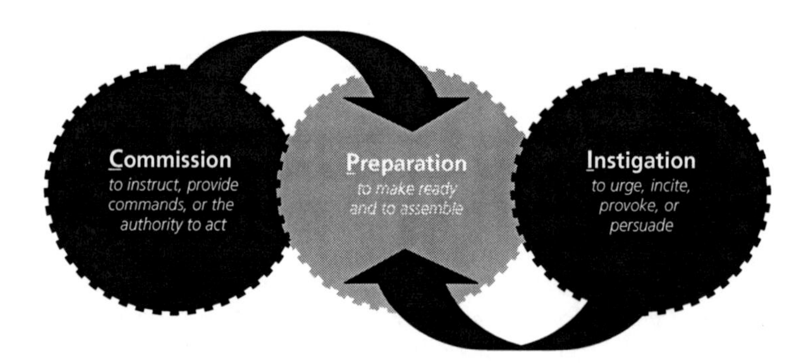

Figure 6.2. Terrorist definition: commission, preparation, instigation.

KEY POINT—RETROSPECTIVE APPLICATION

It is important for those police officers investigating terrorist cases to know that the meaning of 'terrorist' applies retrospectively. Anyone who has been involved in the commission, preparation, or instigation of acts of terrorism even before the Terrorism Act 2000 came into force shall be deemed a 'terrorist' under the law. Terrorist attacks which were conducted many years ago, especially those resulting in murder, may now produce fresh lines of enquiry resulting in cold-case reviews and fresh investigations.

6.5.3 **The meaning of 'terrorist investigation'**

Definition of terrorist investigation

Section 32 of the Terrorism Act 2000 defines a 'terrorist investigation'. This definition applies to powers to use cordons, to obtain search warrants, production orders, and explanation orders, and to make financial orders. Terrorist investigation means an investigation of

a) the commission, preparation, or instigation of acts of terrorism;
b) an act which appears to have been done for the purposes of terrorism;
c) the resources of a proscribed organisation;
d) the possibility of making an order under section 3(3) of the Terrorism Act 2000; or
e) the commission, preparation, or instigation of an offence under the Terrorism Act 2000 or under Part 1 (sections 1–20) of the Terrorism Act 2006 other than an offence under section 1 (encouragement of terrorism) or section 2 (dissemination of a terrorist publication) of that Act.

The terms used in the definition of 'terrorist investigation' will often cover not only investigations into possible criminal offences but also other forms of preparatory work, such as in relation to the proscription of terrorist organisations, and the identification and tracking of transnational terrorism finances.

6.6 Stop and Search

Stop and search powers provide the police service with an essential tool for the detection and prevention of terrorism and the collection of intelligence in order to safeguard communities. There are two primary stop and search powers under anti-terrorism legislation. These are section 43 of the Terrorism Act 2000 which covers the powers to stop and search persons and their vehicles, and new provisions provided under section 47A of the Terrorism Act 2000, amended by the Terrorism Act 2000 (Remedial) Order 2011, which came into effect on 18 March 2011, and which provides powers to exercise stop and search powers in specified areas and places.

6.6.1 **Section 43**

Section 43 of the Terrorism Act 2000 provides a police officer with the power to stop and search anyone whom he or she reasonably suspects is a terrorist, or search anyone who has been arrested under section 41 of the Terrorism Act 2000. Section 43A provides a power for a police officer to stop and search a vehicle, including its driver, any passenger, and anything in or on the vehicle, if he or she reasonably suspects the vehicle is being used for the purposes of terrorism. The police powers under section 43 and 43A are as follows:

Section 43(1) A constable may stop and search a person whom he reasonably suspects to be a terrorist to discover whether he has in his possession anything which may constitute evidence that he is a terrorist.

Section 43(2) A constable may stop and search a person arrested under section 41 to discover whether he has in his possession anything which may constitute evidence that he is a terrorist.

Section 43(4A) Subsection (4B) applies if a constable, in exercising the power under subsection (1) to stop a person whom the constable reasonably suspects to be a terrorist, stops a vehicle,
Section 43(4B) the constable,

a) may search the vehicle and anything in or on it to discover whether there is anything which may constitute evidence that the person concerned is a terrorist, and
b) may seize and retain anything which the constable—
   (i) discovers in the course of such a search, and
   (ii) reasonably suspects may constitute evidence that the person is a terrorist.

Section 43A(1) Subsection (2) applies if a constable reasonably suspects that vehicle is being used for the purposes of terrorism.

Section 43A(2) The constable may stop and search—

a) the vehicle;
b) the driver of the vehicle;
c) a passenger in the vehicle;
d) anything in or on the vehicle or carried by the driver or a passenger;

to discover whether there is anything which may constitute evidence that the vehicle is being used for the purposes of terrorism.

KEY POINTS—REASONABLE SUSPICION

The stop and search powers provided by section 43 of the Terrorism Act 2000 are much wider than the powers under section 1 of the Police and Criminal Evidence Act 1984 as no *reason* is required for the purposes of the stop and search other than a reasonable suspicion that the person is a terrorist. In addition, under subsection 43(4) and 43A(3), any material that the police officer believes is evidence that the person is a terrorist, or that the vehicle is being used for the purposes of terrorism, can be seized and retained. Section 51 of the Criminal Justice and Police Act 2001 provides powers for such material to be taken away and examined elsewhere, such as a police station.

Section 43 can be exercised in any part of the UK and none of the subsections limit where the power can be used, but if it is being applied in a private place, then the police officer would have to have some other lawful reason or consent for being on the premises.

A Code of Practice for the exercise of stop and search powers under sections 43 and 43A of the Terrorism Act 2000, is reproduced in Appendix 2.

6.6.2 **Section 47A**

Section 47A of the Terrorism Act 2000 makes provision for a senior police officer to give authorisation to allow the stop and search of vehicles (including drivers of vehicles, passengers, and anything carried by a pedestrian), and to search for anything that may constitute evidence that a person is a terrorist. The senior officer must reasonably suspect that an act of terrorism will take place and reasonably consider that the authorisation is necessary to prevent such an act. In addition, the senior officer must reasonably consider that the area or place specified in the authorisation is no greater than necessary, and the duration of the authorisation is also no longer than necessary. Once the authorisation has been given, a police officer does not require any reasonable suspicion in order to exercise the powers.

Schedule 6B to the Terrorism Act 2000 provides supplementary provisions in relation to the power under section 47A. There is also a 'Code of Practice (England, Wales and Scotland) for the Authorisation and Exercise of Stop and Search Powers Relating to Section 47A of, and Schedule 6B to, the Terrorism Act 2000'. For the full text, please see Appendix 2.

KEY POINTS—REVIEW OF ANTI-TERROR STOP AND SEARCH POWERS

The new stop and search powers under section 47A of the Terrorism Act 2000 replace the controversial provisions of section 44 Terrorism Act 2000, which Shami Chakrabarti, Director of the National Council for Civil Liberties (Liberty), described as 'a good example of all that was wrong with counter terrorism legislation that trod all over our rights and freedoms'. She continued:

> arming the police with a broadly worded, discretionary power to stop and search individuals without suspicion, not only was this crude and blunt instrument inappropriate, its negative impact on community relations made it entirely counterproductive. While the widespread use of power did nothing to enhance public safety, never leading to an arrest for a terror offence, it did cost us dearly by clamping down on peaceful protestors and disproportionately targeting young Black and Asian men.

The power to stop and search under section 44 of the Terrorism Act 2000 was replaced by the UK government following the successful challenge at the European Court of Human Rights (ECtHR) in the case of *Gillan and Quinton v United Kingdom*.

Case Study *Gillan and Quinton v United Kingdom*

Two pedestrians were stopped and searched by police officers under section 44(2) of the Terrorism Act 2000, under authorisations covering the Metropolitan Police Service area. Kevin Gillan was a PhD student who came to London to protest peacefully against an arms fair, the Defence Systems and Equipment International Exhibition, being held at the Excel Centre, Docklands, in east London. He was riding his bicycle near the centre when he was stopped by two police officers. They searched him and his rucksack and found nothing incriminating. They gave him a copy of the Stop and Search Form 5090 which recorded that he was stopped and searched under section 44 of the Terrorism Act 2000. The whole incident lasted approximately twenty minutes.

Pennie Quinton was a freelance journalist. She went to Excel to film the protests taking place against the arms fair. She was stopped by a female police officer near the Centre and was asked to explain why she had emerged out of some bushes. Wearing a photographer's jacket and carrying a small bag and a video camera, she explained she was a journalist and produced her press pass. The officer searched her, found nothing incriminating, and gave her a copy of Form 5090, which recorded that the objects and grounds of the search were 'POTA' (which the court thought was a reference to the Terrorism Act 2000 rather than the previous Prevention of Terrorism Acts). The form showed the length of the search as five minutes, but Ms Quinton estimated it lasted for 30 minutes.

Gillan and Quinton both challenged the legality of the stop and search all the way through the English courts to the ECtHR. The House of Lords on 8 March 2006 supported their appeals following decisions at the High Court and Court of Appeal to dismiss their cases, but Lord Bingham observed that:

> It is an old and cherished tradition of our country that everyone should be free to go about their business in the streets of the land, confident that they will not be stopped and searched by the police unless reasonably suspected of having committed a criminal offence. So jealously has this tradition been guarded that it has almost become a constitutional principle. But it is not an absolute rule. There are, and have for some years been, statutory exceptions to it. Since any departure from the ordinary rule calls for careful scrutiny, their challenge raises issues of general importance.

Under Article 34 of the Convention for the Protection of Human Rights and Fundamental Freedoms, the case of Gillan and Quinton was lodged at the ECtHR on 26 January 2005 and the completed application form was filed on 30 April 2007. The ECtHR held that the use of coercive powers to require an individual to submit to a detailed search of his or her person, clothing, and belongings amounted to a clear interference with his or her right to respect for private life, contrary to Article 8, European Convention on Human Rights. As a result of the following, the ECtHR held that the interference was *not* justified and therefore was unlawful:

- The police's discretion to authorise stop and search powers, and to use them once authorised, was very wide and there was no real curb on that power.
- The test of 'expedience' in section 44 was much lower than that of 'necessity' and therefore during the authorisation process there was no requirement upon the police or the state to assess the *proportionality* of the authorisation.

- There was no real check on the issuing of authorisations, demonstrated by the fact that the Metropolitan Police Service authorisation had been continually renewed in a 'rolling programme' ever since the very first authorisation had been granted.
- There was a huge discretion bestowed on individual officers deciding to use section 44 powers, as they were not required to have reasonable suspicion. Rather, the decision to search could be based upon a 'hunch' or 'professional intuition'.

The ECtHR referred to the many thousands of searches that had taken place under section 44, and the fact that not a single one had ever led to an arrest for a terrorism-related crime. The ECtHR considered that there was a real risk of arbitrariness in the way the power could be used, and on 28 June 2010 delivered its final judgment that the section 44 powers as enacted by Parliament were not in accordance with the law.

KEY POINTS—LEGAL CHALLENGES

One of the central tenets of the British legal system is a presumption that people are able to 'know' the law to which they are subject. This means that the law must be accessible and foreseeable, formulated with sufficient precision to enable the individual—if need be with appropriate advice—to regulate his or her conduct. Although the details of the Terrorism Act 2000 can be consulted, the extent to which the many conditions that applied to section 44 authorisation are present is not immediately apparent, either to the people who might wish to question the lawfulness of its use or to those who exist to act in their wider interests. The way in which section 44 has been used in some cases would not meet those conditions.

The legal challenges and reviews of counter-terrorism legislation over recent years are now producing a gradual reduction and dilution of some of the more controversial powers introduced in direct response to the threat of terrorism following the events of 9/11 and 7/7. While police officers may be concerned that a reduction in the available options to protect the public, prevent offending, and bring offenders to justice may impact upon their effectiveness, there remains a broad range of legal tools available to combat terrorism effectively. The police service must, however, acknowledge that a key contributory factor in the over-extended use of section 44 was due in part to their poor understanding, awareness, application, and interpretation of stop and search powers under these provisions. Poorly briefed and poorly trained officers led to poorly applied legislation. It also contributes to a mistrust of the police and damage to community relations. With the introduction of the new section 47A powers to stop and search, the police service must focus its efforts and invest in the practical training, education, and exercising of its workforce to deliver anti-terrorism stop and search provisions professionally and proportionately.

Public reassurance

All police officers who have the responsibility to exercise section 47A stop and search powers must understand the provisions it provides and be able to discharge their duties professionally while providing reassurance to the public. The following checklist provides essential guidance and advice for the public when the subject of a search under section 47A.

Stop and Search Public Information—Know Your Rights Checklist

What is section 47A Stop and Search?

Section 47A of the Terrorism Act 2000 gives police the power to search any person or vehicle within a defined geographical area if:

- They reasonably suspect that an act of terrorism will take place, and
- The power is necessary to prevent such an act.

Only senior police officers can issue the power. They must be at least the rank of Assistant Chief Constable and must inform the Secretary of State.

Once the authority has been issued, a police constable may then exercise the power, even if they do not have reasonable grounds to suspect an offence has been committed.

Who can stop you?

- A uniformed police officer.
- A uniformed Police Community Support Officer (PCSO).

Who can search you?

Under the legislation, a police officer in uniform may search:

- You.
- Your clothes.
- Your vehicle.
- Anything you are carrying on your person.
- Anything in or on your vehicle, including passengers.

If you are searched, it will be by an officer of the same gender.

A PCSO in uniform, **under the supervision of a police constable,** may search:

- Anything you are carrying on your person.
- Your vehicle.
- Anything in or on your vehicle, including items carried by passengers.
- If your vehicle is unattended it may still be searched. A receipt will be left with your vehicle to notify you about the search.

Why is it done?

The purpose of section 47A Stop and Search is to deter and detect terrorist activity.

Where can I be stopped and searched?

You can be stopped and searched under section 47A if you and/or your vehicle are within the geographical area defined by the authorisation. If you are in a public place, the officer will only ask you to remove your coat or jacket and your gloves, unless the officer believes you are using your clothes to hide your identity.

If the officer asks you to take off any headgear, or anything you wear for religious reasons, they must take you somewhere out of public view.

What happens if I am stopped and searched?

Stop and Search is for your safety. Being stopped and searched does not mean you are suspected of being a terrorist. Before you are searched the officer should tell you:

- The legislative power that allows the search.
- Your rights.
- His or her identity.
- What he or she is looking for.

You must:

- Stop when requested.
- Stop your vehicle when requested.
- Comply with the search.

If you fail to cooperate, or deliberately obstruct a search, you will have committed an offence and could be arrested.

What happens next?

If you are stopped and searched, the officer will complete an electronic form. He or she will then give you a receipt with a reference number. If you would like to see a copy of the form relating to your stop and search, you can take the reference number into any police station and request one.

The officer will ask you questions and record:

- Your name, address, and date of birth (you do not have to give this information if you do not want to, unless the officer says he or she is reporting you for an offence which may or may not be related to terrorism. In this case, you could be arrested if you do not offer these details).
- A description of you and/or your vehicle.
- Your ethnic background.
- When and where you were stopped and searched.
- The names and/or numbers of the officers involved in the search.

POINT TO NOTE—POLICE COMMUNITY SUPPORT OFFICERS

Provided they have been designated under the provisions of the Police Reform Act 2002, and they are in the company of a constable who is supervising them, under section 47A, Police Community Support Officers (PCSOs) can stop:

- Any pedestrian.
- Any vehicle.

They may then search:

- Anything carried by a pedestrian;
- Anything carried by a driver or passenger;
- Any vehicle;
- Anything on or in a vehicle.

However, a PCSO is NOT authorised to search a person or his or her clothing.

Exercising section 47A stop and search powers

When exercising powers authorised under section 47A police officers **must** be in uniform. They do not need to form any reasonable grounds or suspect any suspicious behaviour to conduct the stop or search. Articles can be seized or retained if it is reasonably suspected they may be used in connection with terrorism, but officers must note that there is **NO** power to retain individuals for questioning. When stopping someone under section 47A, an officer must:

- Identify him or herself;
- Explain why the person or vehicle has been stopped;
- Reassure the individual that the stop is a routine part of counter-terrorist policing;
- Complete a record and explain entitlement to a copy.

When applying the power the search officers should consider the following:

Authorisation—What are the geographical limits?
Person—Does the person fit any description provided by intelligence?
Location—Is the place attractive to terrorists, e.g. critical transport routes?
Time—Is it a significant period of the day, e.g. crowded or rush hour?
Behaviour—Is the person acting in a suspicious manner?
Clothing—Could the clothing conceal a weapon or terrorist paraphernalia?

KEY POINTS—MITIGATING THE RISK OF POTENTIAL DISCRIMINATION

However uncomfortable the reality, senior police officers authorising the use of section 47A must acknowledge that stopping a member of the public under these provisions carries the risk of potential discrimination in the selection of suspects or persons to be searched. All evidence of stop and search powers to counter-terrorism to date strongly indicate that this is the case. The first step for the police service in tackling this discrimination is to accept and recognise the overwhelming evidence from independent research and analysis and from the governmental statistics. This risk must be effectively managed and wherever possible mitigated by the execution of sound intelligence analysis and assessments which provide police officers with a full picture of the specific nature of the terrorist threat they are seeking to prevent.

In order to maintain the community's confidence, supervising officers must monitor the use of stop and search powers. They should consider in particular whether there is any evidence or trend suggesting the powers are being exercised on the basis of stereotyped images or inappropriate generalisations about types of people. The statistical data on these searches must be retained and made available to community representatives. A series of further measures to reduce the risk of discrimination includes the use of clear briefings prior to officers being deployed to use stop and search powers, which should complement existing training provisions which reinforce the stop and search guidelines provided by the Home Office.

6.6.3 Stop and search guidelines

The Home Office has provided detailed guidance for police officers in relation to the appropriate use of terrorism stop and search powers. It specifically highlights the fact that stop and search activity has raised concerns over its disproportional use among black and ethnic minority groups. This is liable to be accentuated by its use in relation to terrorism, especially when countering the threat from international groups. It is not appropriate to stereotype people of a certain faith or ethnicity as terrorists. These factors may prove to be significant but only when taken into consideration as part of a combination of other factors. Some terrorists will adopt behaviours and appearances typical of specific cultures to avoid identification and it is not therefore appropriate to use these factors as a preconceived basis for searches. It is important to remember that where profiles of suspects are available, they are subject to change and can become quickly outdated. All officers conducting stop and search under terrorism legislation should be aware of the cultural sensitivities surrounding the removal of clothing, and especially the removal of headgear. A thorough and sympathetic understanding of religious and cultural differences is an essential element of policing communities.

Prior to exercising stop and search powers under terrorism legislation, police officers should seek to 'PLAN' their actions and be able to answer the questions illustrated in Figure 6.3.

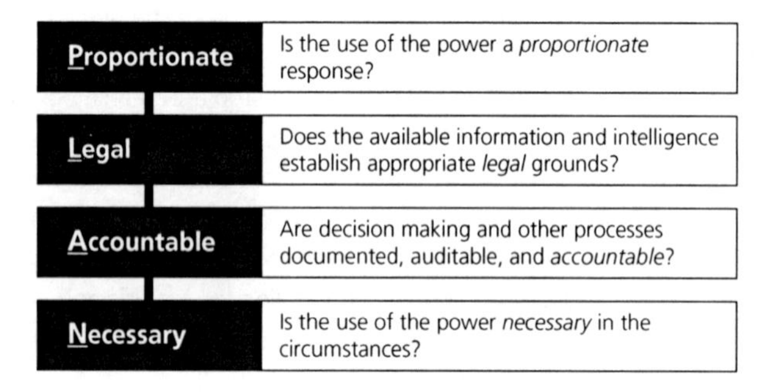

Figure 6.3. Stop and search 'PLAN'.

POINT TO NOTE—THE IMPORTANCE OF BRIEFING

The Home Office Stop and Search Code of Practice stresses the central importance of briefing all officers who may use section 47A powers. The written authorisation and confirmation process requires the authorising officer to set out the details of the planned tactical deployment of the section 47A stops. Officers involved in conducting the stops MUST receive clear instructions as to the intended deployment. For risk management reasons, officers receiving these instructions or briefings should clearly record their content. In order to demonstrate that the powers are used appropriately and proportionately, the briefing process MUST be robust and auditable. **All officers involved in the process should be reminded that they are fully accountable in law for their own actions.**

If the exercise of section 47A powers is challenged, it may prove crucial to any subsequent and required justification that the police are able to show that the officer conducting the search:

- was briefed as to the appropriate and proportionate exercise of the power in the circumstances of the particular authorisation; and
- did not exceed the scope of the briefing, and exercised the section 47A powers proportionately and appropriately.

The briefing may direct that officers are to stop and search pedestrians or vehicles in a certain location at random, provided this formed part of the plan within the original written authorisation, and the necessity to have taken these steps can be demonstrated.

6.6.4 Alternative stop and search powers

Police officers should be reminded that terrorism powers must only be used for terrorism purposes. The Home Office Stop and Search Code of Practice, which recognises that terrorism stop and search powers have been overused leading to the potential for mistrust of the police and damage to community relations, now encourages the use and consideration of alternative and existing stop and search powers which are available to the police. These include:

- **section 60 Criminal Justice and Public Order Act 1994**: to search for offensive weapons and dangerous instruments (prior statutory authorisation is required)
- **section 1 Police and Criminal Evidence Act 1984**: to search for stolen articles, offensive weapons, articles made or adapted for use in the course of or in connection with relevant offences, articles with a blade or point in a public place (reasonable suspicion is required for the exercise of this search)
- **section 139B Criminal Justice Act 1988**: to search for offensive weapons on school premises (reasonable suspicion is required for the exercise of this search)
- **section 47 Firearms Act 1968**: to search for a firearm or ammunition in a public place, or in a vehicle in a public place (reasonable suspicion is required for the exercise of this search)
- **section 27 Sporting Events (Control of Alcohol) Act 1985**: to search for alcohol at sporting events (reasonable suspicion is required for the exercise of this search)

POINT TO NOTE—COOPERATION IS KEY

If the legal tests for the use of any of the alternative stop and search powers are met, then these powers can also be used in a terrorist context if necessary and appropriate. Officers must consider the full range of powers available to them to protect the public but in doing so they must remember that it remains an important goal of contemporary practical policing that it should, wherever possible, be conducted by consent. It is absolutely vital that a person who is about to be searched is given the opportunity to cooperate where practicable, as the use of force where it is unnecessary (that is, where consent could have been given) constitutes assault. While the existence of the legal power and authorisation is a necessary prerequisite for sections 43 and 47A stop and search powers under the Terrorism Act 2000, the cooperation of the person to be searched must be sought in every case, even if the person initially objects to the search. A forcible search may be made only if it is has been established that the person is unwilling to cooperate or resists. Reasonable force may be used as a last resort if necessary to conduct a search. These general observations provide best-practice guidance for the conduct of stop and search powers under terrorism legislation.

6.7 Power of Arrest

Section 41 of the Terrorism Act 2000 provides a power of arrest without warrant to a constable for a person reasonably suspected to be a terrorist. This can be used throughout the UK and there is no requirement for the necessity test to be fulfilled as with those persons arrested under the Police and Criminal Evidence Act 1984. The only requirement of the constable is to reasonably suspect that the person is a terrorist.

KEY POINT—REASONABLE SUSPICION

The test for whether a police officer has reasonable suspicion for an arrest is a simple one, according to *O'Hara v Chief Constable of the Royal Ulster Constabulary* [1997]. The components are a genuine and subjective suspicion in the mind of the arresting officer that the arrestee has been concerned in acts of terrorism, and also objectively reasonable grounds for forming such a suspicion. Thus, there is an objective element to the test in that the grounds must be reasonable. Reasonable suspicion can be formed by the officer based on information he or she has been told either by a more senior officer or an informant. There is no need for the arresting officer to establish first that the information was true, but it must be genuinely believed to be so. Reasonable grounds for suspicion MUST be taken in light of the whole situation which includes the information and the context in which it is received.

Case Study—*Raissi v Metropolitan Police Commissioner*

In *Raissi v Metropolitan Police Commissioner* [2007] person X was arrested as a suspected terrorist. She was the wife of a prime suspect of 9/11, thought at that time to be involved in the terrorist attacks in the US. She was with her husband in a foreign country when it was believed he may have undergone terrorist training at the same time and at the same location as one of the perpetrators of the 9/11 attacks. It was deemed reasonable for the officer to suspect that she may be a terrorist. Person Y was also arrested as a suspected terrorist; he was the brother of the prime suspect, who in turn was thought by the officer to live nearby. The arresting officer had been informed that family links played a part in terrorist activity, and claimed that this was the basis of his suspicions. This did not pass the threshold of reasonable suspicion and the arrest of the brother was deemed unlawful. The Commissioner of the Metropolitan Police Service appealed the decision but the appeal was dismissed.

KEY POINT—EXERCISE WITH CAUTION

The power of arrest without warrant under section 41 of the Terrorism Act 2000 is a broad one, requiring the officer making the arrest simply to hold reasonable suspicion at the time that the person being arrested is a terrorist, and is involved in the commission, instigation, or preparation of an act of terrorism. The development of the reasonable suspicion must take account of the specific circumstances at the time but yet considering the wider context. While legislators were right to include such a wide-ranging power of arrest to ensure a suspected terrorist could be arrested and detained to keep the public safe, it is a power that must be exercised with caution and must NOT be used indiscriminately; there MUST be a real and reasonable suspicion.

6.7.1 **Spontaneous arrests**

Section 41 was designed by legislators for use by not just specialist counter-terrorism police officers but also by officers who, in the course or connection with their routine duties, come across an individual who they reasonably suspect is a terrorist. This may arise following a routine traffic stop, while responding to reports of a suspicious sighting or activity at or near to key national critical infrastructure such as power plants, airports, communications installations, and government buildings. It may also be used when officers are responding to reports of a suspected terrorist incident taking place. Whatever the situation, police officers must have confidence in their use of this important power of arrest. Given that there is no requirement to fulfil the necessity test, unlike conducting an arrest under the provisions of the Police and Criminal Evidence Act 1984 (PACE), an arrest can be made when the police service believe it should be made, even though under PACE provisions there may be insufficient evidence to arrest a person in connection with a specific offence. The advantage of the use of the term 'terrorism' is that the basis for the arrest may be more speculative in terms of a range of possible offences, but it should still be conceived as being equivalent to a criminal act otherwise it may be challenged as an incursion on liberty which lacks legal certainty.

6.7.2 **Pre-planned arrests**

Preventing terrorism necessitates a covert approach, where all the operationally sensitive tools and tactics of surveillance and intelligence collection are used to detect potential terrorist activity. Counter-terrorism intelligence operations can be protracted investigations involving multiple agencies around the world. These long-term, major covert counter-terrorism investigations may yield sufficient suspicion to move on to arrest where the section 41 power of arrest is used. Such arrests are pre-planned but police officers must afford due diligence to the appropriate use of the power and the gradual collection of intelligence and evidence which leads to an arrest without warrant.

Case Study—Operation Pathway

On Wednesday 8 April 2009, the North West Counter Terrorism Unit, working with Merseyside Police, Greater Manchester Police, Lancashire Constabulary, and the Metropolitan Police Service, arrested twelve men under section 41 of the Terrorism Act 2000. The police operation, known as Operation PATHWAY, was believed to have disrupted a terrorist plot to attack crowded places in the north-west of the country. In his independent review of the operation published in October 2009, Lord Carlile, the IRTL, revealed that analysis of intelligence material suggested strongly to the services concerned that this might well be part of a very significant international plot. The initial priorities of the investigation were first, the arrest and detention of the suspects, and secondly, the recovery of any materials that might be used in a terrorist attack. However, it was not originally intended for the arrests to take place as early as they did.

On the morning of Wednesday 8 April 2009 a briefing had taken place at 10 Downing Street where Assistant Commissioner Bob Quick, a very highly regarded officer and one of the most senior figures in the effort to counter terrorism, was photographed by the media entering the front door of Number 10 carrying papers marked 'SECRET'. These papers were not contained in a secure briefcase, or folder, nor were they concealed using any protective covering sheet. This was in breach of clear instructions to all public servants carrying highly confidential material. Sensitive operational details about the investigation were clearly visible in the photographs. As a direct result, the arrest phase of Operation PATHWAY was brought forward which materially affected communities at the locations where the arrests of suspects were carried out, increasing community tension. Lord Carlile's review found no evidence that the change in the timing of the arrest led to any failure to find or the loss of any material evidence. However, he criticised the police, stating that they should have taken immediate steps to inform the Crown Prosecution Service (CPS) about the timing of the arrest, and he emphasised the need for the CPS to provide any required legal advice to the police at an early stage. Lord Carlile recommended that CPS expert vetted lawyers should be informed, well before arrests take place, of ongoing enquiries likely to result in arrests, and that they should be asked to advise on the state of the intelligence, information, and evidence as the enquiry in question progresses, with an eye on the implications and challenges post-arrest. As a result of the incident, Assistant Commissioner Bob Quick tendered his resignation to Boris Johnson, the Lord Mayor of London and chairman of the Metropolitan Police Authority, after admitting that he 'could have compromised a major counter-terrorism operation'.

KEY POINTS—IMMEDIATE NOTIFICATION FOLLOWING ARREST

The section 41 power of arrest may be used for both planned and spontaneous arrests. For those counter-terrorism investigations where arrests are planned, and which form part of an ongoing operation, the recommendations of Lord Carlile should be followed, and the advice and guidance sought from the Crown Prosecution Service. For those arrests that are unplanned, made by officers on routine patrols or in the general course of their duties, the police are advised to alert their local Special Branch, Counter Terrorism Intelligence Unit, or Counter Terrorism Unit as soon as reasonably practicable of the arrest. It is strongly advised that all officers follow local force policy and procedures for alerting specialist counter-terrorism officers, but the sooner this is done, the quicker specialist support, guidance, resources, and force contingency plans can be activated. This kind of swift notification helps to ensure the best possible outcome for investigations. The UK now has a wealth of specialist, trained, and dedicated officers and staff deployed both locally and regionally as part of the police counter-terrorism network whose purpose it is to respond to terrorism-related incidents, events, and arrests. Their expertise must be called upon at the earliest opportunity.

6.7.3 Detention following arrest

Section 41 of, and Schedule 8 to, the Terrorism Act deal with the arrest and detention of suspected terrorists. The Police and Criminal Evidence Act 1984 Code of Practice H deals with the detention, treatment, and questioning by police officers of persons arrested under section 41 of the Terrorism Act 2000 and detained in police custody under section 41 of and Schedule 8 to the Terrorism

Act 2000. A person arrested under the section 41 powers can be detained on the authority of the police for forty-eight hours from the time of arrest. If no extensions are sought or granted under Schedule 8, then the person must be released. It is not within the scope of this chapter to discuss all of the provisions relating to the detention of terrorist suspects, suffice to say that the maximum time a person may be detained in police custody is fourteen days, but only following a period of reviews and the approval of warrants of further detention by the judicial authority/High Court judge. There is no provision for bail under the provisions of the Terrorism Act 2000 before or after charge and all persons in custody must be dealt with expeditiously, and released as soon as the need for detention no longer applies.

KEY POINTS—POLICE AND CRIMINAL EVIDENCE ACT 1984 AND THE TERRORISM ACT 2000

If a person suspected of being a terrorist is arrested using PACE provisions, the provisions under the Terrorism Act 2000 will NOT be available unless further offences are disclosed. If there is any reasonable suspicion that the person is involved in terrorism, it is advisable to use the power of arrest under section 41 and not section 24 of PACE for the following two reasons:

- Once arrested, due to the very sensitive nature of terrorist investigations, there is NO requirement that the suspect be given detailed information of the reasons for his arrest; both the suspect and any representatives need ONLY be informed of legal grounds and basic factual details (for example, 'you are suspected of being a terrorist and have been arrested and detained under section 41 of the Terrorism Act 2000'). However, Article 5.2 of the European Convention on Human Rights allows only a few hours' delay in giving some indication as to the nature of the offences and charges. Not having to provide full details initially allows for greater flexibility in the investigation and formulation of interview strategies.
- Suspects arrested under the Terrorism Act 2000 are subject to extra powers and extended periods of detention after arrest as previously stated.

The important differences between the use of PACE and TACT for the initial progression of post-arrest investigations amplify the need to notify specialist counter-terrorism officers as soon as reasonably practicable following an unplanned arrest under section 41. Alerting trained and experienced custody staff, notifying counter-terrorism officers, and following local force procedures serve likewise the efficiency of the arrest, detention, and continued terrorist investigation.

6.7.4 Personal and operational security

When arresting any person under section 41, it is advisable for personal and operational security and safety that officers provide terrorist suspects with an identification number other than their police collar number wherever possible. The collar number of police officers is a public-facing identification number from which officers' full names can be easily traced. Officers are advised to follow their local force policy and procedure on which number they should provide to arrested terrorist suspects, but the number on the back of officers' warrant cards or personnel numbers provide alternative numbers which fulfil requirements of the law but which also make it more difficult to identify the arresting officer. When police officers and staff are talking to one another in the presence of a detained terrorist suspect they should refrain from using personal details such as nicknames or first names which may lead to the identification of the officer. Wherever possible officers should address each other by their rank only but it is advised that local force policy and procedures should be followed. Personal and operational security and safety is paramount when arresting suspected terrorists—there is no room for complacency.

KEY POINTS—TREATMENT OF ARRESTED TERRORIST SUSPECTS

Any officer arresting a person under the provisions of section 41 must treat the suspected terrorist fairly, responsibly, professionally, and with respect for the removal of their liberty without unlawful discrimination. Everyone in authority is reminded that the Equality Act 2010 makes it unlawful for police officers to discriminate against, harass, or victimise any person on the grounds of age, disability, gender, race, religion or belief, sexual orientation, and marital status when using their powers. Any mistreatment of terrorist suspects detained following arrest has the potential to threaten the effectiveness of the investigation but can also serve to undermine the professionalism of the police service, affecting the public's confidence in the police to treat citizens in their custody fairly. Mistreatment also provides terrorists with fuel for their propaganda programmes.

6.8 Cordons

The Terrorism Act 2000 provides the police with specific statutory powers to establish a cordon in relation to terrorism. In summary, the Act grants the police powers to be used where it is considered expedient for the purposes of a terrorist investigation, to:

- designate areas to be cordoned off with police tape or otherwise;
- do this urgently, if necessary;

- control who and what is present in the area of the cordon while it is in place; arrange for the removal or movement of vehicles within the area; and restrict access to the area;
- extend the duration of the cordon beyond fourteen and up to twenty-eight days.

6.8.1 **Designating a cordoned area**

Sections 33 to 36 of the Terrorism Act 2000 provide for the designation of areas, and the implementations of cordons around those areas, for the purposes of the terrorist investigation. A constable of any rank can erect a cordon if considered necessary by reason of urgency. If a constable makes such a designation, then he or she must do so in writing and also must inform an officer of at least the rank of superintendent that this is being done, as soon as possible. The officer who is told of the designation can confirm or cancel it. It can only be cancelled in writing, giving the reasons for the cancellation. A cordoned-off area is simply an area which has been 'designated' under section 33. Under normal circumstances it is anticipated that the identification of a cordoned area will be made by the use of police tape, but other methods such as barriers, vehicles, or officers could be used to create the cordon if considered appropriate by a constable. It is the duty of the constable to arrange for the cordoned-off area to be demarcated so far as is 'reasonably practicable'.

KEY POINTS—TERRORIST INVESTIGATION

A designation may be made *only* if the person making it considers it expedient for the purposes of a terrorist investigation (please see section 6.5.2, this chapter). It follows from this definition that there *must* be an element of investigation, or intended investigation, in order for an area to be subject to a cordon. The investigation does not need to have started by the time the cordon is in place, and the person making the designation must consider that cordoning the area would be of *significant practical value and utility* for the purposes of a terrorist investigation.

Section 34 of the Act provides details regarding cordons, as illustrated in Table 6.2.

Table 6.2 Designation of areas to be cordoned

Area	Cordon	Force	Rank
Outside Northern Ireland	Wholly or partly within the police area	An officer for that police area	At least Superintendent

Transport network	(except in Northern Ireland) • on track (including bridges, tunnels, level crossings, etc.) • on network (i.e. the system of track and other installations) • in a station (including station approaches, forecourts, and car parks, etc.) • in a light maintenance depot • on other land used for purposes of or in relation to a railway • on other land in which a person who provides railway services has a freehold or leasehold interest	British Transport Police Officer	At least Superintendent
In Northern Ireland	Wholly or partly within the police area	A member of the Police Service of Northern Ireland	At least Superintendent
Ministry of Defence (outside or in Northern Ireland)	Land, vehicles, vessels, aircraft, and hovercraft for naval, military, or air purposes. Includes most Ministry of Defence land. An area relating to a particular incident or operation where the assistance of the Ministry of Defence Police has been requested by another police force under provisions of the Ministry of Defence Police Act 1987	Ministry of Defence Police	At least Superintendent

KEY POINTS—DURATION OF DESIGNATION

A designation has effect during the period from when it was made and ending with a date or time specified in the designation. The maximum period that can be initially specified is fourteen days. A designation may be extended by the person who made it, or a person who could have made it of at least the rank of inspector. The extension must specify the additional period during which the designation is to have effect. A designation shall not have effect after the end of the period of twenty-eight days beginning on the day on which it is made. There is no provision for granting an extension urgently.

6.8.2 **Police powers**

Under section 36(1), a constable in uniform and a Police Community Support Officer (by virtue of the Police Reform Act 2002, Schedule 4, paragraph 14) have the following significant powers in relation to a designated area, *whether or not it has yet been demarcated* by tape or by other means;

- to order a person in a cordoned area to leave it immediately;
- to order a person immediately to leave premises which are wholly or partly in or adjacent to the cordoned area;
- to order the driver or person in charge of a vehicle in a cordoned area to move from the area immediately;
- to arrange for the removal of a vehicle from a cordoned area;
- to arrange for the movement of a vehicle from a cordoned area;
- to prohibit or restrict access to a cordoned area by pedestrians or vehicles.

All of these powers can be exercised in relation to any person. There are no preconditions to be fulfilled in relation to any individual (such as reasonable suspicion). An officer can start to give these orders *before* the cordoned area has been demarcated. It is an offence to fail to comply with an order, prohibition, or restriction imposed by section 36(1). It is a defence to prove a reasonable excuse. As necessity is a general defence in criminal law, a 'reasonable excuse' will include circumstances that would not reach the standard required for a necessity defence such as where, due to physical infirmity, a person might not be able to comply immediately with a direction to leave an area.

KEY POINTS—WIDE-RANGING POWERS

A cordon provides the police with powers to designate an area involved in a terrorist incident or one that they believe may be or become involved in one. Whilst it is a wide-ranging power, the benefits of stopping terrorist acts and preventing the loss of any potential evidence at terrorist crime scenes must outweigh the inconvenience imposed upon the public. That being said, everyone in authority must remember that such laws are a step outside the norms of criminal justice legislation: the obtaining of an authority to cordon an area is a potentially serious interference with the private and economic lives of law-abiding citizens. All police officers, and especially Superintendents, must familiarise themselves with the powers and provisions provided by the designation of cordons which may be required to be put in place urgently.

6.9 **Parking**

Sections 48 to 51 of the Terrorism Act 2000 provide a separate, independent, and relatively uncontroversial power to authorise the imposition of parking restrictions and prohibitions for specified areas. The parking restriction under section

48 of the Act may only be imposed where it is considered expedient for the prevention of acts of terrorism. An authorisation provides any constable in uniform with the power to prohibit or restrict the parking of vehicles on a road specified in the authorisation. Parking authorisations under section 48 can only be granted by a senior police officer as set out in Table 6.3.

Table 6.3 Section 48 authorising officers

Specified area	Police force	Rank
Whole or part of the Metropolitan police district	Metropolitan Police Service	At least Commander
Whole or part of City of London	City of London	At least Commander
Whole or part of Northern Ireland	Police Service of Northern Ireland	Assistant Chief Constable
Any other area	The force for that area	Assistant Chief Constable

The section 48 authorisation *must* be in writing. If an authorisation is given orally, the person giving it shall confirm it in writing as soon as is reasonably practicable. All roads affected *must* be specified in the authorisation, together with the duration. The maximum duration for a parking authorisation is twenty-eight days, although this can be renewed following the same procedure.

6.9.1 **Parking prohibitions**

Once an authorisation has been given, a constable in uniform may prohibit or restrict parking of vehicles on a road specified in the authorisation. This includes suspending parking places. This is to be carried out by placing a traffic sign on the road concerned. A constable in uniform may also order a driver or anyone with control of a vehicle to move it if it is parked in contravention of a restriction or prohibition imposed under the Act.

6.9.2 **Parking offences**

It is an offence for a driver, or someone with control of a vehicle, to park or fail to move a vehicle in contravention of a prohibition or restriction. The penalties are significantly more serious than fixed penalties for normal parking offences. Parking in contravention of a restriction can result in a fine not exceeding level 4 on the standard scale. Defying a constable's request to move a vehicle can result in a fine, a sentence of imprisonment of up to fifty-one weeks, or both.

It is a defence for the person to prove that he had a reasonable excuse for the act or omission in question. However, as for the cordon offences, it is likely to be difficult to establish such a defence. For example, possession of a disabled person's badge is not itself a defence to a contravention offence. It might be reasonable to refuse to move a vehicle if the driver knew that he or she was over the limit for alcohol consumption, or were unable to drive due to being injured or unwell.

6.10 Terrorism Prevention and Investigation Measures

In December 2011, the Terrorism Prevention and Investigation Measures Act 2011 introduced the new system of Terrorism Prevention and Investigation Measures (TPIMs), replacing the controversial Control Orders enacted by the Terrorism Act 2005. TPIMs are designed to protect the public from the small number of people who pose a real terrorist threat but who cannot be prosecuted, or in the case of foreign nationals, deported.

Section 3 of the Terrorism Prevention and Investigation Measures Act 2011 sets out the five conditions that have to be met in order for a TPIMs notice to be issued to an individual by the Secretary of State and are as follows:

- **Condition A:** the Secretary of State reasonably believes that the individual is, or has been, involved in terrorism-related activity.
- **Condition B:** all of the relevant activity is new terrorism-related activity.
- **Condition C:** the Secretary of State reasonably considers that it is necessary for the purposes connected with protecting members of the public from a risk of terrorism, for terrorism-prevention and investigation measures to be imposed on the individual.
- **Condition D:** the Secretary of State reasonably considers that it is necessary, for the purposes connected with preventing or restricting the individual's involvement in terrorism-related activity, for the specified terrorism prevention and investigation measures to be imposed on the individual.
- **Condition E:** the court gives the Secretary of State prior permission from powers and functions of the court granted by section 6 of the Act, or the Secretary of State reasonably considers that the urgency of the case requires terrorism prevention and investigation measures to be imposed without obtaining such permission.

6.10.1 Terrorism-related activity

For the purposes of the Terrorism Prevention and Investigation Measures Act 2011, involvement in terrorism-related activity comprises any one or more of the following:

a) the commission, preparation, or instigation of acts of terrorism;
b) conduct which facilitates the commission, preparation, or instigation of such acts, or which is intended to do so;
c) conduct which gives encouragement to the commission, preparation, or instigation of such acts, or which is intended to do so;

d) conduct which gives support or assistance to individuals who are known or believed by the individuals concerned to be involved in conduct falling within paragraphs (a) to (c).

6.10.2 **New terrorism-related activity**

For the purposes of the Terrorism Prevention and Investigation Measures Act 2011, involvement in new terrorism-related activity comprises any one or more of the following:

a) If no TPIM notice relating to the individual has ever been in force, terrorism-related activity occurring at any time (whether before or after the coming into force of this Act);
b) If only TPIM notices relating to the individual has ever been in force, terrorism-related activity occurring after that notice came into force; or
c) If two or more TPIM notices relating to the individual have been in force, terrorism-related activity occurring after such a notice came into force most recently.

6.10.3 **Secretary of State measures**

Schedule 1 of the Terrorism Prevention and Investigation Measures Act 2011 provides a list of measures that the Secretary of State can impose upon an individual. Only the measures listed in this Schedule can be imposed upon a person subject to a TPIM notice. The full list of measures is shown in Table 6.4.

Table 6.4 Schedule 1—Terrorism Prevention and Investigation Measures

Measure	Description
Overnight residence	Restrictions with regards to the residence in which the individual resides
Travel	Restrictions on an individual leaving the UK, or Great Britain if that is the individual's place of residence
Exclusion	Excludes the individual from certain streets, areas, or towns. For example, an area where it is believed that extremist's contacts are present
Movement directions	Requires that the individual comply with directions in relation to his/her movements given by a police constable. For example, requiring the individual to be escorted to his/her place of residence in order to fit him/her with an electronic tag
Financial services	Requirements on an individual's access to bank accounts and cash

(*continued*)

Table 6.4 Continued

Property	Requirements relating to the transfer of property to or by the individual or in relation to the disclosure of property
Electronic communication device	Restrictions on the possession or use of electronic communication devices by the individual or by other persons in the individual's residence
Association	The Secretary of State may impose restrictions on the individual's association or communication with other persons
Work or studies	Restrictions on the individual's work or studies
Reporting	A requirement for the individual to report to a police station and comply with any direction given by a constable in relation to such reporting
Photography	A requirement for the individual to allow photographs to be taken of him/her at such locations and times as required
Monitoring	A requirement for the individual to cooperate with specified arrangements for enabling the individual's movements to be monitored

KEY POINT—DURATION OF TPIM NOTICE

A TPIM notice remains in force for one year beginning on the date on which it is served, or at a later date specified in the notice. The TPIM notice may be extended for a further year, but can only be extended once. To ensure that the police and their partners are working to establish a traditional criminal evidenced-based investigation upon the person subject to a TPIM notice, the Secretary of State MUST consult with the Chief Officer of the police force concerned on whether there is any evidence that could be used to prosecute the individual. The Chief Officer is then under a statutory duty to consult with the CPS. The Chief Officer MUST also review the investigation into the individual with a view to bringing a prosecution for a terrorism-related offence and MUST report on the investigation progress to the Secretary of State.

6.10.4 **Police powers**

An individual subject to a TPIM notice is guilty of an offence if they contravene, without reasonable excuse, any measures specified in the TPIM notice. Powers are provided to a police constable without a warrant to enter and search premises:

- for the purposes of locating an individual in order to serve a notice;
- in order to ascertain whether an individual subject to a TPIM notice has absconded; and
- for an individual subject to a TPIM notice for the purpose of public safety.

KEY POINT—CONTROVERSIAL CONTROL

Terrorism is capable of killing, injuring, and intimidating the public, so in order to keep them safe, all communities are entitled to use robust means, starting with the ordinary criminal law, to disrupt terrorists and bring them to justice. The most difficult moral issues concern pursuing those who have not been convicted of a criminal offence. The previous Control Order regime was unfair and unsafe and was the most dangerous legislative legacy of the so-called 'war on terror'. When the state imposes restrictions which collectively amount to house arrest for an indefinite period, inflicted on a person who has never been charged or even arrested and questioned for an offence, this represents the height of injustice and can only serve to contravene values of tolerance and respect for human rights and civil liberties. Yet, in the aftermath of the 7 July 2005 terrorist attack, when the UK was confronted with tackling a critical threat from international terrorism, the state did just this. If such powers are to be justified, they can only be so on the basis that they are operationally *necessary* (not merely expedient or desirable) in the interests of national security, applied in a proportionate manner, and subject to the most rigorous judicial control.

The move from Control Orders to TPIMs is regarded by numerous legal commentators as a piece of legislative tinkering motivated by political considerations rather than based on the merits of the argument, but most of the characteristics of Control Orders have been retained within TPIMs. The one major difference is the removal of the power of compulsory relocation, a power which certainly enabled the removal from associates and familiar places of an individual found to be a terrorist. TPIMs represent the latest attempt to control those few individuals who present a clear and present danger to public safety but who cannot be prosecuted. There remains no obvious 'third-way' executive alternative to TPIMs. They have persisted in one shape or form for decades and show no sign of disappearance. Everyone in positions of authority, and especially police officers who have responsibility to manage a person subject to a TPIMs notice, must familiarise themselves with the processes required to be followed for what remains the most controversial piece of anti-terrorism legislation to control suspected terrorist suspects.

6.11 **Officers' Powers and Duties**

The specialist anti-terror provisions contain a number of specific powers and duties which can only be performed by designated police officer ranks. While the executive action phase of pre-planned terrorist investigations may provide police officers with the responsibility of carrying out these duties with time to prepare and refresh their knowledge and understanding of the appropriate Codes of Practice, it may well be for reasons of operational security that officers find themselves being told to carry out such duties at short notice. Spontaneous terrorist events require officers to respond efficiently and effectively to maximise the full potential of the legal tools to tackle terrorism. The primary powers and duties of anti-terror legislation are designated to the ranks of Inspector, Superintendent, and Assistant Chief Constables or Commanders, illustrated in Table 6.5.

Table 6.5 Summary of officers' powers and duties

Inspector	• Recording of interviews and Codes of Practice (power to require appropriate adults leave interview in the absence of a Superintendent under PACE Code H para 11.10) • Detained person status and rights (qualified officer under para 9(1) of Schedule 8 to the Terrorism Act 2000) • Detention review officer, representations and record of review (review of detention under paras 24–28 of Schedule 8 to the Terrorism Act 2000) • Information about security of dangerous substances and about persons with access to such substances (power to give notice to occupier regarding dangerous substances under section 61(1) and (7) of the Anti-terrorism Crime and Security Act 2001)
Superintendent	• Use of Internet for encouragement of terrorism (power to serve notice under section 3 of the Terrorism Act 2006) • Financial information (power to investigate terrorist finance/to apply for a disclosure order that requires financial institutions to provide customer information) • Obtaining information (overview of powers under Schedule 5) • Search warrants, excluded and special procedure material (urgent cases) • Designation of cordons • Police power to enter and search premises, search persons, seize and retain relevant material in cordoned area • Recording of interviews (Superintendent to be consulted where appropriate adult required to leave interview) • Taking of fingerprints and samples (without consent and intimate samples) • Detention, review officer, representations, and record of review • Warrant of further detention (application for such warrant and extension) • Passenger and crew information: police powers (request such information) • Arrest and detention pending control order (delay right to have someone informed/right to legal advice)
Assistant Chief Constables and Commanders	• Authorisation to invoke powers to stop and search in specified locations (section 47a of the Terrorism Act 2000) • Power to restrict parking (power under section 48 of the Terrorism Act 2000) • Detained person status and rights (power to give direction that detained person can consult solicitor within hearing of qualified officer under para 9(2) of Schedule 8 to the Terrorism Act 2000)

KEY POINTS—RANK SPECIFIC POWERS

Inspectors, Superintendents, and Assistant Chief Constables or Commanders may be called upon at short notice to exercise powers under counter-terrorism law. They should be careful to take time to learn their legal responsibilities, which will serve them well when it comes time to use them in live operations.

6.12 Summary

No area of the law, no set of legislative provisions, is of greater current interest to an audience stretching far beyond lawyers, academics, and the police, than counter-terrorism law. Other countries look to the UK often for guidance on drafting and implementing counter-terrorism legislation. The hope is that exceptional powers (and these include almost the entire gamut of counter-terrorism laws), will cease to be necessary. However, unfortunately, the UK and its interests abroad remain a target for terrorists, and there is no sign of this ending.

There exists an acknowledgement that some of the legislation introduced following the events of 9/11 and 7/7 went too far and some laws have been retracted. Misinterpretation and poor application of some powers by police officers has been a contributory factor. Unfortunately the reviews of counter-terrorism legislation and the gradual move towards reducing and diluting some of the most effective powers mean a necessary increase in resources and a reduction in the available options to bring suspected terrorists to justice and prevent offending.

Further reading

- Anderson, D, *Terrorism and Fundamental Rights in the European Courts* (10 May 2013) UK Independent Reviewer of Terrorism Legislation, Irish Centre for European Law. Available at: <terrorismlegislationreviewer.independent.gov.uk/wp-content/uploads/2013/05/TERRORISM-AND-FUNDAMENTAL-RIGHTS.pdf>.
- *Gillan and Quinton v The United Kingdom* (2010) 50 EHRR 45, [2010] Crim LR 415, 28 BHRC 420, [2010] ECHR 28, 50 EHRR 45.
- Masferrer, A, and Walker, C, *Counter-Terrorism, Human Rights and the Rule of Law* (Cheltenham: Edward Elgar Publishing, 2013).
- Staniforth, A, *The Routledge Companion to UK Counter-Terrorism* (Oxford: Routledge, 2012).
- Staniforth, A, and PNLD, *Blackstone's Counter-Terrorism Handbook* 3rd edition (Oxford: Oxford University Press, 2013).
- Staniforth, A, and PNLD, *Blackstone's Handbook of Ports and Border Security* (Oxford: Oxford University Press, 2013).
- Sterba, J, *Terrorism and International Justice* (Oxford: Oxford University Press, 2003).

- The Stop and Search Action Team's *'Stop and Search Manual'*, published by the Home Office and available at: <http://police.homeoffice.gov.uk/news-and-publications/publication/operational-policing/stopandsearch-international1.pdf>.
- The Terrorism Acts in 2012 *'Report of the Independent Reviewer on the operation of the Terrorism Act 2000 and Part 1 of the Terrorism Act 2006'*, available at: <terrorismlegislationreviewer.independent.gov.uk/wp-content/uploads/2013/07/Report-on-the-Terrorism-Acts-in-2012-FINAL_WEB1.pdf>.
- Vaughan, B, and Kilcommins, S, *Terrorism, Rights and the Rule of Law* (Cullompton: Willan Publishing, 2008).
- Walker, C, *Terrorism and the Law* (Oxford: Oxford University Press, 2009).
- Walker, C, *Blackstone's Guide to the Anti-Terrorism Legislation* (Second Edition) (Oxford: Oxford University Press, 2011).

7

Terrorism Offences

7.1	Introduction	158
7.2	Encouraging Terrorism	158
7.3	Terrorist Training	161
7.4	Summary	165

7.1 Introduction

The purpose of this chapter is to introduce all police officers to the terrorism offences that they are most likely to encounter as part of their operational duties. Police officers must understand the extent and limitations of counter-terrorism laws, and understand exactly what actions constitute a terrorist offence.

The coordinated suicide terrorist attacks in London on 7 July 2005, combined with the realisation that home-grown terrorists were being recruited from within UK communities, brought about a series of fresh challenges for the UK government. At the core of many of these changes was a problematic shift to the pre-emption or interception of terrorism. This shift was necessitated by the suicidal component of terrorist tactics, and it had far-reaching implications for national security and in particular for the police service who would receive a broad range of new powers.

Legislators recognised that in order to prevent terrorist acts while successfully prosecuting terrorists, updated laws were required so that terrorists could be stopped before attacks were mounted. The result of this new emphasis upon pre-emption led to the enactment of the Terrorism Act 2006 (TACT 2006). The 2006 Act extended police powers, creating nine new offences and most importantly, it significantly lowered the legal threshold for individuals to be arrested for terrorism offences.

The offences covered under the 2006 Act included actions that may take place before the actual terrorist act is committed, such as encouragement, preparation, and possessing certain items, or taking part in terrorist training. This preventative approach placed the police service at the very heart of national counter-terrorism policy. Front-line police officers now have the legal tools necessary to pursue terrorists and prevent terrorist activities in order to protect the communities they serve. Over recent years the early disruption of terrorist plots in the UK have become primary security concerns for both the police and for Parliament.

The encouragement of terrorism by terrorists and violent extremists helps to influence, recruit, and radicalise vulnerable members of UK communities to the terrorist cause. Preventing citizens from adopting extremist views which may lead to violence and terrorism remains a priority for the police service. Attendance at a terrorist training camp in the UK or overseas is clearly a very risky undertaking for those who wish to act outside the law. In addition, the UK must not be a training or staging post for the export of home-grown terrorists. Police officers engaged in front-line duties and those working within communities are at the forefront of recognising and identifying individuals who may be considering committing grave offences.

7.2 Encouraging Terrorism

Images of individuals openly supporting and actively encouraging terrorist activity were a frequent occurrence in the British media before the terrorist attacks in London on 7 July 2005. Public speeches made by radical Islamist preachers such as Abu Hamza al-Masri and Omar Bakri Mohammed influenced a number of UK citizens who would go on to form alliances with like-minded extremists developing terrorist cells to plan attacks against the UK.

Case Study—Influence of Radical Preachers

Born in Syria in 1958, Omar Bakri Mohammed fled after joining the Muslim Brotherhood in a failed revolt against the government of President Assad in February 1982. During 1985, then living in the Saudi Arabian city of Jeddah, Bakri Mohammed was one of a large number of Islamist dissidents expelled by the Saudis. He came to Britain where he claimed asylum and was granted indefinite leave to remain because of the risk that he would face political persecution if deported to Saudi Arabia. He became a leader of the first UK branch of Hizb ut Tahrir (the Islamic Liberation Party) and preached incendiary sermons.

Bakri Mohammed split with the international leaders of Hizb ut Tahrir in 1996 and established his own organisation, al-Muhajiroun. His followers toured university campuses and shopping precincts touting recruits, and his website carried lurid accounts of Britons martyred in overseas combat, encouraging others to follow in their footsteps. Known as the 'Tottenham Ayatollah', Bakri Mohammed staged marches and rallies across UK cities and appointed himself as the head of Britain's Sharia court, which had no legal standing. This did not prevent his travelling across the country, administering 'justice' for a fee, to 'plaintiffs' who appeared before him to complain about, for example, 'wayward' teenage daughters wearing make-up or sons who preferred computer games to studying the Qur'an.

While helping to run an Islamist magazine, he suggested in one of the articles that it was time that the UK became a Muslim state. In another published piece he claimed that then Prime Minister, John Major, was a legitimate target for attack. Fearing on that occasion that he may have pushed his freedom of speech too far, a flustered Bakri Mohammed felt the need to explain that he only meant that assassins could kill the Prime Minister when he travelled to a Muslim country. He was later interviewed by police officers about this statement, but no charges were brought against him, just one of almost a dozen incidents when the UK legal authorities investigated his outbursts but decided he had not broken the law.

Bakri Mohammed made his mark on many young impressionable people in the UK before disbanding al-Muhajiroun in 2004. During 2005 he left the UK for Lebanon at about the time it emerged that UK authorities might charge him with incitement to treason after having expressed his view that police officers, soldiers, and civil servants would one day become radicalised. He stated that:

> When you start to ask Muslims to join your Army and your police you are making a grave mistake. That British Muslim who joins the police today will one day read the Qur'an and will have an awakening.

In response to the rising tide of extremist rhetoric designed to recruit and radicalise UK citizens, during August 2005, then Home Secretary Charles Clarke published a list of certain types of 'unacceptable behaviours'. These behaviours formed the basis for excluding and deporting individuals from the UK. It is aimed at those who attempt to promote terrorism or provoke others to commit terrorist acts. The list covers any non-UK citizen, whether in the UK or abroad, who uses any means or medium which includes writing, producing, publishing or distributing material, public speaking including preaching, the running of a website, and using a position of responsibility such as teacher, community, or youth leader to express views which:

- foment, justify, or glorify terrorist violence in furtherance of particular beliefs;
- seek to provoke others to terrorist acts;
- foment other serious criminal activity or seek to provoke others to serious criminal acts;
- foster hatred which might lead to inter-community violence in the UK.

The list of 'unacceptable behaviours' provided legislators with a foundation on which to introduce new preventative powers introduced in the Terrorism Act 2006 to curb the encouragement of terrorism.

7.2.1 **Encouragement of terrorism**

Section 1 of the Terrorism Act 2006 creates the offence of encouragement of terrorism which covers direct and indirect encouragement, including the glorification of terrorism.

Section 1 Terrorism Act 2006

1. This section applies to a statement that is likely to be understood by some or all of the members of the public to whom it is published as a direct or indirect encouragement or other inducement to them to the commission, preparation or instigation of acts of terrorism.
2. A person commits an offence if—
    a) he publishes a statement to which this section applies or causes another to publish such a statement; and
    b) at the time he publishes it or causes it to be published, he—
        i) intends members of the public to be directly or indirectly encouraged or otherwise induced by the statement to commit, prepare or instigate acts of terrorism; or
        ii) is reckless as to whether members of the public will be directly or indirectly encouraged or otherwise induced by the statement to commit, prepare or instigate such acts or offences.

The citing of 'members of the public' in this offence means that statements made in private are not covered by this offence but statements that are likely to be understood as a direct or indirect encouragement or other inducement to them to participate in the commission, preparation, or instigation of acts of terrorism include every statement which:

- glorifies the commission, or preparation (whether in the past, in the future, or generally) of such acts or offences; and
- is a statement from which those members of the public could be reasonably expected to infer that what is being glorified is conduct that should be emulated in existing circumstances.

POINT TO NOTE—EXERCISE WITH CAUTION

Police officers are provided with a power of arrest under section 41 of the Terrorism Act 2000 and the power to stop and search under section 43 of the same Act for the offence of encouraging terrorism under section 1 of the Terrorism Act 2006. While the preventative power provides police with the legal tool to take positive action against terrorist suspects, the inclusion of the term 'to glorify' was much criticised when the Act was made, regarded as too wide and too vague, and not sufficiently clearly defined. Some argue that the offence may infringe on freedom of expression and freedom of speech and be contrary to the Human Rights Act 1998. Police officers should therefore exercise the use of special anti-terrorism powers with caution and are advised to consult specialist counter-terrorism police investigators and prosecutors before action is taken wherever practicable. That said, the encouragement of terrorism is a serious offence and is an important tool to prevent terrorism.

7.3 Terrorist Training

Over recent years terrorist training camps have attracted a great deal of attention. Camps can be found in the mountainous border regions of Pakistan or Afghanistan, or in Syria, or Iraq, and individuals from all over the world travel to stay and train in them. These camps are located in very secure locations, and they often move around to avoid identification and capture. Given the usual kinds of terrain in which they are located, they are also difficult to track by military units. It is estimated that at the time of the 9/11 attacks in 2001 there were over 120 training camps in Afghanistan alone. Individuals attending these camps would typically be trained for between one and six months. Terrorist training camps may also be an adventure centre or paintballing facility located anywhere in the UK.

Training camps are often places where further recruitment and indoctrination is conducted. While terrorist training camps have long been established in parts of the Middle East, there has been a growing number of training activities taking place in the UK in support of international terrorism.

Case Study—Operation Overamp

In the immediate aftermath of the terrorist attacks in London on 7 July 2005, Deputy Assistant Commissioner of Specialist Operations (ACSO) Andy Hayman at New Scotland Yard revealed 'We latched on to one group of terrorists running outdoor training camps and put them under surveillance', and 'what we discovered was mind-boggling'. The training camp investigation was developed under Operation OVERAMP, a two-year joint MI5 and police operation focusing upon Atilla Ahmet, aged 43 from Bromley, and Mohammed Hamid, aged 50 from Hackney. ACSO Hayman revealed that Hamid was a veteran of Pakistan military camps who called himself Osama bin London, going on to describe Ahmet as 'an associate of the jailed preacher Abu Hamza'. ACSO Hayman would also reveal that Hamid had key connections with other UK terrorist plots, stating that:

> Hamid had taken two of the 21/7 bombers on a paintballing trip only three weeks earlier. All the bombers had spent camping weekends in the Lake District in Cumbria and Hamid had called or texted them at least 173 times in the months before the attacks.

It was clear from the information gathered at an early stage of Operation OVERAMP that the training camps being arranged were not 'soft-touch camps but a cover for terrorism'. In order to advance the covert investigation, the police and MI5 mounted intrusive surveillance operations and an undercover officer was able to infiltrate the group. This provided excellent coverage of the activities of Hamid and Ahmet which later led to their arrest. Deborah Walsh, Deputy Head of the Crown Prosecution Service Counter Terrorism Division, revealed that, 'Operation OVERAMP was the first prosecution for offences contrary to sections 6 and 8 of the Terrorism Act 2006. It was only possible to charge these offences because of the evidence of the undercover officer who attended the training sessions'. Walsh explained:

> Hamid and Ahmet were also charged with incitement to murder in relation to speeches they made at Friday night meetings at Hamid's address. Evidence to support these offences came from a probe deployed in Hamid's address, an audio recording device from the undercover officer and live evidence from the undercover officer who attended the meetings. The live evidence of the undercover officer was to illustrate the importance of witness testimony in understanding the context of other more technical evidence. Not only did this corroborate the evidence captured by the probe; it also brought it to life. The officer was able to describe the mood of the meeting, expressions on faces and reactions to words spoken and was able to give evidence as to who was present in the room when certain words were spoken. He was able to explain implied meanings of words spoken that could not be gleaned from the probe; for example, when Hamid used the word 'ting' he would demonstrate the use of a gun which the undercover officer explained and which obviously could not be detected from the audio probe.

At the Central Criminal Court in London and at Woolwich Crown Court during 2007 and 2008, seven men investigated under Operation OVERAMP, including Hamid and Ahmet, were convicted of terrorism-related offences. Hamid was found guilty of three counts of soliciting murder and three counts of providing terrorist training, and was jailed on 7 March 2008 under special Imprisonment for Public Protection powers. The judge said Hamid should serve seven and a half years but that he cannot be released until he has reformed. Ahmet pleaded guilty at the Old Bailey in September 2007 to three counts of soliciting to murder and was sentenced to six years and eleven months' imprisonment. Kibley da Costa, aged 24, of south-west London was found guilty of providing terrorist training, two counts of attending terrorist training, and one count of possessing a record containing information likely to be useful to a terrorist and was sentenced to four years and eleven months' imprisonment. Mohammed Al-Figari, aged 44, of East London, was found guilty of two counts of attending terrorist training and two counts of possessing a record containing information likely to be useful to a terrorist and was sentenced to four years and two months' imprisonment. Kader Ahmed, aged 20, was found guilty at Woolwich Crown Court on 20 February 2008 of two counts of attending terrorist training and was sentenced to three years and eight months' imprisonment. Yassin Mutegombwa, aged 22, of Norwood, south-east London, pleaded guilty to attending a terrorist training camp and was sentenced to three years and five months' imprisonment, and Mohammed Kyriacou, aged 18, of south-east London, pleaded guilty to attending a terrorist training camp and was sentenced to three years and five months' imprisonment. In an earlier trial, Hassan Mutegombwa, aged 20, the brother of Yassin, was also found guilty of seeking funding for terrorism overseas while attending one of the camps and was jailed for ten years. The landmark case brought the first conviction under new provisions provided by the Terrorism Act 2006 which created the offence of providing terrorist training or attending a place for terrorist training.

Operation OVERAMP showed that the UK camps were not clandestine in nature and were being carried out in public. People attending these camps did so in full view. Further investigations led to the police and Security Service identifying legitimate venues, such as adventure centres and paintballing facilities, which were being used by extremists to train and indoctrinate their followers. While these venues were not terrorist training camps per se, it was the intent of the individuals attending that meant that those people could be prosecuted for the new offence. The 'training camps' were also used to assess whether potential recruits could adapt to the rigours of trekking over hills and sleeping in tents in the UK, providing an indication of whether they then could operate in harsher conditions to be found in training camps on the mountainous border regions of Pakistan and Afghanistan. The camps also provided a cover for attack plans and logistics to be developed as well as raising funds for terrorist purposes. During Operation OVERAMP, ACSO Hayman revealed,'At one of the camps someone asked the undercover officer for money to pay a one-way ticket to send a suicide bomber to Somalia'. Following the conviction of the Operation OVERAMP suspects,

Deborah Walsh said: 'no-one should be in any doubt as to how serious Hamid and Ahmet were, encouraging their recruits to inflict casualties on innocent people. Hamid is a man for whom the indiscriminate killing of fifty-two people on 7 July 2005 was, in his own words: "not even breakfast for me"'. The court had heard that the defendants had filmed each other undertaking serious military-style training, including manoeuvres that replicated Taliban and Al Qa'ida training methods. ACSO Hayman later said: 'in my view, Hamid was a despicable man, grooming others far younger than him to be terrorists'.

POINT TO NOTE—BRITISH TRAINING CAMPS

Police officers working in both urban and rural areas must be aware that the very lowest level of terrorist training in the UK is more likely to involve outdoor activities which test potential recruits. It may not involve only physical training but can also involve training via supported reading of books and manuals, and the use of the Internet. Training can also be conducted via 'virtual camps' through a 'chat room', conversing with individuals who do not know each other personally, have never met each other, and who may be thousands of miles apart.

7.3.1 **Terrorist training offences**

Section 6 of the Terrorism Act 2006 creates two offences regarding terrorist training. Providing instruction or training for terrorist acts and receiving such instruction or training are covered by these offences. The offences complement other provisions of the anti-terror legal framework but allow for criminal prosecution of forms of training unrelated to weapons, such as surveillance or targeting techniques, or the handling of substances which might then be used for attacks.

To reinforce legal measures against terrorist training camps, section 8 of the Terrorism Act 2006 makes it an offence to attend a place used for terrorist training which includes camps in the UK and overseas. It is important for police officers to understand what makes a paintballing centre or outdoors activity facility into a 'terrorist training camp'. Essentially, the distinguishing factor is the purpose why individuals are at that place at that time. Therefore, terrorist training camps do not need to be clandestine in nature and may be carried out openly. Those persons attending these types of 'camps' in the open countryside do so in full view of the public. Activity centres are clearly legitimate ventures, however, it is the reason why these people attend which may bring them into conflict with the law. The powers introduced by Parliament to address the use of terrorist training camps provide essential tools for tackling contemporary terrorism.

7.4 Summary

The government has enacted a broad range of anti-terror powers to ensure the police may take a preventative approach to countering terrorism and violent extremism. The increasing number of terrorist offences provides a complex legal framework for police officers but the results of police and Crown Prosecutor's efforts in the decade since 9/11 are revealed in government statistics which, as at 31 March 2011, recorded that 119 people were in custody for terrorist-related offences in Britain, of whom twenty-two were classified as domestic extremists/separatists. The majority (70 per cent) of people imprisoned were UK nationals. There were also four people in custody in the UK for historic cases before the Terrorism Act 2000 came into force. In terrorist trials completed during 2010 and 2011, 78 per cent of defendants tried under terrorism legislation were convicted, and 100 per cent of those charged with non-terrorism offences were convicted. In total, thirteen defendants were sentenced to immediate custody, of whom seven were sentenced to less than ten years in jail, and there were four life sentences, and one non-custodial sentence handed down during this time.

The statistics provide evidence of the increasing demands placed upon the criminal justice system and show that in a free, democratic, and legally sophisticated society, a morally justified response to terrorism is to process criminals, no matter how abhorrent their actions may be, via a fair, transparent, and civil legal process. In that regard, the increased training, awareness, and understanding of special powers by police officers continues to be an essential part of the continued struggle against the excesses of extremism. Pursuing terrorists through a public criminal justice system preserves and protects the democratic values of the prosecuting state while ensuring that the rights of all concerned are maintained.

Further reading

- Masferrer, A, and Walker, C, *Counter-Terrorism, Human Rights and the Rule of Law* (Cheltenham: Edward Elgar Publishing, 2013).
- Staniforth, A, *The Routledge Companion to UK Counter-Terrorism* (Oxford: Routledge, 2012).
- Staniforth, A, and PNLD, *Blackstone's Counter-Terrorism Handbook* 3rd edition (Oxford: Oxford University Press, 2013).
- Sterba, J, *Terrorism and International Justice* (Oxford: Oxford University Press, 2003).
- Walker, C, *Terrorism and the Law* (Oxford: Oxford University Press, 2009).
- Walker, C, *Blackstone's Guide to the Anti-Terrorism Legislation* 2nd edition (Oxford: Oxford University Press, 2011).

8

Preventing Terrorism and Violent Extremism

8.1 Introduction 167
8.2 'Prevent' Priorities 168
8.3 'Prevent' Cycle 168
8.4 'Prevent' in Communities 168
8.5 Delivering 'Prevent' 173
8.6 Summary 179

8.1 Introduction

The attacks on London's public transport system on 7 July 2005 highlighted the very disparate origins of terrorism's threats, and the very local nature of the required response. The terrorist threat appeared to be emerging from all sides. Some terrorists were not UK-natives, others apparently returned from overseas where they had received military training or had gained combat experience in Iraq and Afghanistan. The threat was also virtual, with terrorists being recruited, radicalised, trained, and tasked online.

The threat brought about a series of fresh challenges for the authorities. At the core of many of the changes was the shift of focus towards the pre-emption or interception of terrorism. This was necessitated by the suicidal component of terrorist tactics, and it had far-reaching implications for national security, and in particular for the police service. Contemporary terrorism now involved embedded citizens as much as foreign extremists. While that phenomenon may not have been new to other parts of the world, it certainly represented a significant change in the UK.

The way in which members of UK communities were being influenced by the extreme religious ideology promoted by Al Qa'ida was of critical concern for the UK government. This single narrative, when combined with malaise originating in social and economic factors, served to push individuals towards extremist perspectives. Understanding why UK citizens were attracted to these views and creating an alternative to allow them to resist was widely acknowledged as the key challenge in countering the contemporary terrorist threat. As a direct result, the need for credible and actionable intelligence used to monitor and prevent terrorism came to the fore and was added to the more traditional tactic of the pursuit through criminal justice processes. The need to refocus and react to new trends was made manifest in the government's CONTEST strategy which reflected not only concerns for 'Prevent' and 'Pursuit', but also 'Prepare' and 'Protect'. Bringing these responses together produced very significant changes in the policing of political violence.

Concepts such as community involvement, multi-agency working, and public assurance, now widely accepted and practised in local policing, began to migrate into the policing of political violence. All police officers, and not just specialist counter-terrorism officers, had to share in the tasks. Counter-terrorism policing thus became a matter for everyone in the police, for all strategic partners, and for the public. The purpose of this chapter is to provide every police officer and the extended police family with an introduction to the role, responsibility, and challenges of the police service in delivering the *Prevent Strategy* to ensure communities and their citizens can go about their lives freely and with confidence that their safety is assured.

8.2 'Prevent' Priorities

The overall framework of the *Prevent Strategy* focuses upon three key elements: ideology, individuals, and institutions (more commonly referred to as the 3is) and

- responds to the **ideological challenge** of terrorism and the threat the UK faces from those who promote it;
- **prevents people from being drawn into terrorism** and ensures that they are given appropriate advice and support; and
- works with **sectors and institutions** where there are risks of radicalisation which require addressing.

8.3 'Prevent' Cycle

The *Prevent Strategy* is predicated on the right that everyone possesses to live in a safe neighbourhood where they feel they belong. At the same time it identifies the need for everyone in a given neighbourhood to work together to tackle the challenges they face. Preventing terrorism at its source requires a cycle of sustained effort, as illustrated in Figure 8.1.

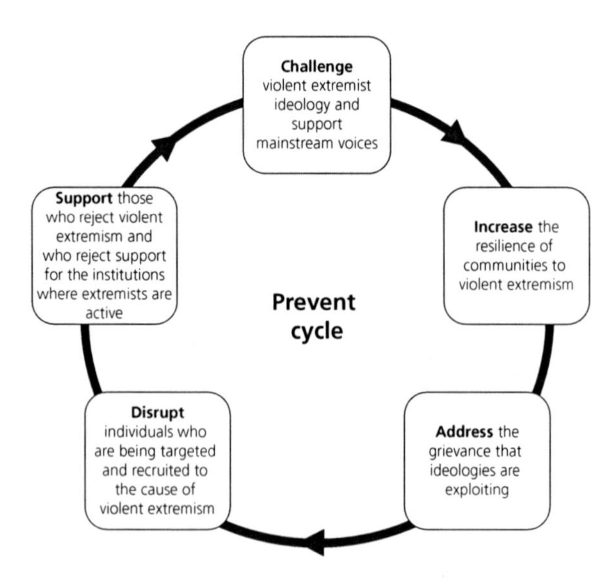

Figure 8.1. The 'Prevent' cycle.

8.4 'Prevent' in Communities

Counter-terrorism research over recent years has focused on answering questions concerning the challenge of radicalisation of individuals, defined as the process by which an individual adopts an interpretation of religious, political, or ideological belief that may lead to him or her believing the use of violence is legitimate. This research contributes to the government's understanding of the precursors, processes, and operational characteristics of radicalisation. Among the 'nodes' of radicalisation, academics and research institutes have identified what they view as the three primary physical venues of concern: radicalised religious premises, educational establishments, and prisons. It is these areas where 'Prevent' activity has been targeted over recent years.

8.4.1 'Prevent' in schools

Schools have an important role to play in preventing violent extremism. Alas, terrorists operating in the UK are intentionally and systematically targeting young people, and individuals as young as 15 have already been implicated in terrorist-related activity. When compared with other types of crime, terrorist offences are relatively few in number, yet analysis indicates that the average age at the time of their arrest is 25. More notably, most of the individuals concerned have been educated in UK schools and several have already exhibited degrees of vulnerability while at school prior to being radicalised as teenagers.

The purpose of 'Prevent' in schools is to offer opportunities to help young people understand the risks associated with violent extremism and to develop knowledge and skills to be able to challenge extremist arguments. Preventing violent extremism from taking root with young people in schools supports the 'Prevent' cycle by:

- using teaching and learning to help young people develop the knowledge and skills to challenge extremist narratives;
- identifying how to prevent harm to pupils by individuals, groups, or others who promote violent extremism;
- providing programmes to support pupils who are vulnerable;
- increasing the resilience of pupils and school communities through the curriculum, other learning opportunities, or activities;
- using teaching styles and curriculum opportunities which allow grievances to be aired.

POINT TO NOTE—A SHARED RESPONSIBILITY

Accepting that the potential radicalisation of school-age children is an issue to be addressed is the first and most important step in countering this threat. It cannot and must not be ignored, and preventive measures in schools require careful consideration. It is widely acknowledged across government that preventing violent extremism from taking root in schools is a challenging issue which needs to be a shared endeavour.

Just as society protects and educates young people in the identification of a variety of risks such as alcohol, tobacco, and drugs, it is also important to support the welfare of pupils who may be particularly vulnerable to recruitment and radicalisation. 'Prevent' in schools highlights the complexity of the threat represented by contemporary terrorism, and the extended reach required of countermeasures to protect the public now and in the future.

8.4.2 'Prevent' in higher education

Universities hold a unique cultural and legal position in the UK. They provide a mix of both educational and social experience to those who attend them. In 2008, the Centre for Social Cohesion commissioned an in-depth, groundbreaking study into attitudes towards Islam on UK university campuses. The research discovered, among other things, that students who are active in their university Islamic society were twice as likely as non-members to hold extreme views, including the opinion that killing in the name of religion is justified. Studies also show that more than 30 per cent of people convicted of Al Qa'ida-associated terrorist offences in the UK between 1999 and 2009 are known to have attended a university. The report of research findings published during 2010 by the Centre for Social Cohesion (*Radical Islam on UK Campuses—A Comprehensive List of Extremist Speakers at UK Universities*) found that a significant number of students and graduates from UK universities have committed acts of terrorism or have been convicted for terrorism-related offences, in the UK and abroad. The report also revealed that more than 30.71 per cent of individuals involved in violent Islamist terrorism in the UK were educated to degree level or higher. Of these, nineteen individuals studied at a UK university; sixteen were graduates; three were postgraduate students, and one had achieved a postgraduate qualification. A further finding of the research identified that at least four individuals involved in acts of terrorism in the UK were members of their student union Islamic society (ISOC), and a further six were studying at a UK university at the time of their arrest. In a number of terrorism cases both in the UK and throughout the world, the individuals involved were reportedly radicalised on UK campuses.

While this evidence strongly suggests that the radicalisation of young adults while studying at university presents a risk, this does not mean that higher educational institutions (HEIs) are to blame in any way for the development of radicalisation. With a large and diverse student population as a potential audience, some extremist organisations target specific institutions with the objective of radicalising and recruiting students. Universities clearly have a role to play in reducing the risk from terrorism by working in partnership with authorities in other agencies to challenge terrorist ideologies, support those who are vulnerable to being radicalised, and work with those institutions where radicalisation takes place.

KEY POINT—ROLE OF THE POLICE

The National Union of Students finds the language and approach of 'Prevent' problematic, whilst academics are concerned at the potential erosion of freedom of speech. It is important that the police should not expect students or staff to readily accept 'Prevent'. In fact, a greater chance of success might be achieved if police who engaged with HEIs embrace challenge and debate whilst being aware of the sensitivities that students and academics might possess.

Universities play a key role in promoting rigorous debate, free speech, and freedom of enquiry within the law, which means that police officers need to be able to tolerate a wide range of political, social, economic, and scientific views, regardless of how unpopular, controversial, or provocative these views are. It is important that academics continue to encourage and expect students to think for themselves and to question existing concepts and authority but when a student begins to develop extremist perspectives, he or she is beginning to move beyond the threshold of what is acceptable and legal. In these circumstances, universities have a duty of care to their students and to wider society and are required to identify and support any student who is vulnerable to radicalisation. Universities also need to recognise that the police service, through 'Prevent', is there to help and support them and the welfare of their students.

To build effective partnerships between police and HEIs, police officers should use the '4R' model for reducing risk of radicalisation at universities (see Figure 8.1).

8.4.3 **Risk reduction in universities**

It is important for the effective delivery of 'Prevent' that police officers engaging with HEIs acknowledge that universities must uphold academic freedom and provide an environment for research and open debate, but it is equally important that HEIs acknowledge the following:

- the potential for radicalisation at HEIs means that the very environment offers a form of risk for their students and staff;
- HEIs staff, students, and the police have a responsibility to help minimise and mitigate against potential risks to public safety;
- sharing information and referring on potential threats is critical;
- a collaborative partnership based on a good working relationship between HEIs and the police form the foundation of future work to identify, mitigate, minimise, and manage risk to public safety.

These themes assist in creating a simple '4R' model for reducing risk at universities shown in Figure 8.2. Police officers and staff who work with HEIs may find the model useful in discussing how 'Prevent' fits in with students and staff. The positive outcome of the model is that risk is reduced by building strong professional relationships.

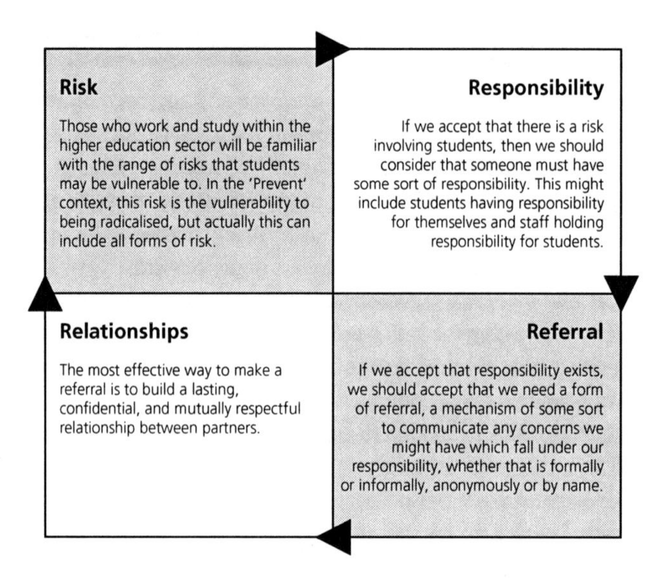

Figure 8.2. Reducing risk of radicalisation in universities—4R 'Prevent' model.

KEY POINT—BUILDING STRATEGIC PARTNERSHIPS

The use of the 4R model as a basic tool to build partnerships between the police service and HEIs offers an effective framework to explain how information sharing and raising awareness of vulnerability can be understood by those who work in universities. It provides a basis on which to build a positive and productive working relationship. In practice, building long-term strategic partnerships means that police and HEIs colleagues must get to know one another, share information appropriately, and work together to solve challenges. From police perspectives, this relationship is not just about gathering intelligence. It is about talking about risks and working together to manage, mitigate, and minimise the risks to public safety by providing support to vulnerable citizens.

8.4.4 'Prevent' in prison

The radicalisation of inmates in prison has become an issue of high priority to public policy-makers throughout the world. Radicalisation in prison is not a new phenomenon in the UK; it is something that has occurred throughout history, especially during the detention of Irish dissidents at the height of The Troubles. However, there are unique challenges that arise from the extreme Islamist genre of terrorism and none more so than the immediacy of the threat, the way in which self-starting groups and individuals are recruited, and the total disregard for human rights in its embrace of suicide martyrdom missions.

Over recent years individuals have emerged from communities as 'home-grown' terrorists. The prison environment is of course a 'community' itself and the government is keen to prevent those individuals within the prison community emerging as 'prison-grown' terrorists upon release. However, prisons are unlike other communities in that they maintain a barrier to social intercourse with the outside, and one of their deliberate and stated purposes is to punish their inmates on behalf of the wider society. Radicalisation within prison is unique when compared to other locations where radicalisation is taking place as it takes place within a self-contained environment resistant to other exterior influences.

In the UK we have learned already that prison is a location which is vulnerable to extremists who propagate their ideas and draw individuals down a path of willingness to condone or even participate in violence for political ends. Extremists are able to exploit the psychological and emotional shock that individuals experience on entering the prison system, as well as the difficulties individuals experience in coming to terms with daily life, and the confined social interaction permissible within the prison environment.

POINTS TO NOTE—UNINTENDED CONSEQUENCES

The UK's relative success in disrupting major attacks and bringing terrorists to justice has resulted in the detention of approximately 130 convicted terrorists in prison. This number includes some suspected terrorists remanded in prison while awaiting trial. As the population of terrorists held in prison grows, so does the challenge of countering the threat of holding a group of like-minded extremists in close proximity to each other. The government, police, and partner agencies are well aware of the risks this threat presents to the safety of the public, and the government has sought to improve the intelligence infrastructure across prisons, developing intervention approaches for extremists in prison and putting in place post-prison supervision procedures. The challenge of tackling radicalisation in prison is not simply confined to the UK; many EU member states, such as Germany and Italy, are also experiencing similar issues. This pan-EU challenge has also drawn research funding from the European Commission Director General of Justice for Freedom and Security to explore the risk of jihadist radicalisation in European prisons with a view to constructing methods and models not only to prevent radicalisation in the first instance, but also to counter radicalisation where it is found to be taking place, and to de-radicalise those inmates who are already adopting an extremist perspective. What is clear from all research conducted thus far is that terrorism will not be defeated by a simple, single blow but instead requires both a complex and concerted effort by everyone in authority.

8.5 Delivering 'Prevent'

The long-term solution to preventing terrorism is to stop people becoming terrorists or becoming involved in violent extremism in the first place. Through the government's *Prevent Strategy*, the police service and its partners have an integral role to play in working with local communities to stop people who are vulnerable to being drawn into criminal activity and to challenge those who support violent extremism. 'Prevent' must not be considered an intelligence-gathering process but rather as an effective tool to safeguard those citizens vulnerable to the process of violent extremist radicalisation.

In April 2008, the Association of Chief Police Officers (ACPO) published a wide-ranging 'Prevent' strategy and delivery plan called *The Policing Response to the Prevention of Terrorism and Violent Extremism*, which set out the national police service contribution to the government's *Prevent Strategy* providing the foundations on which the delivery of 'Prevent' continues to be actioned today.

The main themes of the ACPO *Prevent Strategy* are:

- To incorporate 'Prevent' into day-to-day policing, through neighbourhood policing, community engagement, and related activity;
- To work in partnership to support vulnerable individuals and institutions;
- To ensure a coordinated approach to all police counter-terrorism activity;
- To develop 'Prevent' capability at local, regional, and national level.

8.5.1 **National Prevent Delivery Unit**

ACPO has established a National Prevent Delivery Unit (NPDU) which sits within its Terrorism and Allied Matters (TAM) business area.

The unit comprises seconded police officers and staff from across the police service and supports 'Prevent' activity, providing national coordination as an over-arching umbrella for the policing response to the prevention of violent extremism.

The NPDU team is also responsible for driving forward the national projects set out in the ACPO *Prevent Strategy*. These range from community engagement with women and young people and supporting educational institutions through to the establishment of national information-sharing protocols for the police service and its partners. NPDU also designs and delivers national training and engagement products which form part of the national 'Prevent' toolkit, including Operation Hindsight, ACT NOW, and Channel. The primary purpose for developing national training and engagement products is to ensure consistency in 'Prevent' messaging and to incorporate learning from previous case studies.

The NPDU also provides locally developed products with a national platform in order to share best practice. The innovation used in the delivery of these products has been recognised as an important stepping stone in changing mindsets within the culture of police and partner agencies, and has been encouraged in the other 3 'P's of the CONTEST strategy, as well as within the European Union member states.

A network of regional police 'Prevent' coordinators and managers are now in place across police forces, supported by ACPO 'Prevent' leads, Community

Engagement Field Officers (CEFOs), Counter Terrorism Intelligence Officers (CTIOs), and local Neighbourhood Policing Teams (NPTs). 'Prevent' lies at the heart of the work of local NPTs whose direct contact with the public and local organisations make them ideally placed to support communities against the threat of violent extremism.

Operation Hindsight

Operation Hindsight is an interactive exercise which focuses on creating a wider understanding of the responsibilities of front-line practitioners. A key aim of this exercise is to address the barriers that exist in many instances, which restrict information sharing and multi-agency safeguarding. Without effective mechanisms in this area, a multi-agency approach to countering vulnerability towards violent extremism will be far less effective.

The exercise uses workplace scenarios based on real-life case studies to understand the misconceptions and dilemmas faced by front-line practitioners. It provides further understanding as to what support partner organisations can provide internally for staff, as well as what support is available externally from other associated organisations, including the voluntary and community sector.

The exercise functions as an opportunity for partners to address a fictitious terrorist incident and address key episodes that are featured in an individual's journey toward violent extremism. The exercise scenarios use the perspective of front-line practitioners to address some of the dilemmas and concerns that agencies encounter with information sharing and networking in relation to safeguarding vulnerable individuals.

The scenarios present complex intervention opportunities and demonstrate how authorities may have only one strand of information, which, on its own, may mean nothing until it is pieced together with information from other agencies. Indeed, most practitioners will see the scenarios in isolation and, also, as non-urgent until the full picture comes together.

This process allows agencies to assess the strength of information-sharing and partnership approaches. In very much the same way, if agencies are concerned that individuals are displaying extremist tendencies towards any form of violent personal, religious, or politically motivated ideology, front-line practitioners should be able to consult with other agencies in pre-existing forums to make honest and informed decisions.

ACT NOW

ACT NOW (All Communities Together) is an interactive counter-terrorism exercise which is hosted by a police force or trained facilitator which invites participants to become investigators and work through a fictitious terrorist incident. Throughout the half-day event the participants receive regular media updates which require them to make crucial decisions affecting the lives of their communities. ACT NOW is designed to support engagement between people from different communities, ages, cultures, and faiths. The exercise takes place in a safe and confidential community setting in which sensitive issues around terrorism can be discussed. ACT NOW recognises that community reassurance is an important part of the role-play and during the course of the event participants are required to deal with the media and to brief communities regularly about the incident and the policy response. To address the risk of radicalisation from students attending HEIs, and to support universities and students, a version of ACT NOW has been developed for further education colleges and universities, affording them a safe environment in which to consider and debate decisions in the wake of an unfolding terrorist incident in an academic setting.

Channel

Supporting those who may be vulnerable to being drawn to violent extremism is a key strand of the government's 'Prevent' strategy. All areas throughout the country are required to have local action plans in place to support vulnerable individuals; in some areas this support is provided by a process known as 'Channel'.

Channel provides a mechanism for supporting those who may be vulnerable to violent extremism by assessing the nature and the extent of the potential risk and, where necessary, providing an appropriate support package tailored to an individual's needs. A multi-agency panel decides on the most appropriate action to support individuals, taking their circumstances into account.

Channel focuses on understanding the need for early intervention opportunities and exploiting these to safeguard vulnerability within individuals. Interventions provide a package of measures aimed at diverting the individual away from their chosen path and back into society. The primary challenge is to make a connection with the individual in order to ensure their safety, as well as the wider safety of society.

The partnership-focused structure of Channel is similar to existing, successful partnership initiatives which aim to support individuals and protect them from harm, such as those tackling involvement in drugs and knife and gun crime. Supporting those most at risk focuses on diverting people away from potential risk at an early stage which prevents them from being drawn into criminal activity.

Partnership involvement ensures that those at risk have access to a wide range of support, from diversionary activities through to providing access to specific services such as education, housing, and employment.

Partners may include:

- Statutory partners such as education, health, probation, prisons, police, and others;
- Social services;
- Children's and youth services;
- The Youth Justice Board, through offending teams;

- Voluntary services;
- Credible and reliable communities that demonstrate a commitment to shared values as defined in CONTEST, the government's strategy for tackling international terrorism.

Channel is not about reporting or informing on individuals in order to prosecute them. It is about communities working together to support vulnerable people at an early stage, preventing them from being drawn in to violent extremism.

There are currently twenty-eight local coordinators across more than seventy local authorities. Those in communities who are concerned about individuals who may be vulnerable are advised to contact their local authority, the police, or other trusted local organisation for further advice.

POINT TO NOTE—'PREVENT' TOOLKIT

'Prevent' products previously highlighted represent just some of the tools which the police service has developed to shine a spotlight on key counter-terrorism issues and challenges. The primary drivers for all of the products include sharing experiences and challenges, the development of partnerships, and the creation of a platform from which to engage and raise awareness of the threat from terrorism and violent extremism, in order to ensure communities are safer and feel safer.

8.5.2 National Community Tension Team

The ACPO Prevent Delivery Unit also incorporates the National Community Tension Team (NCTT). The NCTT takes the policing lead for monitoring tensions and encompasses a wide range of issues. To this end, the team works closely with a number of internal and external partners including police forces, national policing units, government departments, and local government offices.

In relation to counter-terrorism and the 'Prevent' agenda specifically, community intelligence derived from monitoring can provide an early indication of the vulnerability of groups or individuals to violent extremism. It also helps build a picture of the 'mood' within communities in order to make policing more responsive to the needs of communities.

The NCTT receives updates from UK police forces on hate crime, critical incidents, community intelligence, and national/international incidents which may impact on community cohesion in the UK. The NCTT also produces Community Impact Assessments (CIA) in response to national and international critical incidents which document specific risks to communities and policing and ways of mitigating these risks.

POINT TO NOTE—LEADING AND DELIVERING 'PREVENT'

A preventive response, led and driven by local partners, is vital to counter the significant threat posed by terrorism.

Violent extremists are constantly seeking to exploit new tactics and technologies in both attack planning and recruitment. The *Prevent Strategy* enables the police service to adapt and strengthen its response to deter people joining the terrorists' recruitment line. It is difficult to measure success yet, but extensive feedback from communities and police partners shows that the police service is beginning to make a difference. The police service is gaining a better understanding of the communities it serves and it is engaging more actively with hitherto hard-to-reach communities and working more closely with key partners. All of these are critical to building an atmosphere of trust rather than grievance and resentment.

'Prevent' is a challenging and complex strategy that requires a cohesive approach by the entire community to empower them to challenge those who espouse violence, and to support those who are vulnerable to the temptations of violent extremism. It will be successful only if the police service continues to build trust and confidence through renewed and consistent engagement activity.

'Prevent' is not a short-term strategy which will be discontinued as soon as the threat level lessens. The threat remains high, and the police service must be ready to respond to any threat, no matter which guise it assumes. 'Prevent' is a shared objective that brings the police service closer to the communities it serves and protects. Evidence is now emerging that it is making a difference to citizen and community safety, supported by the positive outcomes of the Conviction project.

Case Study—The Conviction Project

Andrew Ibrahim was arrested in April 2008 after members of the Muslim community in Bristol alerted the police. In his flat the police found two home-made suicide vests, home-made explosives, a quantity of ball bearings, and airgun pellets. On 17 July 2009 he was given an indeterminate life sentence with a minimum of ten years for terrorist offences. The Conviction project is a twenty-minute DVD with supportive learning materials and was produced in 2011 as a direct result of the Ibrahim case. It aims to highlight the importance of early intervention work, to illustrate how quickly a vulnerable person can be adversely influenced by extremist rhetoric, and to raise awareness of the issues around violent extremism and radicalisation. The Conviction film can be accessed at: <www.convictionfilm.co.uk>. The work of this project has been supported by Andrew Ibrahim and his mother, Vicky Ibrahim, who said

> I feel there is a need to help individuals at risk of radicalisation and guide them. Views should be challenged to prevent incidents like the one that affected Andy happening again. If only others who had become aware of his increasing radicalisation had taken action earlier, then Andy might not have been allowed to continue along his route as far as he did.

8.6 Summary

The early efforts and initial approaches by government to implement preventative counter-terrorism action through CONTEST was by no means welcomed and supported by all. Many in society held the view that the government response through 'Prevent', being driven by the police, was a knee-jerk reaction which failed to create a coordinated, comprehensive policy to tackle the post-7/7 terrorist threat. Some suggested that it played to the public gallery, that being tough on terrorism was an attitude which only suited the government and those in positions of power. Many communities also felt that the 'Prevent' policy was being directed at their religious beliefs alone and this caused some resentment.

Never before had national central government counter-terrorism policy been so directly linked with local community issues as in 'Prevent'. Allegations that authorities were spying on communities and accusing them of being either terrorists, potential terrorists, or potential future terrorists, due to their faith or ideology, were levelled at government and the police. Yet, the challenge of protecting the young and vulnerable in society from recruitment and radicalisation of violent extremists had to be tackled.

For the police service, community engagement is quite properly an important part of the 'Prevent' response to the wider challenge of tackling contemporary terrorism and violent extremism. Inevitably there will be times when police intelligence-based activity, targeted at specific terrorist suspects within communities, will rub up uncomfortably against initiatives to engage with the community more broadly. This is likely to be a recurring theme in counter-terrorist work in the UK in the future. The police service and its partners will need to continue to invest effort in explaining their actions to ensure that they retain public confidence.

As the 'Prevent' strategy has matured, it has been increasingly recognised that many forms of violent extremism need to be addressed in the UK today, not just those linked to the original aim of CONTEST of tackling the Al Qa'ida genre of international terrorism. With a new strategy focusing upon individuals, ideology, and institutions, 'Prevent' has been given a fresh impetus and a clear direction for the future, and has shown that not all measures to counter contemporary terrorism need to be shrouded in secrecy in order for them to be effective. But perhaps most importantly of all, 'Prevent' has proved a vital point to Parliament and to the public through police activities that communities, working together, can prevent terrorism and violent extremism.

Further reading

- Bongar, B, Brown, L, and Beutler, L, *Psychology of Terrorism* (Oxford: Oxford University Press, 2006).
- Coolsaet, R, *Jihadi Terrorism and the Radicalisation Challenge* 2nd edition (London: Ashgate, 2011).

- Daniel Silk, P, Spalek, B, and O'Rawe, M, *Preventing Ideological Violence: Communities, Police and Case Studies of 'Success'—International Law, Crime, and Politics* (London: Palgrave Macmillan, 2013).
- Davies, L, *Educating Against Extremism* (London: Trentham Books, 2008).
- HM Government, *A Strong Britain in an Age of Uncertainty: The National Security Strategy* (2010).
- HM Government, *Countering International Terrorism—The United Kingdom's Strategy* CONTEST (2011).
- HM Government, *Prevent Strategy* (2011).
- Omand, D, *Securing the State* (London: Hurst & Co Publishers Ltd, 2012).
- Silke, A, *Psychology of Counter-Terrorism* (Oxford: Routledge, 2010).
- Spalek, B, *Counter-Terrorism: Community-Based Approaches to Preventing Terror Crime* (London: Palgrave Macmillan, 2012).
- The Centre for Social Cohesion, *Radical Islam on UK Campuses—A Comprehensive List of Extremist Speakers at UK Universities* (2010).

9

Radicalisation

9.1 Introduction 182
9.2 Defining Radicalisation 183
9.3 Drivers of Radicalisation 184
9.4 Models of Radicalisation Processes 191
9.5 Online Radicalisation 196
9.6 Social Media Radicalisation 202
9.7 Summary 203

9.1 Introduction

The purpose of this chapter is to introduce police officers and their partners to the concept of radicalisation within a terrorism and violent extremism context. Understanding how and why people in our communities move towards extremist perspectives, and creating an alternative to allow them to resist adopting such views are key challenges in countering the threat from terrorism.

The police service has a vital role in identifying those individuals and groups who are radicalising and recruiting others to their cause, identifying individuals who are adopting extremist views, and putting in place preventative mechanisms and interventions to stop and deter radicalisation processes at source. Identifying radicalised individuals is a complex task and continues to present an enormous challenge to modern policing. In order to identify the emergence of extremist perspectives everyone in authority must first increase their knowledge and understanding of the process of radicalisation.

This chapter provides police officers with the practical and theoretical underpinning required to improve their understanding of radicalisation and recruitment processes, supported by case studies to reinforce operational implementation. A number of radicalisation development models and theories are offered and are supported by an analysis of the 'push' and 'pull' factors which drive individuals towards adopting extremist perspectives. Most importantly, this chapter provides the operational law enforcement officer with a series of potential signs and indicators which, when contextualised in the given circumstances of the individual case, may provide early warning of the adoption of extremist views.

KEY POINT—DISTINGUISHING BETWEEN RADICALISM, EXTREMISM, AND TERRORISM

The prevention of terrorism and violent extremism remains a vital task for the police service, its partners, and the public, but in identifying potential roots of radicalism, officers must exercise discretion. In a liberal, pluralist, and democratic society, a wide range of political and religious views, even those views which may offend others, are aggressively pursued, or are highly unpopular, is not only acceptable but desirable. A vibrant and mature democracy allows room for these views to be aired in an atmosphere of tolerance and respect for the position of others, and permits legitimate challenges to inevitable differences.

A primary task for police officers, especially those who have direct contact with the communities they serve, is to distinguish between extremism and terrorism; the former does not necessarily lead to the latter, and simply to hold extremist views on the road of radicalisation is neither a criminal offence nor constitutes terrorism itself. To qualify as terrorism (under any generic definition) there must be central elements of violence, intimidation, and coercion. Distinguishing between extremism and terrorism is essential for the police to ensure they uphold and balance the protection of communities with the preservation of fundamental human rights.

9.2 Defining Radicalisation

Defining radicalisation is an important step in understanding the phenomenon, but a national or internationally recognised definition has proved elusive. The following definitions of radicalisation are used throughout the world to support government and academic understanding.

Radicalisation is defined as:

- the growing willingness to support the abolition of the established democratic legal order and which may involve the use of undemocratic methods;
- a process that leads an individual group to accept, support, or encourage the use of violence as a legitimate political means;
- a process of personal development whereby an individual adopts ever more extreme political or political-religious ideas and goals, becoming convinced that the attainment of these goals justifies extreme methods;
- a process of adopting an extreme belief system and the willingness to use, support, or facilitate violence and fear, as a method of effecting changes in society;
- a process by which an individual or group comes to adopt increasingly extreme political, social, or religious ideals and aspirations that reject or undermine the status quo, or reject or undermine contemporary ideas and expressions of freedom of choice;
- the process by which people come to support terrorism and violent extremism;
- the process by which individuals are introduced to an overtly ideological message and belief system that encourages the movement from moderate, mainstream beliefs towards extreme views;
- a growing readiness to pursue and/or support, if necessary by undemocratic means, far-reaching changes in society that conflict with or pose a threat to, the democratic order;
- a process by which a person to an increasing extent accepts the use of undemocratic or violent means, including terrorism, in an attempt to reach a specific political or ideological objective;
- a process by which an individual changes from passiveness or activism to become more revolutionary or militant.

Collectively, the definitions provide a useful framework for identifying the core characteristics and attributes of radicalisation. From these definitions the common themes which emerge indicate that radicalisation is a process of development via which an individual comes to adopt increasingly extreme views, leading to the active willingness to support or use violence in pursuit of a cause contrary to civil societal laws and values. Everyone in authority must learn to distinguish between extremism and terrorism. One does not necessarily lead to the other, and simply to hold extremist views while engaged in the process of radicalisation is neither a criminal offence nor does it constitute terrorism.

9.3 **Drivers of Radicalisation**

There are many potential factors which may tempt an individual towards adopting extremist perspectives. These include not only particular political views or those on religion, race, and ideology, but may also include a sense of grievance or injustices perpetrated against the individual him- or herself, or the community to which that individual belongs. Terrorists recruit and radicalise new members to their cause by providing a particular version of history or recent events, which is usually anti-government. The process of globalisation can also act as a potential driver for radicalisation as those feeling disenfranchised by globalisation's thrust may view their own way of life, their tradition and culture as being undermined by an economic impetus quite beyond their control.

Other factors which may drive individuals towards adopting extremist perspectives include feelings of personal alienation or experiences or perceptions of community disadvantage. These drivers may stem from socio-economic factors such as discrimination, social exclusion, and lack of opportunity. While an individual may not be relatively disadvantaged, he or she may identify with others seen as less privileged. It is important to note that different generations within the same family may have significantly different views about these issues.

Exposure to radical ideas can stem from a variety of sources, including the reading of radical religious or political literature, or surfing the Internet where many types of radical views are promoted. More often, however, radicalisation seems to start with local contacts and come from peers. The influence of exposure to a figure of inspiration who is already committed to extremism should not be underestimated, and the lessons from Al Qa'ida-inspired terrorist cells operating in the UK over recent years has shown that cell members often coalesce around a central and dominant figure who provides spiritual and religious guidance, encouragement, and reassurance. This person may be associated with a particular place, or can be a national or international figure, seen on video, or heard on tapes or video clips on the Internet, whose rise has had a significant impact on the accessibility and flow of radical ideas.

It is widely acknowledged that nobody suddenly wakes up in the morning and decides that he or she is going to make a bomb. Likewise no one is born a terrorist. Becoming involved in violent extremism is a process, it does not happen suddenly. Similarly, the idea that extremists adhere to a specific psychological profile has been abandoned. Empirical work has identified a wide range of potential 'push' and 'pull' factors leading to (or away from) radicalisation. This starts with the fact that terrorist groups fulfil important needs. They offer a clear sense of identity, a strong sense of belonging to a group, the belief that the person is doing something important and meaningful, and also offer a sense of danger and excitement. For some individuals, and particularly for young men, these are very attractive factors. Individuals at risk seem to share a widely held sense of injustice. The exact nature of this perception of injustice varies with respect to the underlying motivation for violence, but the effects are very similar. Personal attributes such as strong political views against government foreign policies regarding conflicts overseas can play an important role in creating initial vulnerabilities.

Police officers must recognise that terrorism is a minority-group phenomenon, not the work of a radicalised mass of people following a twisted version of faith. People are often gradually socialised into this activity, and their involvement deepens only over time. Radicalisation is a social process, which requires an environment that enables and supports a growing commitment. The process begins when enabling environments intersect with personal 'trajectories', allowing the aims of radicalism to resonate with the individual's personal experience. Some of the main elements in the radicalisation process are related to the social network of the individual. Good questions to ask include, for example: who is the person spending time with? who are his or her friends? and whether the interaction takes place in the physical or the cyber world.

Figure 9.1 shows some of the factors which may potentially push or pull an individual towards adopting extremist perspectives.

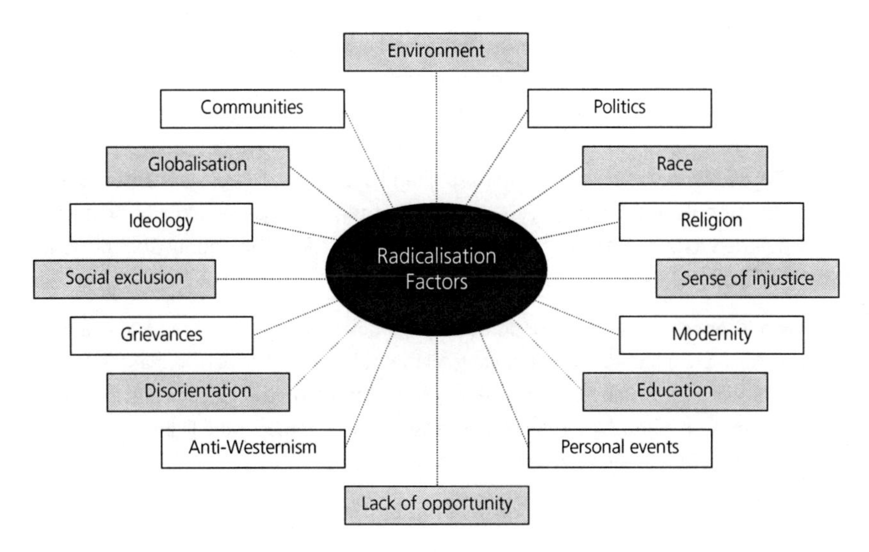

Figure 9.1. Radicalisation factors.

KEY POINT—NO SINGLE RADICALISATION FACTOR PREDOMINATES

The push and pull radicalisation factors shown in Figure 9.1 do not represent a definitive list of all potential drivers, because many factors will influence an individual's radicalisation from his or her specific personal experience and setting. Nor are any of the identified factors conclusive; they are best viewed as considerations for the operational practitioner which may influence the process of radicalisation for any given individual. They do, however, illustrate the range of potential radicalisation factors tempting people towards adopting extremist perspectives but no single radicalisation factor predominates.

The manifestation of individual radicalisation factors may be subtle, resulting in very weak signs and signals of radicalisation development, while other factors may be more visible. Extremists attempting to recruit and indoctrinate individuals from UK communities to the violent jihadist ideology of Al Qa'ida-inspired terrorism will very often, if not always, encourage an often simplistic but virulent anti-Westernism. Fuelling hatred for the West, and in particular for Western foreign policy and interventions overseas, has been shown to be a regular factor contributing to the radicalisation of UK citizens.

Case Study—Foreign Policy Drivers for Radicalisation

Overnight on 9 August 2006, large numbers of police officers were deployed across High Wycombe and Birmingham as part of an operation to disrupt a major terrorist plot. A total of twenty-four terrorist suspects were arrested and questioned in relation to the commission, instigation, and preparation of an alleged transatlantic terrorist attack of 9/11 proportions. The police and Security Service had been monitoring the activities of UK-based Al Qa'ida-inspired terrorists for several years and the executive action taken overnight was the result of the largest operation ever conducted by the Metropolitan Police Service and MI5. A potentially catastrophic terrorist attack had been disrupted, and intelligence and evidence had been painstakingly gathered under Operation OVERT. Then Deputy Commissioner of the Metropolitan Police Service, Paul Stephenson, stated that 'We cannot stress too highly the severity that this plot represented. Put simply this was intended to be mass murder on an unimaginable scale'. The Deputy Commissioner went on to reveal more about the terrorist plot:

> We are confident that we have disrupted a plan by terrorists to cause untold death and destruction and to commit, quite frankly, mass murder. We believe that the terrorists' aim was to smuggle explosives on to aeroplanes in hand luggage and to detonate these in flight. We also believe that the intended targets were flights from the United Kingdom to the United States of America.

In the weeks and months that followed the British public would learn more about the realities of the terrorist plot as the police carried out extensive searches of buildings and vehicles, focusing on a 354-acre wood near High Wycombe. The massive scale of the searches conducted and the resources required to mount this operation presented a significant logistical challenge; more than 200 police officers were on site every day. A variety of different kinds of evidence was gathered including potential bomb-making equipment and chemicals, computers, telephones, and portable storage media such as memory sticks, CDs, and DVDs. As Operation OVERT gathered pace, investigators and prosecutors were soon to identify the drive and motivation behind the terrorist plot.

The covert surveillance activity under Operation OVERT identified three primary terrorist cell members: Abdulla Ahmed Ali, aged 27, the leader of the terrorist cell,

Tanvir Hussain, aged 28, and Assad Sarwar, aged 29, all from High Wycombe. All three men knew each other. Ali was an engineering graduate who chose not to go into industry after leaving City University in London in 2002 but instead had decided to pursue business opportunities in Pakistan. In contrast, Sarwar turned down a place at university in Chichester in Sussex because he became homesick, and his second attempt to study as an undergraduate at Brunel University in Bristol, first with a sports science course, then earth sciences, also failed because he found the work too difficult. Ali and Sarwar were to meet in 2003 when they both went to deliver aid to refugee camps on the Pakistan and Afghanistan border. In the aftermath of 9/11, the US-led military response in the Bush administration's 'war on terror' resulted in coalition forces' ground troops pouring into Afghanistan. As a result many Afghans decided to flee from areas of conflict compounding a decades-old refugee crisis. In support of the worsening situation, the Islamic Medical Association, a charity shop located in Clapton in East London, raised money and collected equipment to send to the refugee camps. Ali and Sarwar were volunteers, distributing aid in what seems to have been a sincere humanitarian endeavour, but their shared experiences at the refugee camps radically altered their world view. Ali, married with a son, was shocked by the appalling conditions in the camps, where he witnessed many people dying. Sarwar would also be dismayed at what he had seen at the camps, later believing that the aid work in which he was engaged was an ineffective way of helping. Both Ali and Sarwar were angered about the situation and decided to tackle what they believed was the root cause of the death and misery they witnessed at the camps—Western foreign policy. Ali and Sarwar turned against the UK and the US and both began to share the kinds of sentiments found in the anti-Western rhetoric of radical Islamism. Ali and Sarwar started to move in Islamist circles which were increasingly calling for attacks on Britain.

When Ali returned from Pakistan in June 2006, the Security Service and anti-terror police were sufficiently interested in him to conduct a covert baggage search of his luggage before it passed through to the arrivals hall at the airport. Inside his luggage they found a powdered soft-drink, and a large number of batteries. The discovery was extremely suspicious and served to attract more attention from MI5. The police and the Security Service needed to identify the purpose of the batteries and the drink bottle because they suspected, while under the influence and instruction of Rashid Rauf, that Ali had made the dangerous transition from Al Qa'ida sympathiser and supporter to Al Qa'ida attack planner. In the coming weeks the Metropolitan Police Service and MI5 mounted Operation OVERT, which later captured Ali sending e-mails to Pakistan. These e-mails were coded messages, thinly veiled communications to his jihadist contact, believed to be Rauf. The e-mails talked about acquiring Calvin Klein aftershave for a business opportunity but instead the plotters were purchasing hydrogen peroxide, a legitimate but potentially lethal component of a home-made explosive. Investigators discovered that the quantities of aftershave referred to in the e-mails bore a striking similarity to the quantities of chemicals being amassed. Mobile surveillance of Sarwar captured him buying household items that could be used to make bombs and MI5 covertly entered the east London flat being used by Ali to install audio- and visual-recording devices. Ali's family had recently purchased the £138,000 two-bedroom flat at 386a Forest Road for cash. MI5 were alarmed by what they saw when they entered the flat as it appeared to be a bomb factory. On 3 August 2006, MI5 recorded Ali and Hussain constructing home-made improvised explosive devices from drink bottles. The covert cameras also captured Hussain drilling a hole in the bottom of a soft-drink bottle in order to replace its contents with concentrated hydrogen peroxide without breaking the seal on the cap. Combined with AA batteries filled with HMTD (hexamethylene triperoxide diamine) and concealed in a disposable camera in hand luggage, the component parts of the bomb were to be assembled mid-flight and detonated over US towns and cities. MI5 found further clues to the transatlantic plot from their intrusive surveillance, recording the conspirators reviewing numbers, talking of '18 or 19'. It was not known whether this meant nineteen devices, targets, or even nineteen co-conspirators. Then mobile surveillance teams observed Ali for over two hours in an internet cafe, researching flight schedules. The disparate jigsaw pieces of extraordinary evidence were finally beginning to reveal a distinct picture. Ali's e-mail traffic continued, and he received the order to go ahead with the project, or 'presentation' as Ali described it. The attack plan had entered a new phase. The plotters now had to find some willing volunteers to join their conspiracy and commit acts of martyrdom on board the transatlantic flights. The tipping point at which executive action would necessitate the arrest of the conspirators was closing in, but events beyond the control of MI5, the police, or government, would dramatically change the carefully planned course of Operation OVERT.

The major covert terrorist investigation mounted against the transatlantic plotters had captured considerable evidence indicating the scale of murder and destruction that they intended to bring about if not stopped. Postponing the arrest of all the suspects called for political courage by the Home Secretary John Reid, and operational leadership by MI5 and the Metropolitan Police. At one critical moment, the Home Secretary told Jonathan Evans, the Director General of the Security Service, that 'If this goes wrong I'm out of a job, you're out of a job, and the government will fall'. Across the Atlantic US Intelligence officials were anxious about the possibility of another Al Qa'ida attack and were concerned that any delay in arresting the plotters may allow time for them to complete their plans. Although unable to determine the timing of arrests in Britain, the Americans brought pressure to bear on the Pakistani authorities to arrest Rashid Rauf. It was extremely important that the arrest of all conspirators, in Pakistan and in the UK, was carefully coordinated so as not to cause a chain of events that would lead to the disclosure that the arrest had been made and the potential escape of the terrorists. Unfortunately, Pakistani authorities decided to arrest Rauf on 9 August 2006 when he was stopped by local police in a taxi in Rawalpindi. The premature arrest brought unwelcomed pressure upon the senior managers leading Operation OVERT. Deputy Assistant Commissioner Peter Clarke stated that:

> We were at a critical point in building our case. If word got out that Rauf had been arrested, evidence might be destroyed or scattered to the four winds. More worrying still was the prospect of a desperate attack.

The arrest phase of Operation OVERT was swiftly brought forward and put into action that same day. When Ali was arrested, found in his possession was a computer memory stick containing details of seven transatlantic flights due to take off from Heathrow Terminal 3 within two and a half hours of each other. For a large part of their combined flight times to cities in the US and Canada, all the aircraft would have been airborne simultaneously. There would have been little chance of surviving the attack which would have brought mass deaths.

As the Operation OVERT post-arrest investigation continued, police recovered a series of videotapes containing 'martyrdom' videos which Sarwar had hidden in his garage. Contained within the videos was the martyrdom recording made by Ali. Wearing a headscarf and a black robe, while jabbing his finger repeatedly at the camera, Ali declared angrily:

> Sheikh Osama warned you many times to leave our land or you will be destroyed, and now the time has come for you to be destroyed and you have nothing but to expect than floods of martyr operations, volcanoes and anger and revenge and raping among your capital and yet, taste that what you have made us taste for a long time and now you have (to) bear the fruits you have sown.

Another recovered pre-recorded martyrdom message showed Hussain in which he warned of further attacks, declaring his regret that he could only be a suicide bomber once. He said:

> For many years, you know, I dreamt of doing this, you know, but I didn't have no chance of doing this. I didn't have any means to do this. You know I only wish I could do this again, you know come back and do this again and just do it again and again until people come to their senses and realise, realise you know, don't mess with the Muslims.

The Crown Prosecution Service, Counter Terrorism Division (CTD), working alongside counter-terrorism police investigators and operatives from the Security Service, prepared the prosecution case for Operation OVERT. Of the twenty-four suspects arrested on 9 August 2006, seventeen were formally charged. Abdulla Ahmed Ali, Assad Sarwar, Tanvir Hussain, Oliver Savant, Arafat Khan, Waheed Zaman, Umar Islam, and Mohammed Gulzar, were charged in connection with the transatlantic plot. The trial began in April 2008 and ran for six months.The three key conspirators, Ali, Sarwar, and Hussain, attempted to convince the jury that the plot had simply been an audacious stunt, intended to direct public attention to a documentary they were making to change opinion on UK foreign policy. They also explained to the court that the suicide videos they had made and stored had been recorded for a documentary they would post on YouTube.

After deliberating for over fifty hours on charges of conspiracy to blow up aircraft, the jury failed to reach a verdict on this specific charge, but they did find Ali, Hussain, and Sarwar guilty of conspiracy to murder. Later, in September 2009, a second trial of the eight men excluding Gulzar but with the addition of Donald Stewart-Whyte, found Ali, Sarwar, and Hussain guilty of the plot. In July 2010, Ibrahim Savant, Arafat Khan, and Waheed Zaman were also found guilty at Woolwich Crown Court in London and sentenced to life in prison for conspiracy to murder. They must serve a minimum of twenty years in prison before being eligible for release. The Home Secretary, Theresa May, welcomed the guilty verdicts and commended the efforts of police, Security Services, and the Crown Prosecution Service in bringing the men to justice. The Home Secretary said: 'I welcome the verdicts in one of the most significant terrorist plots the UK has ever seen. National security is our top priority and this result reflects the continued and serious threat we face'.

KEY POINT—UNINTENDED CONSEQUENCES OF FOREIGN POLICY

Operation OVERT served to show that foreign policy had become a key driver for the radicalisation and recruitment of UK citizens. At that time, Dame Eliza Manningham-Buller, then Director General of the Security Service (MI5), said the radicalisation of teenage Muslims 'from first exposure, to extremism, to active participation in terrorist plotting' was now worryingly rapid, and it was vital that the government rose to the challenge of trying to change the attitudes that 'lead some of our young people to become terrorists'.

Despite the legitimate presence of Western interests, and sometimes military forces, in Muslim countries, this presence is seen by some as an affront and a source of shame. In addition, terrorist recruiters have cited the inconsistency of Western standards in its international behaviour. Conflicts such as Bosnia and Chechnya are highlighted, where Muslims have been the victims of non-Western violence, and it is argued that the Western nations have failed to act quickly or effectively enough to protect them. In particular, this applies to perceptions of relations with Israel and the approach to the Middle East peace process, despite the fact that the UK is actively committed to a two-state solution, with a viable Palestinian state alongside a secure Israel.

POINT TO NOTE—IDENTIFICATION OF RADICALISATION FACTORS

Identifying the factors which may lead to radicalisation, and some of the arguments used to justify it, are important. Setting out these factors does not in any way imply that wider society ought to accept their validity or that resorting to terrorist violence could ever be justified. Nor does it imply that an alienated individual who has become highly radicalised is necessarily a terrorist. Only a small minority of radicalised individuals ever become terrorists.

It is also important to acknowledge that the treatment of individuals at the hands of government agencies, including possible discriminatory and abusive treatment by authorities, can also give rise to extremist behaviour.

9.4 **Models of Radicalisation Processes**

To improve understanding of radicalisation, academics from a number of different disciplines have looked at extremist development processes. Disciplines have included psychology, sociology, and theology as well as security professionals, practitioners, and policy makers. This research has resulted in a number of models and perspectives concerning the radicalisation process.

Table 9.1 shows ten models which are widely recognised as having the most appropriate practical application and interpretation for policing.

Table 9.1 Radicalisation process models

Model	Description
Marc Sageman's four-stage process model (2008)	Radicalisation process progresses in four steps which reinforce each other commencing with the first stage of '*moral outrage*', which is then '*interpreted in a specific way*' by the person during stage two through interactions on online forums. The third stage identifies that radical ideas are '*resonating with own personal experiences*' and are supported by interactions with like-minded people. These groups give the individual and other groups further self-confidence by justifying their ideologies, actions, and beliefs moving to the fourth and final stage of the individual radicalisation by being '*mobilised through a network*'.
Taarnby's eight-stage recruitment process model (2005)	Outlines the structure of a recruitment and radicalisation process in eight stages: 1. Individual alienation and marginalisation 2. A spiritual quest 3. A process of radicalisation 4. Meeting and associating with like-minded people 5. Gradual seclusion and cell formation 6. Acceptance of violence as legitimate political means 7. Connection with a gatekeeper in the know, and finally 8. Becoming operational.

(*continued*)

Table 9.1 Continued

Model	Description
Association of Chief Police Officers (ACPO), Prevent Pyramid model	Radicalisation is described as a gradual change from being part of a broad base of sympathisers to becoming an active terrorist. The gradual change process is divided into four distinct phases of the pyramid as follows: • *Tier 1*—includes all members of the community with a universal approach • *Tier 2*—described as the people who are vulnerable to radicalisation, are not yet committing any violent acts but are providing tacit support requiring a targeted approach • *Tier 3*—described as moving towards extremism requiring an interventionist approach • *Tier 4* —described as actively breaking the law and are active terrorists but relatively few in number requiring a law-enforcement approach.
New York Police Department (NYPD) four-stage radicalisation process model	A four-stage process: • *pre-radicalisation*—a person's life situation before radicalisation creates a vulnerability to radicalisation to 'jihadisation', based on the systematic examination of eleven in-depth case studies of Al Qa'ida-influenced terrorists • *self-identification*—beginning of association with like-minded individuals and adoption of the ideology as their own • *indoctrination*—intensifying of individual's beliefs and finally whole-hearted adoption of the ideology • *'jihadisation'*—the operational phase in which members may carry out acts of violence and terrorist attacks.
Gill's pathway model (2007)	A pathway model for an individual's development across four key stages on their way to becoming a suicide bomber: • *broad socialisation process*—exposure to propaganda which tends towards violence • *catalysts*—catalysts motivate joining an extremist organisation • *pre-existing ties to aid recruitment*—kinship and friendship ties facilitate recruitment phase • *suicide bombers*—internalisation of the group's norms and values.
Wiktorowicz's al-Muhajiroun model (2004)	Focused on the role that social influences play in leading a person to join a radicalised Islamic group. He proposed his model in a four-stage process from cognitive opening to socialisation as follows: • *cognitive opening*—where a person can gain new ideas and world views • *religious seeking*—where a person seeks meaning through a religious framework • *frame alignment*—where the public representation offered by the radical group 'makes sense' to the seeker and attracts their initial interest • *socialisation*—where a person experiences religious instruction that facilitates indoctrination, identity-construction, and value changes.

McCauley and Moskalenko's twelve mechanisms of political radicalisation model (2008)	Identifies twelve 'mechanisms' of political radicalisation. These mechanisms operate across three levels: Individual, Group, and 'The Mass', as follows: *Level 1—Individual*: refers to the role of personal dissatisfaction in the decision to radicalise and includes: 1. personal victimisation 2. political grievance 3. joining a radical group—the slippery slope 4. joining a radical group—the power of love 5. extremity shift in like-minded groups *Level 2—Group*: refers to political grievances based on political events or trends, and includes: 6. extreme cohesion under isolation and threat 7. competition for the same base of support 8. competition with state power 9. within-group competition—fissioning *Level 3—The Mass*: refers to activities such as joining a radical group and starting with small tasks finally leading to violent actions and includes: 10. political activism 11. hatred 12. martyrdom.
Moghaddam's staircase to terrorism model (2007)	Offers a sophisticated 'multi-causal approach' with the aim to understand suicide terrorism by way of metaphor of a staircase housed in a building where everyone lives on the ground floor, but where an increasingly small number of people ascend up the higher floors, and a very few reach the top of the building to carry out a terrorist act. The model comprises three levels, but focuses on the individual (dispositional factors), organisations (situational factors), and the environment (socio-cultural, economic, and political forces). The radicalisation process progresses in six steps illustrated in Figure 9.2.
Davis, Artan, Sageman, and Rijpkema (2009)	A psychological model focusing on the relationship between ideas and behaviours at both the individual and the network level. Their model considers three aspects: 1. radicalisation as changing moral priorities; 2. cognitive dissonance and individual radicalisation; 3. vicarious cognitive dissonance and network radicalisation. The central concept of this model is that cognitive dissonance occurs across networks of individuals observing each other, demonstrating how radicalisation may spread through networks.

(*continued*)

Table 9.1 Continued

Model	Description
European Commission Radicalisation Pyramid (2008)	Provides a six-tiered approach to the radicalisation and recruitment process from pan-European research for the European Commission Directorate-General Justice, Freedom and Security with support from Research, Information and Communications Unit (RICU) Home Office. The six tiers (shown in Figure 9.3) are: • *Tier 1*—ideological experimentation, isolation, disintegration, loss of identity • *Tier 2*—hostility, moral condemnation of Western society, disapproval of Western principles and institutions, isolation from social environment • *Tier 3*—change in outer appearance and/or patterns of behaviour, growing acceptance of violence • *Tier 4*—willingness to use violence • *Tier 5*—readiness to contribute towards violent acts • *Tier 6*—preparation or acts of terror.

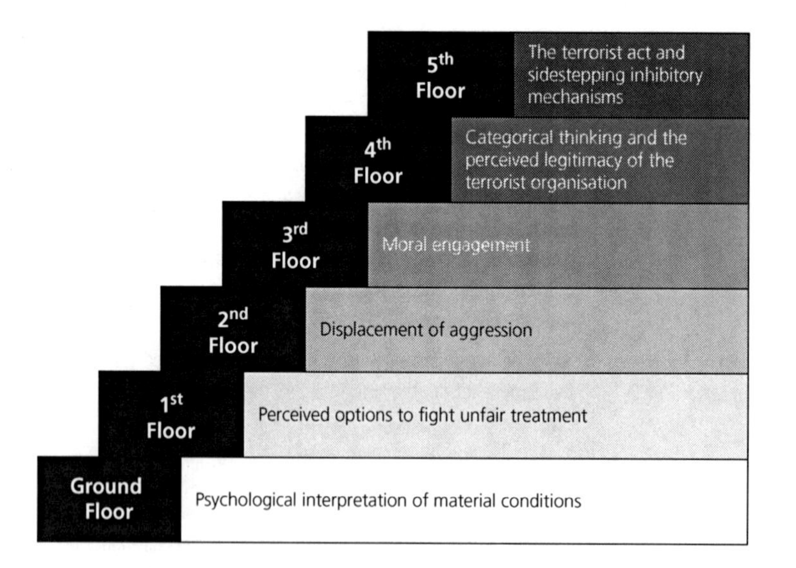

Figure 9.2. The six steps of Moghaddam's staircase to terrorism model.

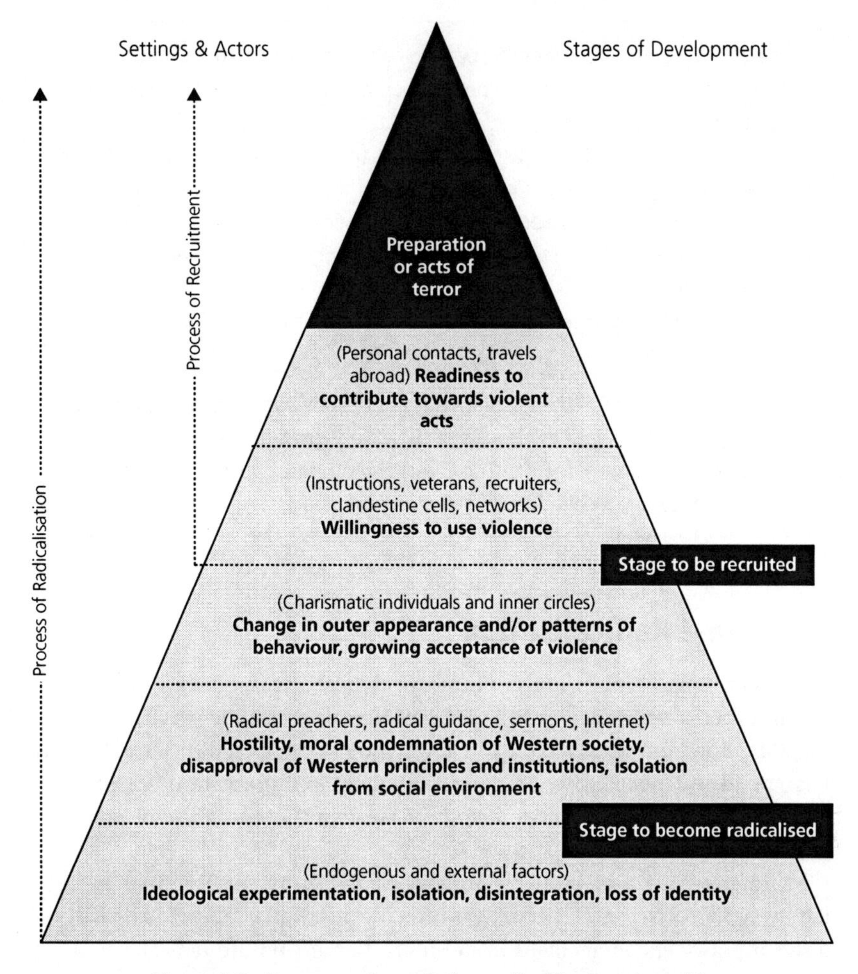

Figure 9.3. European Commission radicalisation pyramid.

KEY POINT—REVIEW OF RADICALISATION FACTOR MODELS

The range of models available help in understanding the complex phenomenon of radicalisation and recruitment process, considered from a broad range of perspectives. Collective understanding of the radicalisation process remains far from perfect. Still, the models do share common traits. For example, there appears to be strong correlation between all models that becoming involved in violent extremism through radicalisation is a process, it does not happen spontaneously. Similarly, the idea that there is a simple psychological profile to describe terrorists has been abandoned. From the review of the chosen models we can draw four lessons which help police practitioners in their understanding of the radicalisation process as follows:

- There is no reliable demographic pattern describing those who become radicalised. Instead, highly developed group bonds seem important precursors to collective radical action.
- A sophisticated ideological basis for radical action is not a necessary precursor of radical action, and violent networks are not distinguishable from the communities they are embedded within by a special sense of moral outrage.
- A formal process of recruitment and 'brainwashing' is not a necessary feature of radicalisation.
- The pathway to violence is typically a gradual one, at both individual and collective levels.

However shared some of the characteristics of the development of a radical may be throughout all of these models, inconsistencies across models also show immense gaps in understanding. Considerably more research is required to identify the factors which influence online radicalisation.

9.5 **Online Radicalisation**

The Internet has changed, and continues to change, the very nature of terrorism. The Internet is well suited to the nature of terrorism and the psyche of the terrorist. It allows the plotter to remain anonymous, or at least difficult to identify. It is a rapid and inexpensive distribution medium for information. And it is very good at attracting new terrorist recruits, very often the young and most vulnerable and impressionable in society.

An ungoverned and probably ungovernable entity, the Internet unfortunately supports 'self-radicalisation'—the radicalisation of individuals without direct input or encouragement from others. Its role in both radicalisation and the recruitment into terrorist organisations is a growing source of concern for security authorities. It lets people connect with like-minded others across the world quickly and easily, and allows them to share their views without censorship.

KEY POINT—LIMITATIONS OF RADICALISATION MODELS

Identifying radicalised individuals is a difficult task. There is still scant research which investigates the psychological profiles of online radicalisers and recruiters, and the models are not yet capable of identifying individuals and their profiles in a comprehensive manner.

All prominent extremist groups have established at least some presence on the Internet. The increasing sophistication and interactivity of extremists online has led to considerable challenges in detecting radical online content, among them the nature of the content, the often ephemeral nature of the content, and the diversity of data formats. The rise of social media has increased the challenge still further, and robust methods are now needed to identify radical online profiles to protect our citizens' use of the Internet.

9.5.1 Tackling online radicalisation

The Home Office has published guidance for those citizens who are responsible for vulnerable individuals and who work within communities to help ensure that the Internet is an environment where terrorist and violent extremist messages can be challenged. As part of their wider efforts to counter the threat of radicalisation on the Internet, a public web page was launched in February 2010 to encourage the public to take action against unacceptable violent extremist websites and other potentially malicious online content. Where individuals believe that material they have located is potentially unlawful they are asked to complete a form on the web page and refer it to the Counter Terrorism Internet Referral Unit (CTIRU), established by ACPO during 2010.

Case Study—Role of the Counter Terrorism Internet Referral Unit

The CTIRU provides a national coordinated response to referrals from the public as well as from government and industry. It also acts as a central, dedicated source of advice for the police service.

The CTIRU provides the UK police service with a unit of experts who can carry out an initial assessment of material located on the Internet. It is also responsible for alerting forces and the units of the UK Police Counter-Terrorism Network to online terrorist offences that may fall within their jurisdiction. Powers under UK terrorism legislation provide for the CTIRU to take a national lead in serving notices on website administrators, web hosting companies, Internet Service Providers (ISPs), and other relevant parties within the UK, to modify or remove any unlawful content.

The CTIRU also focuses on developing and maintaining relationships with the Internet industry, an important part of ensuring the delivery of a safer and more secure online experience for citizens. A further challenge given the global scope of cyberspace for UK law enforcement was the majority of terrorist content online being hosted in other countries outside UK jurisdiction. To counter this challenge the CTIRU continues to forge links with law enforcement counterparts abroad to help target those websites hosted overseas. UK Counter Terrorism and Extremism Liaison Officers (CTELOs) based in countries around the world have a key role in supporting this work. The ACPO national coordinator for Prevent, Assistant Chief Constable John Wright, describes the role of CTIRU as:

providing the opportunity to effectively enforce, and control, access to material believed to be extreme. In addition, the CTIRU will help to develop a culture of collaboration between police, partners and service providers dedicated to making the internet a safer place, particularly for young people.

9.5.2 **Online radicalisation models**

The Internet has become crucial in all phases of the radicalisation process, as it provides conflicted individuals with direct access to unfiltered radical and extremist ideology which drives the aspiring terrorist to view the world through this extremist lens. When combined with widely marketed images of the holy and heroic warrior, the Internet becomes a platform of powerful material communicating terrorist visions of honour, bravery, and sacrifice for what is perceived to be a noble cause.

The prevention of online radicalisation remains an ambitious undertaking. Intelligence and law enforcement agencies across the world have come to learn more about how the process of radicalisation develops, but their collective understanding remains far from perfect. If preventive measures are to have a chance in interdicting at least the most savage excesses of online extremism, countermeasures need to be informed by better definitions of online radicalisation and improved modelling of its causal mechanisms.

Radicalisation-Factor Model

A theory-independent approach to online radicalisation which enables the aggregation of empirical findings into a common framework is provided by the Radicalisation-Factor Model (RFM) created by Akhgar, Bayerl, and Staniforth in 2013, as a result of multidisciplinary research across informatics, research methodologies, and counter-terrorism law enforcement. The RFM provides a framework which allows the integration of known causal factors in online radicalisation. The model considers four interlinked factors as follows:

- **Characteristics of the radicalised individual:** This aspect refers to features of the individual that are linked with a weaker or stronger vulnerability for radicalisation in general or preference for specific ideologies as well as specific patterns of online and radical behaviours. These can include aspects from demographic information to norms, values, or personal experiences.
- **Characteristics of the environment:** This aspect refers to the environment(s) in which not only the individual, but also the ideological groups operate. The environment(s) can be analysed with respect to political, economic, social, technological, and legal characteristics (political system, societal diversity, general level of education, religious observance, internet penetration rate, legal system, etc.).

- **Characteristics of the radical groups and ideologies:** Terrorism comes in many forms based on political, religious fundamentalist, nationalist–separatist, social revolutionary, and extreme right-wing ideologies. Other typologies of terror include state-sponsored terrorism and single-issue terrorism, the latter very often committed by the lone actor or 'lone wolf' terrorist. Identifying the specific genre of terrorism is an important factor in determining the most effective countermeasures to deploy.
- **Characteristics of the technologies related to online radicalisation:** Technologies differ greatly in the extent to which they may lend themselves to online radicalisation or for terroristic behaviours (indicators). Relevant aspects here, for instance, are the degree of anonymity for users, the speed with which information can be sent/accessed, and the number of users to be reached at the same time.

RFM further includes the **usage of technologies by the individual** as well as the **usage of technologies by the ideological group(s)** the individual belongs to or is influenced by. These two aspects consider links between technology (factor 4) and the individual (factor 1) and radical groups (factor 3), respectively. The model thus explicitly addresses the problem of how online behaviour increases or decreases radical behaviour (e.g., radicalising individuals tend to access exclusively networks which adhere to their own ideology which in turn leads to exaggerated views of public support for their own view). Including technology features as well as technology usage patterns, the RFM, shown in Figure 9.4, thus explicitly addresses the context of online radicalisation.

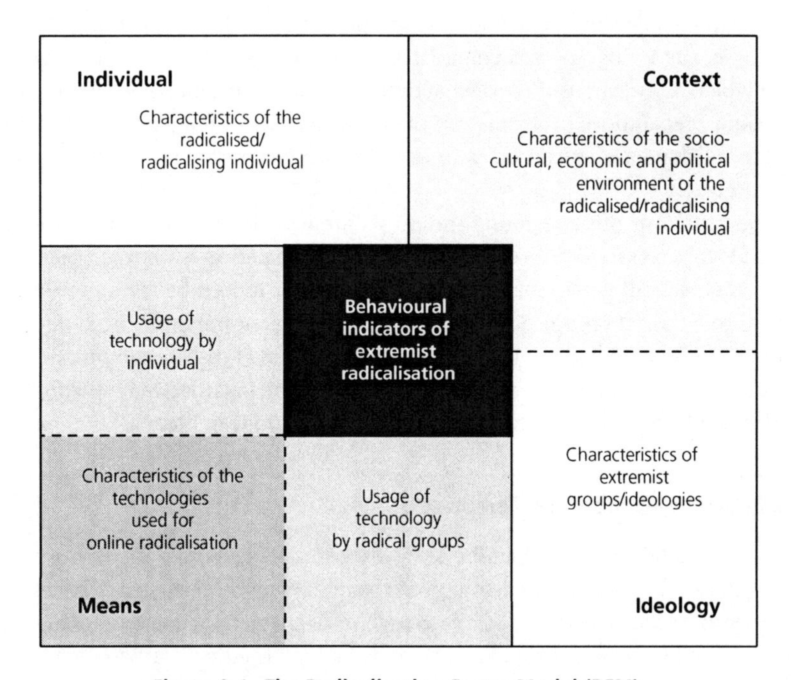

Figure 9.4. The Radicalisation-Factor Model (RFM).

While RFM provides the matrix to outline the causal pathways towards online radicalisation, a second crucial element is to clarify exactly what online radicalisation and radicalism entails. Without a clear definition, it is impossible to unequivocally link influencing factors to online radicalisation. Furthermore, only with a clear view about which behaviours can serve as indicators to radicalisation, is it possible to identify radicalised (or radicalising) individuals. Such conceptual clarity also allows differentiation between those individuals who may pose an actual or acute threat from mere sympathisers. Of course, the transition from sympathiser to active terrorist is not a distinct step. Still, omitting the specification of clear criteria can result in a dangerous blurring of the concept and thus increase the risk of unsystematically expanding the group of targeted individuals (creating the risk of false positives). Moreover, the clear specification of indicators enables the comparison of definitions of online radicalisation as well as comparability of empirical results. Therefore a precise police interpretation of online radicalisation is needed in every application. The RFM proposes three ways of interpreting online radicalisation and extremism as follows:

(a) single behavioural indicators
(b) combinations of behavioural indicators
(c) intensity of one or more behaviours.

By 'behavioural indicators' the RFM refers to the concrete behaviours of a person which indicate that he or she has been radicalised. Some behaviours are very clear and can by themselves indicate radicalisation. Such single indicators are best defined as online behaviours which have crossed the legal threshold; for example, the individual has committed criminal acts of inciting racial hatred and violence, encouraged terrorist activity, or is directly concerned in the commission, preparation, or instigation of acts of terrorism. If a person shows one of these behaviours, it can be assumed with some certainty that radicalisation has occurred.

Combinations of behavioural indicators are less clear; for example, reading radical blogs can stem from different motivations (a person is studying the topic for a high-school paper, may simply be curious, or indeed be trying to obtain access to a radical group). Some behaviours are thus not unambiguous enough to identify unambiguous online radicalisation. In this case, a combination of specific behaviours (i.e. two or more actions occurring together) may still provide a clear indication that radicalisation is taking or has taken place.

Case Study—Schoolboy Terrorist

In June of 2006, Hammad Munshi, a 16-year-old schoolboy from Leeds in the UK was arrested and charged on suspicion of committing terrorism-related offences. He remains the youngest person in Europe to be formally charged and convicted of terrorist offences. Following his arrest, police searches were conducted at his family home where his wallet was recovered from his bedroom. It was found to contain handwritten dimensions of a submachine gun. At the time Munshi had excellent information technology skills; he ran a registered website on which he sold knives and extremist material. He passed on, for example, information on how to make napalm as well as how to make detonators for improvised explosive devices (IEDs). At the time of his arrest Munshi was still a schoolboy and had been directly influenced by being exposed to extremist rhetoric and propaganda on the Internet unbeknown to his family, friends, and wider social network.

While the individual actions by Munshi certainly raise the potential for him to act in extremist ways, the full degree of radicalisation becomes apparent only in their combination. Considering pertinent combinations of behavioural indicators may thus support identification of at-risk individuals at a stage when radicalisation is still at a low level. Taken by itself, online activity may barely leave a trace on authorities' monitoring mechanisms, but in combination with other behavioural and contextual factors it can provide a more comprehensive picture from which authorities can deduce their assessments of potential risk, threat, and harm to society.

In addition to the type of behaviours, the intensity of one or more behaviours can provide important indications for the degree of radicalisation. Intensity refers to how often or how rapidly a certain behaviour occurs. As a simple example, observing a person posting a daily blog or some forum discussion entries may indicate a higher level of radicalisation than a person posting only once a month. While single indicators or indicator combinations consider the qualitative aspects of radicalisation, intensity thus takes into account the quantitative aspects of behaviours.

KEY POINT—A MODEL FOR TACKLING ONLINE RADICALISATION

The primary operational challenge for conducting complex investigations and analysis of online radicalisation is developing a focused strategy. The RFM provides a framework on and parameters within which an online investigation can be methodically advanced, tracked, and monitored. A holistic approach can be taken as practitioners give due consideration to the four linked factors, including the characteristics of the radicalised individual, the environment, the radical groups and ideologies, and the technologies relating to online radicalisation. Working within this framework, counter-terrorism practitioners can identify weak signals, early indicators, and emerging behaviours of individuals on the path towards radicalisation. Early signals can be assessed and prioritised by existing intelligence and law enforcement agency tasking and coordination mechanisms. Appropriate action can then be taken, leading to early preventative interventions, continued monitoring, or executive action.

For the adequate representation of causal mechanisms, the links between the RFM and behavioural indicators is crucial. Starting with a precise definition of online radicalisation the framework looks at influencing factors that are known to affect how an individual is radicalised. In this way, the framework excludes a potentially wasteful approach which has to consider each and every possible cause. Causal variables are exposed, which provide valuable information for further analysis to identify emergent behaviours, trends, and patterns with regard to those being recruited and radicalised online. From this data, new evidenced-based policies and strategies can emerge.

RFM also highlights gaps in collective knowledge and understanding of online radicalisation. Identification of gaps also opens new avenues for research, especially in the psychological and technological domains.

As part of the contemporary counter-terrorism toolkit, the RFM helps to ensure that all in authority are better informed today so that they can tackle the online radicalisation challenges of tomorrow.

9.6 **Social Media Radicalisation**

At 2.20 p.m. on 22 May 2013, Drummer Lee Rigby of the Royal Regiment of Fusiliers was walking outside barracks in Woolwich, south-east London. As he made his way onto Artillery Place, a vehicle swerved from the road onto the pavement and struck him. Two occupants got out of the car and viciously attacked and killed him with a cleaver and a knife. With no prior warning of the ambush, the unarmed Rigby had no chance of defending himself or of making an escape. After the initial attack, his lifeless body was moved to the centre of the road where it was left while the two alleged attackers, Michael Adebowale, aged 22, and Michael Adebolajo, aged 28, engaged in conversation with members of the public as they walked by, encouraging them to look at what had happened. As armed police officers arrived at the scene, the attackers ran towards them brandishing their weapons. Police officers shot and detained the two suspects, arresting them for the murder of the soldier. The horrific and very public death of Drummer Lee Rigby on the streets of London shocked the public. The injuries inflicted upon the victim were so severe that the 25-year-old could only be formally identified by a forensic dentist. His murder showed that the amorphous threat from non-hierarchical terrorist cells of radicalised individuals affiliated to Al Qa'ida was alive and well in the UK.

Citizens who witnessed the killing of Drummer Rigby became evidence gatherers and unaffiliated journalists, reporting images from the scene of the attack to news media and online social networks. They captured the terrorists' justification and motivation for the murder of the British soldier on mobile phones.

Just moments after the attack, a frenzy of social media communications from online users provided commentary about the incident. The attack sparked a great deal of debate online, some of it from violent extremists.

While extremists used the attack to promote their causes and draw attention to their particular grievances, other online users published comments that would have damaging consequences. One online message was posted by Deyka Ayan Hassan, a 21-year-old undergraduate student from Kingston University. Hassan contacted the police after receiving hundreds of Tweets from people threatening to rape and kill her in the aftermath of Drummer Rigby's murder.

At the time of his murder, Drummer Rigby was wearing a T-shirt bearing the logo of a charitable organisation established to support armed forces personnel on their return after active duty. Hassan had posted a message on Twitter which said: 'to be honest, if you wear a Help for Heroes T-shirt you deserve to be beheaded'. The Tweet received a furious backlash from far-right organisations, including threats so severe that Hassan feared for her safety, resulting in her reporting the matter to the police. Appearing at Hendon Magistrates Court in London during June, Hassan was ordered to undertake 250 hours of community service after admitting the charge of sending a malicious electronic message. Magistrate Nigel Orton, Chairman of the Bench, said Hassan could have been jailed by the court for what she had done but the court had accepted her claim that she did not know that it was a soldier who had been killed at the time she had posted the offending Tweet. Mr Orton said:

> The tragic events in Woolwich that day have created a context which made this Tweet appear extreme. It had a huge impact and clearly caused offence and distress. We accept you didn't intend to cause harm and you felt it was a joke. Your act was naive and foolish and without regard to the general public at a time of heightened sensitivity.

KEY POINT—HIJACKING SOCIAL MEDIA

While some online users' comments were not intended to cause offence, evidence from the aftermath of the murder in Woolwich shows that following a terrorist incident, online platforms are swiftly created by extremist groups and individuals in order to espouse their harmful views. The Internet quickly becomes a battleground of views, some extreme, others more moderate, but even the more moderate can be rapidly hijacked by extremists.

9.7 Summary

The tremendous growth in Internet use and mobile connectivity has stimulated widespread security concerns. While the Internet has provided many positive advances in communications, there remain a small number of individuals who seek to destroy our democratic values by harnessing its power to advance extremist causes. Innovative approaches are needed to identify and prevent online radicalisation.

The use of cyberspace to disseminate radical materials and messages has become the predominant method used by extremists to recruit and radicalise individuals, and this is only increasing. Global efforts are being made to monitor and disrupt contemporary cyber avenues of terrorist recruitment. Individuals, particularly young computer-literate males, are becoming self-radicalised through access to sophisticated online materials promoting and justifying extreme views and actions. The identification of these self-radicalised individuals is very difficult indeed.

To prevent contemporary terrorism and to successfully tackle the underlying causes of radicalisation, police officers, the extended police family, and their partners are required to gain a greater understanding of the psychological perspectives of violent extremists and the societal influences which drive them towards developing extremist perspectives. Police officers must recognise that the process of radicalisation is incremental, and that the decision to become a terrorist can be months or years in the making. The key challenge for police officers is how to identify those at risk of radicalisation. Many people fit broad profiles of potential terrorists; they are in the right age group and gender categories, the right social demographics, they are exposed to an environment with a lot of the factors pushing and pulling people towards extremism. Yet only a handful actually adopt extremist perspectives and even fewer continue to become terrorists. Considerably less than 1 per cent of those who visit an extremist website will eventually go on to commit serious crime. These issues present the police service with significant challenges: how to prevent people from adopting extremist perspectives without labelling them, isolating them, or without the authorities distancing themselves from the very communities with whom they wish to engage, and who otherwise could help to prevent pockets of extremism from developing. Effectively tackling the phenomenon of radicalisation remains the greatest contemporary counter-terrorism policing challenge.

Further reading

- Augustus, G, and Clarence, C, *Understanding Terrorism: Challenges, Perspectives, and Issues* (London: SAGE Publications, 2012).
- Bongar, B, Brown, L, and Beutler, L, *Psychology of Terrorism* (Oxford: Oxford University Press, 2006).
- Burke, J, *Al-Qaeda: The True Story of Radical Islam* (London: Penguin, 2007).
- Burke, J, *On the Road to Kandahar: Travels through Conflict in the Islamic World* (London: Penguin, 2007).
- Burke, J, *The 9/11 Wars* (London: Penguin, 2012).
- Coolsaet, R, *Jihadi Terrorism and the Radicalisation Challenge* 2nd edition (London: Ashgate, 2011).

- Crenshaw, M, *Explaining Terrorism: Causes, Processes and Consequences* (Oxford: Routledge, 2010).
- Daniel Silk, P, Spalek, B, and O'Rawe, M, *Preventing Ideological Violence: Communities, Police and Case Studies of 'Success'—International Law, Crime, and Politics* (London: Palgrave Macmillan, 2013).
- Davies, L, *Educating Against Extremism* (London: Trentham Books, 2008).
- HM Government, *A Strong Britain in an Age of Uncertainty: The National Security Strategy* (2010).
- HM Government, *Countering International Terrorism—The United Kingdom's Strategy CONTEST* (2011).
- HM Government, *Prevent Strategy* (2011).
- Silke, A, *Psychology of Counter-Terrorism* (Oxford: Routledge, 2010).
- Spalek, B, *Counter-Terrorism: Community-Based Approaches to Preventing Terror Crime* (London: Palgrave Macmillan, 2012).
- The Centre for Social Cohesion, *Radical Islam on UK Campuses—A Comprehensive List of Extremist Speakers at UK Universities* (2010).

10

Neighbourhood Policing

10.1	Introduction	207
10.2	Evolution of Neighbourhood Policing	208
10.3	Implementing Neighbourhood Policing	209
10.4	Defining 'Neighbourhood' and 'Community'	212
10.5	Neighbourhood Policing Principles	212
10.6	Neighbourhood Policing Works	226
10.7	Neighbourhood Policing Plus	228
10.8	Summary	234

10.1 Introduction

The purpose of this chapter is to introduce all police officers, Police Community Support Officers, and special constables to the growing importance of Neighbourhood Policing in preventing terrorism and violent extremism. Police officers and the wider police family at all levels must understand the full extent to which Neighbourhood Policing can contribute towards national counter-terrorism efforts. The discovery of the home-grown terrorist has meant that the pursuit of terrorists must draw on the information and goodwill of communities from which aberrant extremists come. A major shift towards harnessing the capacity of the public to support the broader counter-terrorism effort has been an important development in the history of UK counter-terrorism practice. The counter-terrorism continuum, the unbroken thread of intelligence that links the neighbourhood to the nation, remains the critical spinal cord of the UK counter-terrorism architecture. The lesson of Al Qai'da-inspired international terrorism is that issues which give rise to low-level crime and the development of violent extremism leading to terrorism begin at the local level. Thus, national security increasingly depends upon neighbourhood security, and good intelligence to prevent terrorism at its source has come to the fore.

While Neighbourhood Policing has been integral to police practice for over a decade, many officers do not fully understand nor appreciate the scale and scope of Neighbourhood Policing and how it has served to reduce crime and the fear of crime significantly. It is essential that all members of the police family understand the philosophy, delivery mechanisms, and key characteristics of Neighbourhood Policing in operation today if they are to contribute towards the prevention of terrorism and violent extremism. At its simplest level, police interaction with the public through Neighbourhood Policing informs communities about the risk from terrorism and reminds the public to remain vigilant. But individual and collective efforts of a professional and positive Neighbourhood Policing Team (NPT), whose members are both informed of the terrorist threats in their locality and conduct their duties with a focus on counter-terrorism efforts, can directly prevent terrorism.

This chapter describes the early development of Neighbourhood Policing and provides a context from which it emerged as the preferred policing system in the UK. This is followed by a clear explanation of Neighbourhood Policing and its guiding principles of community engagement, collaborative problem-solving, partnerships, and its intelligence-led ethos, all of which provide a framework in which effective Neighbourhood Policing can be delivered. One should remember that terrorists already live and work here in the UK. The police force's responsibility is to identify these people and stop them recruiting and radicalising others.

10.2 Evolution of Neighbourhood Policing

The rise of Neighbourhood Policing in the latter half of the twentieth century can be explained in terms of the wider crisis of legitimacy and effectiveness facing the police service in the UK. There are three interrelated points to be made here. First, during the 1990s, questions were raised about whether the criminal justice system was effective in controlling, stopping, and successfully prosecuting crime. Second, in the same period social science studies of policing were directly calling into question the effectiveness of valued extant police strategies, from visible patrol to rapid response times. A particular concern was the attempt to 'professionalise' policing via an emphasis on fast, responsive, 'fire-brigade' models of policing, away from familiar bobbies walking the beat. Police would now increasingly meet the members of the communities they served only at flashpoints rather than on regular patrol. Neighbourhood Policing thus began to appear far more effective as a means of maintaining low-key contact with the public, a way of improving police legitimacy and public relations.

Communities have never been completely homogenous, and the police have long had very different relations with different constituencies in their community. Following the Second World War, communities have become much less homogenous, more individualist and fragmented along socio-economic lines, race and ethnicity, sexuality, political and ethical values and interests.

Neighbourhood Policing is sometimes hailed as a return to more 'traditional' policing, either of the 'golden age' of the 1950s, or of the style of preventive policing envisaged by the architects of the modern police in the nineteenth century. The level of proactive community engagement envisaged in much contemporary Neighbourhood Policing goes beyond what Robert Peel had in mind. The claim that Neighbourhood Policing is simply a return to 'traditional' policing can be worrisome as it rings of nostalgia, with scant evidence that the past was in fact any better than now. However, the claim that Neighbourhood Policing marks a return to more 'traditional' forms of policing is worthy of some consideration as the role of the police officer can be seen as 'peace officer', drawing authority and capacity for social control from the wider web of informal and communal controls in the communities with which they are enmeshed.

KEY POINTS—RESPONDING TO CRISIS

Neighbourhood Policing has shown its significant worth over the last thirty years as a response to specific crisis events. The race riots which erupted across several cities in England during the early 1980s, most infamously those in Brixton and Toxteth in London, and the subsequent inquiry into the causes of those riots by Lord Scarman highlighted the importance of Neighbourhood Policing as they showed quite clearly the effect of a lack of continuing and direct positive engagement between the police and the public.

10.3 Implementing Neighbourhood Policing

The implementation of Neighbourhood Policing was a significant undertaking for the government, the police service, and their partners. The introduction of Police Community Support Officers (PCSOs) during 2002 laid the foundations for visible police reform, pleasing to the public who had long called for a greater presence of the police within their communities in order to address their concerns about crime and anti-social behaviour (ASB). Neighbourhood Policing was initially piloted at ward level as part of the National Reassurance Policing Programme (NRPP) between October 2003 and March 2005. It was framed as 'reassurance policing', which reflected concerns that public anxieties about crime were continuing to rise, or were remaining static, despite the fact that crime rates started to fall in the 1990s. This approach helped to develop and inform the development of NRPP.

International evidence indicated that Neighbourhood Policing's prospects for success were promising in terms of reducing crime and improving public perceptions, particularly when it involved both the public's participation in setting priorities and problem solving. Both were considered critical elements of the programme to introduce Neighbourhood Policing across England and Wales. Early research, however, highlighted the challenges associated with implementing Neighbourhood Policing, suggesting that change required long-term commitment.

The NRPP ran pilots of Neighbourhood Policing in sixteen wards, in eight forces in England, from October 2003 under relatively controlled conditions. Wards were considered to be a convenient geographic unit for the trial because of the availability of administrative data, although the delivery of Neighbourhood Policing was structured at a more local level in some sites. Each site contained between about 7,000 and 20,000 residents. The impact of piloting Neighbourhood Policing at a ward level was assessed in two related studies. The studies provided good evidence of Neighbourhood Policing's efficacy in both the short and longer term, where focused police activity and relatively small-scale organisational change could be achieved. An evaluation of the programme showed that the NRPP delivered, after twelve months, increased public confidence in the police, reduced the numbers of victims of crime, and improved feelings of safety, public perceptions of community engagement, police visibility, and familiarity with the police. The three delivery mechanisms (see next paragraph) were associated with improvements in public confidence. Following the pilot, a three-year Neighbourhood Policing Programme (NPP) was officially launched in April 2005 by which every neighbourhood in England and Wales would have a Neighbourhood Policing Team (NPT) by 2008.

In both the NRPP and NPP, the purpose of Neighbourhood Policing activity was to trigger three delivery mechanisms: high visibility of police foot patrols; community involvement in identifying local priorities; and collaborative problem solving with partners and the public to tackle those priorities (see Figure 10.1).

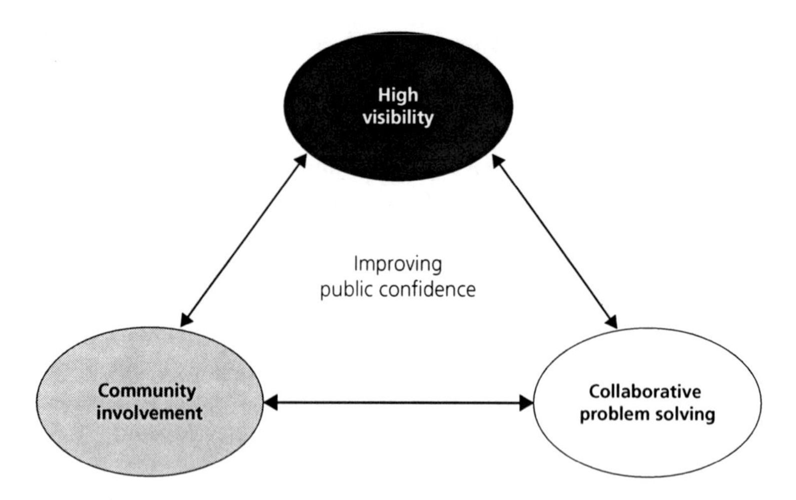

Figure 10.1. Delivery mechanisms of Neighbourhood Policing.

KEY POINTS—IMPROVING PUBLIC CONFIDENCE

When piloted at a local level, Neighbourhood Policing was found to have a significant positive impact on a wide range of measures, including supporting victims of crime, perceptions of anti-social behaviour, and public confidence in the police. Subsequent research found that the vast majority of these improvements were sustained in the longer term. Importantly, the three delivery mechanisms—high visibility foot patrol, community involvement, and problem solving—were all found to be critical in improving the public's confidence in the police.

The early success of Neighbourhood Policing fuelled a range of swift changes to local policing. During 2007 over 16,000 PCSOs had been recruited and were undergoing training to join the ranks of local NPTs. By 2008, there were 3,600 NPTs across England and Wales, comprising 13,500 police officers. The concept of Neighbourhood Policing was also introduced to Scotland at that time, referred to there as 'Community Policing', but the approach and improvement in public confidence and police performance had similar positive outcomes. During 2009 the Neighbourhood Policing approach concentrated on 'citizen focus', made manifest in a national 'Policing Pledge' which was driven by central government and which sought to put communities at the heart of policing and public safety. Further developments were made by the introduction of Neighbourhood Managers in 2010, who were dedicated to the delivery of local community-focused policing through increased emphasis upon partnerships and joint working.

The change of government in 2010 did little to alter the successful development of Neighbourhood Policing. Following the delivery of a safe and secure London 2012 Olympic and Paralympic games, the Metropolitan Police amplified the reach of NPTs, integrating criminal investigators to tackle low-level community-based crimes. The introduction of locally elected Police and Crime Commissioners in 2012 served to strengthen the commitment to Neighbourhood Policing. Despite severe cuts to police budgets from consecutive Comprehensive Spending Reviews, Police and Crime Commissioners and their Chief Constables remained committed to resourcing NPTs. As new five-year Police and Crime Plans were published by elected PCCs during April of 2013, many stated a determination to preserve Neighbourhood Policing; in reality, their Chief Constables were having to work extremely hard behind the scenes to maintain this strategy by recruiting additional Special Constables and volunteers into NPTs. Numbers of fully warranted police constables and sergeants were falling, and not being replaced due to recruitment freezes in the light of reduced government spending targets. To plug the gap left by fewer police officer numbers, and to amplify the role and engagement of wider public services, local police partners, and the communities themselves, police forces are increasingly adopting a 'safer communities' approach to Neighbourhood Policing which recognises that the police force is just one among numerous bodies who have a responsibility and vested interest in keeping citizens and their communities safe.

More than a decade since its creation and integration, Neighbourhood Policing remains the preferred policing model in the UK. A timeline of key developments in Neighbourhood Policing is shown in Figure 10.2. As the police service continues its major transformation, with a renewed focus on collaboration and partnerships, the maintenance and support of Neighbourhood Policing continues to help make communities safe.

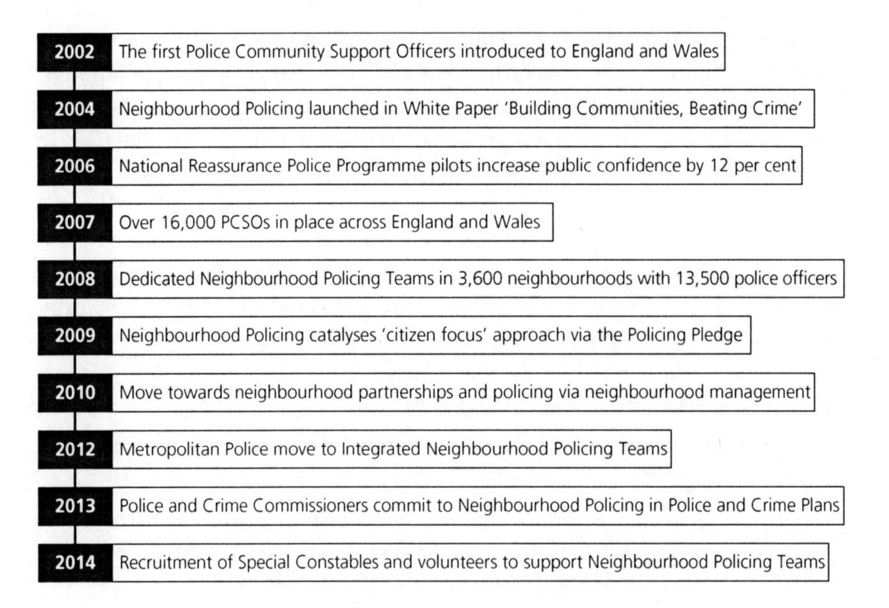

2002
The first Police Community Support Officers introduced to England and Wales
2004
Neighbourhood Policing launched in White Paper 'Building Communities, Beating Crime'
2006
National Reassurance Police Programme pilots increase public confidence by 12 per cent
2007
Over 16,000 PCSOs in place across England and Wales
2008
Dedicated Neighbourhood Policing Teams in 3,600 neighbourhoods with 13,500 police officers
2009
Neighbourhood Policing catalyses 'citizen focus' approach via the Policing Pledge
2010
Move towards neighbourhood partnerships and policing via neighbourhood management
2012
Metropolitan Police move to Integrated Neighbourhood Policing Teams
2013
Police and Crime Commissioners commit to Neighbourhood Policing in Police and Crime Plans
2014
Recruitment of Special Constables and volunteers to support Neighbourhood Policing Teams

Figure 10.2. Neighbourhood policing timeline.

10.4 Defining 'Neighbourhood' and 'Community'

The sense of community, of belonging to a defined geographical location or self-identified social, religious, or ethnic group, and the importance of security, order, and well-being within that community, are fundamental to human well-being. During the early development of Neighbourhood Policing, 'neighbourhood' and 'community' were terms used almost interchangeably but for purposes of clarity, and for operational interpretation and delivery, they are defined as follows:

- **Neighbourhood**—the people resident within a distinct geographical location with recognised physical boundaries;
- **Community**—a group of people united by a shared common interest, cause, faith, or purpose.

Understanding the difference between 'neighbourhood' and 'community' is important for the effective delivery of policing. A 'neighbourhood' for an inner-city resident is very different from someone living in a rural area. For the former, a neighbourhood may include a number of streets, a specific estate, or group of estates. For those living in the countryside, a neighbourhood might be a whole village, group of villages, or parish. A 'community', by contrast, is much less well defined. There may be many individual communities living within a single neighbourhood who share a common interest, purpose, or faith.

10.5 Neighbourhood Policing Principles

The concept of Neighbourhood Policing has proved to be popular and widely used, characterised as the 'new orthodoxy' and 'preferred policing style' amongst senior police officials and leaders all around the world. Neighbourhood Policing has long been recognised as an ambiguous term, one that has become used in very general ways (referring to almost anything that could feasibly have a bearing on police–public relations) as to be largely meaningless. Recognising this, the Association of Chief Police Officers (ACPO) articulated 'Ten Principles of Neighbourhood Policing' in 2006 to clarify what Neighbourhood Policing entailed, as well as to achieve consistency of delivery across England and Wales. These principles are shown in Table 10.1

Table 10.1 Ten Neighbourhood Policing Principles

	Ten Neighbourhood Policing Principles
Principle 1	Neighbourhood Policing is an *organisational strategy* that allows the police, its partners, and the public to work closely together to solve problems of crime and disorder, and improve neighbourhood conditions of security.

Principle 2	Neighbourhood Policing is a mainstream policing activity and integrated with other policing services.
Principle 3	Neighbourhood Policing requires evidence-based deployment of Neighbourhood Policing Teams against identified needs.
Principle 4	Neighbourhood Policing establishes dedicated, identifiable, accessible, knowledgeable, and responsive neighbourhood policing teams which provide all citizens with a named point of access.
Principle 5	Neighbourhood Policing reflects local conditions and is flexible, responsive, and adaptable.
Principle 6	Neighbourhood Policing allows the police service to work directly with the local community to identify the problems that are most important to them, thereby giving people direct influence over local policing priorities.
Principle 7	Neighbourhood Policing establishes a regime for engaging other agencies and the public in problem-solving mechanisms.
Principle 8	Neighbourhood Policing uses the National Intelligence Model as the basis for deployment.
Principle 9	Neighbourhood Policing requires effective engagement, communication and feedback strategies, and a clear explanation of where accountability lies.
Principle 10	Neighbourhood Policing should be subject to rigorous performance management, including clear performance monitoring against a local plan, and commitments made to neighbourhoods.

KEY POINT—FRAMEWORK FOR DELIVERY

The creation of the Ten Principles has served to provide the police service with a framework within which to establish and deliver Neighbourhood Policing. Defining the principles by which a neighbourhood is policed means that inspection and assessment of any Neighbourhood Policing activity can be made against a national standard within general parameters set by the principles. It also provides a base on which good practice in local policing can be identified and shared nationally with all other forces, ensuring that communities across the country can directly benefit from the experiences and lessons learned from each other.

10.5.1 Principle 1: Organisational Strategy

Neighbourhood Policing is an organisational strategy which allows the police, partners, and the public to work together to solve problems of crime and disorder, and improve neighbourhood conditions and security. Neighbourhood Policing is not a set of specific projects; rather, it involves changing decision-making processes and creating a specific culture within police departments. It is an organisational strategy that leaves setting priorities and the means of achieving them largely to residents and the very police who serve in their neighbourhoods. In this regard, Neighbourhood Policing should be viewed as a process rather than a product.

The key elements of a Neighbourhood Policing organisational strategy are 'police, partners, and the public'. To be effective Neighbourhood Policing must be based on partnerships, engaging with communities to identify what local problems are, and then seeking ways in which problems can be tackled and resolved.

KEY POINT—LOCAL COUNTER-TERRORISM STRATEGIES

To ensure that the prevention of terrorism and violent extremism starts at a local community level, elements of counter-terrorist activity must form part of Neighbourhood Policing's organisational strategies. With advice, guidance, and support from specialist counter-terrorism police units, every Neighbourhood Policing strategy must address how to tackle and respond to terrorist activity, terrorist events, or incidents, and it must include measures to address the prevention, emergence, and propagation of extremist perspectives and behaviours. These local plans should show direct links to the wider operational strategies of each police force and the associated Police and Crime plans, which in turn demonstrate commitment and determination to serving the national counter-terrorism interest made manifest by the Strategic Policing Requirements and the government's CONTEST Strategy. Ensuring that such plans address the prevention of terrorism at a local level strengthens the counter-terrorism continuum, from local to national level.

10.5.2 Principle 2: Mainstream Policing Activity

Neighbourhood Policing is mainstream policing activity and must be fully integrated with other policing services, especially counter-terrorism efforts. Experience has shown that a visible policing presence, combined with a focus on signs of crime and disorder, drives crime down and means that the demands for a police presence may diminish over time, as it tends to have a deterrent effect for as long as it is visible. Regular police patrols of Vulnerable Sites and Sectors (VSS) and Economic Key Points (EKPs), such as electricity substations, waterways, military and government installations, landing fields, small ports, and crowded public places, provide an important deterrent against terrorist efforts.

KEY POINT—PERMANENT PRESENCE OF PREVENT

Disorder and crime will return to a neighbourhood if it is believed by offenders that the police presence is token, half-hearted, or intermittent. This is as true for terrorist activity as it is for anti-social behaviour, vehicle crime, or burglary. A continued police presence reinforces the presence of law and order within a community. It is far better if the first time the police and community engage together to tackle terrorism and violent extremism is not in the immediate aftermath of a terrorist event or counter-terrorism police operation being conducted in their locality. Nor ideally should it be following the identification of a suspected terrorist who has been recruited and radicalised from their community. Counter-terrorism preventive policing must be integrated into Neighbourhood Policing from the very start, and it is an activity which requires a permanent presence and continued maintenance.

10.5.3 **Principle 3: Evidence-based Deployment**

Neighbourhood Policing requires evidence-based deployment of NPTs against clearly identified needs. The principle of evidence-based deployment is intended to guide the effective management of scarce resources and aid the prioritisation in instances where not all needs can be met immediately. It is the purpose of the National Intelligence Model (NIM) business process to help the identification, assessment, prioritisation, and management of crime and community safety issues. Continuous and detailed assessment of a community and neighbourhood is required. From a counter-terrorism perspective, all NPTs have access to appropriately sanitised information from their local Special Branch or counter-terrorism units. This information is provided within Counter-Terrorism Local Profiles (CTLPs) which paint a rich picture of each community, and are designed to support Neighbourhood Policing efforts to prevent terrorism and violent extremism in their locality.

10.5.4 **Principle 4: Dedicated Teams**

Neighbourhood Policing must establish dedicated, identifiable, accessible, informed, and responsive NPTs which provide all citizens with a named point of access. This explicit insistence on identifiable NPTs which are dedicated to the neighbourhood is fundamental to the effective deployment of NPTs. Officer distractions to meet competing priorities disrupt the composition and membership of policing teams. All evidence shows that citizens are reassured when they can deal with the same member of an NPT, whose name is known to them and who works on other police business only rarely and when there is overriding operational urgency to do so.

Prevention and reduction

The role of the dedicated NPT is as much about crime prevention and crime reduction as it is about investigating and responding to crime in a given location. This preventive ethos mirrors the approach of preventing terrorism and violent extremism but crime prevention has never been particularly attractive to career police officers, despite its importance. The primary function of the police remains the prevention of crime, the protection of life and property, and preservation of the Queen's peace. Unfortunately, peace-keeping in local communities is less headline-grabbing than audacious acts, whether serious crimes or the capture of criminals. As a result, it is a constant challenge to develop new ways of promoting prevention to officers as well as to their partners and the communities they serve. Anyone involved in Neighbourhood Policing will be expected to support both crime reduction and crime prevention very positively, and this includes the prevention of terrorism and violent extremism.

Neighbourhood Policing Teams

The actual size of a dedicated NPT will depend largely on the neighbourhood to be policed. The NPT shall have responsibility for a neighbourhood that is a geographically designated area which may contain numerous communities. The police do not operationally deploy their resources and assets according to people's lifestyles or culture. Present police organisational architecture and resource deployment continues to be primarily structured around geographical boundaries. There are many local variations of NPTs across the UK, but in essence most are resourced from the following:

- Police officers
- Special Constables
- Police Community Support Officers
- Local Authority staff
- Voluntary organisations
- Police Support Volunteers

Some police forces have larger numbers of Special Constables and PCSOs on their NPT than fully warranted police constables. Some forces will have many volunteer organisations to draw on, while others will not. Some forces may have invested heavily in local partnerships including wardens and parks officials. Some NPTs may be staffed completely by warranted police constables working in shifts led by a police sergeant while other forces may keep sworn officers to a minimum, using constables as local beat managers. Whatever the composition of an NPT, all members are expected to be strongly committed to keeping their neighbourhood safe.

A typical NPT is led by a police sergeant who also has the responsibility of interacting with police colleagues from the borough or division in which the

NPT is located, as well as engaging with the local Tasking and Coordinating Group, the rest of the police force, and liaising with neighbourhood partners. The NPT sergeant is the main link between the NPT and other parts of their police service as well as other agencies, representatives, and community stakeholders. The range of qualities and skills which this role demands is extensive and is pivotal in motivating and encouraging the NPT to be alert to terrorist activity in their locality.

KEY POINT—MOVE TOWARDS INTEGRATED NEIGHBOURHOOD POLICING TEAMS

Recent developments in Neighbourhood Policing have seen the introduction of further specialist resources to support NPTs and extend their mission. The Metropolitan Police Service introduced Integrated Neighbourhood Policing Teams (INPTs) to communities across London during the autumn of 2012. The INPTs, regarded as 'Neighbourhood Policing Plus', comprise personnel of a typical NPT but also include detectives, forensic officers, and other policing specialists operating under the leadership of a police inspector. Expanding the reach of the NPT, the new INPTs teams investigate lower-level neighbourhood crimes, such as thefts, criminal damage, and anti-social behaviour. They proactively target offenders, engage with the public, and work with communities and partners to address problems. The development of new teams must now also include Community Engagement Field Officers (CEFOs) and Prevent police officers who specialise in, are focused on, and dedicated to the prevention of terrorism and violent extremism.

10.5.5 **Principle 5: Locally Dependent**

Neighbourhood Policing must reflect local conditions and must be flexible, responsive, and adaptable. Meeting the fifth principle of Neighbourhood Policing requires constant review and maintenance of individual NPTs because local conditions vary greatly, resulting in there being no definitive prescription for an NPT. Over time, the deployment configurations of established NPTs should change not only to reflect the changes in the community they serve but also to tackle new and emerging challenges. If working effectively, NPTs should not be confronted by any strategic surprises, the very reason why the prevention of terrorism and violent extremism ought to be integrated at a local level from the outset. Sound judgement and initiative are required by police officers and senior management, together with creative and sustained efforts to reach out to sections of the community who may be assessed as 'hard to reach' or 'hard to hear'. These kinds of groups may be hostile to the police or frightened, suspicious, or intimidated by the police, so finding new and innovative ways in which to reach out to them is vital in order to capture and respond to their specific concerns.

10.5.6 **Principle 6: Public Priorities**

The sixth principle of Neighbourhood Policing serves to ensure that the police service works directly with the local community, to identify the problems that are most important to its members, thereby giving people direct influence over local policing priorities. Historically, the police took decisions on how to deal with crime on the basis that they were the experts in this particular field. However, policing is no longer something which is 'done to' people, but is now 'done with' people. The concerns of the public must influence and modify the police approach and should determine local law and order priorities. The introduction of democratically elected Police and Crime Commissioners across England and Wales, alongside the office of the Mayor of London for the Metropolitan Police Service, is increasingly putting the public centre-stage in law enforcement.

To 'work directly' with local communities in identifying problems entails mechanisms that enable local people to air their concerns. In addition, the police and their partners must regularly feed back information on progress about issues of concern, allowing priorities to be reviewed at regular intervals, and for the police to be held accountable for their response to concerns of the community. Capturing community concerns, responding to them, and reporting back is a continual cycle that is integral to the success of Neighbourhood Policing (see Figure 10.3).

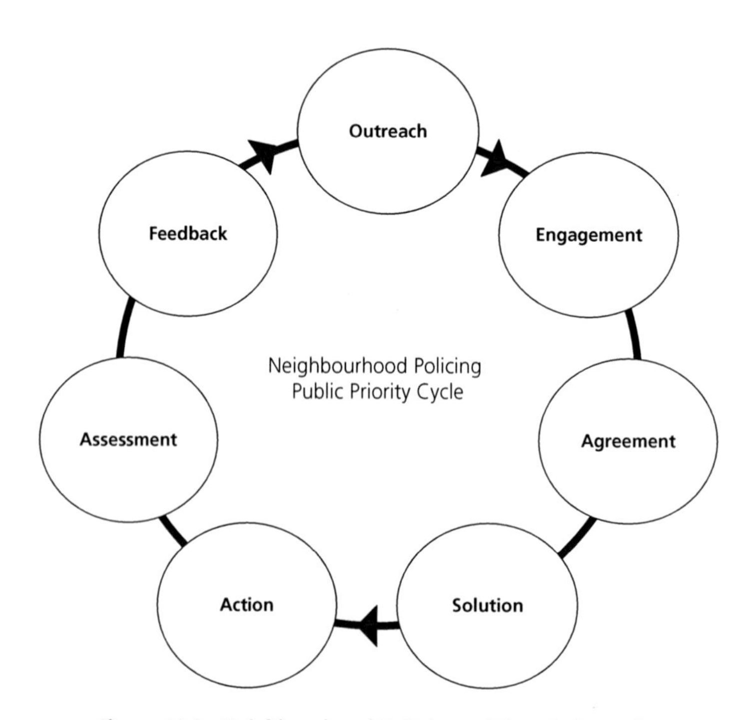

Figure 10.3. Neighbourhood Policing public priority cycle.

10.5.7 **Principle 7: Collaborative Problem Solving**

The seventh principle of Neighbourhood Policing seeks to establish a regime for engaging with other agencies and the public in problem-solving mechanisms. The intention is to develop shared activities in order to identify what a problem is, and how and when it occurs. Solutions may be proposed from any party to the collaboration or consultation, and considerations discussed should include terms of practicality, effectiveness, and cost. What emerges as the best option to deal with the problem is then prioritised and implemented over time, reviewed, and assessed. This approach is essentially a joint process between the police, their partners, and the public, with no one party dominating.

KEY POINT—PARTNERS AND COMMUNITIES TOGETHER

The collaboration between police and the public in the attempt to solve the community's problems is called Police and Communities Together (PACT). Not all police forces have adopted PACT per se but they all have a version of the PACT approach which seeks to engage with communities to listen to their concerns and make positive steps to address them. The aim is to obtain the widest spectrum of participants as possible. One of the inherent problems in Neighbourhood Policing is ensuring that those who attend do genuinely represent all strands of the community. This is an ambitious undertaking, and one which is rarely achieved given the diversity of most inhabitants of any given place in the UK today, but this should not dampen any effort to meet this goal. Unfortunately, all too often, PACT comprises only certain types of members of the community, and the group therefore is not genuinely representative of the whole community. Gatherings are also often dominated by the same, regular attendees who may proclaim themselves representative of their community but who merely represent their own personal or political interests in furtherance of their own agenda. The key is to ensure firm, fair, and neutral chairing and facilitation of such meetings following an agreed agenda so everyone present has an equal opportunity to raise and discuss issues. Inclusivity, not exclusivity, must be the foundation upon which NPTs conduct PACT meetings, and these meetings should also result in defined outcomes and allocated actions which genuinely address public concerns.

While PACT meetings play an important role in solving community problems, sometimes public meetings can be counterproductive. Not all members of the community can attend public meetings all of the time, nor do all citizens enjoy public debate in the presence of authorities. Public meetings may also be inappropriate places in which citizens can raise and discuss sensitive issues, especially those related to terrorism and violent extremism, thus alternative and innovative methods to capture and address the concerns of the community must be available. Such methods may include:

- postal survey
- online survey
- open days
- street briefings
- focus groups
- house-to-house calls
- mobile pop-up police stations
- drop-in surgeries
- online surgeries
- social media forums
- online web forums.

To engage with a broad cross-section of communities, Neighbourhood Policing must seek a variety of ways in which to capture their concerns. As more members of the public are putting more of their lives online, and the Internet and social media are used as primary means of communication, the police force must have a permanent, sustainable, and appropriate online presence to meet the needs of the communities it serves. Evidence from numerous recent research programmes assessing the success of Neighbourhood Policing shows that partnership working for residents and partners has positive outcomes for both parties. Table 10.2 provides a summary of key findings from residents and partners serving to illustrate the positive outcomes of collaborative working.

Table 10.2 Positive outcomes of collaborative working

Benefits of collaborative working for local residents	Benefits of collaborative working for partners
Increased empowerment: Residents who are more directly involved in service delivery in their communities tend to feel that the process of working with local partners increases their sense of empowerment.	**Improved efficiencies:** Partner agencies believe that joint neighbourhood policing and neighbourhood management approaches have the potential to result in more efficient delivery of services.
Perceived reductions in crime and anti-social behaviour: Residents attributed perceptions of reduced crime and anti-social behaviour to the feedback they received in meetings with partners on the actions taken to address local priorities. This in turn led to increased feelings of confidence in partners.	**More effective problem solving:** When issues are dealt with collaboratively by more than one agency, partner representatives and residents feel they are resolved more effectively. Residents therefore felt that joint problem solving increased their confidence in partners' ability to deal with their problems. As a result of their increased confidence they were more likely to engage further with partner organisations by reporting problems and providing information.

Improved perceptions of safety:
Local residents observe an improved perception of safety when increased visibility and accessibility of partners, particularly neighbourhood patrols. Other benefits were attributed to improved perceptions of safety.

Personal fulfilment:
Representatives from partner agencies have an increased sense of personal fulfilment when they see results being achieved in their areas. This was enhanced when partners developed strong and productive personal working relationships which enabled greater communication through organisational barriers.

Key Individual Networks

A Key Individual Network (KIN) is a list of contact details of anyone who may be able to help resolve community problems. Normally held by individual members of an NPT, it is critical that these individual lists are recorded, centralised, and shared with the wider NPT. Contacts ought to be shared between members and passed on to new members arriving on the NPT. A KIN provides a valuable tool, serving to build a rich picture of the cooperative elements within a community. While the contact details of senior community leaders and executives may be helpful to an NPT during a time of crisis, the KIN's more practical use is for contacts who actually perform roles in and on behalf of the locality and who can act as a credible voice in that community. An NPT should ensure that each KIN includes a broad range of contacts from faith leaders, local councillors, landlords, shop owners, and the local and regional media, as well as tradespeople who may be needed to secure a dwelling or repair vandalism. While the majority of contacts within a KIN are primarily of use for tackling lower-level crime and anti-social behaviour, they can also support counter-terrorist activity and each NPT, after consulting their Counter Terrorism Local Profile (CTLP), should seek ways in which to extend their networks to tackle the threats and risks in their community from terrorism and violent extremism. A number of police forces have formalised and extended their use of KINs to Key Individual Networks Extended List (KINEL) to ensure they capture a wide spectrum of contacts who can assist and support the police, their partners, and the public with solving community problems.

KEY POINT—COLLABORATION IN COUNTER-TERRORISM

The prevention of terrorism and violent extremism cannot be tackled by the police or intelligence agencies alone. Collaboration in counter-terrorism at a local level with partners, key stakeholders, and the public is integral in ensuring all communities are safe and feel safer from those individuals and groups who seek to propagate extremism designed to damage and divide neighbourhoods. Every effort must be made by NPTs, closely supported by Prevent-focused counter-terrorism officers and Community Engagement Field Officers, to forge new and long-term partnerships and alliances to tackle problems together. All the evidence indicates that when the public, partners, and the police work as a team, positive outcomes for all are achieved. Focusing on the expansion of neighbourhood networks and investing time and energy to strengthen existing KINs and KINELs is vital in preventing contemporary terrorism. A determined approach will yield positive results for tackling the home-grown terrorist threat, especially the recruitment and radicalisation of young and vulnerable members of our communities to violent extremist causes.

Problem-Orientated Policing

The application of problem-solving theory in policing is known as Problem-Orientated Policing (POP). There are a number of models to support POP in practice but all are based on the premise that the police should be concerned with order, safety, security, and with a neighbourhood's well-being, and that this should include taking action on matters of social concern, rather than merely enforcing the law. There are four distinct stages in problem solving at a local community level:

- Stage 1: defining and researching what the problem is;
- Stage 2: exploring opportunities to resolve the problem;
- Stage 3: gathering reliable information to support solutions;
- Stage 4: developing community support through partners.

POP is a process, and the necessary steps to be taken ensure that a given problem is as amenable to resolution as possible. The process first involves distinguishing causes from symptoms. A useful model to identify underlying causes of any problem is the Scanning, Analysis, Response, and Assessment (SARA) model shown in Figure 10.4.

The SARA analytical methodology offers a staged process for identification, understanding, and resolution of specific problems through scanning, analysis, response, and assessment. The four-stage process is used by a number of police forces to provide a framework to guide them through the challenges of finding solutions to community problems. It is an approach that works well for the prevention of terrorism and violent extremism. Of course, in reality, no theoretical model can cover all potential issues when attempting to work with numerous partners to identify a solution to resolve complex issues. Stages of the SARA cycle may overlap, repeat themselves, and some can remain undeveloped while others move to completion. Simple attempts to define the problem where radicalisation is concerned may not necessarily lead to clarity, and scoping the problem can become an activity in its own right. Police officers do not progress methodically around the four stages of the SARA cycle each and every time. They may use some

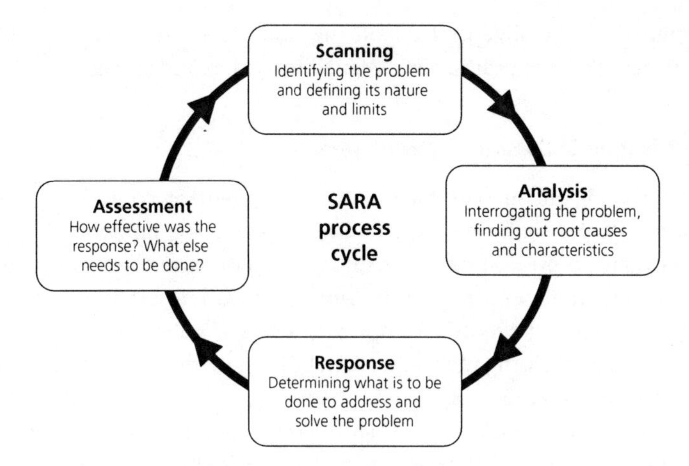

Figure 10.4. The SARA process cycle.

stages and not others, or cut across to use them in different orders, but the SARA cycle provides a methodical approach on which to frame problem-solving activity. Officers charged with the responsibility of policing neighbourhoods following a major terrorist event would be well advised to adopt the model which provides confidence and clarity to their problem-solving decision-making processes.

KEY POINT—LISTENING TO THE COMMUNITY

Neighbourhood Policing Teams might wish to use the SARA model to focus attention on the nature of the problem, rather than as some sort of template for action. Listening to the community may already hold the seeds of a solution which then merely requires coordination to be effective. The NPT role in bringing partners and the public together may be all that is required to reveal the solution to an apparently intractable problem.

10.5.8 **Principle 8: Intelligence-led Deployment**

The eighth principle of Neighbourhood Policing ensures it uses the National Intelligence Model (NIM) process as a basis for deployment. Neighbourhood Policing must be driven by information that has been rigorously analysed and by the disciplines of multi-agency tasking and coordination at appropriate levels which the business approach of the NIM provides. For intelligence-based Neighbourhood Policing to be effective there must be the systematic accruing of data about the locality, from demography to incident logs, from structured Environments Visual Aids (EVAs) to source targeting. To ensure Neighbourhood Policing has an intelligence-led approach, NPTs should digest and implement their Counter Terrorism Local Profiles (CTLPs) which are provided by information from Special Branch and counter-terrorism police units. The NIM and CTLPs are designed for intelligence-led policing and are the mechanisms through which issues can be appropriately assigned for action and resolution.

10.5.9 **Principle 9: Community Engagement**

Neighbourhood Policing must have effective engagement, communication, and feedback strategies, with clear explanations of where accountability lies. This is a vital element in preventing terrorism and violent extremism at a local level, serving to build resilient communities who reject extremist rhetoric and recover quickly from terrorist events. An increased sense of public safety and security helps towards minimising the fear, vulnerability, and insecurity which terrorists seek to instil in communities.

As a concept, 'community engagement' is wide-ranging and involves engaging at an individual or at a group level, and includes residents in decisions that affect them and the areas in which they live. The engagement is a two-way process and the police must listen to the concerns of the community. Police officers know all too well that it is very often the very people in communities who are assessed as either 'hard to reach' or 'hard to hear' who are the ones who require the most support. Articulate, well-resourced, and fully integrated citizens have fewer challenges when attempting to engage with the local police about their specific concerns compared with others less fortunate. These individuals and groups are very often minority communities who may be disadvantaged, discriminated against, demonised, or somehow uninvolved with and detached from society. While these are merely indicative examples, every police force area will include individual citizens or groups who do not normally engage in open dialogue with the police. Every effort must be made by local policing to reach out and engage with individuals, groups, and communities who can support and inform local countermeasures and interventions.

The Association of Chief Police Officers (ACPO) specifies that 'police and partners have a responsibility to engage with communities, their concerns, and their identified priorities'. To engage effectively with the community requires a citizen-focused approach which bridges the gap between what the public wants and what the police can deliver. The shift towards citizen-focused policing is not just an internal police management issue, nor is it merely a public relations issue; it is fundamentally about organisational culture which underpins the ethos of Neighbourhood Policing. The police need to involve the community in decision-making to increase their own accountability and legitimacy. The contemporary citizen is no longer a passive observer of policing, but has become a 'consumer' and 'customer' of the 'policing product' and therefore will not tolerate not being consulted. Citizen-focused policing means that the police must reflect the needs and expectations of individuals and local communities. The objectives of citizen-focused policing are to improve public confidence, to increase satisfaction of police service users, and to increase public involvement in policing. It is not a new area of business or a stand-alone project. It must be embedded through everything the police do and the way it is done, including the prevention of terrorism and violent extremism through Neighbourhood Policing.

One of the most important concepts within Neighbourhood Policing for the prevention of terrorism and violent extremism at a local level is that it is not divorced or separated from other policing or public sector activities. Neighbourhood Policing exists in symbiosis with community engagement and citizen focus to effectively deliver counter-terrorism policing, as Figure 10.5 illustrates.

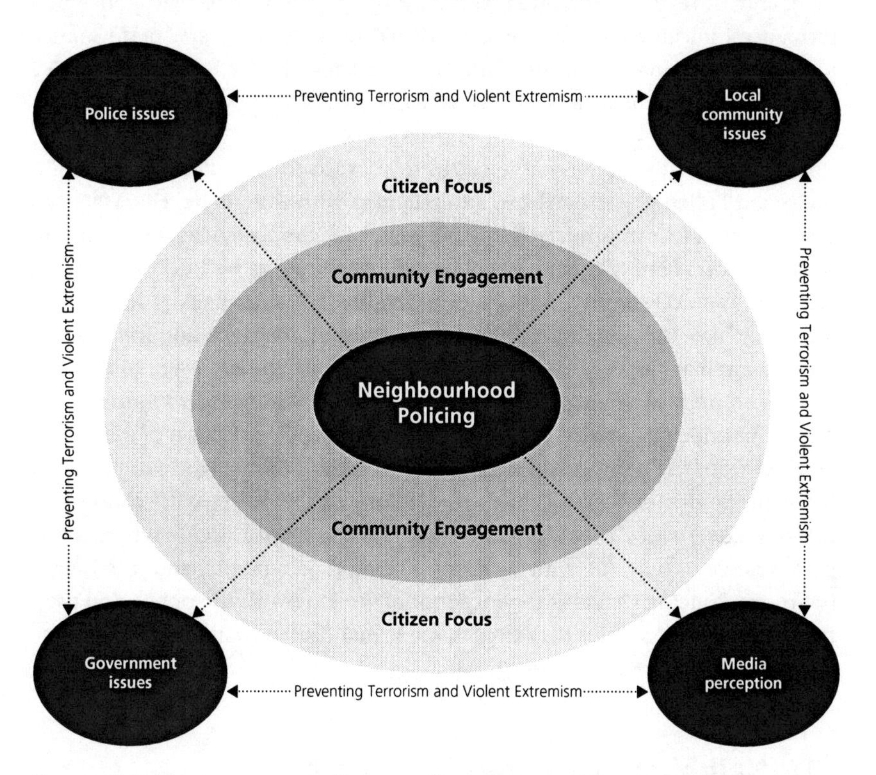

Figure 10.5. The components of community engagement for preventing terrorism and violent extremism.

KEY POINT—SOPHISTICATED COMMUNICATIONS

To reinforce the message of safety and security, the police and partners have to engage in marketing, public relations, and communicating messages with considerable expertise, sensitivity, and sophistication. For the effective delivery of policing terrorism and violent extremism, every effort must be made to engage with individuals, groups, and communities who can support and inform local counter-terrorism preventative measures and interventions. Community engagement strategies concerning terrorism and violent extremism must be embedded into the very culture of day-to-day Neighbourhood Policing.

10.5.10 Principle 10: Performance Management

The final principle of Neighbourhood Policing states that it should be subject to rigorous performance management, including clear monitoring against a local plan and commitments made to neighbourhoods. The police service, driven by central government, has a relentless pursuit of performance so it is little surprise that Neighbourhood Policing should not escape internal and independent review, audit and scrutiny. While the culture of rigid police performance-indicator regimes has diminished over recent years, performance measurement remains an important tool for senior police leaders and Police and Crime Commissioners to assess what works and what needs further thought.

Police forces are regularly assessed in relation to their dedication to Neighbourhood Policing, partnerships, and relations with the public. Her Majesty's Inspectorate of Constabulary (HMIC) assesses factors which relate directly to Neighbourhood Policing such as anti-social behaviour, as well as customer satisfaction and accessibility. Actions of individual NPT members at local street level now have the potential to affect their division, borough, and force assessments as well as their credibility with its citizens, with attendant publicity and media comment. Any negative performance which damages community confidence in policing remains critical to the election and re-election of PCCs, and by extension, the continued employment of Chief Officers who fail to match the expectations of the PCC and the electorate they serve. With changes in policing governance it is ultimately the public who will decide whether the performance of each force meets their policing requirements, and it is Neighbourhood Policing that is at the forefront of working with the public and partners to deliver the service they expect, made manifest in individual force Police and Crime Plans.

10.6 Neighbourhood Policing Works

There is strong evidence from government and independent research that Neighbourhood Policing continues to provide positive results throughout the United Kingdom. There is little doubt that a local, visible, and accessible police presence has contributed towards the continued reduction of crime in the UK. Specifically, five areas of Neighbourhood Policing have been identified as offering primary positive outcomes:

- increased public satisfaction with the police;
- decreased fear of crime;
- reductions in levels of crime and anti-social behaviour or disorder;
- increased community engagement, increasing public 'ownership' of local crime problems, and willingness to play a role in problem solving;
- changing police officers' levels of engagement and satisfaction with the job.

Evidence to support the five positive outcomes of Neighbourhood Policing, summarised from numerous government and independent research and reports over recent years, are outlined in Table 10.3.

Table 10.3 Evidence to support the positive outcomes of Neighbourhood Policing

Increased public satisfaction with the police.	Research studies vary in their findings as to the level of increase in public satisfaction driven by Neighbourhood Policing, from modest improvements to significant gains, but all provide evidence of a positive impact and improvement. There is data to support the contention that it is a visible police presence rather than the quality of resident–police interaction that drives satisfaction with the police and confidence in officer effectiveness.
Decreased fear of crime.	Reductions in the fear of crime, and increases in feelings of safety, range in the evaluation data of research studies from the impressive to the patchy, but all provide evidence of a decreasing fear of crime. As well as reducing fear of crime through directly lowering crime and disorder rates, and attending to quality-of-life issues, there is evidence that Neighbourhood Policing may reduce fear of crime simply through its 'reassuring' presence. While knowledge of the police's local Neighbourhood Policing efforts has been found to be associated with lower fear of crime, often the majority of residents do not know enough about the implementation of Neighbourhood Policing in their locality to benefit from this reassurance.
Reductions in levels of crime and anti-social behaviour or disorder.	Neighbourhood Policing has been seen to reduce both crime and disorder, although there is stronger evidence for its effectiveness in reducing disorder than crime. The positive results in relation to the reduction of disorder have been suggested to be related to two strands of the Neighbourhood Policing approach, in particular: high-visibility foot patrol and collaborative problem solving.
Increased community engagement, increasing public 'ownership' of local crime problems and willingness to play a role in problem solving.	Implementing a variety of strategies to encourage citizen participation in the processes of Neighbourhood Policing has been seen to be more effective than relying only on one method of engagement, for example public meetings. Although programmes have been found to have achieved positive results in relation to public confidence in the police, feelings of safety, problem solving, and police visibility, they have tended to have little effect on calls for service or 'social capacity'; i.e. willingness of neighbours to intervene, or increased voluntary activity.
Changing police officers' levels of engagement with and satisfaction with the job.	There is a wide range of possible beneficial effects of Neighbourhood Policing on police attitudes. In the right implementation context, confidence in and support for Neighbourhood Policing practices can be high among community officers.

KEY POINT—UNINTENDED CONSEQUENCES

In the increasingly complex and multicultural communities of the UK, no single approach to delivering public safety and security through policing can possibly prove successful for everyone all of the time. While Neighbourhood Policing continues to develop, providing positive outcomes for the public and the police, it has, quite naturally, resulted in a series of unintended consequences:

- The apparent popularity of high-visibility policing with members of the public may sometimes stigmatise an area as being a high-crime neighbourhood and therefore dangerous or otherwise unappealing.
- There is a risk that Neighbourhood Policing can become a vehicle for the practical implementation of local punitive attitudes against marginalised or minority groups. Neighbourhood Policing can become problematic if it moves away from a genuine problem-solving ethos through simply appeasing public appetites for enforcement that may function as unduly exclusionary.
- The supposition that freeing up officers' time to allow them to patrol communities will somehow automatically translate into more 'on the ground' community-level problem solving seems to be optimistic, without explicit coordination of community officers' time around Neighbourhood Policing methods and a detailed understanding of what these methods can deliver.

Acknowledging the potential for unintended consequences for the police, their partners, and the public, provides a way in which to positively and pro-actively manage and mitigate any risks that may serve to harm the successful delivery of Neighbourhood Policing. All of these identified consequences can be guarded against, provided that regular reviews of Neighbourhood Policing practices are conducted, and any issues raised are addressed accordingly.

10.7 **Neighbourhood Policing Plus**

The continued success of Neighbourhood Policing provides strong evidence that a team of police officers, visible, accessible, and most importantly, familiar within the community, is the fundamental building-block for all policing. This model of policing also includes the protection of the public from those individuals and groups who seek to divide and destroy communities through acts of violent extremism.

It is now well established that the police, partners, and the public can tackle terrorism together far more effectively than they can alone. The nature of the contemporary terrorist threat demands a collaborative approach to problem solving, an approach which is at the very heart of the Neighbourhood Policing ethos.

Preventing terrorism and violent extremism through community-based police action is best regarded as 'Neighbourhood Policing Plus'. All that is required for existing Neighbourhood Policing machinery to contribute towards countering terrorism is the increased knowledge, awareness, and understanding of all NPTs of the terrorist profile of their locality so that they are better placed to inform the public and conduct their everyday duties through the lens of counter-terrorism.

The new generation of police officers should know that counter-terrorism has not simply been added to the police curriculum since the tragic events of 7 July 2005 in London. Countering terrorism has always been part of the police officer's role but the diverse range, complexity and suicidal component of contemporary terrorism demands a more highly focused response from all those in the force, including Neighbourhood Policing. This intensified response must be achieved through localised sharing of information and intelligence between specialist counter-terrorism units, their Prevent delivery teams, NPTs, and the wider police estate and family. Specialist counter-terrorism units must play their full part in supporting front-line counterparts through internal and open dialogue. Accurate, accessible, and appropriately sanitised information, creatively disseminated via briefings, training, seminars, workshops, and exercises, in which the police, partners, and the public can actively contribute, are all ways in which NPTs can help to identify suspicious behaviours and activities, providing them with a greater opportunity to identify the early signs and indicators of radicalisation emerging from the communities they protect.

KEY POINT—CONTINUED ENGAGEMENT IS KEY

Engagement with all communities at a local level remains the key to building capacity to challenge and resist violent extremism which leads to terrorism, and is also the optimal way of gaining valuable community intelligence which serves to inform the policing response to terrorism at all levels. At its simplest, regular police interaction with the public through Neighbourhood Policing reassures communities about the risk from terrorism and reminds the public to remain vigilant. Through positive, open, and informative dialogue with the public, NPTs can encourage and support people to come forward with information to help keep their own neighbourhood safe. They can also relay messages to reassure communities following police operations and terrorist events.

10.7.1 Suspicious sightings

One of the most important role police officers and members of the public can conduct in support of countering terrorism is to report suspicious activity. The police service is now asking the public to trust their instincts and pass on information which could help stop terrorists in their tracks. Members of the public may unknowingly have information which could prove to be a crucial piece of the investigative jigsaw. To achieve this, however, police officers must be in a position to provide practical guidance and support to members of the public displaying knowledge and understanding of terrorist-related activity. Police officers need to be aware of what the public should be alert to and what type of activity or incident should be reported. This will require officers to have an in-depth knowledge of their local force's intelligence requirements for countering terrorism. Police officers also need to develop a sense of what information is a priority which requires an initial assessment of its potential importance, and what force protocols are in place to report such information locally.

Police officers need to encourage the public to be aware of what is happening around them and to think about anything or anybody that has struck them as unusual in their day-to-day lives. Police officers also need to ask members of the public to think carefully about anyone they know whose behaviour has changed suddenly. What has changed? Could it be significant? What about the people they associate with? Have they noticed activity where they live which is not the norm? The checklist below highlights key issues for practitioners to assess whether suspicious activity could be linked to terrorist activity.

Checklist—If You Suspect It, Report It

- Terrorists need transport—If you work in commercial vehicle hire or sales, has any rental made you suspicious?
- Terrorists use multiple identities—Do you know someone with documents using different names for no obvious reason?
- Terrorists need communication—Anonymous, pay-as-you-go, and smart phones are typical. Have you seen someone using more than one mobile phone, or with large quantities of mobile phones, that has made you suspicious?
- Terrorists need information—Observation and surveillance help terrorist attacks. Have you seen anyone taking pictures of security arrangements?
- Terrorists use chemicals—Do you know of someone buying large or unusual quantities of chemicals for no obvious reason?
- Terrorists use protective equipment—Handling chemicals is dangerous. Maybe you have seen goggles or masks dumped somewhere?
- Terrorists need funding—Cheque and credit-card fraud are ways terrorists generate cash. Have you seen any suspicious transactions?
- Terrorists use computers—Do you know someone who visits terrorist-related websites?
- Terrorists need to travel—Meetings, training, and planning can take place anywhere. Do you know someone who travels but is vague about where they are going?
- Terrorists need storage—Lock-ups, garages, and sheds can all be used to store equipment. Are you suspicious of anyone renting a commercial property?

POINT TO NOTE—TRUST YOUR INSTINCTS

If you suspect that any of the activity described in the Checklist is taking place, or have received reports from partners or members of the public about such activity, think about terrorist tactics, trust your instincts, and report it. In an emergency which is believed as presenting an immediate threat such as a person observed acting suspiciously, or a vehicle, unattended package or bag which might pose an imminent danger, then the **999** emergency services telephone number should be used by members of the public at all times. There should be no delay in responding to such a perceived threat. The confidential anti-terrorism hotline number, **0800 789 321**, which is staffed around the clock by specialist counter-terrorism police officers and staff, provides an additional service and is waiting to receive information. As an alternative to speaking directly to police officers or staff an online form is also available to complete which can be located at <http://www.met.police.uk/so/athotline>.

Police officers must be aware that the anti-terrorism hotline service is available for members of the public to report terrorism-related information confidentially. Members of the public may be concerned and have reservations about contacting the police, either because their friends or family may find out, or their suspicions may prove to have innocent explanations, but police officers must reassure the public that all calls and information received by the anti-terrorism hotline number are treated in the strictest of confidence. All information received is thoroughly researched and investigated before any police action is taken. No one should be complacent. Everyone has a responsibility to remain vigilant. Anyone who has any concerns about possible terrorist-related activity should contact the police through the Anti-Terrorist Hotline.

10.7.2 **Contact management**

Within policing, and especially in cases of issues related to terrorism, one of the key points from which all actions and perceptions derive is the initial contact between the public and the police. This first contact is critical for the delivery of counter-terrorism policing at a local level. Whether this contact is by calling the police via telephone or meeting a police officer in person, for the member of the public initiating the interaction and coming forward, it is a crucial time. The member of the public contacting the police, implicitly or explicitly asks himself three questions:

- Will my concern be taken seriously?
- Will I receive the service I expect?
- Will I get satisfaction from what has occurred?

If this initial contact is handled well, then the subsequent actions are based on a good foundation. To prevent terrorism and violent extremism emerging from communities the police require the full support of the public, so when members of the public have the courage to come forward to report and discuss sensitive issues, police officers must have due regard to managing this contact positively. Counter-terrorism contact management must be a priority not just for Neighbourhood Policing but for all of policing. Figure 10.6 provides a model for the delivery of effective counter-terrorism contact management, ensuring that reports from the public are appropriately prioritised, taken seriously, and the member of the public is kept informed and is satisfied with the police response.

Figure 10.6. Effective counter-terrorism contact management.

KEY POINT—COMPLACENCY IN COUNTER-TERRORISM

All police officers must understand that first impressions really do count. The courteous, professional, and positive contact with members of the public and partners is important for all policing activities, including the prevention of terrorism and violent extremism. Above all else, matters reported to the police regarding terrorism and violent extremism must be taken seriously. There is no room for complacency when it comes to counter-terrorist initiatives. When dealing with reports concerning terrorism or violent extremism, all officers must **LISTEN** to members of the public:

Listen to citizens and take their concerns seriously
Inspire confidence and provide reassurance
Support with information, advice, and guidance
Take ownership and record citizen concerns
Explain what will be done and why
Notify supervision and report concerns to counter-terrorism specialists

10.7.3 **Investment in Neighbourhood Policing**

The continued development of Neighbourhood Policing is vital for the effective delivery of counter-terrorism policing. More than a decade since its first introduction as the preferred policing model in the UK, Neighbourhood Policing requires constant review and investment to ensure it maintains its relevance and effectiveness in delivering safer communities from new and emerging terrorist threats. Investing in Neighbourhood Policing and extending its reach will yield positive outcomes for the police, partners, and the public. Putting Neighbourhood Policing at the centre of policing activity is an approach embraced by the Metropolitan Police.

Case Study—Local Policing in London

The communities in London received an extra 2,000 officers in Neighbourhood Policing Teams in the autumn of 2012 following the London 2012 Olympic and Paralympic Games. This investment in Neighbourhood Policing was part of the Metropolitan Police Service's total war on crime and part of their renewed approach for total victim care.

The new proposals formed part of a major investment programme in Neighbourhood Policing which has seen a new set of promises of how the Metropolitan Police serve and protect the communities of London. The programme ensures that each ward keeps their dedicated officers and PCSOs in local policing teams, who now operate under a new 'local policing model' being part of newly formed Integrated Neighbourhood Policing Teams (INPTs). The new INPTs comprise uniformed officers, detectives, forensic and other officers under the leadership of a police inspector.

These teams now investigate 'lower-level' neighbourhood crimes, such as thefts, criminal damage, and anti-social behaviour. They proactively target offenders, engage with the public, and work with communities and partners to address problems. The INPTs agree on a number of promises with local communities, such as patrolling certain areas at certain times, or visiting every secondary school and every place of worship in the area at least once a month.

More complex and serious investigations have remained the responsibility of Criminal Investigation Departments (CID), who prioritise the pursuit and disruption of harmful criminals and gang members, as well as supporting vulnerable people, such as victims of hate crime or domestic violence.

Putting the public first has meant changing shift patterns so more officers are on duty at key times, such as late at night and at weekends, and they have been used in a more intelligence-led way in the areas where crime is taking or could take place. And, in a renewed focus on victim care, any person who suffers a crime, whether a stolen bicycle or serious assault, is offered a visit by police.

The staffing level of an additional 2,000 officers has been achieved through transferring officers from back-room and non-operational roles, and from merging existing squads, while senior management costs are being reduced to ensure that there are as many constables out in communities as possible. This investment in Neighbourhood Policing to Neighbourhood Policing Plus sees the introduction of war-room-style 'Grip and Pace' centres where senior officers will have daily conferences with key staff, armed with the latest intelligence and data to coordinate police activities, and ensure all the right resources are being used in the right places at the right times.

Announcing the changes at a meeting of Metropolitan Police borough commanders on Monday 19 March 2012, Assistant Commissioner Simon Byrne, head of Territorial Policing said:

> Neighbourhood Policing will be the foundation of our total war on crime and our total care for victims. Our refreshed approach to local policing will see us being more visible to the public, more flexible in how we use our resources, and more focused on meeting the needs of victims and people affected by crime. Our new policing model will see a number of firm commitments to the public.
>
> We will increase visibility in neighbourhoods by putting significantly more uniformed officers where the public want to see them. We will operate with greater pace, flexibility and momentum, while leadership will be more visible and more intrusive. We will seize every opportunity to cut crime, tackle offending and support victims. And we will speak to and listen to people, and respond to their concerns.
>
> Last year we announced changes to the number of sergeants on Safer Neighbourhood teams to make the supervisory ratios more in line with other police forces. Our new model now increases the number of police officers in local communities at a time when the Metropolitan Police is facing budget challenges so this step is a clear statement of our commitment to local policing.

10.8 **Summary**

When Neighbourhood Policing was first introduced in England and Wales, many senior police leaders and experts publicly dismissed the idea, arguing that providing reassurance and focusing on the public's crime priorities would not cut crime or improve public confidence. Some added that the policy was conceived by people who had no real knowledge about the front line. Now that it has helped to sustain record reductions in crime and is held up as a beacon of best practice around the world, the Neighbourhood Policing model is fiercely protected and promoted by senior officers, ACPO, the Home Office, and all major political parties. It is, perhaps, the best example of a successful innovation in British policing. The journey from conception to world-renowned innovation (in policing circles, at least) was not an easy one, made harder by institutional resistance to change and a culture that often sees promising ideas rejected.

Despite an inherent risk-averse approach to change and innovation, police officers leading the charge to develop and implement Neighbourhood Policing passionately believed that it would deliver safer communities based upon the ten founding principles of Neighbourhood Policing. Drawing upon a wealth of practical operational experience, the creation of Neighbourhood Policing has delivered in essence what the police service already knew: that a team of dedicated police officers, visible, accessible, and most importantly, familiar within the community, is the fundamental building-block for all policing, including counter-terrorism. Engagement with all communities at a local level remains the key to building capacity to challenge and resist the kind of violent extremism which leads to terrorism, and is also the optimal way of gaining valuable community intelligence which serves to inform the policing response to terrorism at all levels. At its simplest, regular police interaction with the public through Neighbourhood Policing reassures communities about the risk from terrorism and reminds the public to remain vigilant. Through positive, open, and informative dialogue with the public, Neighbourhood Policing Teams can encourage and support people to come forward with information to help keep their own neighbourhood safe. They can also relay messages to reassure their communities following police operations and terrorist events, and address concerns in the community. The individual and collective efforts of a professional Neighbourhood Policing Team, who are both informed about the terrorist profiles in their locality, and conduct their duties through the lens of counter-terrorism, can directly prevent terrorism and protect the communities they serve from those individuals and groups who seek to divide communities and destroy our free and democratic way of life.

Further reading

- Association of Chief Police Officers, *Practice Advice on Professionalising the Business of Neighbourhood Policing* (2006). Available at <http://www.neighbourhoodpolicing.co.uk>.
- Brain, T, *A History of Policing in England and Wales from 1974: A Turbulent Journey* (Oxford: Oxford University Press, 2010).
- Brain, T, *A Future for Policing in England and Wales* (Oxford: Oxford University Press, 2013).
- Caless, B, *Blackstone's PCSO Handbook* 2nd edition (Oxford: Oxford University Press, 2010).
- Caless, B, *Blackstone's Policing for the Special Constable* (Oxford: Oxford University Press, 2013).
- Caless, B, Harfield, C, and Spruce, B, *Blackstone's Police Operational Handbook: Practice and Procedure: Part 3 Neighbourhood Policing* 2nd edition (Oxford: Oxford University Press, 2013).
- Clements, P, *Policing a Diverse Society* (Oxford: Oxford University Press, 2008).
- Home Office, *Policing in the 21st Century: Reconnecting police and the people* (2010), Available at: <http://www.homeoffice.gov.uk/publications/consultations/policing-21st-century>.
- Reiner, R, *The Politics of the Police* (Oxford: Oxford University Press, 2010).

- Rogers, C, *Crime Reduction Partnerships*, (Oxford: Oxford University Press, 2012).
- Staniforth, A, *The Routledge Companion to UK Counter-Terrorism* (Oxford: Routledge, 2012).
- Staniforth, A, and PNLD, *Blackstone's Counter-Terrorism Handbook* 3rd edition (Oxford: Oxford University Press, 2013).

Appendix 1

List of Proscribed Terrorist Organisations

There are fifty-one international terrorist organisations proscribed under the Terrorism Act 2000. Of these, two organisations are proscribed under powers introduced in the Terrorism Act 2006 as glorifying terrorism. Fourteen organisations in Northern Ireland are proscribed under previous legislation. The proscribed terrorist groups and their aims include;

17 November Revolutionary Organisation (N17)
Aims to highlight and protest against what it deems to be imperialist and corrupt actions, using violence. Formed in 1974 to oppose the Greek military Junta, its stance was initially anti-Junta and anti-US, which it blamed for supporting the Junta.

Abu Nidal Organisation (ANO)
ANO's principal aim is the destruction of the state of Israel. It is also hostile to 'reactionary' Arab regimes and states supporting Israel.

Abu Sayyaf Group (ASG)
The precise aims of the ASG are unclear, but its objectives appear to include the establishment of an autonomous Islamic state in the southern Philippine island of Mindanao.

Al-Gama'at al-Islamiya (GI)
The main aim of GI is to overthrow the Egyptian government and replace it with an Islamic state via any means, including the use of violence. Some members also want the total removal of Western influence from the Arab world.

Al Ghurabaa
Al Ghurabaa is a splinter group of Al-Muhajiroun and disseminates materials that glorify acts of terrorism.

Note: The government laid orders, in January 2010 and November 2011, which provide that Al-Muhajiroun, Islam4UK, Call to Submission, Islamic Path, London School of Sharia and Muslims Against Crusades should all be treated as alternative names for the organisation which is already proscribed under the names Al Ghurabaa and The Saved Sect.

Al Ittihad Al Islamiya (AIAI)
The main aims of AIAI are to establish a radical Sunni Islamic state in Somalia, and to regain the Ogaden region of Ethiopia as Somali territory via an insurgency campaign. Militant elements within AIAI are suspected of having aligned themselves with the 'global jihad' ideology of Al Qa'ida, and to have operated in support of Al Qa'ida in east Africa.

Al Qa'ida (AQ)
Inspired and led by Osama Bin Laden, its aims are the expulsion of Western forces from Saudi Arabia, the destruction of Israel, and the end of Western influence in the Muslim world.

Note: The government laid an order, in July 2013, which provided that the al-Nusra Front (ANF) and Jabhat al-Nusra li-ahl al Sham should be treated as alternative names for the organisation already proscribed under the name Al Qa'ida.

Al Shabaab
Al Shabaab is an organisation based in Somalia which has waged a violent campaign against the Somali Transitional Federal Government and African Union peacekeeping forces since 2007, employing a range of terrorist tactics including suicide bombings, indiscriminate attacks, and assassinations. Its principal aim is the establishment of a fundamentalist Islamic state in Somalia, and the organisation has also publicly pledged its allegiance to Osama Bin Laden and announced an intention to combine its campaign in the Horn of Africa with Al Qa'ida's aims of global jihad.

Ansar al-Islam (AI)
AI is a radical Sunni Salafi group from northeast Iraq around Halabja. The group is anti-Western, and opposes the influence of the US in Iraqi Kurdistan and the relationship of the KDP and PUK to Washington. AI has been involved in operations against Multi-National Forces-Iraq (MNF-I).

Ansar al-Sunna (AS)
AS is a fundamentalist Sunni Islamist extremist group based in central Iraq and what was the Kurdish Autonomous Zone (KAZ) of northern Iraq. The group aims to expel all foreign influences from Iraq and create a fundamentalist Islamic state.

Ansarul Muslimina Fi Biladis Sudan (Vanguard for the Protection of Muslims in Black Africa) (Ansaru)
Ansaru is an Islamist terrorist organisation based in Nigeria. They emerged in 2012 and are motivated by an anti-Nigerian Government and anti-Western agenda. They are broadly aligned with Al Qa'ida.

Armed Islamic Group (Groupe Islamique Armée) (GIA)
The aim of the GIA is to create an Islamic state in Algeria using all available means, including violence.

Asbat Al-Ansar ('League of Partisans' or 'Band of Helpers')
Sometimes going by the aliases of 'The Abu Muhjin' group/faction or the 'Jama'at Nou', this group aims to enforce its extremist interpretation of Islamic law within Lebanon and, increasingly, further afield.

Babbar Khalsa (BK)
BK is a Sikh movement that aims to establish an independent Khalistan within the Punjab region of India.

Baluchistan Liberation Army (BLA)
BLA comprise tribal groups based in the Baluchistan area of eastern Pakistan. It aims to establish an independent nation encompassing the Baluch-dominated areas of Pakistan, Afghanistan, and Iran.

Basque Homeland and Liberty (Euskadi ta Askatasuna) (ETA)
ETA seeks the creation of an independent state comprising the Basque regions of both Spain and France.

Boko Haram (Jamā'at Ahl as-Sunnah lid-da'wa wal-Jihād) (BH)
Boko Haram is a terrorist organisation, based in Nigeria, that aspires to establish Islamic law in Nigeria. It has carried out a number of terrorist attacks that have targeted all sections of Nigerian society.

Egyptian Islamic Jihad (EIJ)
The main aim of the EIJ is to overthrow the Egyptian government and replace it with an Islamic state. However, since September 1998, the leadership of the group has also allied itself to the global jihad ideology expounded by Osama Bin Laden and has threatened Western interests.

Groupe Islamique Combattant Marocain (GICM)
The traditional primary objective of the GICM has been the installation of a governing system of the caliphate to replace the governing Moroccan monarchy. The group also has an Al Qa'ida-inspired global extremist agenda.

Hamas Izz al-Din al-Qassem Brigades
Hamas aims to end Israeli occupation in Palestine and establish an Islamic state.

Harakat-ul-Jihad-I-Islami (HUJI)
The aim of HUJI is to achieve through violent means accession of Kashmir to Pakistan, and to spread terror throughout India. HUJI has targeted Indian security positions in Kashmir and conducted operations in India.

Harakat-ul-Jihad-I-Islami (Bangladesh) (HUJI-B)
The main aim of HUJI-B is the creation of an Islamic regime in Bangladesh modelled on the former Taliban regime in Afghanistan.

Harakat-ul-Mujahideen/Alami (HuM/A) and Jundallah.
The aim of both HuM/A and Jundallah is the rejection of democracy of even the most Islamic-oriented style, and to establish a caliphate based on Sharia law, in addition to achieving accession of all Kashmir to Pakistan. HuM/A has a broad anti-Western agenda.

Harakat Mujahideen (HM)
HM, previously known as Harakat ul-Ansar (HuA), seeks independence for Indian-administered Kashmir. The HM leadership was also a signatory to Osama Bin Laden's 1998 fatwa, which called for attacks against US and Western interests anywhere in the world.

Hezb-i-Islami Gulbuddin (HIG)
Led by Gulbuddin Hekmatyar who is in particular very anti-American, HIG is anti-Western and wants the creation of a fundamentalist Islamic State in Afghanistan.

Hizballah Military Wing
Hizballah is committed to armed resistance to the state of Israel, and aims to seize all Palestinian territories and Jerusalem from Israel. Its military wing supports terrorism in Iraq and the Palestinian territories.

Indian Mujahideen (IM)
IM aims to establish an Islamic state and implement Sharia law in India using violent means.

International Sikh Youth Federation (ISYF)
ISYF is an organisation committed to the creation of an independent state of Khalistan for Sikhs within India.

Islamic Army of Aden (IAA)
The IAA's aims are the overthrow of the current Yemeni government and the establishment of an Islamic State following Sharia law.

Islamic Jihad Union (IJU)
The primary strategic goal of the IJU is the elimination of the current Uzbek regime. The IJU would expect that following the removal of President Karimov, elections would occur in which democratic Islamic political candidates would pursue goals shared by the IJU leadership.

Islamic Movement of Uzbekistan (IMU)
The primary aim of IMU is to establish an Islamic state in the model of the Taliban in Uzbekistan. However, the IMU is reported also to seek to establish a broader state across the entire Turkestan area.

Jaish-e-Mohammed (JeM)
JeM seeks the 'liberation' of Kashmir from Indian control as well as the 'destruction' of America and India. JeM has a stated objective of unifying the various Kashmiri militant groups.

Jammat-ul-Mujahideen Bangladesh (JMB)
JMB first came to prominence on 20 May 2002 when eight of its members were arrested in possession of petrol bombs. The group has claimed responsibility for numerous fatal bomb attacks across Bangladesh in recent years, including suicide bomb attacks in 2005.

Jemaah Islamiyah (JI)
JI's aim is the creation of a unified Islamic state in Singapore, Malaysia, Indonesia, and the southern Philippines.

Khuddam ul-Islam (KUI) and splinter group Jamaat Ul-Furquan (JuF)
The aim of both KUI and JuF is to unite Indian-administered Kashmir with Pakistan, to establish a radical Islamist state in Pakistan, the 'destruction' of India and the USA, to recruit new jihadis, and the release of imprisoned Kashmiri militants.

Kongra-Gel Kurdistan (PKK)
PKK/KADEK/KG is primarily a separatist movement that seeks an independent Kurdish state in south-east Turkey. The PKK changed its name to KADEK and then to Kongra-Gel Kurdistan, although the PKK acronym is still used by parts of the movement.

Lashkar-e-Tayyiba (LeT)
LeT seeks independence for Kashmir and the creation of an Islamic state using violent means.

Note: The government produced an order in March 2009 which provides that Jama'at-ud-Da'wa (JuD) should be treated as another name for the organisation which is already proscribed, known as Lashkar-e-Tayyiba.

Liberation Tigers of Tamil Eelam (LTTE)
The LTTE is a terrorist group fighting for a separate Tamil state in north and east Sri Lanka.

Libyan Islamic Fighting Group (LIFG)
The LIFG seeks to replace the current Libyan regime with a hard-line Islamic state. The group is also part of the wider global Islamist extremist movement inspired by Al Qa'ida. The group has mounted several operations inside Libya, including a 1996 attempt to assassinate Muammar Gaddafi.

Minbar Ansar Deen (also known as Ansar al-Sharia UK)
Minbar Ansar Deen is a Salafist group based in the UK that promotes and encourages terrorism. Minbar Ansar Deen distributes content through its online forum which promotes terrorism by encouraging individuals to travel overseas to engage in extremist activity, specifically fighting. The group is not related to Ansar al-Sharia groups in other countries.

Palestinian Islamic Jihad–Shaqaqi (PIJ)
PIJ aims to end the Israeli occupation of Palestine and to create an Islamic state. It opposes the existence of the state of Israel, the Middle East peace process, and the Palestinian Authority, and has carried out suicide bombings against Israeli targets.

Revolutionary People's Liberation Party—Front (Devrimci Halk Kurtulus Partisi-Cephesi) (DHKP-C)
DHKP-C aims to establish a Marxist-Leninist regime in Turkey by means of armed revolutionary struggle.

Salafist Group for Call and Combat (Groupe Salafiste pour la Predication et le Combat) (GSPC)
Its aim is to create an Islamic state in Algeria using all necessary means, including violence.

Saved Sect or Saviour Sect
The Saved Sect is a splinter group of Al-Muhajiroun and disseminates materials that glorify acts of terrorism.

Note: The government laid down orders, in January 2010 and November 2011, which provide that Al-Muhajiroun, Islam4UK, Call to Submission, Islamic Path, London School of Sharia, and Muslims Against Crusades should be treated as alternative names for the organisation which is already proscribed under the names Al Ghurabaa and The Saved Sect.

Sipah-e-Sahaba Pakistan (SSP) (aka Millat-e-Islamia Pakistan (MIP)–SSP was renamed MIP in April 2003 but is still referred to as SSP) and splinter group Lashkar-e-Jhangvi (LeJ)
The aim of both SSP and LeJ is to transform Pakistan by violent means into a Sunni state under the total control of Sharia law. Another objective is to have all Shia declared

Kafirs (infidels) and to participate in the destruction of other religions, notably Judaism, Christianity, and Hinduism.

Note: Kafirs means non-believers: literally, one who refused to see the truth. LeJ does not consider members of the Shia sect to be Muslim, hence they can be considered a 'legitimate' target.

Tehreek-e-Nafaz-e-Shariat-e-Mohammadi (TNSM)
TNSM regularly attacks coalition and Afghan government forces in Afghanistan and provides direct support to Al Qa'ida and the Taliban. One faction of the group claimed responsibility for a suicide attack on an army training compound on 8 November 2007 in Dargai, Pakistan, in which forty-two soldiers were killed.

Tehrik-e Taliban Pakistan (TTP)
Tehrik-e Taliban Pakistan has carried out a high number of mass casualty attacks in Pakistan and Afghanistan since 2007. The group has announced various objectives and demands, such as the enforcement of Sharia law, resistance against the Pakistani army, and the removal of NATO forces from Afghanistan. The organisation has also been involved in attacks in the West, such as the attempted Times Square car-bomb attack in May 2010.

Teyre Azadiye Kurdistan (TAK)
TAK is a Kurdish terrorist group currently operating in Turkey.

(Note: Mujahedin-e Khalq (MeK) was removed from the list of proscribed organisations in June 2008, as a result of judgments of the Proscribed Organisations Appeals Commission and the Court of Appeal).

List of Proscribed Northern Irish Groups

Continuity Army Council
Cumann na mBan
Fianna na hEireann
Irish National Liberation Army
Irish People's Liberation Organisation
Irish Republican Army
Loyalist Volunteer Force
Orange Volunteers
Red Hand Commando
Red Hand Defenders
Saor Eire
Ulster Defence Association
Ulster Freedom Fighters
Ulster Volunteer Force

Appendix 2

Terrorism Act 2000 (Issued under S47AB as amended by the Protection of Freedoms Act 2012) Code of Practice (England, Wales and Scotland) for the Exercise of Stop and Search Powers under Sections 43 and 43A of the Terrorism Act 2000, and the Authorisation and Exercise of Stop and Search Powers Relating to Section 47A of and Schedule 6B to the Terrorism Act 2000

1. Introduction

1.1. The Purpose of this Code is

1.1.1. To set out the basic principles for the use of powers by police officers under sections 43 and 43A of the Terrorism Act 2000 and the authorisation and use of powers by police officers under section 47A of, and Schedule 6B to, the Terrorism Act 2000.

1.1.2. To reflect that the powers under section 47A and Schedule 6B entirely replace those previously found in sections 44–47 of the 2000 Act and are not simply a modification of those provisions. As such they carry different criteria for both authorisation and use.

1.1.3. In respect of the powers under section 47A and Schedule 6B, to provide clarity that the threshold for making an authorisation is higher under these powers and the way in which the powers may be exercised is also different from under the provisions of sections 44–47. There is far greater circumscription in the use of these powers and the manner in which these powers are to be implemented by the police. Section 47A powers should only be authorised where other powers or measures are insufficient to deal with the threat and, even where authorised, officers should still consider whether section 47A powers are the most appropriate to use.

1.1.4. To promote the fundamental principles to be observed by the police and to preserve the effectiveness of, and public confidence in, the use of police powers to stop and search. If these fundamental principles are not observed, public confidence in the use of these powers to stop and search may be affected. Failure to use the powers in the proper manner also reduces their effectiveness.

1.1.5. To ensure that the intrusion on the liberty of the person stopped and searched is as limited as possible and to clarify that detention for the purposes of a search should take place at or near the location of the stop and last only as long as necessary.

1.1.6. To set out that those using the powers may be required to justify the use of such powers, in relation both to individual searches and the overall pattern of their activity in this regard, to their supervisory officers or in court. Any misuse of the powers is likely to be harmful to counter-terrorism policing and lead to mistrust of the police. Officers must also be able to explain their actions to the member of the public searched. The misuse of these powers can lead to disciplinary action. Proportionate use of the powers can contribute towards the primary purpose of counter-terrorism work: ensuring the safety of the public.

1.1.7. To reiterate guidance found in the Police and Criminal Evidence Act 1984 (PACE)[1] Code A that officers must not search a person, even with his or her consent, where no power to search is applicable.[2] Even where a person is prepared to submit to a search voluntarily, the person must not be searched unless the necessary legal power exists, and the search must be in accordance with the relevant power and the provisions of this code. The only exception, where an officer does not require a specific power, applies to searches of persons entering sports grounds or other premises carried out with their consent given as a condition of entry.

1.2. Basic Application of this Code

1.2.1. This code applies to any authorisation or exercise of relevant stop and search powers by a police officer, which commences after midnight on the day the Terrorism Act 2000 (Codes of Practice for the Exercise of Stop and Search Powers) Order 2012 comes into force.

1.2.2. This code of practice is issued under section 47AB of the Terrorism Act 2000.

1.2.3. The effect of this code is set out in section 47AE of the Terrorism Act 2000: constables must have regard to the code and the code is admissible in criminal or civil proceedings (although a breach of the code itself does not make a person liable to any such proceedings).

1.2.4. Powers to stop and search must be used fairly, responsibly, and in accordance with the Equality Act 2010.

1.2.5. Chief Constables, police authorities and the Mayor's Office for Policing and Crime have a duty to have regard to this code of practice when discharging a function to which this code relates. This code must be followed unless there is good reason not to do so, in which case the decision not to follow this code should be recorded in writing.

1.2.6. This code of practice must be readily available at all police stations for consultation by police officers, police staff, detained persons and members of the public.

---

[1] PACE does not apply in Scotland.

[2] This does not affect the position in Scotland where there can be voluntary compliance with a search in terms of Scottish common law.

1.2.7. This code of practice applies to all police forces in England, Wales and Scotland, including the British Transport Police, the Ministry of Defence Police and the Civil Nuclear Constabulary. It does not apply to police forces in Northern Ireland—a separate code governs those police forces.

1.2.8. References to police authorities refer only to police authorities in England and Wales, the Mayor's Office for Policing and Crime, the British Transport Police Authority, Civil Nuclear Police Authority and Ministry of Defence Police Committee.

1.2.9. References in this code to the information required in an authorisation refer to a written authorisation or written confirmation of an oral authorisation.

2. Scope of this Code

2.1. Powers of Stop and Search:

2.1.1. This code concerns the

a) exercise of stop and search powers conferred by section 43 and 43A of the Terrorism Act 2000, and
b) authorisation and exercise of powers to stop and search in specified areas or places at specified times contained in section 47A of, and Schedule 6B to, the Terrorism Act 2000.

2.1.2. Sections 43, 43A and 47A of the Terrorism Act 2000 as amended by the Protection of Freedoms Act 2012.

2.2. Definition of Terrorism

2.2.1. Terrorism is defined by section 1 of the Terrorism Act 2000. In summary the term 'terrorism' in the 2000 Act means the use or threat of action where:

- the action used or threatened:
  - involves serious violence against a person or serious damage to property;
  - endangers a person's life, other than that of the person committing the action;
  - creates a serious risk to the health or safety of the public or a section of the public; or
  - is designed seriously to interfere with or seriously to disrupt an electronic system;
- the use or threat is designed to influence the government or an international governmental organisation, or intimidate the public or a section of the public; and
- the use or threat is made for the purpose of advancing a political, religious, racial or ideological cause.

3. Section 43 of the Terrorism Act 2000

3.1. Legal Background

3.1.1. Section 43(1) of the Terrorism Act 2000 provides a power for a constable to stop and search a person whom he or she reasonably suspects is a terrorist, to discover whether that person has anything in their possession which may constitute evidence they are a terrorist.

3.1.2. Section 43(2) of the Terrorism Act 2000 provides a power for a constable to search a person arrested under section 41 of that Act to discover whether that person has anything in their possession which may constitute evidence they are a terrorist. It does not require prior reasonable suspicion that such evidence may be found.

3.1.3. There are two powers to stop and search a vehicle with reasonable suspicion, introduced by amendments to the Terrorism Act 2000. The first is under section 43(1), where the officer reasonably suspects a person in a vehicle to be a terrorist and stops the vehicle in order to carry out a search. Under section 43(4B), the officer may also search the vehicle and anything in it or on it during the course of a search. The second is under section 43A, which provides a power for a constable to stop and search a vehicle which he or she reasonably suspects is being used for the purposes of terrorism, to search the vehicle and its occupants for evidence that it is being used for those purposes.

3.1.4. Given they require reasonable suspicion in order to be exercised, the use of powers under sections 43(1) and 43A should be prioritised for the purposes of stopping and searching individuals for the purposes of preventing or detecting terrorism. The authorisation of the no suspicion powers under section 47A should only be considered as a last resort, where reasonable suspicion powers are considered inadequate to respond to the threat. Use of the search powers under section 47A should only be made (in an authorised area) when the powers in sections 43 and 43A are not appropriate.

3.2. Stopping and Searching Persons and Vehicles under section 43(1)

3.2.1. A police officer may stop and search a person under section 43(1) of the Terrorism Act 2000 if they reasonably suspect that the person is a terrorist, to discover whether or not they have in their possession anything which may constitute evidence that they are a terrorist. This power may be used at any time or in any place when the threshold of reasonable suspicion is met. No authorisation is required.

3.2.2. If, when exercising the power to stop a person under section 43(1), a constable stops a vehicle, he or she may search the vehicle, and anything in or on it, under section 43(4B).

3.2.3. A person who is in the same vehicle as someone an officer reasonably suspects to be a terrorist may not be searched by virtue of this power, solely on the basis that they are with a person whom an officer reasonably suspects is a terrorist. However, anything otherwise in or on the vehicle may be searched to discover whether there is anything that may constitute evidence that the person the officer suspects to be a terrorist is a terrorist. The person may only be searched (under section 43(1)) if the officer reasonably suspects that they too are a terrorist.

3.2.4. The powers under section 43 to search a person include the power to search anything that person is carrying with them, such as a bag, container or other object.

3.2.5. For searches of persons under section 43, the statutory requirement for the officer to be of the same sex as the persons to be searched has been repealed but where an officer of the same sex as the person to be searched is readily available, they should carry out the search. However, if an officer of the same sex is not available, searches may be carried out by an officer of the opposite sex (see paragraph 3.2.8.). Officers should have particular regard to the sensitivities of some religious communities in respect of being searched by a member of the opposite sex.

3.2.6. An officer need not be in uniform to carry out a stop and search of a person under section 43(1). However, in accordance with section 2(9)(b) of PACE, a constable stopping a vehicle under section 43(4A) or section 43A, must be in uniform.

3.2.7. A person can only be required to remove more than an outer coat, jacket or gloves if the search takes place out of public view and is near the place where that person was stopped. Unlike searches authorised under section 47A, a person cannot be required to remove their headgear and footwear in public. This does not, however, prevent an officer from placing his or her hand inside the pockets of the outer clothing, or feeling round the inside of collars, socks and shoes if this is considered reasonably necessary in the circumstances to look for the object of the search or to remove and examine any item reasonably suspected to be the object of the search. For the same reasons, subject to the restrictions on the removal of headgear, a person's hair may also be searched in public.

3.2.8. Where on reasonable grounds it is considered necessary to conduct a more thorough search (e.g. by requiring a person to take off a T-shirt), this must be done out of public view, for example, in a police van or police station if there is one nearby. Any search involving the removal of more than an outer coat, jacket, gloves, headgear or footwear, or any other item concealing identity, should only be conducted by an officer of the same sex as the person searched and may not be made in the presence of anyone of the opposite sex unless the person being searched specifically requests it. If a search involves exposure of intimate parts of the body and a police station is not nearby, particular care must be taken to ensure that the location is suitable in that it enables the search to be conducted in accordance with the requirements of paragraph 11 of Annex A to PACE Code C.

3.3. Stopping and Searching Vehicles under section 43A

3.3.1. Section 43A of the Terrorism Act 2000 allows a constable to stop and search a vehicle which he or she reasonably suspects is being used for the purposes of terrorism, for evidence that the vehicle is being used for such purposes. The constable may search anything in or on the vehicle or any person (including drivers, crew and passengers) in the vehicle to discover whether there is anything which may constitute evidence that the vehicle is being used for the purposes of terrorism. Section 43A may be used to search unattended vehicles where an officer reasonably suspects the vehicle is being used for the purposes of terrorism.

3.3.2. If the officer reasonably suspects a person in a vehicle of being a terrorist, but does not suspect the vehicle is being used at that time for the purposes of terrorism, the power under section 43(1) should be used.

3.3.3. The power in section 43A may be used on the basis of information or intelligence about (for example) ownership or user(s) of the vehicle, previous involvement of the vehicle in terrorist or suspected terrorist activity or observation of how the vehicle is being used (for instance, if a vehicle is parked outside a potential target for long periods, or if a vehicle appears to be following a suspicious or repetitive route) or the nature of the vehicle or its contents (for example, if a non-commercial vehicle appears to be carrying gas canisters).

3.3.4. Searches may be undertaken of anything in or on the vehicle, but care should be taken not to damage a vehicle as part of a search, or in the case of an unattended vehicle, in order to gain entry into it.

3.3.5. Vehicles stopped under section 43A and persons in those vehicles may be detained only for as long as is necessary to carry out the searches—at or near the place the vehicle was stopped.

3.4. Reasonable Grounds for Suspicion

3.4.1. Reasonable grounds for suspicion depend on the circumstances in each case. There must be an objective basis for the suspicion (that the person is a terrorist or that the vehicle is being used for the purposes of terrorism) based on relevant facts, information, and/or intelligence. Reasonable suspicion must rely on intelligence or information about, or behaviour by, the person or vehicle concerned. Unless the police have a description of a suspect, a person's physical appearance (including any of the 'protected characteristics' set out in the Equality Act 2010), cannot be used alone or in combination with each other or with any other factor, as the reason for searching that person. Reasonable suspicion cannot be based on generalisations or stereotypical images of certain groups or categories of people as more likely to be involved in terrorist activity.

3.4.2. Reasonable suspicion may exist without specific information or intelligence but on the basis of the behaviour of a person. For example, reasonable suspicion that a person is a terrorist may arise from the person's behaviour at or near a location which has been identified as a potential target for terrorists.

3.4.3. However, reasonable suspicion should normally be linked to credible and current intelligence or information, such as information describing an article being carried, a suspected terrorist, or intelligence about a particular or general threat insofar as it relates to a specific target or type of potential target. Searches based on credible and current intelligence or information are more likely to be effective.

3.4.4. Searches are more likely to be effective, legitimate, and secure public confidence when reasonable suspicion is based on a range of factors. The overall use of these powers is more likely to be effective when up to date and accurate intelligence or information is communicated to officers and they are well-informed about the nature of the terrorist threat, potential targets and ways in which terrorists are known to operate.

3.4.5. An officer who has reasonable grounds for suspicion may detain the person concerned in order to carry out a search. Before carrying out a search the officer may ask questions: for example about the person's behaviour or presence in circumstances which gave rise to the suspicion. As a result of this conversation with the person, the reasonable grounds for suspicion necessary to search may remain or, because of a satisfactory explanation, may be eliminated—in which case no search should be conducted. The conversation may also reveal reasonable grounds to suspect the possession of unlawful articles such as drugs or non-terrorist related articles, in which case a search may be continued using a different, appropriate search power. Reasonable grounds for suspicion however cannot be provided retrospectively by a conversation with the individual or by their refusal to answer any questions asked (see paragraph 3.4.10.).

3.4.6. Where the powers under section 43(1) or 43(4A) and 43(4B) are exercised in Scotland, the officer should administer a formal caution at common law prior to conducting the search. Failure to do so may affect the admissibility of statements made in response to anything found as a result of a search.

3.4.7. In some circumstances preparatory questioning may be unnecessary, but in general a brief conversation or exchange will be desirable not only as a means of avoiding unsuccessful searches, but by providing an opportunity to explain the grounds for the stop/search (see paragraph 5.2.1.), to gain co-operation and reduce any tension there might be surrounding the stop/search.

3.4.8. Where a person is lawfully detained for the purpose of a search, but no search in the event takes place, the detention will not thereby have been rendered unlawful.

3.4.9. If, as a result of questioning before a search, or because of other circumstances which come to the attention of the officer, there cease to be reasonable grounds for suspecting that the person is a terrorist or the vehicle is being used for the purposes of terrorism, the officer may not conduct a search under section 43 or 43A. In the absence of any other lawful power to search or detain, the person is free to leave at will at that stage and must be so informed.

3.4.10. There is no power to stop or detain a person in order to find grounds for a search. Police officers have many encounters with members of the public which do not involve detaining people. If reasonable grounds for suspicion emerge during such an encounter, the officer may search the person, even though no grounds existed when the encounter began. If an officer is detaining someone for the purpose of a search, he or she should inform the person as soon as detention begins.

3.4.11. The grounds for stopping and searching a person under section 43A are the same as the grounds for arrest under section 41 of the Terrorism Act 2000: reasonable suspicion that the person is a terrorist. Stop and search is a less intrusive power than arrest and will be more appropriate in many situations e.g. in encounters with individuals where a stop and search may help to allay suspicions. Stop and search should not be used in any situation where it is more appropriate to arrest or where an officer believes it may put him, or members of the public, in danger.

4. Authorisations under section 47A

4.1. Meeting the Test for Making an Authorisation

4.1.1. The powers to stop and search under section 47A represent a significant divergence from the usual requirement to have reasonable suspicion when exercising stop and search powers. The powers are therefore only exercisable by a constable in uniform in an area where and during a period when an authorisation given by a senior officer is in force. The test for authorising section 47A powers is that the person giving it: must reasonably suspect that an act of terrorism will take place and considers that the powers are necessary to prevent such an act and that the area(s) or place(s) specified in the authorisation are no greater than is necessary and the duration of the authorisation is no longer than is necessary to prevent such an act.

4.1.2. An authorisation under section 47A may only be made by an officer of ACPO or ACPOS rank (i.e. at least the rank of assistant chief constable or, in the case of the Metropolitan and City of London Police, a commander). Authorising officers must be either substantive or on temporary promotion to the qualifying rank. Officers who are acting in the rank may not give authorisations.

4.1.3. The Secretary of State must be notified of any authorisation and must confirm any authorisation specified to exceed 48 hours, if it is to remain in force beyond 48 hours.

4.1.4. An authorisation may only be given where there is intelligence or circumstances which lead the authorising officer to reasonably suspect that an act of terrorism will take place. The authorising officer must also be satisfied that the powers are 'necessary' to prevent such an act of terrorism. This will involve an assessment that other powers are not sufficient to deal with the situation. Authorising officers should always consider whether it is appropriate to authorise the powers in the particular circumstances, with regard to:

- the safety of the public;
- the safety of officers; and
- the necessity of the powers in relation to the threat.

4.1.5. The following may be taken into account when deciding whether to give an authorisation, but should not form the sole basis of such a decision:
a) There is a general high threat from terrorism;
b) A particular site or event is deemed to be 'high risk' or vulnerable.

4.1.6. An authorisation may not be given on the basis that:
a) The use of the powers provides public reassurance;
b) The powers are a useful deterrent or intelligence-gathering tool.

4.1.7. An authorisation should not provide for the powers to be used other than where they are considered necessary to prevent the suspected act of terrorism. Authorisations must be as limited as possible and linked to addressing the suspected act of terrorism. In determining the area(s) or place(s) it is necessary to specify in the authorisation, an authorising officer may need to consider the possibility that terrorists may change their method or target of attack, or that there are a number of potential targets. It will be necessary to consider what the appropriate operational response to the intelligence is (e.g. whether to conduct stop and search around suspected target sites or areas or routes which could allow the police to intercept a terrorist or vehicle). However, any authorisations must be as limited as possible and based on an assessment of the existing intelligence.

4.1.8. One authorisation may be given which encompasses a number of different places or areas within a police force area (whether those are included in response to the same or different threats). The authorisation must set out the necessity for including each of these areas or places and the necessity for the length of time for which the authorisation lasts in respect of each area or place.

4.1.9. A new authorisation should be given if there is a significant change in the nature of the particular threat (or the authorising officer's understanding of it) which formed the basis of an existing authorisation. In such circumstances it will be appropriate to cancel the earlier authorisation.

4.1.10. The authorisation should also include details of how the exercise of the powers is necessary to prevent the act of terrorism. This means an explanation of how the authorisation will counter the threat i.e. why the stopping and searching of individuals and/or vehicles without suspicion is necessary to prevent the suspected act of terrorism. The consideration of necessity will also involve an assessment of why other measures (in particular the stop and search powers in section 43 of the 2000 Act) are not sufficient to address the threat.

4.1.11. If during the currency of an authorisation, the authorising officer no longer reasonably suspects that an act of terrorism of the description given in the authorisation will take place or no longer considers that the powers are necessary to prevent such an act, the authorising officer must cancel the authorisation immediately and inform the Secretary of State.

4.1.12. If, during the currency of an authorisation, the authorising officer believes that the duration or geographical extent of the authorisation is no longer necessary for the prevention of such an act of terrorism, he or she must substitute a shorter period, or more restricted geographical area. In that instance, the officer must inform the Secretary of State but the Secretary of State need not confirm such changes.

4.2. Information in Support of an Authorisation

4.2.1. Authorisations should where practicable, be given in writing. Where an authorisation is given orally, it should be confirmed in writing as soon as possible after it is given. Written authorisations and written confirmation of oral authorisations should include the information set out in this section and be provided on the form in Annex C.

4.2.2. Intelligence Picture: The authorising officer should provide a detailed account of the intelligence which has given rise to the reasonable suspicion that an act of terrorism will take place. This should include classified material where it exists, which should be provided to the Secretary of State, with the authorisation, by a secure means of communication. References to classified reporting may be used instead of verbatim reports or quotes, but the reporting referenced must have been considered by the authorising officer in making the authorisation, and must be available to the Secretary of State when considering whether to confirm an authorisation.

4.2.3. Geographical Extent: Detailed information should be provided to identify the geographical area(s) or place(s) covered by the authorisation. Where possible, maps of the authorised area should be included. The area authorised should be no wider than necessary. Authorisations which cover entire force areas are not justifiable under section 47A and Schedule 6B, unless there are exceptional circumstances which support such an authorisation.[3]

4.2.4. If an authorisation is one which covers a similar geographical area to one which immediately preceded it, information should be provided as to how the intelligence has changed since the previous authorisation was given, or if it has not changed, that it has been reassessed in the process of deciding on giving the new authorisation, and that it remains pertinent, and why.

4.2.5. Duration: The maximum period for an authorisation is 14 days. An authorisation should be given for no longer than necessary and should not be made for the maximum period unless it is necessary based on intelligence about the specified threat. Justification should be provided for the length of an authorisation, setting out why the intelligence supports the amount of time authorised. If an authorisation is one which is similar to another immediately preceding it, information should be provided as to why a new authorisation is justified and why the period of the initial authorisation was not sufficient. Where different areas or places are specified within one authorisation, different time periods may be specified in relation to each of these

[3] Force-wide authorisations may be justifiable in respect of City of London Police, purely because of the size of the force area. However, the geographical area should still be no greater than necessary.

areas or places—indeed the time period necessary for each will need to be considered and justified.

4.2.6. Briefing Provided: Information should be provided which demonstrates that all officers involved in exercising section 47A powers receive appropriate briefing in the use of the powers, including the provisions of this code, and the reason for the use of the powers on each relevant occasion.

4.2.7. Tactical Deployment: The authorising officer should provide information about how the powers will be used and why. The extent to which there are objective factors (see paragraph 4.9.3. for examples) that can be used as a basis for the powers' tactical deployment will depend on the intelligence available and will, therefore, vary. Where the intelligence is very limited, officers may not be able to use behavioural indicators or information contained in the intelligence and may have to conduct stop and searches in a less targeted way. Constables must not, however, stop and search an individual or vehicle where they consider that there is no possibility of the individual being a terrorist or the vehicle being used for terrorism.

4.2.8. Given the powers are generally being used on the basis of objective factors, constables should consider whether powers requiring reasonable suspicion are more appropriate and should only use the powers conferred by a section 47A authorisation, if they are satisfied that they cannot meet a threshold of reasonable suspicion sufficient to use other police powers.

4.3. Successive or Replacement Authorisations

4.3.1. Once an authorisation is coming to an end, a new authorisation may be given. However, authorising officers should remember that the powers under sections 44 to 46 of the Terrorism Act 2000, under which authorisations were made by some forces on a virtually indefinite basis, have been repealed. 'Rolling' authorisations are not permitted under the powers in section 47A of, and Schedule 6B to, the Terrorism Act 2000.

4.3.2. A new authorisation covering the same or substantially the same areas or places as a previous authorisation may be given if the intelligence which informed the initial authorisation has been subject to fresh assessment and the officer giving the authorisation is satisfied that the test for authorisation is still met on the basis of that assessment. Where a successive authorisation is given, it may be given before the expiry of the existing authorisation, but that existing authorisation should be cancelled.

4.3.3. In the exceptional circumstances where a new authorisation is given in respect of a different threat during the currency of an existing authorisation in that force area, that existing authorisation need not be cancelled if it continues to be necessary.

4.4. Information for Authorising Officers

4.4.1. Authorising officers should always consider whether giving an authorisation under section 47A is the most appropriate power to use in the circumstances.

4.4.2. An authorisation may be given orally or in writing. If given orally, the authorisation must be confirmed in writing as soon as possible. All authorisations must include the time and date they were given and the time or date of expiry (or, times or dates where more than one area is authorised and where applicable). This must be no later than 14 days from the date on which the authorisation was given (although the maximum 14 days may only be authorised where necessary to address the particular threat (see paragraph 4.2.5.)). The maximum 14 day period should not be seen as the 'norm'—it is a maximum. An authorisation must specify an end time no later than 23:59hrs on the 14th day after it was given (or if only the date is given, that date must be the 14th day—and the time will be taken as 23:59hrs on that date):

- For example, if an authorisation is made at 08:00hrs on 1st November, the specified end time must be no later than 23:59hrs on 14th November, rather than 07:59 on 15th November.

4.4.3. Authorisations begin at the point at which they are signed, or when they are given orally by the authorising officer before being confirmed in writing. The written authorisation, or written confirmation of an oral authorisation, must state the time at which the authorising officer gave it. A new authorisation covering a similar area as an existing authorisation may be given before the expiry of the previous one if necessary, to avoid the need to give the subsequent authorisation at the exact time the existing one expires (see paragraphs 4.3.1.– 4.3.3.).

4.4.4. When a section 47A authorisation has been given, the authorising officer should ensure that officers who will take part in any subsequent stop and search operations are briefed on the fact of the authorisation, its intended use and on the provisions of section 47A of, and Schedule 6B to, the Terrorism Act 2000 and the provisions of this code. Officers should also be briefed on the availability of other powers and the circumstances in which these may be more appropriate (see paragraph 4.9.1.).

4.4.5. In terms of the requirement to inform the Secretary of State of each authorisation and the requirement for an authorisation to be confirmed by the Secretary of State if it is to last beyond 48 hours, the relevant Secretary of State is the Home Secretary.

4.5. Confirmation within the Home Office

4.5.1. Where practicable, an authorising officer should inform the Home Office that he or she intends to give an authorisation and provide a draft of that authorisation before it is given.

4.5.2. The authorising officer must inform the Secretary of State as soon as reasonably practicable once an authorisation under section 47A of the Terrorism Act 2000 has been given. In practice, the police force should aim to have provided the written authorisation to the Home Office within 2 hours of an authorisation being given.

4.5.3. Authorisations remain lawful for up to 48 hours without Secretary of State approval. If the authorisation is not confirmed within a 48 hour period, it ceases to have effect at the end of the 48 hours. If confirmed, the authorisation remains in effect until the expiry time specified in the authorisation by the authorising officer (or an earlier time subsequently substituted by the Secretary of State or a senior officer) or until it is cancelled by a senior officer or by the Secretary of State.

4.6. Notification of Other Police Forces and the Police Authority

4.6.1. Home Office and Scottish forces should notify any non-Home Office force when an authorisation covers areas for which both forces have a responsibility (i.e. British Transport Police, Ministry of Defence Police or Civil Nuclear Constabulary). Similarly, where an authorisation is given by a senior officer in the British Transport Police, the Ministry of Defence Police or the Civil Nuclear Constabulary, the authorising officer should notify the Home Office police force(s) which has responsibility for the police area where the authorisation is given. The authorising officer should also notify their police authority.[4] The authorisation provided to the Home Secretary should include confirmation that both such notifications (to other police forces and to the relevant police authority) have taken place.

4.7. Short-Term Authorisation—Under Forty-Eight Hours

4.7.1. In the event an authorisation for the use of section 47A powers is given for a period of less than 48 hours the authorising officer must inform the Secretary of State of the authorisation as soon as reasonably practicable. Where it is reasonably practicable to do so, the Secretary of State may confirm or cancel the authorisation prior to its expiry.

4.7.2. Where practicable, the authorising officer should inform the Secretary of State that he or she intends to make a short term authorisation in advance of doing so.

4.7.3. The test for a short term authorisation is the same as an authorisation of longer duration. 'Rolling' short term authorisations are not permitted.

4.8. Internal Waters

4.8.1. For the purposes of the Terrorism Act 2000, the term 'vehicle' includes any vessel or hovercraft. And the term 'driver' includes the captain or any person in control of the vehicle, or any member of its crew.[5]

4.8.2. Section 47A authorisations can specify any place or area within a police force area. Police force areas cover inland waters such as lakes, reservoirs and rivers and extend to the low water line at the coast. Police force areas do not cover the sea below the low water line.

4.8.3. Internal waters are defined in detail by the United Nations Convention on the Law of the Sea (UNCLOS); but are typically bays, the estuaries of large rivers and the sea near larger islands. Further information on the extent of internal waters can be obtained by contacting police marine units or the Law of the Sea Division of the United Kingdom Hydrographic Office (UKHO), by email at los@ukho.gov.uk or telephone: 01823 337 900. A map indicating the extent of internal waters can be found on their website by following the links to UK Territorial Sea Limits at http://www.ukho.gov.uk.

4.8.4. A section 47A authorisation can cover any internal waters adjacent to the area specified in the authorisation.

[4] Authorising officers within the Metropolitan Police Service should notify the Mayor's Office for Policing and Crime. Authorising officers within the Ministry of Defence Police should notify the MoD Police Committee.

[5] The term 'vehicle' also includes an aircraft and a train, and the term 'driver' includes a pilot or any person in control of the aircraft or any member of the crew and any member of the train's crew.

4.8.5. Section 47A powers cannot be authorised in territorial seas that are not internal waters. If officers need to stop and search a vessel in UK territorial waters then other powers should be used.

4.9. Exercising Stop and Search Powers under section 47A General Use

4.9.1. When exercising section 47A powers, officers should have a basis for selecting individuals or vehicles to be stopped and searched. This basis will be set by the tactical briefing on the use of powers described in paragraph 4.2.7. Constables should still consider whether powers requiring reasonable suspicion are more appropriate and should only use the powers conferred by a section 47A authorisation if they are satisfied that they cannot meet a threshold of reasonable suspicion.

4.9.2. Searches conducted under section 47A may be carried out only for the purpose of discovering whether there is anything that may constitute evidence that the vehicle being searched is being used for the purposes of terrorism, or the individual being searched is a terrorist.[6] The search can therefore only be carried out to look for anything that would link the vehicle or the person to terrorism.

4.9.3. When selecting individuals to be stopped and searched, officers should consider the following:

- Deciding which power to use—If a section 47A authorisation is in place, the powers conferred by that authorisation may be used as set out in paragraph 4.9.1. above. However, if there is a reasonable suspicion that a person is a terrorist or a vehicle is being used for the purposes of terrorism, then powers requiring reasonable suspicion in section 43 or 43A of the Terrorism Act 2000 should be used as appropriate instead.
- Selecting an individual or vehicle using indicators:
  a) Geographical extent—What are the geographical limits of the authorisation and what are the parameters within which the briefing allows stops and searches to be conducted?
  b) Behaviour—is the person to be stopped and searched acting in a manner that gives cause for concern, or is a vehicle being used in such a manner?
  c) Clothing—could the clothing conceal an article of concern, which may constitute evidence that a person is a terrorist?
  d) Carried items—could an item being carried conceal an article that could constitute evidence that a person is a terrorist or a vehicle is being used for the purposes of terrorism?
- Explanation—officers should be reminded of the need to explain to people why they or their vehicles are being searched.

4.9.4. A constable exercising the power conferred by an authorisation under section 47A may not require a person to remove any clothing in public except for headgear, footwear, an outer coat, a jacket or gloves. Officers should be aware of the cultural sensitivities that may be involved in the removal of headgear.

4.10. Briefing and Tasking

4.10.1. Officers should use the information provided in a briefing to influence their decision to stop and search an individual. Officers should also be fully briefed on and

[6] A 'terrorist' in the context of these powers means a person within the meaning of section 40(1)(b) of the Terrorism Act 2000 (i.e. a person who is or has been concerned in the commission, preparation or instigation of acts of terrorism).

aware of the differences between searches under sections 43, 43A and 47A of the Terrorism Act 2000, and the circumstances in which it is appropriate to use these powers.

4.10.2. The stop and search powers under section 47A of the Terrorism Act 2000 should only be used by officers who have been briefed about their use.

4.10.3. Officers should be reminded that other powers of stop and search may be more appropriate to use.

4.10.4. Officers should be reminded of the need to record information and provide anyone who is stopped and searched, or whose vehicle is stopped and searched, with written confirmation that the stop and search took place and details of the power used. Accurate recording of information is essential in order to monitor the use of the powers, safeguard against misuse and provide individuals with information about the powers which have been used.

4.10.5. The briefing should make officers aware of relevant current information and intelligence including potential threats to locations. Briefings should be as comprehensive as possible in order to ensure officers understand the nature and justification of the operation (which will in turn help officers to understand what evidence they are looking for in the course of a search), while recognising that it may not be possible or appropriate to communicate highly sensitive intelligence to all officers.

4.10.6. Officers should be reminded of the grounds for exercising the powers i.e. only for the purpose of discovering whether there is anything that may constitute evidence that the vehicle being searched is being used for the purposes of terrorism, or the individual being searched is a terrorist. The purpose of the search must therefore be to look for items which connect the vehicle or individual being searched to terrorism, rather than generally for items which could be used (e.g. by another individual in different circumstances) in connection with terrorism.[7]

4.10.7. Briefings should also provide officers with a form of words that they can use when explaining the use of stop and search powers under section 47A of the Terrorism Act 2000. Officers should be reminded at the briefing of the importance of providing the public with as much information as possible about why the stop and search is being undertaken. The following list can help officers to explain the use of the powers when dealing with the public:

- The power that is being used and the fact that an authorisation is in place;
- That the powers conferred by section 47A can be exercised without reasonable suspicion;
- What the operation is seeking to do, e.g. to prevent terrorist activity in response to a specific threat;
- Why the person or vehicle was selected to be searched; and
- What entitlements the person has.

4.10.8. It may also be useful to issue officers with an aide-memoire of search powers in relation to terrorism.

4.10.9. In order to demonstrate that the powers are used appropriately and proportionately, the briefing process must be robust and auditable. All officers involved in

[7] Section 45 of the Terrorism Act 2000 (which is no longer applicable) specified that the purpose of the search under the repealed powers was to search for articles of a kind which could be used in connection with terrorism. Officers should note the different purpose of the search under section 47A.

the process should be reminded that they are fully accountable in law for their own actions. For further information on briefing, see ACPO (2006) Guidance on the National Briefing Model.

4.10.10. Officers should be given clear instructions about where, when and how they should use their powers. If a section 47A authorisation is in place, officers should be clearly tasked so that the power is used appropriately and proportionately. For further information see ACPO (2006) Practice Advice on Tasking and Co-ordination.

4.10.11. There may be exceptional circumstances where it is impractical to brief officers before they are deployed. Where this occurs, supervisors should provide officers with a briefing as soon as possible after deployment.

4.11. Avoiding Discrimination

4.11.1. The Equality Act 2010 makes it unlawful for police officers to discriminate against, harass or victimise any person on the grounds of age, disability, gender reassignment, race, religion or belief, sex, sexual orientation, marriage or civil partnership, pregnancy or maternity in the discharge of their powers. When police forces are carrying out their functions they also have a duty to have due regard to the need to eliminate unlawful discrimination, harassment and victimisation, to advance equality of opportunity and to foster good relations.

4.11.2. Racial or religious profiling is the use of racial, ethnic, religious or other stereotypes, rather than individual behaviour or specific intelligence, as a basis for making operational or investigative decisions about who may be involved in criminal activity.

4.11.3. Officers should take care to avoid any form of racial or religious profiling when selecting people to search under section 47A powers. Profiling in this way may amount to an act of unlawful discrimination, as would selecting individuals for a search on the grounds of any of the other protected characteristics listed in paragraph 4.11.1. Profiling people from certain ethnicities or religious backgrounds may also lose the confidence of communities.

4.11.4. Great care should be taken to ensure that the selection of people is not based solely on ethnic background, perceived religion or other protected characteristic. A person's appearance or ethnic background will sometimes form part of a potential suspect's description, but a decision to search a person should be made only if such a description is available.

4.11.5. Following the failed attacks on the London Underground on 21 July 2005, the approximate age and visible ethnicity of the suspects were quickly identified but little else was immediately known about them. In similar circumstances it may be appropriate to focus searches on people matching the descriptions of the suspects.

4.11.6. Terrorists can come from any background; there is no profile for what a terrorist looks like. In recent years, criminal acts motivated by international terrorism and aimed against people in the United Kingdom have been carried out or attempted by White, Black and Asian British citizens.

4.12. Health and Safety

4.12.1. When undertaking any search, officers should always consider their own safety and the health and safety of others. Officers should have an appropriate level of personal safety training and be in possession of personal protective equipment. Officers carrying out searches should use approved tactics to keep themselves and the public safe. For further information on personal safety training, see ACPO Guidance on Personal Safety Training.

4.12.2. If, during the course of a stop and search, there is a suspicion that a person is in possession of a hazardous device or substance, an officer should immediately request the assistance of officers appropriately trained and equipped to deal with the situation. For further information, refer to local force policy and the ACPO 2009 Manual of Guidance on the Management, Command and Deployment of Armed Officers.

4.13. Photography/Film

4.13.1. There has been widespread concern amongst photographers and journalists about the use of stop and search powers in relation to photography. It is important that police officers are aware, in exercising their counter-terrorism powers, that:

a) members of the public and media do not need a permit to film or photograph in public places;
b) it is not an offence for a member of the public or journalist to take photographs/ film of a public building; and
c) the police have no power to stop the filming or photographing of incidents or police personnel.

4.13.2. Police officers can under section 47A stop and search someone taking photographs/film within an authorised area just as they can stop and search any other member of the public in the proper exercise of their discretion in accordance with the legislation and provisions of this code (see paragraph 4.9.3.). But an authorisation itself does not prohibit the taking of photographs or digital images.

4.13.3. Further guidance on the use of counter-terrorism powers and photography can be found on the Home Office and police websites.

4.13.4. On the rare occasion that an officer reasonably suspects that photographs/ film are being taken as part of hostile terrorist reconnaissance, a search under section 43(1) of the Terrorism Act 2000 or an arrest should be considered. Whilst terrorists may undertake hostile reconnaissance as part of their planning and this could entail the use of a camera or video equipment, it is important that police officers do not automatically consider photography/filming as suspicious behaviour. The size of the camera/video equipment should not be considered as a risk indicator.

4.13.5. Film and memory cards may be seized as part of the search if the officer reasonably suspects they are evidence that the person is a terrorist, or a vehicle is being used for the purposes of terrorism, but officers do not have a legal power to delete images or destroy film. Cameras and other devices should be left in the state they were found and forwarded to appropriately trained staff for forensic examination. The person being searched should never be asked or allowed to turn the device on or off because of the danger of evidence being lost or damaged.

4.13.6. Seizures of cameras etc. may only be made, following a stop and search, where the officer reasonably suspects that they constitute evidence that the person is a terrorist or that the vehicle is being used for the purposes of terrorism as the case may be.

4.14. Seizure of Items

4.14.1. An officer may seize and retain anything which he or she discovers in the course of a search and reasonably suspects may constitute evidence that the person concerned is a terrorist within the meaning of section 40(1)(b) of the Terrorism Act 2000 or the vehicle concerned is being used for the purposes of terrorism.

4.14.2. Anything seized may be retained for as long as necessary in all the circumstances. This includes retention for use as evidence at a trial for an offence.

4.14.3. A record should be made of any item seized or retained and made available with a copy of the record of the stop and search (see sections 5.3. and 5.4.). If reasonable suspicion ceases to apply, the item should be returned to the individual from whom it was seized, or the person in charge of the vehicle from which it was seized unless there are other grounds for retaining it (e.g. in respect of the investigation of a separate offence). If there appears to be a dispute over the ownership of the article, it may be retained for as long as necessary to determine the lawful owner.

5. General

5.1. Conduct of Stops and Searches

5.1.1. All stops and searches must be carried out with courtesy, consideration and respect for the person concerned. Individuals who understand the reason for being stopped and searched are more likely to have a positive experience of an encounter. This has a significant impact on public confidence in the police. Every reasonable effort must be made to minimise the embarrassment that a person being searched may experience. The co-operation of the person to be searched must be sought in every case, even if the person initially objects to the search. A forcible search may be made only if it has been established that the person is unwilling to co-operate or resists. Reasonable force may be used as a last resort if necessary to conduct a search or to detain a person or vehicle for the purposes of a search.

5.1.2. The length of time for which a person or vehicle may be detained must be reasonable and kept to a minimum. The search must be carried out at or near the place where the person or vehicle was first stopped. A person or vehicle may be detained under the stop and search powers at a place other than where the person or vehicle was first stopped, only if that place, be it a police station or elsewhere, is nearby. Such a place should be located within a reasonable travelling distance using whatever mode of travel (on foot or by vehicle) is appropriate.

5.2. Steps to be Taken Prior to a Search

5.2.1. Before any search of a detained person or attended vehicle takes place the officer must take reasonable steps to give their identification number and name of police station (see paragraph 5.3.1.) to the person to be searched or to the person in charge of the vehicle to be searched and to give that person the following information:

a) that they are being detained for the purposes of a search;
b) the legal search power which is being exercised; and
c) a clear explanation of:
    (i) the object of the search (i.e. to search for evidence that the person is a terrorist or that a vehicle is being used for the purposes of terrorism);

(ii) in the case of section 47A of the Terrorism Act 2000, the nature of the power, the fact an authorisation has been given and a brief explanation of why individuals are being stopped and searched, or

(iii) in the case of section 43 or 43A, the grounds for suspicion.

d) that they are entitled to a copy of the record of the search if one is made if they ask within 3 months from the date of the search[8] and that:

(i) if they are not arrested and taken to a police station as a result of the search and it is practicable to make the record on the spot, then immediately after the search is completed they will be given (subject to being called to an incident of higher priority (see paragraphs 5.3.1.–5.3.3.)) if they request, either:

- a copy of the record, or
- a receipt which explains how they can obtain a copy of the full record or access to an electronic copy of the record.[9]

(ii) if they are arrested and taken to a police station as a result of the search, that the record will be made at the station as part of their custody record and they will be given, if they request, a copy of their custody record which includes a record of the search as soon as practicable whilst they are at the station.

5.2.2. A person who is not provided with an immediate copy of a stop and search record may request a copy within 3 months of being stopped and searched. In addition a person is also entitled, on application, to a written statement that they were stopped by virtue of the powers conferred by section 47A(2) or (3), if requested within 12 months of the stop taking place.

5.2.3. If the person to be searched, or person in charge of a vehicle to be searched, does not appear to understand what is being said, or there is any doubt about the person's ability to understand English, the officer must take reasonable steps to bring information regarding the person's rights to his or her attention. If the person is deaf or cannot understand English and is accompanied by someone, then the officer may try to establish whether that person can interpret or otherwise help the officer to give the required information.[10] This does not preclude an officer from conducting a search once he or she has taken reasonable steps to explain the person's rights. In some situations forces should consider having information leaflets produced in languages other than English.

5.3. Recording Requirements

Searches which do not result in an arrest

5.3.1. When an officer carries out a search under sections 43(1), 43A or in the exercise of powers conferred by an authorisation under section 47A and the search does not result in the person searched or person in charge of the vehicle searched, being arrested and taken to a police station, a record must be made of it at the time, electronically or on paper, unless there are circumstances which make this wholly impracticable (see paragraph 5.2.1.d) and section 5.3.3.). If a record is not made at the time of the

[8] Not applicable in Scotland.

[9] A receipt may take the form of a simple business card which includes sufficient information to locate the record should the person ask for a copy, for example, the date and place of the search or a reference number.

[10] The officer may consider a language line service more appropriate.

stop and search, the officer must make the record as soon as practicable after the search is completed. There may be situations in which it is not practicable to obtain the information necessary to complete a record, but the officer should make every reasonable effort to do so. If it is not possible to complete a record in full, an officer must make every reasonable effort to at least record details of the date, time and place where the stop and search took place, the power under which it was carried out and the officer's identification number.

5.3.2. If the record is made at the time, the person who has been searched or who is in charge of the vehicle that has been searched must be asked if they want a copy of the record and if they do, they must (subject to paragraph 5.3.3.) be given immediately, either:

(i) a copy of the record, or
(ii) a receipt which explains how they can obtain a copy of the full record or access to an electronic copy of the record.

5.3.3. An officer is not required to provide a copy of the full record or a receipt at the time if they are called to an incident of higher priority.

5.3.4. In situations where it is not practicable to provide a written copy of the record or immediate access to an electronic copy of the record or a receipt at the time, the officer should give the person details of the police station at which they may request a copy of the record.

Searches which result in an arrest

5.3.5. If a search in the exercise of any power to which this Code applies results in a person being arrested and taken to a police station, the officer carrying out the search is responsible for ensuring that a record of the search is made as part of their custody record. The custody officer must then ensure that the person is asked if they want a copy of the record and if they do, that they are given a copy as soon as practicable.

5.4. Record of Search

5.4.1. The record of a search must always include the following information:

a) a note of the self-defined ethnicity, and, if different, the ethnicity as perceived by the officer making the search, of the person searched or of the person in charge of the vehicle searched (as the case may be) (see paragraph 5.4.2.);
b) the date, time and place the person or vehicle was searched;
c) the object of the search;
d) in the case of:
    (i) the powers under section 47A of the Terrorism Act 2000, the nature of the power, the fact an authorisation has been given and the reason the person or vehicle was selected for the search;
    (ii) the powers under section 43 or 43A, the grounds for suspicion;
e) the officer's warrant number or other identification number (see paragraph 5.4.4.).

5.4.2. Officers should record the self-defined ethnicity of every person stopped according to the categories used in the 2001 census question listed at Annex B. The person should be asked to select one of the five main categories representing broad ethnic groups and then a more specific cultural background from within this group. An additional 'Not stated' box is available but should not be offered to respondents explicitly. Officers should be aware and explain to members of the public, especially where concerns are raised, that this information is required to obtain a true picture of stop and search activity and to help improve ethnic monitoring, eliminate any discriminatory practice, and promote effective use of the powers. If the person gives what appears to the officer to be an 'incorrect' answer (e.g. a person who appears to be white states that they are black), the officer should record the response that has been given and then record their own perception of the person's ethnic background by using the PNC classification system.

5.4.3. For the purposes of completing the search record, there is no requirement to record the name, address and date of birth of the person searched or the person in charge of a vehicle which is searched and the person is under no obligation to provide this information.[11] An officer may remind a person that providing these details will ensure that the police force is able to provide information about the stop and search in future should the person request that information (see paragraphs 5.2.1.d) and 5.2.2.) or if it is otherwise required.

5.4.4. The names of police officers are not required to be shown on the search record in the case of operations linked to the investigation of terrorism or otherwise where an officer reasonably believes that recording names might endanger the officers. In such cases (including in relation to section 47A searches) the record must show the officers' warrant or other identification number and duty station.

5.4.5. A record is required for each person and each vehicle searched. However, if a person is in a vehicle and both are searched, and the object and grounds of the search are the same, only one record need be completed. If more than one person in a vehicle is searched, separate records for each search of a person must be made. If only a vehicle is searched, the self-defined ethnic background of the person in charge of the vehicle must be recorded, unless the vehicle is unattended.

5.4.6. The record of the grounds for making a search must, briefly but informatively, explain the reason for suspecting the person concerned, by reference to the person's behaviour and/or other circumstances, or, in the case of searches under section 47A, the reason why a particular person or vehicle was selected.

5.4.7. After searching an unattended vehicle, or anything in or on it, an officer must leave a notice in it (or on it, if things on it have been searched without opening it) recording the fact that it has been searched.

5.4.8. The notice must include the name of the police station to which the officer concerned is attached and state where a copy of the record of the search may be obtained and how (if applicable) an electronic copy may be accessed and where any application for compensation should be directed.

5.4.9. The vehicle must, if practicable, be left secure.

5.5. Monitoring and Supervising the Use of Stop and Search Powers

5.5.1. Supervising officers must monitor the use of stop and search powers. They should consider in particular whether there is any evidence that they are being exercised on the basis of stereotyped images or inappropriate generalisations. Supervising officers should satisfy themselves that the practice of officers under their supervision in

[11] This does not apply in Scotland for a search carried out with reasonable grounds for suspicion where section 13 of the Criminal Procedure (Scotland) Act 1995 applies.

stopping, searching and recording is fully in accordance with this code. Supervisors must also examine whether the records reveal any trends or patterns which give cause for concern, and if so take appropriate action to address this.

5.5.2. Supervision and monitoring must be supported by the compilation of comprehensive statistical records of stops and searches at force, area and local level. Any apparently disproportionate use of the powers by particular officers or groups of officers or in relation to specific sections of the community should be identified and investigated. Statistical data on the use of the powers should be provided quarterly (in arrears) to the Home Office.

5.5.3. In order to promote public confidence in the use of the powers, forces in consultation with police authorities must make arrangements for the records to be scrutinised by representatives of the community, and to explain the use of the powers at a local level. Arrangements for public scrutiny of records should take account of the right to confidentiality of those stopped and searched.

5.6. Use of Powers by PCSOs (England & Wales only)

5.6.1. Under the Police Reform Act 2002, Police Community Support Officers (PCSOs) may (where an authorisation is in place) search vehicles and anything carried by individuals under section 47A, provided they have been designated under the 2002 Act by their chief constable, and that they are in the company of a constable who is supervising them. PCSOs may not, however, search people or people's clothing under the section 47A powers. PCSOs can stop:

- any pedestrian; and
- any vehicle;

and search

- anything carried by a pedestrian;
- any vehicle;
- anything carried by a driver or passenger; and
- anything on or in a vehicle.

5.6.2. Authorising officers may consider whether to include PCSOs within a stop and search operation authorised by section 47A. If PCSOs are to use the powers available, they should be properly briefed on the limitations set out in this section, as well as being briefed on the appropriate use of the powers.

6. Community Engagement

6.1. Community Engagement

6.1.1. Stop and search is one of the ways in which the police can protect communities from terrorism. Ongoing community engagement is essential in improving relationships with the community and can help to:

a) Increase confidence in the Police Service through a greater understanding of why the powers of stop and search are needed and the reasons for their use;
b) Improve public reassurance;
c) Increase the flow of information and intelligence from the community to the Police Service, which can help to assist with investigations and, ultimately, the prevention of terrorist activity; and
d) Minimise any possible negative impact of police activities within communities.

6.1.2. Police forces may, for example, use existing community engagement arrangements. However, where stop and search powers affect sections of the community with whom channels of communication are difficult or non existent, these should be identified and put in place. For example, if section 47A authorisations have primarily been made around transport hubs, effort should be made to engage with people using those hubs.

6.1.3. When planning a counter-terrorism search operation, police authorities and the local CONTEST prevent strategic partnership should be involved at the earliest opportunity to provide advice and assistance in identifying mechanisms for engaging with communities. For further information on the government's counter-terrorism strategy, see http://www. homeoffice.gov.uk/counter-terrorism/uk-counter-terrorism-strat/.

6.1.4. If a force has a 'PREVENT' lead officer they should be engaged with the planning process. Police forces may also consider using the media to inform and reassure the community. Note: use of the media is not an alternative to community consultation.

6.1.5. Other stakeholders that the Police Service should consider engagement with include:

(i) Community Safety Partnerships (CSPs);
(ii) Local Criminal Justice Boards (LCJBs);
(iii) Local Strategic Partnerships (LSPs); and
(iv) Neighbourhood Panels.

6.2 Retrospective and Ongoing Engagement

6.2.1. The stop and search powers under section 47A of the Terrorism Act 2000 are only for use in circumstances where the authorising officer reasonably suspects an act of terrorism will take place and it will not always be possible to carry out community engagement prior to authorisation. In these circumstances, police forces should carry out a retrospective review of the use of the powers, including the stakeholders above.

6.2.2. Police forces should continue to monitor the use of section 47A powers for the duration of an authorisation, both in discussion with community representatives and by explaining how and why the powers are being used to individuals who are stopped and searched.

6.2.3. Officers should be ready to explain to individuals why the powers are in place, insofar as this can be communicated without disclosing sensitive intelligence or causing undue alarm. Stop and search operations should form part of wider counter-terrorism policing, and public awareness of the powers should be considered as part of any wider communications strategy associated with an operation.

6.3 The Role of Police Authorities

6.3.1. Police authorities continue to have a role in working with their local force to build community confidence in the appropriate use of stop and search.

6.3.2. The Association of Police Authorities (APA) has developed guidance for police authorities which offers both practical advice and examples of good practice to help raise awareness of stop and search.

6.3.3. Where section 47A searches under the Terrorism Act 2000 have been carried out in a particular police force area, the police authority may review the use of these powers by that force. For searches carried out within the metropolitan police district, the Mayor's Office for Policing and Crime may review the use of these powers. Such a review may focus on supervision, briefing and analysis of the statistics recorded. This review may also involve members of the community.

For details of the annexes to this Code of Practice, please go to <http://www.homeoffice.gov.uk/publications/counter-terrorism/stop-search-code-of-practice>.

Bibliography

Books and Reports

ACPO *Interim Practice Advice on Stop and Search in Relation to the Terrorism Act 2000* (ACPO and NCPE, 2005).

ACPO *Practice Advice on Professionalising the Business of Neighbourhood Policing* (ACPO 2006).

ACPO *Neighbourhood Policing Performance Guide* (ACPO, 2007).

ACPO *National Counter-Terrorism Policing Structure—Building Capacity* (ACPO, 2008).

Augustus, G, and Clarence, C, *Understanding Terrorism: Challenges, Perspectives, and Issues* (London: SAGE Publications, 2012).

Baylis, J, and Smith, S, *The Globalization of World Politics: An Introduction to International Relations* 2nd edn (Oxford: Oxford University Press, 2007).

Bergen, P, *The Longest War: America and Al-Qaeda Since 9/11* (London: The Free Press, 2011).

Beuter, LE, Bongor, B, Brown, LM, Breckenridge, JN, and Zimbardo, PG, *Psychology of Terrorism* (Oxford: Oxford University Press, 2007).

Bongar, B, Brown, L, and Beutler, L, *Psychology of Terrorism* (Oxford: Oxford University Press, 2006).

Bowers, R, Jones, A, and Lodge, HD, *Blackstone's Guide to the Terrorism Act 2006* (Oxford: Oxford University Press, 2006).

Brain, T, *A History of Policing in England and Wales from 1974: A Turbulent Journey* (Oxford: Oxford University Press, 2010).

Brain, T, *A Future for Policing in England and Wales* (Oxford: Oxford University Press, 2013).

Brown, D, *Combating International Crime: The Longer Arm of the Law* (Oxford: Routledge-Cavendish, 2008).

Bruce, S, *The Red Hand: Protestant Paramilitaries in Northern Ireland* (Oxford: Oxford University Press, 1992).

Burke, J, *Al-Qaeda: The True Story of Radical Islam* (London: Penguin, 2007).

Burke, J, *On the Road to Kandahar: Travels through Conflict in the Islamic World* (London: Penguin, 2007).

Burke, J, *The 9/11 Wars* (London: Penguin, 2012).

Caless, B, *Blackstone's PCSO Handbook* (Second Edition) (Oxford: Oxford University Press, 2010).

Caless, B, Harfield, C, and Spruce, B, *Blackstone's Police Operational Handbook: Practice and Procedure* (Second Edition) (Oxford: Oxford University Press, 2013).

Carlile, Lord A, *Operation Pathway Report Following Review* (2009).

Chandler, M, and Gunaratna, R, *Countering Terrorism: Can We Meet the Threat of Global Violence?* (London: Reakton Books Ltd, 2007).

Combs, CC, *Terrorism in the 21st Century* 3rd edn (New Jersey: Prentice Hall, 2003).

Coogan, P, *The IRA* (London: Harper Collins, 1995).

Coolsaet, R, *Jihadi Terrorism and the Radicalisation Challenge* (second edition) (London: Ashgate, 2011).

Crenshaw, M, *Explaining Terrorism: Causes, Processes and Consequences* (Oxford: Routledge, 2010).

Daniel Silk, P, Spalek, B, and O'Rawe, M, *Preventing Ideological Violence: Communities, Police and Case Studies of 'Success'—International Law, Crime, and Politics* (London: Palgrave Macmillan, 2013).

Davies, B, *Terrorism: Inside A World Phenomenon* (London: Virgin Books Ltd, 2003).

Davies, L, *Educating Against Extremism* (Staffordshire: Trentham Books Limited, 2008).

English, R, *Armed Struggle: The History of the IRA* (London: Pan, 2012).

Harfield, C, and Harfield, K, *Covert Investigation* (Oxford: Oxford University Press, 2005).

Harnden, T, *Bandit Country: The IRA and South Armagh* (London: Hodder, 2000).

HM Government *Countering International Terrorism: The United Kingdom's Strategy* (2006a).

HM Government *Report into the London Terrorist Attacks on 7 July 2005* (2006b).

HM Government *Threat Levels—The System to Assess the Threat from International Terrorism* (2006c).

HM Government *The Definition of Terrorism—A Report by Lord Carlile of Berriew Q.C. Independent Reviewer of Terrorism Legislation* (2007).

HM Government *Preventing Violent Extremism—A Strategy for Delivery* (2008a).

HM Government *Report on the Operation in 2007 of the Terrorism Act 2000 and of the Terrorism Act 2006* (2008b).

HM Government *The National Security Strategy of the United Kingdom—Security in an Interdependent World* (2008c).

HM Government *The Prevent Strategy—A Guide for Local Partners in England and Wales* (2008d).

HM Government *London 2012 Olympic and Paralympic Safety and Security Strategy* (2009).

HM Government *The United Kingdom's Cyber Security Strategy* (2009).

HM Government *The United Kingdom's Strategy for Countering International Terrorism-CONTEST* (2009).

HM Government *The Prevent Strategy* (2011).

HM Government *The United Kingdom's Strategy for Countering International Terrorism-CONTEST* (2011).

HM Revenue & Customs *Protecting Society against Crime and Terrorism* (2006).

Home Office *Extremism: Protecting People and Property* (2001).

Home Office *Our Shared Values—A Shared Responsibility*: First International Conference on Radicalisation and Political Violence (2007).

Home Office *From The Neighbourhood To The National: Policing Our Communities Together*: Green Paper (2008a).

Home Office *Working Together To Protect The Public: The Home Office Strategy 2008–11* (2008b).

Home Office and UK Border Agency, *A Strong New Force at the Border* (2008c).

Home Office and UK Border Agency, *Enforcing the Deal—Our Plans for Enforcing the Immigration Laws in the United Kingdom's Communities* (2008d).

Horgan, J, T*errorism Studies: A Reader* (Oxford: Routledge, 2011).

Houck, M, *Forensic Science: Modern Methods of Solving Crime* (London: Preager, 2007).

Jackson, R, *Terrorism: A Critical Introduction* (London: Palgrave Macmillan, 2011).
Kegley, C, *The New Global Terrorism: Characteristics, Causes, Controls* (London: Pearson, 2002).
Kilcommins, S, and Vaughan, B, *Terrorism, Rights and the Rule of Law: Negotiating Justice in Ireland* (Devon: Willan Publishing, 2008).
Lambert, R, *Countering Al-Qaeda in London: Police and Muslims in Partnership* (London: C Hurst & Co Publishers Ltd, 2011).
Masferrer, A, and Walker, C, *Counter-Terrorism, Human Rights and the Rule of Law: Crossing Legal Boundaries in Defence of the State* (London: Edward Elgar Publishing Ltd, 2013).
Moloney, E, *A Secret History of the IRA* 2nd edn (London: Pearson Penguin Books, 2007).
Neumann, P, *Old and New Terrorism* (London: Polity Press, 2009).
Niksch, L, *Abu Sayyaf: Target of Philippine—US Anti-Terrorism Co-operation* (Washington: The Library of Congress, 2002).
Omand, D, *Securing the State* (London: Hurst & Co Publishers Ltd, 2012).
Patterson, H, *Ireland Since 1939: The Persistence of Conflict* (London: Pearson Penguin Books, 2007).
Rapoport, DC, *Inside Terrorist Organisations* 2nd edn (London: Frank Cass, 2001).
Ratcliffe, J, *Intelligence-Led Policing* (Devon: Willan Publishing, 2008).
Reiner, R, *The Politics of the Police* (Oxford: Oxford University Press, 2010).
Rogers, C, *Crime Reduction Partnerships*, (Oxford: Oxford University Press, 2006).
Sageman, M, *Leaderless Jihad: Terror Networks in the Twenty-first Century* (Pennsylvania: University of Pennsylvania Press, 2000).
Sageman, M, *Understanding Terror Networks* (Pennsylvania: University of Pennsylvania Press, 2004).
Silke, A, *Terrorists, Victims and Society: Psychological Perspectives on Terrorism and its Consequences* (Chichester: Wiley, 2003).
Silke, A, *Psychology of Counter-Terrorism* (Oxford: Routledge, 2010).
Sinclair, A, *An Anatomy of Terror: A History of Terrorism* (London: Macmillan, 2003).
Spalek, B, *Counter-Terrorism: Community-Based Approaches to Preventing Terror Crime* (London: Palgrave Macmillan, 2012).
Staniforth, A, *The Routledge Companion to UK Counter Terrorism* (Oxford: Routledge, 2012).
Staniforth, A, and Police National Legal Database, *Blackstone's Counter-Terrorism Handbook* 3rd edn (Oxford: Oxford University Press, 2013).
Staniforth, A, and Police National Legal Database, *Blackstone's Handbook of Ports and Border Security* (Oxford: Oxford University Press, 2013).
Sterba, JP, *Terrorism and International Justice* (Oxford: Oxford University Press, 2003).
Sutherland, Lord, *Opinion of the High Court of Justiciary at Camp Zeist, Netherlands* (1998).
Taylor, P, *The Provos: The IRA and Sinn Fein* (London: Bloomsbury, 1998).
Thomas, P, *Responding to the Threat of Violent Extremism: Failing to Prevent* (London: Bloomsbury Academic, 2012).
Walker, C, *Blackstone's Guide to Anti-Terrorism Legislation* (Oxford: Oxford University Press, 2006).
Walker, C, *Terrorism and the Law* (Oxford: Oxford University Press, 2009).

Whittaker, DJ, *The Terrorism Reader* (London: Routledge, 2001).

Whittaker, DJ, *Terrorism: Understanding the Global Threat* (London: Longman, 2002).

Wright, L, *The Looming Tower: Al-Qaeda's Road to 9/11* (New York: Penguin Books, 2006).

Online articles

BBC (1997), 'IRA Prisoners Taste Freedom' <http://news.bbc.co.uk/1/hi/uk/40874.stm> accessed August 2013.

BBC (1988a), 'On This Day—Debris of Disaster' <http://news.bbc.co.uk/onthisday/hi/witness/december/21/newsid3332000/3332069.stm> accessed June 2013.

BBC (1988b), 'On This Day—Harrods Bomb Blast Kills Six' <http://news.bbc.co.uk/onthisday/hi/dates/stories/december/17/newsid2538000/25381.stm> accessed July 2013.

BBC (2001a), 'Republican Fugitives Freed on Licence' <http://news.bbc.co.uk/1/hi/northern_ireland/1244975.stm> accessed September 2013.

BBC (2001b), 'Y2K Bomb Plot Man Convicted' <http://news.bbc.co.uk/1/hi/world/americas/1265159.stm> accessed September 2013.

BBC (2003a), 'Golden Temple Attack' <http://news.bbc.co.uk/go/pr/fr/-/1/hi/world/south_asia/3774035.stm> accessed September 2013.

BBC (2003b), 'Profile: Gulbuddin Hekmatyar' <http://news.bbc.co.uk/1/hi/world/middle_east/2701547.stm> accessed October 2013.

BBC (2005a), 'Call for Police to Solve Sikh Murder' <http://news.bbc.co.uk/1/hi/uk/4354435.stm> accessed September 2013.

BBC (2005b), 'Millennium Bomber Gets 22 Years' <http://news.bbc.co.uk/go/pr/fr/-/1/hi/world/americas/4722409.stm> accessed September 2013.

BBC (2006a), 'Groups Banned by New Terror Law' <http://news.%20bbc.co.uk/1/hi/uk_;politics/5188136.stm> accessed October 2013.

BBC (2006b), 'Militants jailed for Bali attacks' <http://news.bbc.co.uk/1/hi/world/asia-pacific/5322498.stm> accessed October 2013.

BBC (2006c), 'Video of 7 July Bomber Released' <http://news.bbc.co.uk/2/hi/uk_news/5154714.stm> accessed July 2013.

BBC (2007a), 'Glasgow Airport attack man dies' <http://news.bbc.co.uk/2/hi/uk_news/scotland/glasgow_and_west/6928854.stm> accessed October 2013.

BBC (2007b), 'Police Avert car bomb carnage' <http://news.bbc.co.uk/2/hi/uk_news/6252276.stm> accessed October 2013.

BBC (2008), 'Profile: Ayman al-Zawahiri' <http://news.bbc.co.uk/1/hi/world/middle-east/7216127.stm> accessed June 2013.

BBC (2009) 'Three arrested over PC Caroll murder' <http://news.bbc.co.uk/1/hi/northern_ireland/8505672.stm> accessed July 2013.

BBC (2009) 'Murder police examine base CCTV' <http://news.bbc.co.uk/1/hi/northern_ireland/7931774.stm> accessed October 2013.

Burgess, M (2002), 'In The Spotlight—Islamic Movement of Uzbekistan (IMU)' <http://www.cdi.org/terrorism/imu.cfm> accessed October 2013.

CBC News (2005), 'Air India: Key Characters' <http://www.cbc.ca/news/background/airindia/key_characters.html> accessed September 2013.

Daily Telegraph (2009) 'Bob Quick Resigns Over Terror Blunder' <http://www.telegraph.co.uk/news/uknews/5129561/Bob-Quick-resigns-over-terror-blunder.htm> accessed March 2013.

Hensher, P, and Margoyles, M (2006), 'The fight against terror: Surveillance UK' The Independent <http://www.independent.co.uk/news/uk/crime/the-fight-against-terror-surveillance-uk> accessed June 2013.

Jenkins, R, and McGory, D (2007), 'How Al-Qaeda tried to bring Baghdad to Birmingham' <http://www.timesonline.co.uk/tol/news/uk/crime/article1308572.ece> accessed April 2013.

National Commission on the Terrorist Attacks upon the United States (2002), '9/11 Commission Report' <http://www.gpoaccess.gov/911> accessed August 2013.

Newspaper and Journal articles

Clarke, P, 'Learning from Experience—Counter-Terrorism in the UK since 9/11' The Inaugural Colin Cramphorn Memorial Lecture, Policy Exchange (London, 2007).

Gardham, D, and Rayner, G, 'British suicide bombers planned to blow airliners out of the sky', *Daily Telegraph*, 4 April 2008.

Fresco, A, McGory, D, and Norfolk, A, 'Video of Suicide Bomber Released', *The Times*, 6 July 2006.

Manningham-Buller, Dame E, 'Partnership and Continuous Improvement in Countering Twenty-First Century Terrorism', *Policing: A Journal of Policy and Practice*, Vol. I, No. 1 (Oxford: Oxford University Press, 2007).

Index

3/11 (Madrid train bombings, 2004) 38–40, 47–8
7/7 (London tube bombings, 2005) 38, 40, 74–9, 133, 155, 179
9/11 (New York City WTC attack, 2001) 30, 47, 59, 68, 72, 88, 110, 121–4, 133, 141, 155, 161, 165, 186–7
  economic impact 9/11 37–40
17 November Revolutionary Organisation (N17) 237 (App 1)

Abu Nidal Organisation (ANO) 237 (App 1)
Abu Sayyaf Group (ASG) 237 (App 1)
Al-Gama'at al-Islamiya (GI) 237, 241 (App 1)
Al Ghurabaa 237 (App 1)
Al Ittihad Al Islamiya (AIAI) 237 (App 1)
Al Qa'ida (AQ)
  3/11 (Madrid train bombings) 39–40, 47–8, 72
  7/7 (London tube bombings) 76–9
  9/11 (WTC, New York) 38, 72
  in the Arabian Peninsula (AQ-AP) 11–12, 16
  Bali bombings 47
  CONTEST Strategy 88, 167, 179
  counter-terrorism investigations 120
  cyber terrorism 28–9
  followers of ideology 14–16
  Frankfurt Cell 71–2
  hostile reconnaisance 71–2
  in Iraq (AQ-I) 11
  justification for actions 50
    belief system 51
  Kurdish battalions (AQ-KB) 11
  legislative framework 123
  lone-actor terrorists 17–18
    online radicalisation 17–18
  in the Maghreb (AQ-M) 11–12
  national threat 8–12, 19, 25–6
    affiliates 10–11, 93
    conflicts overseas 19
    foreign fighters 19
    international vs. domestic terrorism 25–6
    leadership 9–10
    UK threat 10 *fig.*, 12, 93, 167, 202
  NIRT, comparison with 25–6
  objectives 50–1, 88
  Operation Gamble 73–4
  prosecution 114
  'Pursue' strategy 93
  radicalisation
    drivers of 184–92
    online 17–18
  religious ideology 14–16, 167, 186, 237
  resilience 30
  Ricin Plot 69
  suicide terrorism 37, 76
  terrorist organisations and networks 55, 59, App 1
    organisational structure 59–60, 63
  training methods 164
  universities and 170
  weaknesses of 30
  see also World Trade Center (WTC)
Al Shabaab 238 (App 1)
  Armed Assault 16–17
All Communities Together Now (ACT NOW)
  National Prevent Delivery Unit (NPDU) 174–6
AMISOM (African peacekeeping force)
  attacks against 16
Ansar al-Islam (AI) 238 (App 2)
Ansar al-Sunna (AS) 238 (App 2)
Ansarul Muslimina Fi Biladis Sudan 238 (App 2)
Anti-Social Behaviour (ASB)
  community response 85
  Key Individual Networks (KIN) 221
  neighbourhood policing 209–10, 215, 221
    reducing levels of ASB 226–7
  perceptions of 210
    perceived reductions 220
anti-terror legislation 119–55
  definitions 126–9
    retrospective application 128

anti-terror legislation (*cont.*)
'terrorism' 127
'terrorist' 127–8
'terrorist investigation' 129
effective application 120
independent oversight 124–6
asset-freezing 125
non-statutory functions 126
statutory functions 125–6
terrorism acts 125
TPIMs 125
legal framework 121–4
guiding principles 121–2
new 122–4
UK 123 *fig.*
Officers' powers and duties 153–5
rank specific 155
operational reality 120–1
see also cordons; parking; power of arrest; stop and search powers; Terrorism Prevention and Investigation Measures (TPIMs)
Anti-Terrorism Crime and Security Act 2001 (ATCSA) 122
Armed Islamic Group (GIA) 238 (App 2)
As Low As Reasonably Practicable (ALARP) 88
Asbat Al-Ansar 238 (App 2)
Association of Chief Police Officers (ACPO)
ACPOS Coordinator Counter Terrorism 111
armed officers App 2 (258)
authorisations App 2 (249)
briefing App 2 (257)
Counter Terrorism Internet Referral Unit (CTIRU) 197–8
domestic extremism 112
National Prevent Delivery Unit (NPDU) 174
neighbourhood policing principles 212–26, 234
personal safety training App 2 (258)
Prevent Strategy 174–7
Prevent Pyramid model 192
tasking and co-ordination App 2 (257)

Babbar Khalsa (BK) 238 (App 1)
Baluchistan Liberation Army (BLA) 239 (App 1)
Basque Homeland and Liberty, *see* ETA
Beslan Siege (2004) 74–5
Boko Haram (BH)
political objectives 239 (App 2)
UK national threat 12–13
Border Policing Command (BPC)
National Crime Agency (NCA) 113
objectives and purpose 113
roles and responsibilities 102 (table 4.2)

Cabinet Office (CO)
Cabinet Office Briefing Room (COBR) 107–9
organisation 107–8
strategic objectives 107–8
CONTEST roles and responsibilities 100 (table 4.2)
intelligence community 106
objectives and purpose 107
UK counter-terrorism strategy 97
UK Security and Intelligence Coordinator 88
CCTV (Closed Circuit Television)
7/7 76–8
Armed Assaults of Lashkar-e-Tayyiba 64
London Nail Bomber 62–3
Centre for the Protection of the National Infrastructure (CPNI)
CONTEST roles and responsibilities 100 (table 4.2)
NaCTSO 102 (table 4.2)
Chemical, Biological, Radiological, Nuclear or Explosive (CBRNE) 68–9
Al Qa'ida Ricin Plot 69
'Prepare' strategy 111
Child Exploitation and Online Protection Centre (CEOP)
CONTEST roles and responsibilities 102 (table 4.2)
National Crime Agency (NCA) 114
commission, preparation, or instigation (CPI)
definition of 'terrorist' 127
Community Engagement Field Officers (CEFOs)
neighbourhood policing 217, 222
Community Impact Assessment (CIA)
National Community Tension Team (NCTT) 177
Conflict-Engaged Citizens (CEC)
conflicts overseas 19–23
CONTEST (COuNter-TErrorism STrategy) 88–104
construction 88–9

challenges 103, 179
community engagement 264 (App 2)
CONTEST 2 88
CONTEST 3 88, 104
counter-terrorism policing 111, 113
governance 98–9
launch 88
neighbourhood policing 214
'Prepare' strategy 95–7, 111, 167, 174
cycle 97–8
key objectives 99 *fig.*
'Prevent' strategy 90–1, 111, 167
Act Now 175–6
Channel 176–7
in communities 168–9
The Conviction Project 178
cycle 168
delivery 173–9
in higher education 170
NCTT 177
NPDU 174–7
Operation Hindsight 175
permanent presence 215
priorities 168
in prison 172–3
risk reduction in universities 171–2
role of the police 171
in schools 169–70
unintended consequences 173
'Protect' strategy 93–6, 111, 167, 174
key objectives 96 *fig.*
'Pursue' strategy 91–3, 111, 167, 174
responses 84–6
community 85–6
criminal justice 85
military 84–5
roles and responsibilities 99–103
shared values 177
strategic aim 89, 107, 179
strategy structure 89
twelve rules 86–7
see also Overseas CONTEST Group (OCG)
Continuity Army Council 242 (App 1)
Continuity Irish Republican Army (CIRA)
murder of PC Stephen Caroll 24
cordons 145–8
designating a cordoned area 146–7
duration of designation 147
police powers 148
terrorist investigation 146
see also anti-terror legislation
Counter-Terrorism Act 2008 (C-TACT)
anti-terror legislation 122
Counter Terrorism Division (CTD)
Deputy Head 162
establishment 114
Operation OVERT 189
role and responsibilities 116
see also Special Crime and Counter Terrorism Division (SCCTD)
Counter Terrorism and Extremism Liaison Officers (CTELOs)
role and responsibilities 197
Counter Terrorism Intelligence Units (CTIU)
counter-terrorism policing 111
Counter Terrorism Internet Referral Unit (CTIRU)
establishment 197
online radicalisation 197
role and responsibilities 197–8
Counter-Terrorism Local Profile (CTLP)
neighbourhood policing principles 215, 221, 223–4
counter-terrorism policing 111–14
domestic extremism 112
National Crime Agency 113–14
strategic policing requirements 112–13
widening police portfolio 114
Crown Prosecution Service (CPS) 114–15
Code for Crown Prosecutors 115–16
criminal justice system 116
SCCTD 114–15
counter terrorism strategy, *see* **CONTEST (COuNter-TErrorism STrategy)**
Counter Terrorism Units (CTU)
operational realities 120
Police Counter Terrorism Network 111
Cumann na mBan 242 (App 1)
Cyber Terrorism (CyT)
cyber terrorist 007 28–9
cyber threats 29
GCHQ cyber threats 110
National Crime Agency 114
online radicalisation and 185, 204
public order maintenance 113
UK national security strategy 4, 6, 8, 9 *fig.*, 28, 96, 100 (table 4.2)
see also Counter Terrorism Internet Referral Unit (CTIRU)

Defence Intelligence Staff (DIS)
intelligence community 106, 110
Department for Business, Innovation and Skills (BIS)
CONTEST roles and responsibilities 100 (table 4.2)
Department for Communities and Local Government (DCLG)
CONTEST roles and responsibilities 100 (table 4.2)
Department for Education (DfE)
CONTEST roles and responsibilities 100 (table 4.2)
Department of Energy & Climate Change (DECC)
CONTEST roles and responsibilities 100 (table 4.2)
Department for Environment, Food and Rural Affairs (DEFRA)
CONTEST roles and responsibilities 100 (table 4.2)
Department of Health (DH)
CONTEST roles and responsibilities 101 (table 4.2)
Department for International Development (DFID)
CONTEST roles and responsibilities 100 (table 4.2)
Department for Transport (DfT)
CONTEST roles and responsibilities 101 (table 4.2)
devolved administrations 101 (table 4.2)
Distinguished Service Order (DSO) 65

Economic Crime Command (ECC)
CONTEST roles and responsibilities 102 (table 4.2)
National Crime Agency (NCA) 114
Economic Key Points (EKP)
mainstream policing activity 214
Egyptian Islamic Jihad (EIJ) 239 (App 1)
Environments Visual Aids (EVA)
intelligence-led deployment 223
European Court of Human Rights (ECtHR)
stop and search powers 131–3
Euskadi Ta Askatasuna (ETA)
3/11 accusations 47
nationalist terrorism 44
political objectives 238
Extreme Left-Wing (XLW) terrorism
definition 41–2
ideological terrorism 44
Extreme Right-Wing (XRW) terrorism
definition 41
ideological terrorism 44
national threats 8, 9 *fig.*
Radicalisation-Factor Model (RFM) 198
UK national security 26–7
Martin Gilleard case 26–7

Federal Bureau of Investigation (FBI)
description of terrorism 34–5
Federal Emergency Management Agency (FEMA)
9/11 and 38
Federally Administered Tribal Areas (Pakistan)(FATA)
Al Qa'ida followers 14
Al Qa'ida leadership 9
Fianna na hEireann 242 (App 1)
Foreign and Commonwealth Office (FCO)
CONTEST roles and responsibilities 101 (table 4.2)

Glasgow Central Mosque terror threats (2012) 21–2
Government Communications Headquarters (GCHQ)
CONTEST roles and responsibilities 101 (table 4.2)
cyber threats 29
intelligence community 106, 109–10
Government Liaison Officer (GLO)
Cabinet Office role 108
Government Office for Science (GO-S/ GO-Science)
CONTEST roles and responsibilities 101 (table 4.2)
Gross Domestic Product (GDP)
United States 38
Groupe Islamique Combattant Marocain (GICM) 239 (App 1)

Hamas Izz al-Din al-Qassem Brigades
home-grown terrorism 21
political objectives 239 (App 1)
Harakat Mujahideen (HM) 239 (App 1)
Harakat-ul-Jihad-I-Islami (HUJI) 239 (App 1)
Harakat-ul-Jihad-I-Islami (Bangladesh) (HUJI-B) 239 (App 1)

Harakat-ul-Mujahideen/Alami (HuM/A) 239 (App 1)
Her Majesty's Inspectorate of Constabulary (HMIC)
neighbourhood policing 226
Her Majesty's Treasury
asset freezing 125
CONTEST roles and responsibilities 101 (table 4.2)
Hezb-i-Islami Gulbuddin (HIG) 239 (App 1)
Higher Education Institutions (HEIs)
radicalisation and 170–2, 176
Hizballah Military Wing 239 (App 1)
Home-Made Explosives (HME)
Al Qa'ida Hostile Reconnaissance 71
Lockerbie bombing 66–8
London Nail Bomber 62
Operation Overt 187–8
right-wing terrorism 27
Home Office (HO)
anti-terror powers 92
authorisations:
confirmation of 253 (App 2)
notification of police authorities 254 (App 2)
Boko Haram case 12–13
briefing, importance of 138
Intelligence Services Act (1994), elements of 96
neighbourhood policing 234
online radicalisation 197
photography and counter-terrorism 258 (App 2)
'Prepare' strategy 95
proscribed terrorist organisations 14, 237–42 (App 1)
Research, Information and Communications Unit (RICU) 194
stop and search guidelines 137–9, 156
monitoring and supervision 263 (App 2)
UK threat level 8
see also Office of Security and Counter-Terrorism (OSCT); United Kingdom Border Agency (UKBA)

ideology
definition 43
Improvised Explosive Device (IED)
3/11 and 47
Al Qa'ida in the Arabian Peninsula 11
online radicalisation 201
tactics by UK extremists 80
Independent Reviewer of Terrorism Legislation (IRTL)
non-statutory functions 126
Operation Pathway 142
statutory functions 125
Indian Mujahideen (IM) 240 (App 1)
Integrated Neighbourhood Policing Teams (INPTs)
establishment 217
local policing model 233
International Security Assistance Force (ISAF)
Al Qa'ida leadership 9
conflicts overseas 19
International Sikh Youth Federation (ISYF) 240 (App 1)
internet, *see* Cyber Terrorism (CyT); radicalisation
Internet Strategy Group (ISG)
CONTEST Board 99
Irish National Liberation Army (INLA)
assassination of Airey Neave 65–6
Irish People's Liberation Organisation 242 (App 1)
Irish Republican Army (IRA), *see* Continuity Irish Republican Army (CIRA); Provisional Irish Republican Army (PIRA); Real Irish Republican Army (RIRA)
Islamic Army of Aden (IAA) 240 (App 1)
Islamic Jihad Union (IJU) 240 (App 1)
Islamic Movement of Uzbekistan (IMU) 240 (App 1)

Jaish-e-Mohammed (JeM) 240 (App 1)
Jamaat ul-Furquan (JuF) 240 (App 1)
Jammat-ul Mujahideen Bangladesh (JMB) 240 (App 1)
Jemaah Islamiyah (JI) 240 (App 1)
Joint Terrorism Analysis Centre (JTAC)
CONTEST roles and responsibilities 102 (table 4.2)
establishment and purpose 110
intelligence community 106, 110
national threat level system 7, 110
Jundallah 239 (App 1)

Kenya Defence Forces (KDF)
Al-Shabaab Armed Assault 16

Key Individual Network (KIN)
Key Individual Networks Extended List (KINEL) 221–2
neighbourhood policing 221–2
Khuddam ul-Islam (Kul) 240 (App 1)
Kongra-Gel Kurdistan (PKK) 240

Lashkar-e-Jhangvi (LeJ) 241–2 (App 1)
Lashkar-e-Tayyiba (LeT)
armed assaults 64–5
FATA terrorist organisation 14–15
political objectives 240–1 (App 2)
Lead Government Department (LGD)
COBR 108
DECC 100 (table 4.2)
DEFRA 100 (table 4.2)
Liberation Tigers of Tamil Eelam (LTTE) 241 (App 1)
Libyan Islamic Fighting Group (LIFG) 241 (App 1)
Lockerbie disaster (1988) 67–8
London Nail Bomber attack (1999) 62–3
London Stock Exchange (LSE)
7/7 and 40
Loyalist Volunteer Force (LVF) 242 (App 1)

Metropolitan Police Service (MPS)
Authorising officers 149, 254n (App 2)
domestic extremism 112
Gillan and Quinton v United Kingdom 131–2
neighbourhood policing 217–18, 233
Operation Overt 187
Operation Pathway 142
parking authorisation 149
power of arrest 141
radicalisation 186
Raissi v Metropolitan Police Commissioner 141
Specialist Operations business group 112
stop and search powers 131–3
Military Cross (MC) 65–6
Minbar Ansar Deen (Ansar al-Sharia UK) 241 (App 1)
Ministry of Defence (MoD)
CONTEST roles and responsibilities 102 (table 4.2)
cordons 147 (table 6.2)
Defence Intelligence Staff (DIS) 110
Police Act (1987) 147 (table 6.2)
stop and search powers 245 (App 2)
MoD Police 245 (App 2), 254 (App 2)
MoD Police Committee 245 (App 2)
notification of police authorities 254 (App 2)
Ministry of Justice (MoJ)
CONTEST roles and responsibilities 102 (table 4.2)
MI5 Security Service (Military Intelligence section 5)
CONTEST roles and responsibilities 103 (table 4.2), 109
intelligence community 106, 109
Operation Gamble 74
Operation Overamp 162
Operation Overt 187–8
radicalisation 186–8, 190
MI6 Secret Intelligence Service (Military Intelligence section 6)
intelligence community 108–9
Mumbai Massacre (2008) 15–16

National Community Tension Team (NCTT)
'Prevent' strategy 177
National Counter-Terrorism Security Office (NaCTSO)
CONTEST roles and responsibilities 102 (table 4.2)
National Crime Agency (NCA)
CONTEST roles and responsibilities 102 (table 4.2)
counter-terrorism policing 113–14
see also Border Policing Command (BPC); Child Exploitation and Online Protection Centre (CEOP); Economic Crime Command (ECC); Organised Crime Command (OCC)
National Domestic Extremism Team (NDET)
domestic extremism 112
National Domestic Extremism Unit (NDEU)
domestic extremism 112
National Extremism Tactical Coordination Unit (NETCU)
domestic extremism 112
National Intelligence Model (NIM)
evidence-based deployment 215
intelligence-led deployment 223–4
National Prevent Delivery Unit (NPDU)
'Prevent' strategy 174–5

National Public Order Intelligence Unit (NPOIU)
domestic extremism 112
National Reassurance Policing Programme (NRPP)
neighbouring policing pilots 209, 211
National Security Council (NSC)
CONTEST governance 98
CONTEST roles and responsibilities 102 (table 4.2)
establishment 5
national risks 5–6
see also Cabinet Office (CO)
National Security Risk Assessment (NSRA)
national risks 5–6
neighbourhood policing 207–36
community (definition) 212
delivery mechanisms 210 *fig.*
effectiveness 226–7
positive outcomes 227 (table 10.3)
unintended consequences 227
evolution 208
implementation 209–11
improving public confidence 210
neighbourhood (definition) 212
Neighbourhood Policing Plus 228–34
complacency 232
contact management 231–2
continued engagement 229
investment 232–3
local policing in London 233–4
suspicious sightings 229–30
trust your instincts 231
Neighbourhood Policing Programme (NPP):
purpose 209
Neighbourhood Policing Teams (NPT):
community engagement 111–12, 229
community, listening to 223
counter-terrorism structure 111–12
crime prevention and reduction 216
dedicated teams 211, 215
evidence-based deployment 215
integration of 217
intelligence-led deployment 223
Key Individual Networks (KIN) 221–2
local conditions 207, 217, 228–9
national strategy 209
PACT meetings 219
performance management 226
'Prevent' strategy 175
prevention and reduction 216
recruitment and training 210–11
size and variations 216–17
see also Integrated Neighborhood Policing Teams (INPTs)
responding to crisis 208
ten principles 212–13 (table 10.1)
collaborative problem-solving 219–23
community engagement 224–5
dedicated teams 215
evidence-based deployment 215
intelligence-led deployment 223–4
local dependency 217
mainstream policing activity 214–15
organisational strategy 213–14
performance management 226
public priorities 218
timeline 211 *fig.*
NGOs (Non-Governmental Organizations)
conflict-engaged citizens 21
independent oversight 124
Non-Departmental Public Body (NDPB)
Youth Justice Board 102 (table 4.2)
North East Counter Terrorism Unit (NECTU)
right-wing terrorism 27
Northern Ireland Office (NIO)
CONTEST roles and responsibilities 102 (table 4.2)
Northern Ireland-Related Terrorism (NIRT)
assassination of Airey Neave 65–6
Castlereagh 'Room 2-20' (2002) 72–3
coded warnings 25
cordons 146–7 (table 6.2)
deaths recorded 23
devolved administrations 101 (table 4.2)
Good Friday Agreement (GFA) 23
legislation, emergency provisions 87, 121–2, 124, 127
murder at Massereene Barracks 23–4
murder of PC Ronan Kerr 25
murder of PC Stephen Caroll 23, 24–5
National Security Strategy for 6
national threats 8, 9 *fig.*, 23
Omagh Bombing (1998) 56–7
police forces 245 (App 2)
Policing Board of Northern Ireland 72
proscribed terrorist organisations 14, 237–42 (App 1)
resurgence of terrorist activity 25, 30

Northern Ireland-Related Terrorism (NIRT) (*cont.*)
support for 23
the 'Troubles' 23–4
VBIEDs, use in assassinations 65–6
Warrington Bombings (1993) 48
see also Northern Ireland Office (NIO); Police Service of Northern Ireland (PSNI); *see also under individual terrorist organisations*

Office of Security and Counter-Terrorism (OSCT)
CONTEST roles and responsibilities 101 (table 4.2)
HM Treasury and 101 (table 4.2)
Home Office (HO) and 101
'Prepare' strategy 95
role and functions 96–7
terrorist financing 101 (table 4.2)
Operation Gamble 73–4
Operation Gird 126
Operation Hindsight 174–5
Operation Overamp 162–4
Operation Overt 186–90
Operation Pathway 126, 142–3
Operation Seagram 94–5
Orange Volunteers 242 (App 1)
Organised Crime Command (OCC)
CONTEST roles and responsibilities 102 (table 4.2)
National Crime Agency (NCA) 113
Overseas CONTEST Group (OGC)
CONTEST Board 99

Palestinian Islamic Jihad-Shaqaqi (PIJ) 241 (App 1)
parking 148–50
offences 149–50
prohibitions 149
Section 48 authorising officers 149
see also anti-terror legislation
Partners and Communities Together (PACT)
public meetings 219
Police and Crime Commissioners (PCC)
election and re-election 211, 218, 226
police and crime plans 211
strategic policing requirements 112–13
Police and Criminal Evidence Act 1984 (PACE)
officers' powers and duties 154 (table 6.5)
spontaneous arrest 141–2
stop and search powers 244 (App 2)
body searches 247 (App 2)
uniformed officers 246 (App 2)
Terrorism Act 2000 and 144
terrorist suspects 144
Police Community Support Officer (PCSO)
local London policing 233
neighbourhood policing 209
recruitment and training 210–11, 216
restrictions on authorisation 136
stop and search powers 134–6, 263 (App 2)
UK terrorist threat 2
Police Counter Terrorism Board (CTB)
'Prepare' strategy 97, 99
Police National Counter Terrorism Network (PNCTN)
CONTEST roles and responsibilities 102 (table 4.2)
Police National Legal Database (PNLD)
anti-terror legislation 119
Police Service of Northern Ireland (PSNI)
authorising officers 148 (table 6.3)
cordons 147 (table 6.2)
murder of PC Stephen Caroll and 24–5
parking 149 (table 6.3)
politics (definition) 41
power of arrest 140–5
detention following arrest 143–4
exercise with caution 141
immediate notification following arrest 143
PACE and TACT provisions 144
personal and operational security 145
pre-planned arrests 142–3
reasonable suspicion 140–1
spontaneous arrests 141–2
treatment of suspects 145
see also anti-terror legislation
Prevention of Terrorism Act 2005 (PoT)
Control Orders 122, 125
Gillan and Quinton v United Kingdom 132
renewal of earlier legislation 124
terrorism, definition of 127
UK anti-terror legal framework 123
Problem-Orientated Policing (POP) 222–3
see also SARA (Scanning, Analysis, Response, and Assessment model)

prosecution 114–17
 see also Crown Prosecution Service (CPS)
Provisional Irish Republican Army (PIRA)
 Castlereagh 'Room 2-20' (2002) 73
 terrorist organisations 55
 Warrington Bombings (1993) 48

radicalisation 182–205
 definition 183
 drivers of 184–90
  foreign policy 186–90
 extremism and terrorism vs. 182
 factors 185
  identification of 190–1
 online 196–2
  limitations of models 196–7
  'Schoolboy terrorist' (2006) 200–1
  tackling 197–8, 201–2
 process models 191–6
  ACPO Prevent Pyramid 192 (table 9.1)
  eight-stage recruitment 191 (table 9.1)
  European Commission pyramid 194–5
  four-stage 191 (table 9.1)
  NYPD four-stage 192 (table 9.1)
  pathway model 192 (table 9.1)
  psychological model 193 (table 9.1)
  review of 195–6
  socialisation model 192 (table 9.1)
  staircase to terrorism 193 (table 9.1), 194 *fig.*
  twelve mechanisms of 'political' radicalisation 193 (table 9.1)
 Radicalisation-Factor Model (RFM) 198–202
  factors 198–9
  interpretation 200
  model schema 199 *fig.*
  online radicalisation 200–2
  usage of technologies 199
 social media 202–3
  hijacking 203
  murder of Drummer Lee Rigby 202–3
Real Irish Republican Army (RIRA)
 murder at Massereene Barracks 23
 Omagh Bombing 1998 56–7
Red Hand Commando 242 (App 1)
Red Hand Defenders 242 (App 1)
Regulation of Investigatory Powers Act 2000 (RIPA)
 counter-terrorism 96
religion (definition) 42
Revolutionary People's Liberation Party–Front (DHKP-C) 241 (App 1)

Salafist Group for Call and Combat (GSPC) 241 (App 1)
Saor Eire 242 (App 1)
SARA (Scanning, Analysis, Response, and Assessment model)
 police-orientated policing 222–3
 SARA process cycle 223
Saved Sect or Saviour Sect 237, 241 (App 1)
Scotland Office
 CONTEST roles and responsibilities 102 (table 4.2)
Secret Intelligence Service (SIS)
 CONTEST roles and responsibilities 103 (table 4.2)
 intelligence community 106, 108–10
Serious Organised Crime Agency (SOCA)
 Security Service 109
Sipah-e-Sahaba Pakistan (SSP) 241–2 (App 1)
social media, *see* radicalisation
Special Branch (SB)
 Castlereagh 'Room 2-20' (2002) 72–3
 CONTEST roles and responsibilities 102 (table 4.2)
 counter-terrorism policing 111
 evidence-based deployment 215
 intelligence-led deployment 223
 operational realities 120
 power of arrest 143
 right-wing extremism 26
Special Crime and Counter Terrorism Division (SCCTD)
 Crown Prosecution Service 114–16
 role in criminal justice system 116
stop and search powers 129–40
 alternative powers 139
 briefing, importance of 138–9
 Code of Practice 243–65 (App 2)
 cooperation 139–40
 guidelines 137–9
 legal challenges 133
 'Plan' 138 *fig.*
 police community support officers 136
 public information ('know your rights') 134–6
 public reassurance 134

stop and search powers (*cont.*)
reasonable suspicion 130
review of 131
risk of potential discrimination 137
Section 43 129–30
Section 47A 131, 136–7
see also anti-terror legislation
Strategic Policing Requirement (SPR)
counter-terrorism policing 112–13, 121, 214
student union Islamic society (ISOC)
'Prevent' in higher education 170
Syrian Conflict (2011) 20

Taliban (Tehrik-e Taliban Pakistan (TTP))
Al Qa'ida followers 14
political objectives 242 (App 1)
terrorist organisations and 239, 242 (App 1)
training methods 164
Tehreek-e-Nafaz-e-Shariat-e-Mohammadi (TNSM) 242 (App 1)
terrorism
audience and victim relationship 37 *fig.*
characteristics 46–50
human rights 49–50
indiscriminate 47–8
police abuse of power 50
pre-meditated 46–8
core motivations 36 *fig.*, 50–2
ideological 43, 44
justification of beliefs 50–1
nationalistic 44
personality profile 51–2
political 41, 43–4
religious 42, 43–4
definition 33–5
legal definition 35
extremism vs. 41
global context 2–4
wave theory 2–4
impact 37–40
economic 38–40
national risks 5–6
national security risk assessment 5–6
national security 4–5
globalisation, impact of 4
strategy 4–5
national threats 7–29
conflict-engaged citizens 21–5
conflicts overseas 19
cyber terrorism 28–9
domestic vs. international 25–6
exporting terrorism 20–1
foreign fighters 19–20
level system 7–8
public information 7
right-wing terrorism 26–7
threat analysis 8
to the UK 7–30
single-issue extremism 44–6
anarchism 45
animal rights 45
anti-war protests 45
capitalism 45
democratic rights and freedoms 46
environmentalism 45
fascism 46
globalisation 45
state legitimacy 37
state sponsored 44
typology of 43–6
understanding 35–43
Terrorism Act 2000 (TACT)
Asst. Chief Constables and Commanders' powers and duties 154 (table 6.5)
cordons 145–6
detention following arrest 143–4
historic cases 165
Inspector powers and duties 154 (table 6.5)
legal definition of terrorism 35–6, 122–3, 125, 126–8
'terrorist' 127, 255n (App 2)
'terrorist investigation' 129
legislative framework 122–5
statutory functions 125
PACE provisions 144
power of arrest 140–2, 161
proscribed terrorist organisations 13–14, 55, 122, 237–42 (App 1)
stop and search powers 129–33, 243–65 (App 2)
Terrorism Act 2006 (TACT 2006)
encouragement of terrorism 160–1
legislative framework 122–3
police powers 158
Operation Overamp 162
statutory functions 126
Superintendent powers and duties 154 (table 6.5)
terrorist training 163–4
'unacceptable behaviours' 160

Terrorism and Allied Matters (TAM)
National Prevent Delivery Unit (NPDU) 174
Terrorism Case Management Judge (TCMJ)
role in Crown Prosecution Service 115
Terrorism Prevention and Investigation Measures (TPIMs)
anti-terror legal framework 122–3
annual review 125
Conditions A–E 150
Control Orders and 122, 153
duration of TPIM notice 152
new terrorism-related activity 151
police powers 152–3
Secretary of State measures 151–2
statutory functions 125–6
terrorism-related activity 150–1
new 151
see also anti-terror legislation
terrorism offences 158–65
encouraging terrorism 158–61
exercise with caution 161
radical preaching 159
terrorist training 161–4
British Camps 164
offences 164
terrorist organisations 55–82
centralised 55–8
Corporate cell structure 58
Duo-cell structure 57
Tri-cell structure 57–8
IRA 56–7
decentralised 59–63
Fused cell structure 61
Link cell structure 60
Lone actor 62
Star cell structure 60–1
organisational structures 63
tactics 64–81
armed assaults 64–5
assassinations 65–6
biological weapons 68–9
bombings 66–8
chemical weapons 68–9
domestic extremism 79–81
explosives 68–9
fundraising/finance 69–70
hostile reconnaissance 70–2
infiltration 72–3
kidnap 73–4
nuclear weapons 68–9
radiological weapons 68–9
reporting suspicious activity 72
security of public officials 66
siege 74
suicide bombings 75–9
Teyre Azadiye Kurdistan (TAK) 242 (App 1)

UK Border Agency (UKBA)
CONTEST roles and responsibilities 103 (table 4.2)
Ulster Defence Association (UDA) 242 (App 1)
Ulster Freedom Fighters (UFF) 242 (App 1)
Ulster Volunteer Force (UVF) 242 (App 1)
universities, *see* Higher Education Institutions (HEIs)

Vehicle-Borne Improvised Explosive Devices (VBIED)
Northern Ireland assassinations 65
Vulnerable Sites and Sectors (VSS)
regular police patrols 214

Wales Office
CONTEST roles and responsibilities 103 (table 4.2)

Lightning Source UK Ltd.
Milton Keynes UK
UKOW04f2350140414

229967UK00001B/1/P

MOVING FORWARD

ISBN: 1456561030
ISBN-13: 9781456561031

About the Author

Andrew Fitzgerald has worked with disabled children since he was a teenager and has finally decided to combine his passion for writing with his passion for his job. He wrote from a very young age and hopes this is the first of many novels. If you would like to contact him about any of the issues raised in this book or would like further information please visit him on his facebook page or email him on andrew_fitzgerald@hotmail.co.uk.